Application of
Nursing Process and
Nursing Diagnosis

An Interactive Text for Diagnostic Reasoning

Application of
Nursing Process and
Nursing Diagnosis

An Interactive Text for Diagnostic Reasoning

THIRD EDITION

Marilynn E. Doenges, RN, BSN, MA, CS
Clinical Specialist
Adult Psychiatric/Mental Health Nursing
Adjunct Faculty
Beth-El College of Nursing & Health Science,
CU-Springs
Colorado Springs, Colorado

Mary Frances Moorhouse, RN, CRRN, CLNC
Nurse Consultant
TNT-RN Enterprises
Colorado Springs, Colorado

Joseph T. Burley, RN, MNED
College of Nursing
University of Florida
Gainesville, Florida

F. A. DAVIS COMPANY • Philadelphia

F. A. Davis Company
1915 Arch Street
Philadelphia, PA 19103

Printed in the United States of America

Last digit indicates print number: 10 9 8 7 6 5 4 3 2 1

Publisher: Robert Martone
Production Manager: Samuel A. Rondinelli
Production Editor: Jessica Howie Martin
Cover Designer: Louis J. Forgione

As new scientific information becomes available through basic and clinical research, recommended treatments and drug therapies undergo changes. The author(s) and publisher have done everything possible to make this book accurate, up to date, and in accord with accepted standards at the time of publication. The authors, editors, and publisher are not responsible for errors or omissions or for consequences from application of the book, and make no warranty, expressed or implied, in regard to the contents of the book. Any practice described in this book should be applied by the reader in accordance with professional standards of care used in regard to the unique circumstances that may apply in each situation. The reader is advised always to check product information (package inserts) for changes and new information regarding dose and contraindications before administering any drug. Caution is especially urged when using new or infrequently ordered drugs.

Library of Congress Cataloging-in-Publication Data

Doenges, Marilynn E., 1922–
    Application of nursing process and nursing diagnosis : an interactive text for diagnostic
reasoning / Marilynn E. Doenges, Mary Frances Moorhouse, Joseph T. Burley.—3rd ed.
        p. cm.
    Includes bibliographical references and index.
    ISBN 0-8036-0467-X
        1. Nursing.   2. Nursing assessment.   3. Nursing diagnosis.   I. Moorhouse, Mary Frances,
1947– II. Burley, Joseph T. III. Title.
    [DNLM: 1. Nursing Process.   2. Nursing Diagnosis—methods. WY 100 D615a 1999]
    RT41 .D54 1999
    610.73—dc21
                                                                        99-042874

To our families, who support us in all we do and who continue to support our
dreams, fantasies, and obsessions:
With special thanks to:
Marilynn's late husband, Dean, and Mary's and Joe's spouses, Jan and Jolene;
our children and grandchildren,
Nancy, Jim, Jennifer, and Jonathan Daigle; David, Monita, Matthew, and Tyler
Doenges; Jim Doenges; Barbara Doenges, and Bob Lanza; John, Holly, Nicole,
and Kelsey Doenges; Paul Moorhouse; Jason, Alexa, and Mary Moorhouse;
Joel and Justin Burley, and granddaughter Malia;
Alice Geissler, for being available when we need help;
The staff at Memorial Hospital library, for cheerfully filling in all the blanks and pa-
tiently helping us find those elusive references.
To the students of Beth-El College of Nursing and the students of the College of
Nursing, University of Florida, who continue to challenge us to make the nursing
process and nursing diagnosis understandable.
To our colleagues, who continue to provide a sounding board and feedback for our
professional beliefs and expectations. We hope this interactive text will help you
and your students at all stages to clarify and apply these concepts.
Kudos to the F. A. Davis staff,
To our publisher and friend Robert (Bob) Martone;
To Ruth DeGeorge, who has shown great patience and served as a buffer for all
involved;
To Bob Butler, Jessica Howie Martin, and all who facilitated the revision process
to get this project completed in a timely fashion.
Lastly, to the nurses who have patiently awaited this revision, we hope it will help
in applying theory to practice and enhance the delivery and effectiveness of
your care.

Notes To The Educator

The nursing process has been used for over 25 years as a systematic approach to nursing practice. The process is an efficient and effective method for organizing nursing knowledge and clinical decision making in providing planned patient care. Although it has been undergoing constant re-evaluation and revision, the concepts within the process still remain central to nursing practice.

Healthcare accrediting agencies and nursing organizations have developed standards of nursing practice that focus on the tenets of the nursing process, that is, assessing, diagnosing, planning, implementing, evaluating, and documenting patient care. Although the formats used to document the plan of care may change with the interpretation and evaluation of standards, the nursing responsibilities and interventions required for planned patient care still need to be learned, shared, performed, evaluated, and documented.

The nursing process is by its nature an interactive method of practicing nursing. This text mirrors that interactive focus by presenting a step-by-step problem-solving design to help students develop an understanding of the meaning and language of nursing. We have included definitions and professional standards that will serve as a solid foundation for your students to understand and apply the nursing process. The vignettes, practice activities, work pages, and case studies provide an opportunity to examine and scrutinize patient situations and dilemmas in practice, consider alternatives, and evaluate outcomes. The worksheets serve as graphic summaries that provide students with criteria to evaluate their decisions and demonstrate their understanding of the concepts and integration of the material presented. Tear-out pages for independent learning provide an opportunity for practical application and beginning mastery of the nursing process. These pages can be taken to the clinical area to reinforce selected aspects of the nursing process. Finally, review of patient situations and the Code for Nurses can serve as a catalyst for philosophical and ethical discussions. All these activities encourage the student to actively seek solutions rather than passively assimilate knowledge, thus stimulating the student's critical thinking ability.

CHAPTER 1, THE NURSING PROCESS: DELIVERING QUALITY CARE

This introductory chapter presents an overview of the nursing process. Students are introduced to the definitions of nursing and nursing diagnosis and the American Nurses Association's Standards of Clinical Nursing Practice.

CHAPTER 2, THE ASSESSMENT STEP: DEVELOPING THE PATIENT DATABASE

This chapter introduces students to the first step of the nursing process. Organizational formats for constructing nursing assessment tools are discussed and both the physical and psychosocial aspects of assessment are blended into the interview process. Examples of patient data assist students to identify categories of nursing diagnostic labels.

CHAPTER 3, THE PROBLEM/NEED IDENTIFICATION STEP: ANALYZING THE DATA

The definition and concepts of nursing diagnosis are presented in this chapter. We use the term *Patient Diagnostic Statement* to describe the combination of the NANDA-approved label, the patient's related factors (etiology), and associated defining characteristics (signs/symptoms). A six-step diagnostic reasoning process is presented to assist students in their beginning efforts to accurately analyze the patient's assessment data. The remainder of this chapter focuses on ruling out, synthesizing, evaluating, and constructing the patient diagnostic statement.

CHAPTER 4, THE PLANNING STEP: CREATING THE PLAN OF CARE

Information on developing the individualized outcomes for the patient is provided in this chapter. A focus on correctly writing measurable outcomes is initially presented. In addition, examples from the standardized nursing language for outcomes, Nursing Outcomes Classification (NOC) are also presented. Nursing interventions are defined and acknowledgment of the work by the Iowa Intervention Project's Nursing Interventions Classification (NIC) is included. The topics, priorities of interventions, discharge planning, and selecting appropriate nursing interventions are discussed along with examples of a fourth standardized language, the Omaha System. A practice activity for recording the steps of the nursing process learned thus far is included to provide the student a realistic application. An interactive plan of care worksheet is used to present examples and guidelines for developing the patient's outcome statement, selecting nursing interventions, and providing rationales for nursing interventions.

CHAPTER 5, THE IMPLEMENTATION STEP: PUTTING THE PLAN OF CARE INTO ACTION

Information is presented about the validation and implementation of the plan of care. Concerns regarding the day-to-day organization of the nurse's work is creatively used in a practice activity where students use time management to plan the day's patient care interventions. Change-of-shift reporting principles are also discussed and practiced.

CHAPTER 6, THE EVALUATION STEP: DETERMINING WHETHER DESIRED OUTCOMES HAVE BEEN MET

The crucial step of evaluation and its accompanying reassessment and revision processes are presented in this chapter on the last step of the nursing process. A practice activity is provided to help students evaluate the plan of care partially constructed in Chapter 4. Revisions to the plan of care are necessary and the activity provides a realistic exercise for this final step. The interactive plan of care worksheet is designed to ask your students questions about their patient's progress and the effectiveness of their implemented nursing interventions.

CHAPTER 7, DOCUMENTING THE NURSING PROCESS

This chapter introduces students to ways of successfully documenting their use of the nursing process. Communication, legal responsibilities, and reimbursement are a few of the topics introduced in this chapter. The documentation systems of SOAP and FOCUS CHARTING™ are presented to depict two possible methods of documenting the nursing process. The last section of the interactive worksheet focuses the students' attention on three important aspects of documentation: the reassessment data, interventions implemented, and the patient's response.

CHAPTER 8, INTERACTIVE CARE PLANNING: FROM ASSESSMENT TO PATIENT RESPONSE

This final chapter provides an evaluation checklist that can be used to evaluate your students' progress in all aspects of the nursing process. The checklist is designed to include the criteria listed on the Interactive Care Plan Worksheets, ANA Standards of Clinical Nursing Practice, and the JCAHO nursing standards. The chapter ends with a case study that gives your students an opportunity to apply all the steps of the nursing process. The evaluation checklist along with the TIME OUTS included in the plan of care worksheets provide the students with the required guidance when constructing their first complete plan of care.

APPENDICES

A listing of the North American Nursing Diagnosis Association nursing diagnoses are included in Appendix A. Each nursing diagnosis' definition, related/risk factors, and defining characteristics are provided to assist the student in accurately selecting the appropriate nursing diagnosis.

Appendix B provides an adult medical-surgical assessment tool as referenced in Chapter 2 along with excerpts from assessment tools developed for the psychiatric and obstetrical settings. The tools are helpful in assisting students in assessing the patient's response to health problems as well as gathering physical assessment data.

Appendix C organizes the NANDA diagnostic labels within Maslow's hierarchy of needs to aid in visualizing and determining priorities for providing patient care.

Appendix D, Code for Nurses, was included for your use both in the classroom and during clinical rounds to share with your students the values that guide nursing practice today. A reference to the Code and the introduction of a discussion of beliefs that affect nursing practice are contained in Chapter 1 and an ethical activity is presented in Chapter 5.

Appendices E and F provide tools for the student to measure the accuracy of their choice of nursing diagnosis labels. The Ordinal Scale of Accuracy of a Nursing Diagnosis assigns a point value to a diagnosis that is consistent with the number of cues and disconfirming cues identified. This tool aids students in validating their analysis of the collected data and choice of nursing diagnosis. The Integrated Model for Self-Monitoring of the Diagnostic Process provides direct feedback to students but can also be shared with you to demonstrate the students' progress in data analysis and diagnosis.

Appendix G is a sample of a Clinical (Critical) Pathway, providing you with the opportunity to address alternate forms for planning and evaluating care.

Appendix H presents some commonly accepted charting abbreviations, which may be useful in your discussion of the documentation process.

Appendix I provides a glossary of common terms.

Appendix J outlines the 16 Likert scales used to measure the variability in the patient's state, behavior, or perception as depicted in NOC outcomes.

Finally, Appendices K and L are the Keys to the Learning Activities provided in the text.

The National League for Nursing emphasizes the need for graduates of nursing programs to think critically, make decisions, and formulate independent judgments. To achieve this outcome, you as an instructor are encouraged to use teaching strategies that will "stimulate higher-order critical thinking in both theory and practice situations" (Klaassens, 1988). These strategies include: questioning, analysis, synthesis, application, writing, problem-solving games, and philosophical discussions.

It is our hope that the interactive features of this text will provide the strategies to assist you in successfully sharing with your students the meaning and language of the nursing process and in making a smooth and effective transition from the classroom to any clinical setting.

Marilynn E. Doenges
Mary Frances Moorhouse
Joseph T. Burley

Notes To The Student

The nursing process will be described by your instructors as a systematic approach to the practice of nursing. You will shortly find that this process is an efficient and effective method for organizing both nursing knowledge and practice. The process will also assist you in accurately performing clinical decision making activities in planning your patient's care. The process has been continually refined since its inception in the 1960s. However, to date, the concepts within the process still remain central to nursing practice. Through the use of this text, your instructors will share the meaning of the concepts and this evolving nursing practice language with you.

The nursing process is an interactive method of practicing nursing with the components fitting together in a continuous cycle of thought and action. This interactive focus was used in developing and writing this text for you. The text focuses on the steps of the nursing process and provides information and exercises to aid your understanding and application of the process. Included are practice activities, ongoing reference to simulated clinical experiences through the use of vignettes, and end-of-chapter work pages to promote your understanding. Definitions of both nursing and the nursing process, along with the American Nurses Association's (ANA) Standards of Clinical Nursing Practice, are presented to provide a solid foundation for you to build an understanding of the language and knowledge of nursing and application of the nursing process.

In addition, a six-step diagnostic reasoning/critical thinking process is presented for accurately analyzing the patient's assessment data. It will assist you in ruling out, synthesizing, evaluating, and constructing the patient diagnostic statement, which is pivotal for developing individualized plans of care for your patients. A practice activity for writing a nursing plan of care was developed to provide a realistic application of your newly learned knowledge. An example of a typical day's work requirements is used in a practice activity where you are given the opportunity to use time management principles and skills to plan your patient's care within an 8-hour shift. A third practice activity is provided to give you a chance to choose patient information you would include in a change-of-shift report to communicate the outcomes of your use of the nursing process.

Next, you are given an opportunity to test your beginning skills in developing a complete plan of care. A set of step-by-step forms is provided for you to document your clinical judgment by selecting patient diagnostic statements, developing the goals/outcomes, and identifying the nursing interventions. Finally, an evaluation checklist is provided to serve as a valuable self-assessment of the appropriateness and accuracy of your comprehension of the planning exercise and future plans of care that you will design for your patients.

At the end of the chapters, a bibliography and list of suggested readings are included to guide you in further and future reading and understanding of both nursing knowledge and nursing process. In Chapter 1, a suggested reading list provides a listing of publications from a historical perspective. The listing should be helpful to you in searching out the meaning of nursing and the nursing process. The list may also prove valuable in writing varied required papers on similar topics. Use and enjoy. The second section gives you the most current listing of publications at the time of the printing of this edition. Once again, the selected publications are provided to assist you in this learning process.

The perforated tear-out pages for the end-of-chapter work pages, interactive care plan worksheets, and the evaluation checklist were especially designed for your independent learning. These tear-out pages can be taken to the clinical area to reinforce selected aspects of the nursing process. It is our hope that the interactive features of this text will assist you in making the successful and effective transition from the classroom to your assigned clinical setting. We wish you well in this beginning phase of your new profession.

Marilynn E. Doenges
Mary Frances Moorhouse
Joseph T. Burley

Acknowledgments

To Jean Jenny, MS, MEd, BScNEd, RN
Former Professor
Faculty of Health Sciences
University of Ottowa
School of Nursing
Ottowa, Ontario
Canada

To Barbara Ogden, RN, MSN
Assistant Professor
College of Nursing
University of Florida
Gainesville, Florida
a mentor, colleague, and friend. Thank you.

To Paladin Productions
whose computer talents clarified our ideas and made them visible.

Contents

CHAPTER 6

The Evaluation Step: Determining Whether Desired Outcomes Have Been Met 117

CHAPTER 7

Documenting the Nursing Process 131

CHAPTER 8

Interactive Care Planning: From Assessment to Patient Response 157

Practice Activities and
Work Pages

CHAPTER 1

The Nursing Process: Delivering Quality Care

The Nursing Profession

Nursing is both a science and an art concerned with the physical, psychological, sociological, cultural, and spiritual concerns of the individual. The science of nursing is based on a broad theoretical framework; its art depends on the caring skills and abilities of the individual nurse. The importance of the nurse within the health-care system is being recognized in many positive ways, and the profession of nursing is itself acknowledging the need for its practitioners to be professional and accountable.

In its early developmental years, nursing did not seek or have the means to control its own practice. Florence Nightingale, in discussing the nature of nursing, observed that "nursing has been limited to signify little more than the administration of medicines and the application of poultices" (Nightingale, 1859). Although this attitude still persists in some cases, the nursing profession has defined what makes nursing unique and has identified a body of professional knowledge.

Thus, barely a century after Miss Nightingale noted that "the very elements of nursing are all but unknown," (Nightingale, 1859) the American Nurses' Association (ANA) developed the first Social Policy Statement (1980) defining nursing as "the diagnosis and treatment of human responses to actual or potential health problems." Recently the statement was revisited, updated, and titled Nursing's Social Policy Statement (1995). The new policy statement acknowledges that since the release of the original statement, nursing has been influenced by many social

Definition of Nursing
Nursing is the diagnosis and treatment of human responses to health and illness (ANA, 1995).

1

and professional changes, as well as by the science of caring. Nursing has integrated these changes with the 1980 definition to include treatment of human responses to health and illness.

The new statement provides four essential features of today's contemporary nursing practice:

1. Attention to the full range of human experiences and responses to health and illness without restriction to a problem-focused orientation
2. Integration of objective data with knowledge gained from an understanding of the patient's or group's subjective experience
3. Application of scientific knowledge to the processes of diagnosis and treatment
4. Provision of a caring relationship that facilitates health and healing (ANA, 1995, pp. 3–4)

In the modern world of nursing, therefore, human responses, defined as people's experiences with and responses to health and illness, are the phenomena of concern for nurses. Thus, nursing's role includes health promotion as well as activities that contribute to recovery from or adjustment to illness. Also, nurses support the right of patients to define their own health-related goals and engage in care that reflects their values.

In your journey to discover, understand, and apply this body of knowledge, each chapter guides and presents the knowledge of nursing diagnoses, nursing interventions, and nursing outcomes. These three components of nursing knowledge are applied in practice activities and end-of-chapter work pages to further your understanding and correct application of this knowledge.

You will soon be introduced to the language described in the nursing process. This introduction includes the North American Nursing Diagnosis Association's (NANDA) classification of nursing diagnosis, the Iowa Intervention and Outcome Projects: Nursing Intervention Classification (NIC) and the Nursing Outcomes Classification (NOC), and the Omaha Classification System (NANDA, 1999; Iowa Intervention Project, 1996; Iowa Outcome Project, 1997; Martin & Scheet, 1992). The Omaha Classification System combines all three aspects of the language plus an evaluation process. The four patient scenarios presented in the text use examples from NANDA, NIC, NOC, and the Omaha Classification to provide you with differing ways of seeing the nursing process in action.

Now, let's move on and describe the nursing process.

The Nursing Process

Nursing leaders have identified a process that "combines the most desirable elements of the art of nursing with the most relevant elements of systems theory, using the scientific method" (Shore, 1988). This process incorporates an interactive/interpersonal approach with a problem-solving and decision-making process (Peplau, 1952; King, 1971; Travelbee, 1971; Yura & Walsh, 1988).

The nursing process was first introduced in the 1950s as a three-step process of assessment, planning, and evaluation based on the scientific method of observing, measuring, gathering data, and analyzing the findings. Years of study, use, and refinement have led nurses to expand the nursing process to five distinct steps that provide an efficient method of organizing thought processes for clinical decision

Definition of Nursing Process

The nursing process consists of five-steps:

1. Assessment
2. Problem/Need Identification/Analysis (Nursing Diagnosis)
3. Planning
4. Implementation
5. Evaluation

The nursing process provides an orderly, logical problem-solving approach for administering nursing care so that the patient's needs for such care are met comprehensively and effectively.

BOX 1–1

STEPS OF THE NURSING PROCESS

The nursing process consists of five specific steps:

1. *Assessment:* A systematic collection of data relating to patients.
2. *Problem/Need Identification:* Analysis of collected data to identify the patient's problems and/or needs.
3. *Planning:* A two-part process: first, the identification of goals and the patient's desired outcomes to correct the assessed health problem or need, and second, the selection of appropriate nursing interventions to assist the patient in attaining the outcomes.
4. *Implementation:* Putting the plan of care into action.
5. *Evaluation:* Determining the patient's progress toward attaining the identified outcome, and the patient's response to and effectiveness of the selected nursing interventions. Then changing the plan if indicated.

---

making; problem solving; and delivery of higher quality, individualized patient care. Box 1–1 shows the steps and their order. These five steps are central to nursing actions in any setting. The nursing process is now included in the conceptual framework of nursing curricula and is accepted as part of the legal definition of nursing in the Nurse Practice Acts of most states.

When a patient enters the healthcare system, whether as an inpatient, clinic outpatient, or a home care client, the steps of the nursing process are set into motion. The nurse collects data, identifies patient problems/needs (nursing diagnoses), establishes goals, identifies outcomes, and selects nursing interventions to assist the patient in achieving these outcomes and goals. Finally, after these interventions have been implemented, the nurse evaluates the patient's responses and the effectiveness of the plan of care in reaching the desired outcomes and goals to determine whether or not the problems have been resolved and the patient is ready to be discharged from the care setting. If the identified problems remain unresolved, further assessment, additional problem identification, alteration of outcomes and goals, and/or changes of interventions are required.

Although we use the terms *assessment, problem/need identification, planning, implementation,* and *evaluation* as separate, progressive steps, in reality they are interrelated. Together these steps form a continuous circle of thought and action, which recycles throughout the patient's contact with the healthcare system. Figure 1–1 shows a model of how this cycling process can be visualized. You can see that the nursing process uses the nursing diagnosis (the clinical judgment product of critical thinking). Based on this judgment, nursing interventions are selected and implemented. These two products of critical thinking—the clinical judgment and the implementation of selected nursing interventions—are reviewed in upcoming chapters.

Figure 1–1 further shows how the progressive steps of the nursing process create an understandable model of both the products and processes of critical thinking contained within the nursing process. The model graphically emphasizes both the dynamic and cyclic characteristics of the nursing process.

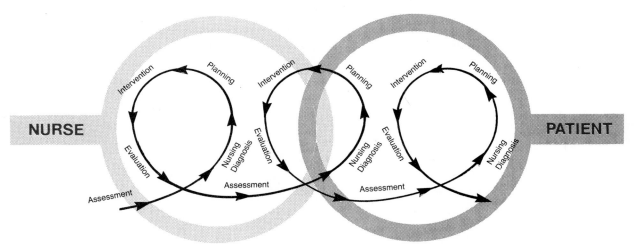

FIGURE 1–1. Diagram of the nursing process. The steps of the nursing process are interrelated, forming a continuous circle of thought and action that is both dynamic and cyclic.

How the Nursing Process Works

The scientific method of problem solving introduced in the previous section is used almost instinctively by most people, without conscious awareness, as noted in Box 1–2. Because the nursing process is based on this method, it may seem somewhat familiar. You only need to learn the new terms required by the nursing process, rather than having to think about each step (assessment, problem identification, planning, implementation, and evaluation) in an entirely new way.

To effectively use the nursing process, there are some basic abilities that the nurse must possess and be able to apply. Particularly important is a thorough knowledge of science and theory, not only as applied in nursing, but also in other related disciplines such as medicine and psychology. Creativity is needed in the ap-

---

BOX 1–2

PROBLEM SOLVING: EVERYDAY USE OF THE NURSING PROCESS

You have celebrated completion of your semester finals with a very spicy, late-evening dinner. You awaken during the night with a burning sensation in the center of your chest. You are young and in good health and note no other symptoms. (*Assessment*). You decide that your pain is the result of the spicy food you have eaten (*Problem Identification*). You then determine that you need to relieve the discomfort before you will be able to return to sleep (*Planning*). You take a liquid antacid for your discomfort (*Implementation*). Within a few minutes, you note the burning sensation is relieved, and you return to bed without further concern (*Evaluation*).

This is a process you routinely use to solve problems in your own life that can be readily applied to patient-care situations.

plication of nursing knowledge, as well as adaptability in handling change and the many unexpected happenings that occur. As a nurse, you must make a commitment to practice your profession in the best possible way, trusting in yourself and your ability to do your job well and displaying the necessary leadership to organize and supervise as your position requires. In addition, intelligence, well-developed interpersonal skills, and competent technical skills are essential.

> **FOR EXAMPLE:** A patient's irritable behavior could be a sign of anger or it could arise from a sense of helplessness regarding life events. However, it could also be the result of low serum glucose or the effects of excessive caffeine intake. A single behavior may have varied causes. It is important that your nursing assessment skills identify the underlying etiology to provide appropriate care.

In addition to these abilities, several fundamental beliefs (Box 1–3) provide guidance for the application of the nursing process and enhance the quality of nursing care. To further increase your knowledge and clinical decision-making skills, Appendix D contains the 11 statements of the ANA Code for Nurses (ANA, 1985). We suggest you take the time to read, think about, and incorporate these 11 statements into your professional practice and refer to the complete work for interpretation of the code statements.

The practice responsibilities presented in the definitions of nursing and the nursing process are explained in detail in the publication *Standards of Clinical Nursing Practice* (1991). The standards provide workable guidelines to ensure that the practice of nursing can be carried out by each individual nurse. Table 1–1 presents an abbreviated description of the standards of clinical practice. With the ultimate

---

BOX 1–3

FUNDAMENTAL PHILOSOPHICAL BELIEFS IN NURSING

Several fundamental philosophical beliefs are essential to the practice of nursing and need to be kept in mind when using the nursing process. The recent update of the ANA's Nursing's Social Policy Statement includes several values and assumptions that are included in the following list:

- The patient is a human being who has worth and dignity.
- Humans manifest an essential unity of mind/body/spirit (ANA, 1995).
- There are basic human needs that must be met (see Chapter 2, Maslow's Hierarchy).
- When these needs are not met, problems arise that may require intervention by another person until the individuals can resume responsibility for themselves.
- Human experience is contextually and culturally defined (ANA, 1995).
- Health and illness are human experiences (ANA, 1995).
- Patients have a right to quality health and nursing care delivered with interest, compassion, and competence with a focus on wellness and prevention.
- The presence of illness does not preclude health nor does optimal health preclude illness (ANA, 1995).
- The therapeutic nurse-patient relationship is important in the nursing process.

TABLE 1–1. ANA Standards of Clinical Nursing Practice

Standards of Care
Describes a competent level of nursing care as demonstrated by the nursing process that encompasses all significant actions taken by the nurse in providing care, and forms the foundation of clinical decision making.
1. **Assessment:** the nurse collects client health data.
2. **Diagnosis:** the nurse analyzes the assessment data in determining diagnoses.
3. **Outcome Identification:** the nurse identifies expected outcomes individualized to the client.
4. **Planning:** the nurse develops a plan of care that prescribes interventions to attain expected outcomes.
5. **Implementation:** the nurse implements the interventions identified in the plan of care.
6. **Evaluation:** the nurse evaluates the client's progress toward attainment of outcomes.

Standards of Professional Performance
Describes roles expected of all professional nurses appropriate to their education, position, and practice setting.
1. **Quality of Care:** the nurse systematically evaluates the quality and effectiveness of nursing practice.
2. **Performance Appraisal:** the nurse evaluates his/her own nursing practice in relation to professional practice standards and relevant statutes and regulations.
3. **Education:** the nurse acquires and maintains current knowledge in nursing practice.
4. **Collegiality:** the nurse contributes to the professional development of peers, colleagues, and others.
5. **Ethics:** the nurse's decisions and actions on behalf of clients are determined in an ethical manner.
6. **Collaboration:** the nurse collaborates with the client, significant others, and healthcare providers in providing client care.
7. **Research:** the nurse uses research findings in practice.
8. **Resource Utilization:** the nurse considers factors related to safety, effectiveness, and cost in planning and delivering client care.

goal of quality healthcare, the effective use of the nursing process will result in a viable nursing-care system that is recognized and accepted as nursing's body of knowledge and that can be shared with other healthcare professionals.

Practice Advantages of the Nursing Process

Practice Advantages of the Nursing Process:

Organizing framework
Human response focus
Structured decision making
Patient involvement
Common language
Economic contributions

There are many advantages to the use of the nursing process:

- The nursing process provides a framework for meeting the individual needs of the patient, the patient's family/significant other(s), and the community.
- The steps of the nursing process focus the nurse's attention on the "individual" human responses of a patient/group to a given health situation, resulting in a holistic plan of care addressing their specific problems/needs.
- The nursing process provides an organized, systematic method of problem solving, which may minimize dangerous errors or omissions in caregiving and avoid time-consuming repetition in care and documentation.
- The use of the nursing process promotes the active involvement of the patient in his or her own health care, enhancing consumer satisfaction. Such participation increases the patient's sense of control over what is happening to him or her, stimulates problem solving, and promotes personal responsibility, all of which strengthen the patient's commitment to achieving identified goals.

- The use of the nursing process enables you as a nurse to have more control over your own practice. This enhances the opportunity for you to use your knowledge, expertise, and intuition constructively and dynamically to increase the likelihood of a successful patient outcome. This, in turn, promotes greater job satisfaction and professional growth.
- The use of the nursing process provides a common language for practice, unifying the nursing profession. Using a system that clearly communicates the plan of care to coworkers and patients enhances continuity of care, promotes achievement of patient goals, provides a vehicle for evaluation, and aids in the developing of nursing standards. In addition, the structure of the process provides a format for documenting the patient's response to all aspects of the planned care.
- The use of the nursing process provides a means of assessing nursing's economic contribution to patient care. The nursing process supplies a vehicle for the quantitative and qualitative measurement of nursing care that meets the goal of cost effectiveness and still promotes holistic care.

Summary

In using the nursing process to administer nursing care to patients, the nursing profession has identified a body of knowledge that contributes to the prevention of illness as well as to the maintenance and/or restoration of the patient's health (or relief of pain/discomfort and provision of support when a return to health is not possible). The nursing process is the basis of all nursing actions and is the essence of nursing. It can be applied in any healthcare or educational setting, in any theoretical or conceptual framework, and within the context of any nursing philosophy. The process is flexible and yet sufficiently structured to provide a base for nursing actions.

The following chapters identify, discuss, and clarify each step of the nursing process. As noted, each step of the process builds on and interacts with the other steps, ensuring an effective practice model. Inclusion of the standards of clinical nursing practice in the appropriate chapters provides additional information to reinforce your understanding and opportunities to apply your knowledge by means of Practice Activities and a Work Page at the end of each chapter. Four patients help you in your learning process by sharing their personal experiences.

- Robert is a 72-year-old African-American male admitted to a medical inpatient unit for a recurrence of bilateral lower lobe pneumonia. He is a retired truck driver, living alone since his wife's death 5 years ago. He is concerned about his future and about losing control of his life, which presents you with ethical concerns and challenges in dealing with family dynamics.
- Sally is a 30-year-old female who is pregnant and experiencing beginning labor. This is her third pregnancy. Sally completed her evening shift as a respiratory therapist although she noted early signs of labor at 8:00 PM. You will follow Sally through labor, delivery, and home visits by a public health nurse to enhance your understanding of the continuity of care.
- Michelle, a 14-year-old female, has suffered multiple injuries in a mountain bike accident. She is a ninth grader at the local high school and lives with her parents (who immigrated from Vietnam 16 years ago), an older brother, and a younger sister. You will find pain management a major aspect of your nursing interventions for Michelle along with several cultural concerns.

- Donald, a 46-year-old male, is being treated for depression after the loss of his position as a loan banker because of his chronic absenteeism and poor job performance related to alcohol abuse. He has been drinking heavily recently and is suffering alcohol withdrawal since his admission. You will follow Donald through his other assessed healthcare needs of nutrition, coping, and changes in his role expectations.

The use of these vignettes provides many clinical examples throughout the text, offering a simulated practice environment and a touch of reality in planning the required continuity of patient care.

Two suggested reading lists are included at the end of this first chapter to assist you in your journey of understanding the historical development of the nursing process and to become knowledgeable about current publications describing these topics. We suggest that sometime during your busy program you take the time to read and reflect on these early authors' meaning and the language of nursing and the nursing process.

1. The ANA has defined nursing as: _____
_____
_____

2. My own definition of nursing is: _____
_____
_____

3. How has the information in this chapter affected your definition? _____
_____

4. The ANA Social Policy Statement defines the phenomena of concern for nurses as:

5. The definition of nursing process is: _____
_____
_____

6. Name and define the five steps of the nursing process and provide an example of each step:

Steps	Definition	Example
a. _____	_____	_____
b. _____	_____	_____
c. _____	_____	_____
d. _____	_____	_____
e. _____	_____	_____

7. List three advantages of using the nursing process:
   a. _____
   b. _____
   c. _____

8. List two of the fundamental philosophical beliefs that you believe are basic to decision making within the nursing process:
   a. _____
   b. _____

9. Identify the steps of the nursing process by placing the appropriate number of the activity in the space following the data presented in the following vignette:

   1 = Assessment; 2 = Problem/Need Identification;
   3 = Planning; 4 = Implementation; 5 = Evaluation.

VIGNETTE: Robert, a 72-year-old African-American male, is admitted with recurrent bilateral lower lobe pneumonia.

He reports this is his second episode in 6 months. _____

Temperature is 101°F, skin hot and flushed. _____

He reports frequent, hacking cough with moderate amount of thick greenish mucus. _____

Auscultation of the chest reveals scattered rhonchi throughout. _____

His mucous membranes are pale, and his lips are dry and cracked. _____

He says when he was sick last month, the doctor prescribed an antibiotic, which he discontinued after 6 days because he was feeling better. _____

You determine Robert has an airway clearance problem, a fluid volume deficit, and is not managing his therapeutic regimen effectively and thus requires teaching to promote adequate self-care and to prevent recurrence. _____

You establish the following outcomes:

- Expectorates secretions completely with breath sounds clear and respiration noiseless. _____
- Demonstrates adequate fluid balance with moist mucous membranes and loose respiratory secretions. _____
- Verbalizes understanding of cause of condition and rationale for therapeutic regimen. _____

You decide to set up a regular schedule for respiratory activities and fluid replacement. _____

In addition, you formulate a teaching plan to cover the identified concerns for self-care and illness prevention. _____

You provide a tube of petroleum jelly for Robert to use on his lips. _____

Every 2 hours you visit Robert to encourage him to deep-breathe, cough, change his position, and drink a glass of fluid of his choice. _____

You use this time to discuss avoidance of crowds and individuals with upper respiratory infections and continuing the treatment plan after discharge. _____

The following day, Robert's skin is no longer hot and flushed, temperature is 99°F, secretions are loose and readily expectorated, and breath sounds are clearing. _____

Robert's lips and oral mucous membranes are moist. He is able to explain in his own words how to care for himself and how to prevent pneumonia. _____

You decide that the current treatment plan is achieving the identified outcomes and to continue the plan as written. _____

BIBLIOGRAPHY

American Nurses' Association. (1980). *Nursing: A Social Policy Statement*. Kansas City, MO: Author.

American Nurses' Association. (1985). *Code for Nurses with Interpretive Statements*. Kansas City, MO: Author

American Nurses' Association. (1991). *Standards of Clinical Nursing Practice*. Kansas City, MO: Author

American Nurses' Association. (1995). *Nursing's Social Policy Statement*. Washington, DC: Author.

Iowa Intervention Project. (1996). *Nursing Intervention Classification (NIC),* ed 2. St. Louis: Mosby.

Iowa Outcome Project. (1997). *Nursing Outcomes Classification (NOC)*. St. Louis: Mosby.

King, L. (1971). *Toward a Theory for Nursing: General Concepts of Human Behavior*. New York: Wiley.

Martin, K.S., & Scheet, N.J. (1992). *Omaha System: Applications for Community Health Nursing*. Philadelphia: W.B. Saunders.

Nightingale, F. (1859). *Notes on Nursing: What It Is and What It Is Not* (Facsimile edition). Philadelphia: J.B. Lippincott, 1946.

North American Nursing Diagnosis Association (1999). *Nursing Diagnoses: Definitions & Classification*. Philadelphia: Author.

Peplau, H.E. (1952). *Interpersonal Relations in Nursing: A Conceptual Frame of Reference for Psychodynamic Nursing.* New York: Putnam.

Shore, L.S. (1988). *Nursing Diagnosis: What It Is and How to Do It, a Programmed Text.* Richmond, VA: Medical College of Virginia Hospitals.

Travelbee, J. (1971). *Interpersonal Aspects of Nursing,* ed 2. Philadelphia: F.A. Davis.

Yura, H., & Walsh, M.B. (1988). *The Nursing Process: Assessing, Planning, Implementing, Evaluating,* ed 5. Norwalk, CT: Appleton & Lange.

SUGGESTED READINGS

Classical Publications

American Nurses' Association. (1973). *Standards of Nursing Practice.* Kansas City, MO: Author.

American Nurses' Association. (1987). *The Scope of Nursing Practice.* Kansas City, MO: Author.

Aspinall, M.J., & Tanner, C.A. (1981). *Decision Making for Patient Care: Applying the Nursing Process.* New York: Appleton-Century-Crofts.

Bloch, D. (1974). Some crucial terms in nursing: What do they really mean? *Nursing Outlook, 22*(11):669–694.

Carlson, J.H., Craft, C.A., & McGuire, A.D. (1982). *Nursing Diagnosis.* Philadelphia: W.B. Saunders.

Carnevali, D.L. (1983). *Nursing Care Planning: Diagnosis and Management,* ed 3. Philadelphia: J.B. Lippincott.

Little, D.E., & Carnevali, D.I. (1976). *Nursing Care Planning,* ed 2. Philadelphia: J.B. Lippincott.

Orem, D.E. (1971). *Nursing: Concepts of Practice.* New York: McGraw-Hill.

Orlando, I.J. (1961). *The Dynamic Nurse-Patient Relationship: Function, Process, and Principles.* New York: Putnam.

Patterson, J.G., & Zderad, L.T. (1976). *Humanistic Nursing.* New York: Wiley.

U.S. Department of Health and Human Services. (1980). A classification scheme for client problems in community health nursing. DHHS Publication No. HRA 80-16.

Wiedenbach, E. (1964). *Clinical Nursing: A Helping Art.* New York: Springer.

Yura, H., & Walsh, M.B. (Eds.). (1967). *The Nursing Process.* Washington, DC: Catholic University of America Press.

Current Publications

Alfaro-Lefevre, R. (1998). *Applying Nursing Process: A Step-by-Step Guide,* ed 4. Philadelphia: Lippincott.

Bulechek, G.M., & McCloskey, J.C. (Eds.). (1985). *Nursing Interventions: Treatments for Nursing Diagnoses.* Philadelphia: W.B. Saunders.

Carnevali, D.L., Mitchell, P.H., Woods, N.F., & Tanner, C.A. (1984). *Diagnostic Reasoning in Nursing.* Philadelphia: J.B. Lippincott.

Carnevali, D.L., & Thomas, M.D. (1993). *Diagnostic Reasoning and Treatment Decision Making in Nursing.* Philadelphia: J.B. Lippincott.

Carpenito, L.J. (1997). *Nursing Diagnosis: Application to Clinical Practice,* ed 7. Philadelphia: Lippincott.

Cox, H., et al. (1997). *Clinical Applications of Nursing Diagnosis: Adult, Child, Women's Psychiatric, Gerontic, and Home Health Considerations,* ed 3. Philadelphia: F.A. Davis.

Craft, M.J., & Denehy, J.A. (1990). *Nursing Interventions for Infants and Children.* Philadelphia: W.B. Saunders.

Gordon, M. (1994). *Nursing Diagnosis: Process and Application,* ed 3. St. Louis: Mosby.

Hannah, K.J., Reimer, M., Mills, W.C., & Letourneau, S. (Eds.). (1987). *Clinical Judgment and Decision Making: The Future with Nursing Diagnosis.* New York: Wiley.

Iowa Intervention Project. (1997). Nursing interventions classification (NIC): An overview. In M.J. Rantz & P. LeMone (Eds.) *Classification of Nursing Diagnosis: Proceedings of the Twelfth Conference North American Nursing Diagnosis Association.* Glendale, CA: Cinahl Information Systems, pp 32–41.

Leuner, J.D., Manton, A.M., Kelliher, D.B., Sullivan, S.P., & Doherty, M. (1990). *Mastering the Nursing Process: A Case Study Approach.* Philadelphia: F.A. Davis.

Maas, M.L. (1997). Nursing-sensitive outcomes classification (NOC): Completing the essential comprehensive languages of nursing. In M.J. Rantz & P. LeMone (Eds.) *Classification of Nursing Diagnosis: Pro-*

ceedings of the Twelfth Conference North American Nursing Diagnosis Association. Glendale, C: Cinahl Information Systems, pp 40–47.

Maas, M., Buckwalter, K.C., & Hardy, M. (1991). *Nursing Diagnosis and Interventions for the Elderly.* Menlo Park, CA: Addison-Wesley.

Martin, K.S. (1997). The Omaha System. In M.J. Rantz & P. LeMone (Eds.) *Classification of Nursing Diagnosis: Proceedings of the Twelfth Conference North American Nursing Diagnosis Association.* Glendale, CA: Cinahl Information Systems, pp 16–21.

Martin, K.S., & Scheet, N.J. (1992). *Omaha System: A Pocket Guide for Community Health Nursing.* Philadelphia: W.B. Saunders.

CHAPTER 2

The Assessment Step: Developing the Patient Database

■ **ANA STANDARD 1:** Assessment: The nurse collects client health data.

The Patient Database

The **ASSESSMENT** step of the nursing process is an organized dynamic process involving three basic activities:

ASSESSMENT: the first step of the nursing process, during which data are collected.

- Systematically gathering data
- Sorting and organizing the data collected
- Documenting the data in a retrievable format

13

Using a number of techniques, you focus on eliciting a profile of the patient that allows you to identify patient problems or needs and corresponding nursing diagnoses, plan care, implement interventions, and evaluate outcomes. This profile is called the **PATIENT DATABASE,** and it serves as the fundamental pool of knowledge about the patient from which all other steps of the nursing process proceed.

The patient database supplies a sense of the patient's overall health status, providing a picture of the patient's physical, psychological, sociocultural, spiritual, cognitive, and developmental levels; economic status; functional abilities; and lifestyle. It is a combination of data gathered from the history-taking interview (a method of obtaining **SUBJECTIVE** information by talking with the patient and/or significant other(s) and listening to their responses); the physical examination (a "hands-on" means of obtaining **OBJECTIVE** information); and data gathered from the results of *laboratory/diagnostic studies.* To be more specific, subjective data are what the patient/significant others perceive, and objective data are what you observe.

Because consistency is important, the same data collection model should be used for both the patient interview (history) and the physical examination, whether that model is a nursing framework, a systems approach, a head-to-toe review, or a combination defined by your own agency. Frequently, to enhance efficiency and effectiveness, these two activities are combined into one interactive process in which physical data are gathered while interview questions are asked.

FRAMEWORK FOR DATA COLLECTION

Several nursing models may be used to guide your data collection. Three of the commonly used models are shown in Table 2–1: Doenges and Moorhouse's Diagnostic Divisions, Gordon's Functional Health Patterns, and North American Nursing Diagnosis Association's (NANDA's) Human Response Patterns.

The use of a nursing model as a framework for data collection rather than a body systems approach (assessing the heart, moving on to the lungs) or the commonly known head-to-toe approach has the advantage of identifying and validating nursing diagnoses as opposed to **MEDICAL DIAGNOSES.** An assessment model such as the Assessment Tool shown in Appendix B limits repetitious collection of medical data and focuses data collection on the nurse's phenomena of concern—the human responses to health and illness. Such responses include self-care limitations; impaired functioning in areas such as sleep, rest, nutrition, and elimination; pain; deficiencies in decision making; problematic relationships; or a desire simply to improve one's well-being (ANA, 1995).

THE INTERVIEW PROCESS

Information in the patient database is obtained both from the patient and from family members/significant others (as appropriate) through conversation and by observation during a structured interview. The nursing interview may take place over several contact sessions, but each contact should yield information, verify information already gathered, and/or clarify data. A well-conducted interview can be the first step in establishing a beneficial nurse-patient relationship and the rapport needed for good communication.

However, the interview is not merely the routine completion of the items on a standardized form by whomever is available. Rather, it is a tool of communication that permits an interactive exchange of information, a process that produces a

PATIENT DATABASE: the compilation of data collected about a patient; it consists of the nursing history, physical examination, and results of diagnostic studies.

SUBJECTIVE DATA: what the patient reports, believes, or feels.

OBJECTIVE DATA: what can be observed, for example, vital signs, behaviors, diagnostic studies.

MEDICAL DIAGNOSIS: illness/conditions for which treatment is directed by a licensed physician; medical diagnoses focus on correction/prevention of the pathology of specific organs/body systems.

Remember:
• The better you are prepared for the interview, the better your chances of asking something revealing that provides new insights about the patient, which in turn will help you to ask more pertinent questions.

TABLE 2–1. Comparison of Nursing Models for Data Collection

DIAGNOSTIC DIVISIONS (DOENGES AND MOORHOUSE, 2000)	FUNCTIONAL HEALTH PATTERNS (GORDON, 1995)	HUMAN RESPONSE PATTERNS (FITZPATRICK, 1991)
Activity/Rest: Ability to engage in necessary/desired activities of life (work and leisure) and to obtain adequate sleep/rest.	**Health Perception/Health Management:** Client's perception of general health status and well-being. Adherence to preventive health practices.	**Choosing:** To select between alternatives; the action of selecting or exercising preference in regard to a matter in which one is a free agent; to determine in favor of a course; to decide in accordance with inclinations.
Circulation: Ability to transport oxygen and nutrients necessary to meet cellular needs.	**Nutritional-Metabolic:** Patterns of food and fluid intake, fluid and electrolyte balance, general ability to heal.	**Communicating:** To converse; to impart, confer, or transmit thoughts, feelings, or information, internally or externally, verbally or nonverbally.
Ego Integrity: Ability to develop and use skills and behaviors to integrate and manage life experiences.	**Elimination:** Patterns of excretory function (bowel, bladder, and skin), and client's perception.	**Exchanging:** To give, relinquish or lose something while receiving something in return; the substitution of one element for another; the reciprocal act of giving and receiving.
Elimination: Ability to excrete waste products.	**Activity/Exercise:** Pattern of exercise, activity, leisure, recreation, and ADL; factors that interfere with desired or expected individual pattern.	
Food/Fluid: Ability to maintain intake of and use nutrients and liquids to meet physiological needs.	**Cognitive-Perceptual:** Adequacy of sensory modes, such as vision, hearing, taste, touch, smell, pain perception, cognitive functional abilities.	**Feeling:** To experience, a consciousness, sensation, apprehension or sense; to be consciously or emotionally affected by a fact, event, or state.
Hygiene: Ability to perform activities of daily living (ADL).	**Sleep/Rest:** Patterns of sleep and rest-relaxation periods during 24-hour day, as well as quality and quantity.	**Knowing:** To recognize or acknowledge a thing or a person; to be familiar with by experience or through information or report; to be cognizant of something through observation, inquiry or information; to be conversant with a body of facts, principles, or methods of action; to understand.
Neurosensory: Ability to perceive, integrate, and respond to internal and external cues.	**Self-Perception/Self-Concept:** Individual's attitudes about self, perception of abilities, body image, identity, general sense of worth and emotional patterns.	
Pain/Discomfort: Ability to control internal/external environment to maintain comfort.	**Role/Relationship:** Client's perception of major roles and responsibilities in current life situation.	**Moving:** To change the place or position of a body or any member of the body; to put and/or keep in motion; to provoke an excretion or discharge; the urge to action or to do something; to take action.
Respiration: Ability to provide and use oxygen to meet physiological needs.	**Sexuality/Reproductive:** Client's perceived satisfaction or dissatisfaction with sexuality. Reproductive stage and pattern.	**Perceiving:** To apprehend with the mind; to become aware of by the senses; to apprehend what is not open or present to observation; to take fully or adequately.
Safety: Ability to provide safe, growth-promoting environment.	**Coping/Stress Tolerance:** General coping pattern, stress tolerance, support systems, and perceived ability to control and manage situations.	**Relating:** To connect, to establish a link between, to stand in some association to another thing, person or place; to be borne or thrust in between things.
Sexuality: (Component of Ego Integrity and Social Interaction) Ability to meet requirements/characteristics of male/female role.	**Value-Belief:** Values, goals, or beliefs that guide choices or decisions.	
Social Interaction: Ability to establish and maintain relationships.		**Valuing:** To be concerned about, to care; the worth or worthiness; the relative status of a thing, or the estimate in which it is held, according to its real or supposed worth, usefulness, or importance; one's opinion of liking for a person or thing; to equate in importance.
Teaching/Learning: Ability to incorporate and use information to achieve healthy lifestyle/optimal wellness.		

> ### BOX 2–1
>
> ## SUBJECTIVE DATA COMPARED WITH OBJECTIVE DATA
>
> **Subjective data** are what the patient/significant other(s) say reflecting their own thoughts, feelings, and perceptions:
>
> "My hip hurts."   "I can't walk that far."
> "I'm worried about surgery."   "I don't know what to do to lower
> "She didn't sleep well."   my cholesterol level."
> "I can't give my husband a shot."   "His usual weight is 160 pounds."
> "I haven't had a bowel movement   "I don't think I'll ever get better."
>   for 3 days."
>
> **Objective data** are observable and measurable and include information gathered during the physical assessment and diagnostic studies:
>
> Restless/agitated   Cardiac murmur
> Temperature 99.2°F   Putrid odor
> Old surgical scar   Bloody vomitus
> Flabby muscle tone   Facial grimacing
> Hb 12.4   Glucose 107

- The better listener you are, the better your chance of hearing something meaningful in the patient's responses.
- The more perceptive you are, the better your chances of seeing new relationships among the data collected.

higher level of understanding than that which either person could achieve alone. The nursing interview thus has a specific purpose: the collection of a set of specific data (information) from the patient and/or significant others through both conversation (subjective data) and observation (objective data). Box 2–1 provides some examples to clarify the distinction between these two forms of data.

Clearly, the interview involves more than simply exchanging and processing data. Nonverbal communication is as important as the patient's choice of words in providing the data. The ability to collect data that are meaningful to the patient's health concerns depends heavily on your own knowledge base; the choice and sequence of questions; and the ability to give meaning to the patient's responses, integrate the data gathered, and prioritize the resulting information. Your knowledge, understanding, and insight into the nature and behavior of the patient are essential elements as well.

Now take a few moments to read through Box 2–2, which identifies 10 key elements for a successful interview. As you begin to understand and apply these patient interviewing techniques, you will see that they provide an opportunity for the patient to use descriptive terms and to explain more fully the meaning of an answer. You will want to keep these tips in mind as you complete the practice activities in this chapter.

The interview question is the major tool you will use to obtain information. Box 2–3 lists nine effective data collection questioning techniques. How you phrase the question is a skill that is important in obtaining the desired results and getting the information necessary to make accurate nursing diagnoses. However, be aware that even with a properly phrased question, there will be times when the answer you are seeking will not be given. It is important to remember, too, that the patient has the right to refuse to answer any question at all, no matter how reasonably phrased. Box 2–4 highlights some questioning strategies to be avoided because

BOX 2–2

ELEMENTS OF A SUCCESSFUL INTERVIEW

A successful interview has 10 key elements: (1) a clear sense of the underlying purpose for conducting the interview, (2) preliminary or background research before the interview begins, (3) a formal request of the interviewee to conduct the interview, (4) sound interviewing strategy, (5) effective use of icebreakers, (6) smoothly addressing the business of the interview, (7) good rapport between nurse and patient, (8) sensitivity to the patient's needs during the interview process, (9) adequate time for recovery following discussion of sensitive areas, and (10) closure.

1. **Underlying purpose:** The information gathered during the interview will be used in formulating the plan of care. Knowing the underlying purpose provides guidance in asking and answering questions, especially when areas that appear to be unrelated to the current situation may need to be pursued.

2. **Preliminary research:** Investigate the patient's and the family's current and previous situation. You can use resources such as records from the doctor's office, receiving department (e.g., emergency department) or prior admissions, as well as other health-team members. Make notes to identify key points because research often generates questions that should be written down so they are not lost. This preparation will assist you when formulating questions in the interview. The end result of the interview depends on what is put into it.

3. **Request to conduct the interview:** Formally requesting the interview is courteous and can clearly promote a positive interaction. Identify yourself to the patient and explain precisely the purpose of collecting the data and how those data will be used. Together, set a time for the interview, giving consideration to the needs and severity of the patient's condition and the availability of significant others. Allow yourself as much time as possible to prepare. Your approach and attitude are important in helping the patient be comfortable and understand the importance of the interview. "Mr. Jones, I would like to ask you some questions about yourself and your health status, so that together we may plan your care," is a more positive approach than, "I need to know your history." The first approach not only sells the interview but stimulates the patient's thinking. The result is a more productive interview.

4. **Interview strategy:** Cover the details of the interview in accordance with the definition of its purpose with the patient. Preparation and planning gives a sense of security and a plan to fall back on if things go slowly or unexpectedly wrong. This also allows a comfortable departure from the plan when conversation takes an unexplored path into productive channels. A new twist and a refreshing insight are the gold nuggets of interviewing, leading to information that otherwise might not have been remembered or shared.

Continued

ELEMENTS OF A SUCCESSFUL INTERVIEW (Continued)

5. **Icebreakers:** Icebreakers are the words and phrases that can put the patient at ease, set the stage, and promote a relaxed situation. They are the first bond of human communication and trust in this new relationship. How the icebreakers are used during the first few minutes may determine how and if the interview proceeds because the participants make important decisions concerning the future of this relationship. The patient and/or significant others are making judgments about you (that you are sincere, trustworthy, sensitive, professionally competent, or not).

   Some examples of icebreakers that might be used are the acknowledgement of what you know and see: "You've been admitted for surgery." A comment about the weather may also put the patient at ease. Offering something to drink, if allowed, and asking the patient how he or she prefers to be addressed also serves to promote an atmosphere of relaxation. When you sit down and appear relaxed and interested, this goal is more readily achieved.

6. **Business:** Get to the business at hand. Ask your prepared questions, using terminology the patient understands. Listen for answers and clues that will lead to other questions that you may not have anticipated. The relaxed informality that you have achieved needs to continue through this phase. Do not expect insights immediately; they usually come with time, increased comfort level, and trust.

7. **Rapport:** Call the participants by name, and monitor reactions to questions. Be careful not to bore or intimidate them with embarrassing questions. It is important to know when to shift gears, speed up, or slow down, or when to ask more challenging questions. Do not hurry the interview, and maintain eye contact as appropriate based on cultural belief systems.

8. **Sensitivity:** It may be necessary to ask questions about issues that involve sensitive areas for the patient. For example, questions about sexuality, lifestyle, or behaviors that put the person at risk for sexually transmitted diseases (STDs, including human immunodeficiency virus/acquired immunodeficiency syndrome [HIV/AIDS]) may be perceived as threatening. The nurse needs to proceed gently toward these sensitive areas. Be alert to verbal/nonverbal cues that may indicate that the area of discussion is particularly sensitive for the individual. Ceasing exploration at this point demonstrates respect for the individual's rights/privacy and can enhance the trust between participants. At a future point in the interview, the patient's level of comfort may allow you to revisit the topic and gather necessary data.

9. **Recovery:** Recover the rapport. If the sensitive areas have been approached slowly, the recovery period should be fairly easy to accomplish. Warmth and caring evidenced by a smile and the touch of the hand are helpful.

10. **Closure:** Conclude the interview by summarizing the highlights of the interview and leave the door open for further communication by asking the patient if he or she has anything else to add or any questions to ask of you.

BOX 2–3

EFFECTIVE DATA COLLECTION TECHNIQUES

- **Open-ended questions** allow the patient maximum freedom to respond in his or her own way, impose no limitations on how the question may be answered, and can produce considerable information. For example, "How do you feel about your new medications?" or "Explain the injection technique to me."
- **Hypothetical questions** pose a situation and ask the patient how it might be handled. You can learn whether the patient has accurate information and can think about how a similar situation might be handled. For example, "What would you do if you felt dizzy?" These questions may be very useful in determining the extent to which the patient has learned previously presented material.
- **Reflecting or "mirroring"** responses are useful techniques in getting at underlying meanings that might not be verbalized clearly. The patient might say, "Some days I'd like to throw this needle out the window." A mirror response would be, "You feel angry about the needle?" Now the patient is encouraged to verbalize what she or he is actually angry about. This response is nonevaluative and nonthreatening.
- **Focusing** shows the patient that you are attending to what is being said and consists of eye contact (within cultural limits), body posture, and verbal responses, that is, "Tell me more about that."
- **Giving broad openings** encourages the patient to take the initiative about what is to be talked about: "Where would you like to begin?"
- **Offering general leads** encourages the patient to continue: ". . . and then?"
- **Exploring** pursues a topic in more detail: "Would you describe it more fully?"
- **Verbalizing the implied** gives voice to what has been suggested; for instance, the patient says, "It's no use taking this medicine anymore." You respond, "You're concerned that it isn't making a difference for you?"
- **Encouraging evaluation** helps the patient to consider the quality of his or her own experience, such as: "How does that seem to you?"

they are generally ineffective in eliciting information from patients. At this point, take a moment to complete Practice Activity 2–1.

The Nursing Interview: Questioning and Listening

The patient's **MEDICAL DIAGNOSIS** can provide a starting point for the nursing interview. Your knowledge about the anatomy and physiology of the disease/condition helps in choosing and prioritizing questions. Remember, though, that when using a nursing model assessment tool, the results of the focused interview will point to the human responses to health and illness and to the development of nursing (rather than medical) diagnoses. Let us visit our first patient, Robert. Although you will ask

---

BOX 2–4

GENERALLY INEFFECTIVE DATA COLLECTION TECHNIQUES

- **Closed-ended questions** (such as "Why?") allow little or no freedom in choosing a response, such as, "Do you take your medicine?" (patient responds "No") or "How long have you been taking insulin?" (patient responds "3 years"). Typically there are only one or two possible answers to the question. The interviewer remains in close control over the interview because of the rigid structure. Although the closed-ended question may be useful in an emergency situation (when it is necessary to gather information in a short time), it is important to provide an opportunity for asking the patient to explain the answers to these questions in greater detail.
- **Leading questions** typically suggest the desired response, such as, "The infection seems to be getting better, don't you agree?" and thereby reduce the range of responses because the interviewee most commonly agrees with any leading statement. Highly emotional questions, tone of voice, or inflection ("Where *did* you learn that injection technique?") may be heard as challenging, provoking the interviewee to "attack" or become defensive, thereby blocking communication.
- **Probing** is a persistent questioning, a demand for more information than is given willingly. "Now tell me about. . . ." This creates an uneasy feeling in the patient and may be interpreted as an invasion of privacy, resulting in a defensive response or withholding of information.
- **Agreeing/disagreeing** implies that the patient is "right" or "wrong" rather than promoting the patient's idea as separate from your own. This can block exploration of an issue. "I agree, that would be the thing to do," or "You didn't mean to do that, did you?"

Robert about the signs and symptoms associated with his pneumonia, your nursing focus is:

- How does his shortness of breath affect his ability to care for himself? (Hygiene)
- Have the coughing episodes resulted in chest-wall pain or loss of sleep? (Pain/Discomfort, Activity/Rest)
- Has his appetite been affected by his frequent expectoration of purulent mucus? (Food/Fluid)
- How does he protect others from transmission of infection? (Safety, Teaching/Learning)

In addition, you need to keep an open mind and pay attention to clues that may identify other areas requiring investigation.

THE PATIENT HISTORY

The history is more than simply recording information. You must review the data, organize and determine the relevance of each item (value the data), and document the facts. The quality of a history improves with your knowledge and experience

PRACTICE ACTIVITY 2–1

Determining Types of Data

1. Identify Subjective (S) versus Objective (O) data:
   _____ Skin cool/damp
   _____ Sputum pale yellow
   _____ Allergic to eggs and sulfa
   _____ Pitting edema of feet and ankles
   _____ Usually voids three times per day
   _____ Chest pain lasting 15 minutes

2. Match the technique in column A to the statements in column B:

Column A	Column B
a. Open-ended question	_____ The next time this comes up, what would you do to handle it?
b. Hypothetical question	_____ That feeling in your chest, can you describe it more fully?
c. Reflection	_____ Do you use alcohol regularly?
d. Closed-ended question	_____ What would you like to talk about?
e. Leading question	_____ You're feeling better today, aren't you?

3. Rewrite the following using effective data collection techniques (see Box 2–3):

   a. You felt like crying, didn't you? _____

   b. You're in pain again? _____

   c. Do you want to change occupations? _____

   d. Since your doctor has talked with you, you don't have any questions, do you?_____

   _____

   e. Did you eat lunch? _____

with the history-taking process. Although such assessments are often lengthy and time-consuming in the beginning, more time is eventually saved by avoiding the necessity to retrace steps, correct misinformation, and undo actions. With practice, the time required for this activity will decrease.

GUIDELINES FOR HISTORY-TAKING

Listen Carefully

Be a good listener: You need to listen attentively to what the individual is saying. Listen for whole thoughts and ideas, not merely isolated facts. Facts may not be as important as the ideas that bind them together. For example, Robert tells you, "Sure, my doctor ordered some pills for me [antibiotics for pneumonia], last month." But Robert's tone of voice, facial expression, and body language communicate the idea that he may not be following his treatment regimen. Robert's non-verbal communication requires validation by asking either reflecting or open-ended questions as described in Box 2–3. For example, "You seem to have a lack of enthusiasm as you tell me about your medication. What is that about?"

Active-Listening

ACTIVE-LISTENING: reflecting back what the other person has said to validate your understanding of the meaning. A restatement of the other person's total communication, including the words and the feelings.

Use skills of Active-listening, silence, and acceptance to provide ample time for the person to respond: Give your full attention to the interview and do not interrupt. Save your own comments until the speaker is completely finished. Finally, ask related questions to stimulate the individual's memory if blocks occur. Once again, "facts" may not be as important as the patient's perception of reality. As you gain more experience in professional practice, you will begin to understand how important the patient's perception is. This is especially true in your assessment, understanding, management, and treatment of your patient's reported perception of pain.

Objectivity

Be as objective as possible: Identify only the patient's and/or significant others' contributions to the history, and do not try to interpret the data at this point. Record subjective data from the patient/significant others just as they were stated during the interview. Failure to do so may cause confusion and lead to inaccurate diagnoses. However, lengthy responses may need to be paraphrased.

Your initial responsibility is to observe, collect, and record data without drawing conclusions or making judgments/assumptions. Your self-awareness is a crucial factor in the interaction, because perceptions, judgments, and assumptions can easily color the assessment findings unless they are recognized. We all have a responsibility to understand how our biases affect the conclusions we draw from the data and not be influenced by them. It may be useful to review the beliefs cited in Chapter 1 (p. 00) and the Code for Nurses contained in Appendix D.

Manageable Detail

Keep the amount of detail manageable: The data collected about the patient and/or significant others contain a vast amount of information, some of which may be repetitious. However, some of it will be valuable for eliciting information that was not recalled or volunteered previously.

Enough material needs to be noted in the history so that a complete picture is presented, and yet not so much that the information will not be read or used. "Necessary" information includes all data (positive and negative) that are relevant to the situation. For example, let us return to your patient Robert. He was admitted with the diagnosis of pneumonia. During the history he reports, "I've been coughing a lot lately." Necessary information in this case would be to clarify what Robert means by "coughing a lot lately." You need to know the frequency and time of coughing and factors that bring about or terminate an episode of coughing. Along with the cough you would want the necessary information about whether or not the cough was productive. So you would want to know the descriptive characteristics of the mucus. What color was it? How much mucus does he expectorate? As you can see, the "necessary" information is that which clarifies and makes the communication of Robert's subjective data to other healthcare providers both useful and meaningful.

Sequence Information

Order is imperative: Develop and use a form that makes it easy to find information, identify problems, and choose nursing diagnoses. In addition, present the current health problems in chronological order and include relevant events from the past. It is also useful to express topics in a uniform manner. For example, expressing the age at which events/illnesses/surgery occurred instead of just the year events occurred: "age 67/born 1932"; or "hysterectomy, age 35/1968."

Document Clearly

Write legibly: This required skill improves the communication and comprehension of your findings, decreasing the chance of misunderstanding, saving time for you and other healthcare professionals who rely on your records.

Record Data in a Timely Way

Record the data during the interview, or write the history as soon as possible after gathering the information: This helps ensure greater accuracy of the data. The longer you wait to record, the more likely it is the data and specific details will fade and be more difficult to recall. A word of advice, data not written are data lost.

Physical Examination: The Hands-On Phase

You perform the physical examination to gather objective information and also as a screening device. For the data collected during the physical examination to be meaningful, you need to know the normal physical and emotional characteristics of human beings sufficiently well enough to be able to recognize deviations.

FOCUS AND PREPARATION

To gain as much information as possible from the assessment procedure, approach the patient with a positive, sincere attitude. Such an attitude conveys competence, interest, kindness, thoroughness, orderliness, and confidence. It may be frightening for the patient if you give the impression that you do not know what you are doing, or if you are awkward in performing assessment tasks. Give the patient a clear explanation of the procedures you will be using. Then, proceed with the examination according to the format you have previously chosen to gather and record the data: a nursing model (as suggested earlier), a systems approach (cardiovascular, respiratory, gastrointestinal, and so on), a head-to-toe review (head, neck, chest, and so on), or a combination of these. The same format should be used each time you perform a physical examination to lessen the possibility of omissions and to increase your confidence and efficiency in completing the task.

However, the patient's state of health/severity of condition may require you to place priority on specific portions of your assessment. This priority in data collection is based in part on the measurement criteria developed by the ANA. "The priority of data collection is determined by the client's immediate condition or needs" (ANA, 1991). For example, when examining a patient with severe chest pain, you would probably choose to evaluate the pain and the cardiovascular system before addressing other areas. Likewise, the duration and length of any physical examination depend on circumstances such as the condition of the patient and the urgency of the situation.

During the examination, emotional support and care should be offered as indicated. Your professional judgment needs to be used in selecting the steps and sequencing the assessment to provide emotional support as needed. The patient with resolving chest pain may want to talk about his embarrassment of being perceived as "weak" during the episode of chest pain. Interrupting your examination to support and listen to your patient is not only a correct intervention, but also demonstrates the sensitive blending of the art and science of nursing.

It is also important to provide the patient with as much feedback as possible. While completing the examination process, you will find this is an excellent opportunity to provide education on associated procedures, assessment findings, and health teaching in general. Perceptual and observational skills are especially important in determining what your patient needs.

ASSESSMENT METHODS

Four common methods used during the physical examination are inspection, palpation, percussion, and auscultation. These techniques incorporate the senses of sight, hearing, touch, and smell:

1. *Inspection* is a systematic process of observation that is not limited to vision but also includes the senses of hearing and smell.

    Sight: Observing the skin for color, discolorations, lacerations; the lesion for drainage; the respiratory pattern for depth and symmetry; body language, movement, and posture, use of extremities, presence of physical limitations; the face for expressions.

    Hearing: Listening to the nature of a cough, the integrity of a joint, the tone of a voice or content of interactions with others.

    Smell: Detecting significant odors.

2. *Palpation* is the touching or pressing of the external surface of the body with the fingers.

    Touch: Feeling a lump; noting temperature, degree of moistness, and texture of skin; or determining strength of uterine contraction.

    Pressure: Determining the character of a pulse, evaluating edema, noting position of the fetus, or pinching (tenting) to observe skin turgor.

    Probing deeper: Reveals muscle tone/tension or an abnormal pain response.

3. *Percussion* is the direct or indirect tapping of a specific body surface to ascertain information about underlying tissues or organs.

    Using fingertips: Tap the chest and listen for the sound indicating the presence or absence of fluid, masses, or consolidation.

    Using a percussion hammer: Tap the knee and observe the presence or absence of lower leg movement/reflexes.

4. *Auscultation* is listening for sounds within the body with the aid of a stethoscope and describing or interpreting them.

    Hearing: Listening at the antecubital space for blood pressure, the chest for heart/lung sounds, the abdomen for bowel sounds or fetal heart tones.

FOLLOW-UP CONSIDERATIONS

After completion of the physical examination, your patient may require assistance. The patient may need to be helped down off the examination table for safety reasons or may require help with dressing. Consideration of these sometimes forgotten needs enhances the rapport and trust developed during the examination. Including these interventions personalizes the patient-nurse interaction and makes the assessment process much more than just your hasty gathering of required data.

You may need to verify or clarify communication associated with the physical examination. By repeating aloud what you have observed, you give the patient the opportunity to validate the accuracy of the information obtained and misunderstandings can be avoided. For example, Observation: "I noticed that you flinched when I palpated your abdomen"; Response: "Yes, your hand was cold and I'm ticklish."

Laboratory Tests and Diagnostic Procedures: Supporting Evidence

Laboratory and other diagnostic studies are a part of the information-gathering stage. They aid in the management, maintenance, and restoration of health. Some tests are used to diagnose disease, whereas others are useful in following the course of a disease or adjusting therapy. Your knowledge about the purpose, procedure, and results of various scans, x-rays, performance tests (e.g., treadmill electrocardiogram, pulmonary function) and numerous laboratory studies is necessary for the success of the study and to promote timely nursing intervention and a positive patient outcome through properly preparing and educating the patient about the prescribed studies.

In reviewing and interpreting laboratory tests, it is important to remember that the origin of the test material does not always correlate to an organ or body system. For example, a urine test might be done to detect the presence of bilirubin and urobilinogen, which could indicate liver disease, biliary obstruction, or hemolytic disease. In some cases, the relationship of the test to the pathology is clear, whereas in others, such as obtaining renal function studies in the presence of cardiac failure, it is not. This is a result of the interrelationships between the various organs and systems of the body. In a few cases the results of a test are nonspecific because they only indicate a disorder or abnormality and do not indicate the location of the cause of the problem. For example, an elevated erythrocyte sedimentation rate (ESR) suggests the presence but not the location of an inflammatory process.

In evaluating laboratory tests, it is advisable to consider which drugs are being administered to the patient because these may have the potential to blur or falsify results, creating a misleading diagnostic picture.

FOR EXAMPLE:

- Heparin prolongs blood clotting times.
- Oral iron preparations cause a false-positive result when the stool is tested for occult blood.
- Phenazopyridine (Pyridium) is a urinary tract analgesic that can color the urine red.

- Use of promethazine (Phenergan), an antiemetic, can cause a false-negative result in a pregnancy test.

In some cases, it is necessary to note at what time medication was administered. Serum levels can be drawn to determine the varied concentrations of administered medications. Terms such as *peak* and *trough* levels are used to determine both the possible toxic effects and the therapeutic ranges of the medication.

There are also several mechanisms that may alter the laboratory results through the introduction of interfering materials.

FOR EXAMPLE:

- Foods that give a yellow color to blood serum (e.g., carrots, yams) alter a bilirubin test.
- Food may contribute to the presence of substances in body fluids/excretions, such as hemoglobin and myoglobin in meat, which may lead to a misdiagnosis of occult blood in the stool.
- Intramuscular injections can elevate creatine phosphokinase (CPK) levels used to diagnose acute myocardial infarction.

Organizing Information Elements

CLUSTERING THE COLLECTED DATA

Data gathered in the interview, in the physical examination, and from other records/sources are organized and recorded in a concise systematic way and clustered into similar categories. Various formats have been used to accomplish this, including a review of body systems. The body systems approach has been used by both medicine and nursing for many years but is actually more useful for the physician in making a medical diagnosis than for a nurse in identifying nursing diagnoses. Currently nursing is developing and fine-tuning its own tools for recording and clustering data (e.g., Doenges & Moorhouse, 2000; Gordon, 1994; Guzzetta, et al., 1989). Organizing data using a nursing framework (Box 2–5) assists you in focusing your attention and in choosing specific nursing diagnosis labels to describe the data accurately. However, it is important to be aware of the advantages of each type of framework and to follow the approach recommended by your school or

---

BOX 2–5

ASSESSMENT DATA FOR ROBERT WITH APPLICATION TO EXCERPT FROM DOENGES AND MOORHOUSE DIAGNOSTIC DIVISIONS ASSESSMENT TOOL

Respiration

Reports (Subjective)

Dyspnea, related to: Climbing stairs/walking more than 2 blocks, close places/crowds

   Cough/sputum: Thick, yellow, approximately ¼ tsp, 6 to 10 times/day, especially with activity

Continued

ASSESSMENT DATA FOR ROBERT WITH APPLICATION TO EXCERPT FROM DOENGES AND MOORHOUSE DIAGNOSTIC DIVISIONS ASSESSMENT TOOL (Continued)

History of:
    Bronchitis: Diagnosed 1991
    Asthma: No   *Tuberculosis:* No
    Emphysema: Diagnosed 1991
    Recurrent pneumonia: Yes; last admission approximately 6 months ago
    Exposure to noxious fumes: Not aware of past exposures (was a diesel trucker)
Smoker: **Cigarettes (pack/day):** 1 × 45 years, ½ × 8 years (since 1991)
    Number of pack/years: 49
Use of respiratory aids: Inhaler and PO meds
Oxygen: No/"Doctor suggested I use oxygen at night, but I don't think I'm that bad."

Exhibits (Objective)

Respiratory: Rate: 28 at rest   *Depth:* Shallow
    Symmetry: Increased AP diameter
Use of accessory muscles: Yes
Nasal flaring: None observed
Fremitus: Increased tactile   *Egophone:* Resonance increased
    Percussion: Hyperresonate
Breath sounds: Diminished, bronchovesicular, basilar inspiratory crackles bilateral, scattered rhonchi—limited clearing with cough
Cyanosis: Oral mucous membranes pale
Clubbing of fingers: Slight
Sputum characteristics: Yellow, tenacious, scant amount during assessment
Mentation/restlessness: Alert; responds to all questions; no restlessness
Other: Verbal responses slow; breathless—phrases four to five words long
Results chest x-ray: Bilateral lower lobe infiltrates

On reviewing the collected data for this patient with pneumonia and noting cues (signs and symptoms) in the Respiration section of the database, you are referred to the Respiration section of the Diagnostic Divisions. Four possible labels are suggested: Airway Clearance, ineffective; Aspiration, risk for; Breathing Pattern, ineffective; and Gas Exchange, impaired.

agency. Remember, consistency is the key. Before you meet Donald and complete Practice Activity 2–2, it is suggested you read about Michelle in Box 2–6 and return to Table 2–1 to review the definitions of the 13 diagnostic divisions and the 11 functional health patterns.

REVIEWING AND VALIDATING FINDINGS

VALIDATION is an ongoing process that occurs during the data collection phase and on its completion, when the data are reviewed and compared. You review the data

VALIDATION: the process of assuring that data are factual.

PRACTICE ACTIVITY 2–2

Organizing Data: Diagnostic Divisions and Functional Health Patterns

Donald has been admitted to the psychiatric hospital inpatient substance abuse unit for treatment of depression and withdrawal from alcohol.

Organize the data below according to diagnostic divisions and functional health patterns. Place the number of the listed data next to the category where you believe it fits (see Table 2–1).

1. 46-year-old male
2. Divorced, not currently involved in a relationship
3. Loan banker, laid off 7 months ago
4. Unsteady gait
5. Clothes rumpled, has not shaved for 2 days, dry skin
6. Eats 1 or 2 meals a day—donuts, sandwiches, meat and potatoes, no vegetables or fruits; coffee 4+ cups/day
7. Stools have been loose, 3 to 4/day
8. BP 136/82 (right arm/sitting), radial pulse 92
9. Alert and oriented
10. Catholic, not practicing
11. Sleeps usually 3 to 4 hours a night, awakens around 5 AM
12. "I've been drinking a lot lately." Bourbon 1 fifth/day
13. Worries about financial situation, unable to make child support payments
14. Congested nonproductive cough
15. Reports constant throbbing pain, left knee—old sports injury
16. Genogram:

GENOGRAM: graphic representation of a family (may include several generations) reflecting medical data and relationships/roles.

Continued

PRACTICE ACTIVITY 2–2

Organizing Data: Diagnostic Divisions and Functional Health Patterns (Continued)

Diagnostic Divisions	Functional Health Patterns
Activity/Rest:	Health Perception/Health Management:
Circulation:	Nutritional/Metabolic:
Ego Integrity:	Elimination:
Elimination:	Activity/Exercise:
Food/Fluid:	Cognitive/Perceptual:
Hygiene:	Sleep/Rest:
Neurosensory:	Self-Perception/Self-Concept:
Pain/Discomfort:	Role/Relationship:
Respiration:	Sexuality/Reproductive:
Safety:	Coping/Stress Tolerance:
Sexuality:	Value/Belief:
Social Interaction:	
Teaching/Learning:	

to be sure that what has been recorded is factual and to identify errors of omission or inconsistencies that require additional investigation. Validation is particularly important when the data are conflicting, when the source of the data may not be reliable, or when serious harm to the patient could result from any inaccuracies. Ask questions of the patient or others to verify your impressions; for example, "Tell me more about that." "What I heard you say is. . . ." Validating the information gathered can avoid the possibility of making wrong inferences or conclusions that can lead to inaccurate nursing diagnoses, incorrect outcomes, and/or inappropriate nursing actions. This can be done by sharing your assumptions with the individuals involved and having them verify the accuracy of those conclusions.

Data that are grossly abnormal are rechecked, and objective and subjective data are compared for congruencies and/or inconsistencies. For example, the patient reports upper right abdominal pain, although musculature appears relaxed and the patient does not flinch on abdominal palpation. Additional investigation reveals that the pain is episodic and usually follows meal times. Temporary factors that may affect the data are also identified/noted. For example, you note the patient's right hand is cool in comparison with the left hand. On questioning her, you discover she had been holding a glass of ice water in her right hand.

Finally, the patient may remember something, or feel more comfortable in sharing information with you, and although the data collected by any healthcare professional are confidential, it may be appropriate or necessary to share the information. For example, you may have a greater opportunity to observe interactions between family members during the assessment process that could have an impact on the diagnostic process and/or the plan of care. Some of these findings may need to be brought to the attention of other healthcare professionals, such as the physician, dietician, or physical therapist. Sharing these additional data aids in collaborative planning of care.

BOX 2–6

ORGANIZING ASSESSMENT DATA FOR MICHELLE USING A NURSING FRAMEWORK

You obtained the following information for the patient database during your assessment of Michelle (following her admission to the orthopedic unit having had an external fixation device applied for multiple compound fractures of the right lower leg). The data have been clustered in each of three nursing frameworks by means of the identifying numbers for each data element.

Assessment Data

1. 14-year-old female
2. High-school student
3. Practicing Buddhist
4. Single
5. Living with parents, one older brother, one younger sister
6. Temperature 100°F
7. Sharp severe pain, right lower leg, "toes to knees," rated "9" on 0 to 10 scale, and right-sided headache rated "4."
8. Hospitalized for tonsillectomy 4 years ago—1995/age 11
9. Alert and oriented, brief loss of consciousness at time of injury
10. Respirations 26, lungs clear, splinting with deep inspiration
11. Weight 98 pounds
12. Indwelling catheter in place, urine clear, amber
13. Independent in self-care
14. Usually sleeps 8 hours each night
15. Right lower leg—wound packed with sterile dressing; multiple puncture sites (external fixator in place)
16. Menarche at age 13
17. Manages stress by talking with friends, exercise (distance runner and mountain biking), meditation
18. States has no allergies
19. Concerned that injury will leave scars and affect participation in track activities
20. P 110, BP 100/78 (left arm/supine)

How you organize these data depends on the format you choose for recording. On occasion, data may be recorded in more than one section because the divisions/patterns are based on human responses instead of specific body systems. The above data could be recorded in three different nursing formats, thus:

Doenges and Moorhouse: Diagnostic Divisions

Activity/Rest: 2, 9, 14, 17	Pain/Discomfort: 7
Circulation: 20	Respiration: 10
Ego integrity: 3, 4, 17, 19	Safety: 6, 15, 18
Elimination: 12	Sexuality: 1, 4, 16

Continued

ORGANIZING ASSESSMENT DATA FOR MICHELLE USING A NURSING FRAMEWORK (Continued)

Doenges and Moorhouse: Diagnostic Divisions (continued)

Food/Fluid: 11   Social interaction: 4, 5
Hygiene: 13   Teaching/Learning: 2, 8
Neurosensory: 9

Gordon's: Functional Health Patterns

Health Perception/Health   Self-perception/Self-concept: 19
   Management: 7, 8   Role/Relationship: 1, 2, 4, 5
Nutritional/Metabolic: 6, 10, 11, Sexuality/Reproductive: 4, 16
   15, 18, 20   Elimination:12
Coping/Stress Tolerance: 17   Activity/Exercise: 10, 13, 17
Value/Belief: 3   Sleep/Rest: 14
Cognitive/Perceptual: 9

NANDA: Human Response Patterns

Exchanging: 6, 8, 10, 11, 12, 15, Moving: 13, 14
   18, 20   Perceiving: 19
Communicating: 0   Knowing: 9
Relating: 1, 2, 4, 5, 16   Feeling: 7
Valuing: 3   Choosing: 17

Summary

The assessment step of the nursing process emphasizes and should provide a holistic view of the patient. The generalized assessment done during the overall gathering of data creates a profile of the patient. A focused assessment may be done to obtain more information about a specific issue that needs expansion or clarification. Both types of assessment are important and complement each other. A successfully completed assessment provides data on the patient's state of wellness, response to health problems, and risk factors.

To assist you in your assessment assignments and future applications of this first step of the nursing process an extensive review of the current literature is provided. The Suggested Readings at the end of this chapter provide assessment references for adult health, the pediatric or geriatric patient, telephone assessment, home health, and long-term care. Also included is a separate bibliography on genograms. A genogram is displayed in Practice Activity 2–2.

Now, before we briefly describe the next chapter, let us return to the first ANA Standard of Clinical Nursing Practice and review the measurement criteria necessary to achieve and ensure compliance with the standard. The knowledge and skills required to meet the criteria listed in Box 2–7 have been described in this chapter.

The next chapter presents the second step of the nursing process—Problem/Need Identification. In this upcoming chapter, the diagnostic reasoning process is

BOX 2-7

MEASUREMENT CRITERIA FOR ANA STANDARD I

Assessment: The nurse collects client health data.

1. Data collection involves client, significant others, and healthcare providers when appropriate.
2. The priority of data collection activities is determined by the client's immediate condition or needs.
3. Pertinent data are collected using appropriate assessment techniques and instruments.
4. Relevant data are documented in a retrievable form.
5. The data collection process is systematic and ongoing.

used to analyze/synthesize the information obtained from the patient database and identify the patient healthcare needs or nursing diagnoses that form the basis for the development of the plan of care.

1. Rewrite the following questions so that they are open-ended:

   a. You're feeling better after the respiratory treatment, aren't you? _____

   _____

   b. Have you taken your medicine today? _____

   _____

   c. Do you understand these directions? _____

   _____

2. Using the technique of reflection, write a question to clarify these patient statements:

   a. Do you think I should tell my doctor about my concern? _____

   _____

   b. What do you want to talk about today? _____

   _____

   c. I don't think I can go on without my husband. _____

   _____

   d. Do you think it is important to get married? _____

   _____

   3. When might a closed-ended question be helpful? _____

   _____

4. Describe the three components of the patient database:

   a. _____   b. _____   c. _____

5. The four activities involved in the physical assessment are:

   a. _____   b. _____   c. _____   d. _____

6. The patient database is important to the provision of patient care because _____

   _____

7. For assessment purposes the difference between subjective data and objective data is _____

   _____

   _____

8. Underline the subjective data and circle the objective data in the following vignette:

VIGNETTE: Sally comes to the obstetric department for evaluation of her stage of labor. Back pains began about 3 hours ago (8 PM) while on her job as a respiratory therapist. Contractions are 5 minutes apart, lasting 30 seconds for the last 45 minutes. BP 146/84 (left arm/lying), P 110, respirations 24. Weight 155 pounds (up 4 pounds this week). Cervix dilated 4 cm, membranes intact. Fetal head engaged, heart tones slightly muffled in right lower quadrant, rate 132. Nauseated since a dinner of fried chicken 4 hours ago. Appears anxious and seems irritated that her physician is not here. Voided 1 hour ago, has not had a bowel movement for 2 days. Stopped smoking 8 months ago. Lungs clear. No allergies. Married, husband plans to attend the birth. Two children are in the care of their grandmother tonight. Appearance is well-groomed with a well-fitting maternity uniform and low-heeled shoes. Requests to leave contacts in to observe the birth. Last physical examination 1 week ago. Gestation 37 weeks, with due date 3 weeks off—3/11/99.

9. An important benefit of doing "research" or reviewing available information before an interview is

_____

_____

10. An interview should be "requested" because _____

_____

11. Check those information resources that can be useful in helping the nurse to prepare for the interview:

_____ Family/significant other   _____ Physician notes

_____ Old medical records   _____ Textbooks/reference journals

_____ Diagnostic studies   _____ Other nurses/healthcare providers

12. Sensitivity of the nurse is important during the interview process to _____

_____

13. List three abilities of the nurse that are necessary in order to collect a relevant patient database.

a. _____ b. _____ c. _____

14. In the following vignette, cluster and record the assessment data (following the numbers) into the appropriate diagnostic divisions listed below. Refer to Table 2–1 as needed for the type of data included in the specific divisions to assist you in clustering the data.

VIGNETTE: Robert, a 72-year-old (1) African-American male admitted to the medical unit at 1:00 PM for (2) bilateral lower lobe pneumonia. (3) Has had liquids only by mouth for several days. (4) Last BM—2 days ago, brown/formed stool, (5) voided at 1:20 PM—clear, dark amber. He reports (6) "My chest hurts", as he splints chest while coughing. (7) Small amount, thick, yellow sputum expectorated with cough. (8) Appears anxious, fidgeting with sheets, face tense, watching nurse intently. (9) Tympanic temperature (TMT) 101°F, (10) BP 178/102 (left arm/lying), P 100/regular, (11) respirations 28/shallow. (12) Skin warm, moist, color pale. (13) Has difficulty hearing questions, left hearing aid (R ear) at home. (14) Reports "This is the second episode in a month." (15) Doctor did prescribe antibiotic (drug unknown) a month ago, patient did not complete treatment. (16) States he lives alone (widower), and is (17) responsible for meeting his own needs. In reviewing diagnostic studies, you note the (18) chest x-ray reveals infiltrates both lower lobes and a (19) Gram stain of the sputum reveals gram-negative bacteria.

DIAGNOSTIC DIVISIONS

Activity/Rest: _____   Hygiene: _____   Safety: _____

Circulation: _____   Neurosensory: _____   Sexuality: _____

Ego Integrity: _____   Pain/Discomfort: _____

Social Interaction: _____   Elimination: _____

Respiration: _____   Teaching/Learning: _____

Food/Fluid: _____

BIBLIOGRAPHY

American Nurses' Association. (1991). *Standards of Clinical Nursing Practice.* St. Louis, MO: Author.

American Nurses' Association. (1995). *Nursing's Social Policy Statement.* Washington, DC: Author.

Doenges, M.E., & Moorhouse, M.F. (2000). *Nurse's Pocket Guide: Diagnoses, Interventions, and Rationales,* ed 6. Philadelphia: F.A. Davis.

Doenges, M.E., Moorhouse, M.F., & Geissler, A.C. (2000). *Nursing Care Plans: Guidelines for Individualizing Patient Care,* ed 5. Philadelphia: F.A. Davis

Fitzpatrick, J.J. (1991). In R.M. Carroll-Johnson (Ed.) *Classification of Nursing Diagnosis: Proceedings of the Ninth Conference.* Philadelphia: J.B. Lippincott.

Gordon, M. (1995). *Nursing Diagnosis: Process and Application,* ed 3. St. Louis, MO: Mosby.

Guzzetta, C.E., Bunton, S.D., Prinkey, L.A., Sherer, A.P., & Seifert, P.C. (1989). *Clinical Assessment Tools for Use with Nursing Diagnoses.* St. Louis, MO: Mosby.

SUGGESTED READINGS

Allen, J.E. (1997). *Long Term Care Facility Resident Assessment Instrument User's Manual: For Use with Version 2.0 of HCFA: Minimum Data Set Resident Assessment Protocols and Utilization Guidelines, October 1995, Plus HCFA's 249 Questions and Answers, August 1996.* New York: Springer.

Barkauskas, V.H., Staltenberg-Allen, K., & Baumann, L. (1998). *Health & Physical Assessment,* ed 2. St. Louis: Mosby.

Barry, P.D. (1989). *Psychosocial Nursing Assessment and Intervention: Care of the Physically Ill Person,* ed 2. Philadelphia: Lippincott.

Bates, B. (1995). *A Visual Guide to Physical Examination,* ed 3. Philadelphia: Lippincott.

Billings, P.C. (1996). *Instant Nursing Assessment: Pediatric.* Albany: Delmar.

Bowers, A.C., & Thompson, J.M. (1992). *Clinical Manual of Health,* ed 4. St. Louis: Mosby-Year Book.

Cohen-Cole, S.A. (1991). *The Medical Interview: The Three-Function Approach.* St. Louis: Mosby.

Coulehan, J.L., & Block, M.R. (1997). *The Medical Interview: Mastering Skills for Clinical Practice,* ed 3. Philadelphia: F.A. Davis.

Eliopoulos, C. (1990). *Health Assessment of the Older Adult,* ed 2. Redwood City, CA: Addison-Wesley Nursing.

Engel, K. (1996). *Pocket Guide to Pediatric Assessment.* St. Louis: Mosby.

Expert 10-Minute Physical Examinations. (1997). St. Louis: Mosby.

Fuller, J., & Schaller-Ayers, J. (1994). *Health Assessment: A Nursing Approach,* ed 2. Philadelphia: Lippincott.

Giger, J.N., & Davidhizar, R.E. (Eds.). (1995). *Transcultural Nursing: Assessment and Intervention,* ed 2. St. Louis: Mosby.

Guzzetta, C.E., Bunton, S.D., Prinkey, L.A., & Sherer, A. (1989). *Clinical Assessment Tools for Use with Nursing Diagnoses.* St. Louis: Mosby.

Hogstel, M.O., & Keen-Payne, R. (1996). *Practical Guide to Health Assessment: Through the Lifespan,* ed 2. Philadelphia: F.A. Davis.

Jackson, J.E., & Neighbors, M. (1990). *Home Care Client Assessment Handbook.* Rockville, MD: Aspen.

Jaffe, M.S., & Skidmore-Roth, L. (1997). *Home Health Nursing: Assessment and Care Planning,* ed 3. St. Louis: Mosby.

Leasia, M.S., & Monahan, F.D. (1997). *A Practical Guide to Health Assessment.* Philadelphia: W.B. Saunders.

Mezey, M.D., Hauckhorst, L.H., & Stokes, S.A. (1993). *Health Assessment of the Older Individual,* ed 2. New York: Springer.

Murray, R.B., & Zenter, J.P. (1997). *Nursing Assessment and Health Promotion Strategies Through the Life Span,* ed 6. Norwalk, CT: Appleton & Lange.

Pesut, D.F., & Herman, J. (1999). *Clinical Reasoning: The Art and Science of Critical and Creative Thinking.* Albany, NY: Delmar.

Seidel, H.M., Ball, J.W., Dains, J.E., & Benedict, G.W. (1995). *Mosby's Guide to Physical Examination,* ed 3. St. Louis: Mosby.

Simonsen, S.M. (1996). *Telephone Health Assessment: Guidelines for Practice.* St. Louis: Mosby.

Thompson, J.M., & Wilson, S.F. (1996). *Health Assessment for Nursing Practice.* St. Louis: Mosby.

Weber, J. (1997). *Nurses' Handbook of Health Assessment,* ed 3. Philadelphia: Lippincott.

GENOGRAM REFERENCES

Beauchesne, M., Kelley, B., & Gauthier, M.A. (1997). News, notes & tips. The genogram: A health assessment tool. *Nurse Educator, 2*(3):9, 16.

Beck, R. (1987). The genogram as process. *American Journal of Family Therapy, 15:*343–351.

Engelman, S.R. (1988). Use of the family genogram technique with spinal cord injured patients. *Clin Rehab, 2:*7–15.

Friedman, H., Rohrbaugh, M., & Krakauer, S. (1988). The time-line genogram: highlighting temporal aspects of family relationships. *Fam Process, 27*(3):293–303.

Herth, K.A. (1989). The root of it all: genograms as a nursing assessment tool. *Journal of Gerontological Nursing, 15:*32–37.

Hurley, P.M. (1982). Family assessment: Systems theory and the genogram. *Children's Health Care, 10:*76–82.

Like, R.C., Rogers, J., & McGoldrick, M. (1988). Reading and interpreting genograms: a systematic approach. *J Fam Prac,* (4):407–412.

Marinelli, R.D. (1995). The genogram in health education. *Journal of Health Education, 26*(4):243–244.

Puskar, K., & Nerone, M. (1996). Genogram: a useful tool for nurse practitioners. *Journal of Psychiatric and Mental Health Nursing, 3*(1):55–60.

Richards, W.R., Burgess, D.E., Petersen, F.R., & McCarthy, D.L. (1993). Genograms: A psychosocial assessment tool for hospice. *Hospice Journal: Physical, Psychosocial, and Pastoral Care of the Dying, 9*(1):1–12.

Rogers, J.C., & Rohrbaugh, M. (1991). The SAGE-PAGE trial: do family genograms make a difference? *J Am Board Fam Pract, 4*(5):319–326.

Rogers, J.C., Rohrbaugh, M., & McGoldrick, M. (1992). Can experts predict health risk from family genograms? *Fam Med, 24*(3):209–215.

Shore, W.B., Wilkie, H.A., & Croughan-Minihane, M. (1994). Family of origin genograms: Evaluation of a teaching program for medical students. *Fam Med, 26*(4):238–243.

Visscher, E.M., & Clore, E.R. (1992). The genogram: A strategy for assessment. *Journal of Pediatric Health Care, 6*(6):361–367.

Waters, I., Watson, W., & Wetzel, W. (1994). Genograms: Practical tools for family physicians. *Can Fam Physician, 40:*282–287.

CHAPTER 3

The Problem/Need Identification Step: Analyzing the Data

■ **ANA STANDARD 2:** Diagnosis: The nurse analyzes the assessment data in determining diagnoses.

The second step of the nursing process is often referred to as **ANALYSIS,** as well as **PROBLEM/NEED IDENTIFICATION** or **NURSING DIAGNOSIS.** Although all of these terms may be used interchangeably, the purpose of this step of the nursing process is to draw conclusions regarding a patient's specific problems or needs so that effective care can be planned and delivered. We have chosen to label this step of the nursing process **PROBLEM/NEED IDENTIFICATION.** To be more specific, this is a process of data analysis using diagnostic reasoning (a form of clinical judgment) in which judgments, decisions, and conclusions are made about the meaning of the data collected to determine whether or not nursing intervention is indicated.

The **DIAGNOSIS** of patient needs has been done by nurses on an informal basis since the early beginnings of the profession. The term came into formal use in the nursing literature during the 1950s (Fry, 1953), although its meaning continued to be seen in the context of medical diagnosis. A group of interested nursing leaders met and held a national conference in 1973 (Gebbie & Lavin, 1975). Their purpose

ANALYSIS: the process of examining and categorizing information to reach a conclusion about a patient's needs.

PROBLEM/NEED IDENTIFICATION: the second step of the nursing process, in which the data collected are analyzed and, through the process of diagnostic reasoning, specific patient diagnostic statements are created.

DIAGNOSIS: Forming a clinical judgment identifying a disease/condition or human response through scientific evaluation of signs/symptoms, history, and diagnostic studies.

NURSING DIAGNOSES: Noun: a label approved by NANDA identifying specific patient problems/needs. The means of describing health problems amenable to treatment by nurses; may be physical, sociological, or psychological. **Verb:** the process of identifying specific patient problems/needs; used by some as the title of the second step of the nursing process.

was to identify the patient needs that fall within the scope of nursing, label them, and develop a classification system that could be used by nurses throughout the world. This group called these labels **NURSING DIAGNOSES.** Regional, national, and international workshops and conferences continue to be held since the first conference. The North American Nursing Diagnosis Association (NANDA) meets every 2 years to review their work on the development and classification of nursing diagnoses, as well as the work of other nursing groups, representing various clinical specialties and healthcare settings.

American Nurses' Association (ANA) standards of practice were first developed in 1973, and with the acceptance of the ANA Social Policy Statement in 1980, which defined nursing as the "diagnosis and treatment of human responses to actual or potential health problems," and the 1995 update description as the "diagnosis and treatment of human responses to health and illness" (ANA, 1995), the movement for broad use of a common language was enhanced. The system developed by NANDA provides a standard terminology that is accepted by ANA and various specialty groups and is being used across the United States and in many countries around the world. NANDA has established a liaison with the International Council of Nursing to support and contribute to the global effort to standardize the language of healthcare with the goal that NANDA labels will be included in the International Classification of Diseases (ICD-II). (NANDA nursing diagnoses are included in the United States version of ICD-10 CM.)

Today, the use of the nursing process and nursing diagnoses is rapidly becoming an integral part of an effective system of nursing practice. It is a system that can be used within existing conceptual frameworks, because it is a generic approach adaptable to all academic and clinical settings. In addition, as mentioned in the first chapter, organizing schema of nursing problems other than NANDA are used within the profession. Additional schema include the Omaha System, the Patient Care Data Set, and Home Health Care Classification (see individual bibliographies for each of these three additional schema). In this edition we introduce you to the Omaha System by presenting associated Omaha System problems with the NANDA diagnoses in the case studies.

Defining Nursing Diagnosis

PATIENT DIAGNOSTIC STATEMENT: the outcome of the diagnostic reasoning process; a three-part statement identifying the patient's problem/need, the etiology of the problem/need, and the associated signs/symptoms.

Distinguishing between Medical and Nursing Diagnoses. . . .

The term *nursing diagnosis* has been used as both a verb and a noun. This may result in confusion. Nursing diagnosis is used as a noun in reference to the work of NANDA. For the purposes of this text, *nursing diagnosis* refers to the NANDA list of nursing diagnosis labels (Table 3–1) that form the stem of the **PATIENT DIAGNOSTIC STATEMENT.**

Although nurses work within the nursing, medical, and psychosocial domains, nursing's phenomena of concern are patterns of human response, *not* disease processes. Therefore, nursing diagnoses do not parallel medical/psychiatric diagnoses but *do* involve independent nursing activities as well as collaborative roles and actions.

The nursing diagnosis is a conclusion drawn from the data collected about a patient that serves as a means of describing a health need amenable to treatment by nurses. A uniform or standardized way of identifying, focusing on, and labeling specific phenomena allows the nurse to deal effectively with individual patient responses.

TABLE 3–1. Nursing Diagnoses

Accepted for Use and Research (1999)

Activity Intolerance [specify level]
Activity Intolerance, risk for
Adaptive Capacity: Intracranial, decreased
Adjustment, impaired
Airway Clearance, ineffective
Anxiety [specify level]
*Anxiety, death
Aspiration, risk for
[Autonomic] Dysreflexia
Autonomic Dysreflexia, risk for

Body Image disturbance
Body Temperature, risk for altered
Bowel Incontinence
Breastfeeding, effective
Breastfeeding, ineffective
Breastfeeding, interrupted
Breathing Pattern, ineffective

Cardiac Output, decreased
Caregiver Role Strain
Caregiver Role Strain, risk for
Communication, impaired verbal
Community Coping, ineffective
Community Coping, potential for enhanced
Confusion, acute
Confusion, chronic
Constipation
Constipation, perceived
*Constipation, risk for
Coping, defensive
Coping, Individual, ineffective

Decisional Conflict (specify)
Denial, ineffective
*Dentition, altered
*Development, risk for altered
Diarrhea
Disuse Syndrome, risk for
Diversional Activity deficit

Energy Field, disturbance
Environmental Interpretation Syndrome, impaired

*Failure to Thrive, adult
Family Coping, ineffective: compromised
Family Coping, ineffective: disabling
Family Coping: potential for growth
Family Processes, altered
Family Processes, altered: alcoholism
Fatigue
Fear
Fluid Volume deficit [hyper/hypotonic]

Fluid Volume deficit [isotonic]
Fluid Volume excess
Fluid Volume risk for deficit
*Fluid Volume risk for imbalance

Gas Exchange, impaired
Grieving, anticipatory
Grieving, dysfunctional
*Growth, risk for altered
Growth & Development, altered

Health Maintenance, altered
Health-Seeking Behaviors (specify)
Home Maintenance Management, impaired
Hopelessness
Hyperthermia
Hypothermia

Infant Behavior, disorganized
Infant Behavior, risk for disorganized
Infant Behavior, organized, potential for enhanced
Infant Feeding Pattern, ineffective
Infection, risk for
Injury, risk for

Knowledge Deficit [Learning Need] (specify)

*Latex Allergy
*Latex Allergy, risk for
Loneliness, risk for

Memory, impaired
*Mobility, impaired bed
Mobility, impaired physical
*Mobility, impaired wheelchair

*Nausea
Noncompliance [Compliance, altered] (specify)
Nutrition: altered, less than body requirements
Nutrition: altered, more than body requirements
Nutrition: altered, risk for more than body requirements

Oral Mucous Membrane, altered

Pain [acute]
Pain, chronic
Parental Role conflict
Parent/Infant/Child Attachment, risk for altered
Parenting, altered
Parenting, risk for altered
Perioperative Positioning Injury, risk for
Peripheral Neurovascular risk for dysfunction
Personal Identity disturbance
Poisoning, risk for
Post-Trauma Syndrome

Continued

TABLE 3–1. Nursing Diagnoses (Continued)

*Post-Trauma Syndrome, risk for	Suffocation, risk for
Powerlessness	*Surgical Recovery, delayed
Protection, altered	Swallowing, impaired
Rape-Trauma Syndrome	Therapeutic Regimen: Community, ineffective management
Rape-Trauma Syndrome: compound reaction	Therapeutic Regimen: Families, ineffective management
Rape-Trauma Syndrome: silent reaction	Therapeutic Regimen: Individual, effective management
Relocation Stress Syndrome	Therapeutic Regimen: Individuals, ineffective management
Role Performance, altered	Thermoregulation, ineffective
	Thought Processes, altered
Self-Care deficit [specify]: feeding, bathing/hygiene,	Tissue Integrity, impaired
dressing/grooming, toileting	Tissue Perfusion, altered (specify): cerebral, cardiopulmonary,
Self-Esteem, chronic low	renal, gastrointestinal, peripheral
Self-Esteem disturbance	Transfer Ability, impaired
Self-Esteem, situational low	Trauma, risk for
Self-Mutilation, risk for	
Sensory/Perceptual alterations (specify): visual, auditory,	Unilateral Neglect
kinesthetic, gustatory, tactile, olfactory	Urinary Elimination, altered
Sexual dysfunction	Urinary Incontinence, functional
Sexuality Patterns, altered	Urinary Incontinence, reflex
Skin Integrity, impaired	[Urinary] Incontinence, stress
Skin Integrity, risk for impaired	[Urinary] Incontinence, total
*Sleep Deprivation	[Urinary] Incontinence, urge
Sleep Pattern disturbance	*Urinary Incontinence, risk for urge
Social Interaction, impaired	Urinary Retention [acute/chronic]
Social Isolation	
*Sorrow, chronic	Ventilatory Weaning Response, dysfunctional (DVWR)
Spiritual Distress (distress of the human spirit)	Violence, [actual/]risk for directed at others
*Spiritual Distress, risk for	Violence, [actual/]risk for self-directed
Spiritual Well-Being, potential for enhanced	
Spontaneous Ventilation, inability to sustain	*Walking, impaired

*New Diagnoses for 1999–2000.
Information that appears in brackets has been added by the authors to clarify and facilitate the use of nursing diagnoses.

- **Medical Diagnoses** are illnesses/conditions, reflecting alteration of the structure or function of organs/systems, verified by medical diagnostic studies, such as diabetes, heart failure, hepatitis, cancer, and pneumonia. The medical diagnosis usually does not change.
- **Nursing Diagnoses** address human responses to actual and potential health problems/life processes, such as Activity Intolerance (specify level); Health

Although there are different definitions of the term *nursing diagnosis*, NANDA has accepted the following:

Nursing diagnosis is a clinical judgment about individual, family, or community responses to actual and potential health problems/life processes. Nursing diagnoses provide the basis for selection of nursing interventions to achieve outcomes for which the nurse is accountable.

The nursing diagnosis is as correct as the current data allow because it is supported by these data. It says what the patient's situation is at the present time and reflects changes in the patient's condition as they occur. Each decision the nurse makes is time dependent and, with additional information gathered later, decisions may change. Unlike medical diagnoses, nursing diagnoses change as the patient progresses through various stages of illness/maladaptation, to resolution of the problem or to the conclusion of the condition. For example, for a patient undergoing cardiac surgery, initial problems/needs may be Pain [acute]; decreased Cardiac Output; ineffective Airway Clearance; and risk for Infection. As the patient progresses, problems/needs may shift to risk for Activity Intolerance; Knowledge Deficit [Learning Need] (specify); and altered Role Performance.

The Use of Nursing Diagnoses

Although not yet comprehensive, the current NANDA list of diagnostic labels defines/refines professional nursing activity. The list of labels is now at a point where nurses need to use the proposed diagnoses on a daily basis, becoming familiar with the parameters of each individual diagnosis, and identifying its strengths and weaknesses, thus promoting research and further development.

A frequently asked question is "Why should we use a nursing diagnosis . . . what is its value to the nursing profession?" The use of a nursing diagnosis can provide many benefits. The accurate choice of a nursing diagnosis to label a patient problem/need:

- **Gives Nurses a Common Language:** Promotes improved communication among nurses, other healthcare providers, and alternate care settings.

  FOR EXAMPLE: Using the nursing diagnosis "Airway Clearance, ineffective" instead of saying "difficulty breathing" conveys a distinct image. When hearing the former, a clear picture begins to develop in your mind, as your thoughts focus on the musculature of the upper airway, mucus production, and cough effort. With the second label, you do not have a clear idea as to what is happening with this patient, and you question whether the patient is experiencing a problem of maintaining an airway, movement of the chest, or perfusion to the lungs.

  This improved communication may result in improved quality and continuity of the care provided to the patient.

- **Promotes Identification of Appropriate Goals:** Aids in the choice of correct nursing interventions to alleviate the identified problem/need and provides guidance for evaluation. Whereas nursing actions were once based on variables such as **SIGNS and SYMPTOMS,** test results, or a medical diagnosis, nursing diagnosis is a uniform way of identifying, focusing on, and dealing with specific patient responses to health and illness (i.e., the phenomena of concern for nurses).

  FOR EXAMPLE: "Risk for infection" compared with "presence of urinary catheter." The risk or potential threat of an infection brings to mind specific goals/outcomes and interventions to protect the patient, but what is your concern, if any, with the urinary catheter?

- **Provides Acuity Information:** Ranks the amount of work that requires nursing care and can serve as a basis for patient classification systems. This method of ranking can be used to determine individual staffing needs. It can also serve as documentation to provide justification for third-party reimbursement.

  FOR EXAMPLE: Nursing diagnoses can be given different, weighted values according to the degree of nursing involvement required; that is, "impaired Gas Exchange" may require a considerable amount of skilled nursing time to promote adequate ventilation, to provide oxygen and respiratory treatments, and to monitor laboratory studies. "Acute Urinary Retention" may

Maintenance, altered; Airway Clearance, ineffective; Self Care deficit (specify). The nursing diagnoses change as the patient's situation or perspective changes/resolves.

SIGN: objective or observable evidence or manifestation of a health problem.

SYMPTOM: subjectively perceptible change in the body or its functions that indicates disease or the kind or phases of disease.

Remember . . . nursing diagnoses may be a physical, sociological, or psychological finding.

Physical Nursing Diagnoses include those that pertain to circulation (e.g., Tissue Perfusion, altered [specify]), ventilation (e.g., Airway Clearance, ineffective), elimination (e.g., Constipation), and so on.

Psychosocial Nursing Diagnoses include those that pertain to the mind (e.g., Thought Processes, altered), emotion (e.g., Anxiety [specify level]), or lifestyle/relationships (e.g., Sexuality Patterns, altered, or Social Isolation).

require a much shorter period of time to insert a catheter into the bladder and periodically measure the urine output.

In addition, some third-party payors (such as Medicare and other insurance companies) include nursing diagnoses when considering extended length of stay or delayed discharge.

- **Can Create a Standard for Nursing Practice:** Provides a foundation for quality assurance programs, a means of evaluating nursing practice, and a mechanism of costing-out delivery of nursing care.

    FOR EXAMPLE: Did the nursing interventions address and resolve the problem? Did the patient experience the desired result (e.g., alleviation of pain)? Were the goals met, or is there documentation of the reasons why they were not met? Were the expected outcomes changed to meet changing patient needs?

- **Provides a Quality Improvement Base:** Clinicians, administrators, educators, and researchers can document, validate, or alter the process of care delivery, which then improves the profession.

    FOR EXAMPLE: The use of universally understood labels enhances retrieval of specific data for review to determine accuracy, to validate and/or change nursing actions related to specific nursing diagnoses, and to evaluate an individual nurse's performance.

Identifying Patient Problems/Needs

During the Assessment step, the collection, clustering, and validation of patient data flow directly into the Problem/Need Identification step of the nursing process, where you sense problems and choose nursing diagnoses.

DIAGNOSTIC REASONING: ANALYZING THE PATIENT DATABASE

Identifying patient problems/needs and then selecting a nursing diagnosis label involves the use of experience, expertise, and intuition on your part. There are six steps involved in problem identification that comprise the activities of diagnostic reasoning. The result is the creation of a patient diagnostic statement that identifies the patient problem or need, suggests its potential cause or etiology, and notes its signs and symptoms. This is known as the **PES** format, reflecting **P**roblem, **E**tiology, and **S**igns/symptoms (Gordon, 1976).

PES: format for combining a nursing diagnosis label, patient-specific etiology, and signs/symptoms to create an individualized diagnostic statement.

Step 1: Problem-Sensing

CUE: a signal that indicates a possible need/direction for care.

Data are reviewed and analyzed to identify **CUES** (signs and symptoms) suggesting patient problems or needs that can be described by nursing diagnosis labels. If the data have been recorded in a nursing format (e.g., Diagnostic Divisions, Functional Health Patterns, or Human Responses), the nurse is automatically guided to specific groups of nursing diagnoses when certain cues from the data are identified (Box 3–1). This helps to focus attention on appropriate diagnoses. Reviewing the NANDA definitions of specific diagnoses (see Appendix A) can be of further assistance in deciding between two or more similar diagnostic labels; for instance, there are five different diagnoses for urinary incontinence (see step 4).

BOX 3-1

NURSING DIAGNOSES ORGANIZED ACCORDING TO DIAGNOSTIC DIVISIONS

After data have been collected and areas of concern/need identified, consult the Diagnostic Divisions framework to review the list of nursing diagnoses that fall within the individual categories. This will assist with the choice of the specific diagnostic labels to accurately describe the data from the patient database. Then, with the addition of etiology (when known) and signs and symptoms, the patient diagnostic statement emerges.

Diagnostic Division: Activity/Rest

Ability to engage in necessary/desired activities of life (work and leisure) and to obtain adequate sleep/rest

Diagnoses

Activity Intolerance [specify level]
Activity Intolerance, risk for
Disuse Syndrome, risk for
Diversional Activity deficit
Fatigue
Mobility, impaired bed
Mobility, impaired wheelchair
Sleep Deprivation
Sleep Pattern disturbance
Transfer Ability, impaired
Walking, impaired

Diagnostic Division: Circulation

Ability to transport oxygen and nutrients necessary to meet cellular needs

Diagnoses

Adaptive Capacity: Intracranial, decreased
[Autonomic] Dysreflexia
Autonomic Dysreflexia, risk for
Cardiac Output, decreased
Tissue Perfusion, altered (specify): cerebral, cardiopulmonary, renal, gastrointestinal, peripheral

Diagnostic Division: Ego Integrity

Ability to develop and use skills and behaviors to integrate and manage life experiences

Diagnoses

Adjustment, impaired
Anxiety [specify level]
Anxiety, death
Body Image disturbance
Coping, defensive

Continued

NURSING DIAGNOSES ORGANIZED ACCORDING TO DIAGNOSTIC DIVISIONS (Continued)

Coping, Individual, ineffective
Decisional Conflict (specify)
Denial, ineffective
Energy Field disturbance
Fear
Grieving, anticipatory
Grieving, dysfunctional
Hopelessness
Personal Identity disturbance
Post-Trauma Syndrome
Post-Trauma Syndrome, risk for
Powerlessness
Rape-Trauma Syndrome
Rape-Trauma Syndrome: compound reaction
Rape-Trauma Syndrome: silent reaction
Relocation Stress Syndrome
Self-Esteem, chronic low
Self-Esteem disturbance
Self-Esteem, situational low
Sorrow, chronic
Spiritual Distress (distress of the human spirit)
Spiritual Distress, risk for
Spiritual Well-Being, potential for enhanced

Diagnostic Division: Elimination

Ability to excrete waste products

Diagnoses

Bowel Incontinence
Constipation
Constipation, perceived
Constipation, risk for
Diarrhea
Urinary Elimination, altered
Urinary Incontinence, functional
Urinary Incontinence, reflex
[Urinary] Incontinence, stress
[Urinary] Incontinence, total
[Urinary] Incontinence, urge
Urinary Incontinence, risk for urinary urge
Urinary Retention [acute/chronic]

Diagnostic Division: Food/Fluid

Ability to maintain intake of and utilize nutrients and liquids to meet physiological needs

Continued

NURSING DIAGNOSES ORGANIZED ACCORDING TO DIAGNOSTIC DIVISIONS (Continued)

Diagnoses

Breastfeeding, effective
Breastfeeding, ineffective
Breastfeeding, interrupted
Dentition, altered
Failure to Thrive, adult
Fluid Volume deficit [hyper/hypotonic]
Fluid Volume deficit [isotonic]
Fluid Volume excess
Fluid Volume risk for deficit
Fluid Volume risk for imbalance
Infant Feeding Pattern, ineffective
Nausea
Nutrition: altered, less than body requirements
Nutrition: altered, more than body requirements
Nutrition: altered, risk for more than body requirements
Oral Mucous Membrane, altered
Swallowing, impaired

Diagnostic Division: Hygiene

   Ability to perform activities of daily living

Diagnoses

Self-Care deficit (specify): feeding, bathing/hygiene, dressing/grooming, toileting

Diagnostic Division: Neurosensory

   Ability to perceive, integrate, and respond to internal and external cues

Diagnoses

Confusion, acute
Confusion, chronic
Infant Behavior, disorganized
Infant Behavior, risk for disorganized
Infant Behavior, organized, potential for enhanced
Memory, impaired
Peripheral Neurovascular risk for dysfunction
Sensory-Perceptual alterations (specify): visual, auditory, kinesthetic, gustatory, tactile, olfactory
Thought Processes, altered
Unilateral Neglect

Diagnostic Division: Pain/Discomfort

   Ability to control internal/external environment to maintain comfort

Continued

NURSING DIAGNOSES ORGANIZED ACCORDING TO DIAGNOSTIC DIVISIONS (Continued)

Diagnoses

Pain [acute]
Pain, chronic

Diagnostic Division: Respiration

Ability to provide and use oxygen to meet physiological needs

Diagnoses

Airway Clearance, ineffective
Aspiration, risk for
Breathing Pattern, ineffective
Gas Exchange, impaired
Spontaneous Ventilation, inability to sustain
Ventilatory Weaning Response, dysfunctional (DVWR)

Diagnostic Division: Safety

Ability to provide safe, growth-promoting environment

Diagnoses

Body Temperature, risk for altered
Environmental Interpretation Syndrome, impaired
Health Maintenance, altered
Home Maintenance Management, impaired
Hyperthermia
Hypothermia
Infection, risk for
Injury, risk for
Latex Allergy
Latex Allergy, risk for
Mobility, impaired physical
Perioperative Positioning Injury, risk for
Poisoning, risk for
Protection, altered
Self-Mutilation, risk for
Skin Integrity, impaired
Skin Integrity, risk for impaired
Suffocation, risk for
Surgical Recovery, delayed
Thermoregulation, ineffective
Tissue Integrity, impaired
Trauma, risk for
Violence, [actual/]risk for directed at others
Violence, [actual/]risk for self-directed

Continued

NURSING DIAGNOSES ORGANIZED ACCORDING TO DIAGNOSTIC DIVISIONS (Continued)

Diagnostic Division: Sexuality

[Component of Ego Integrity and Social Interaction] Ability to meet requirements/characteristics of male/female role

Diagnoses

Sexual dysfunction
Sexuality Patterns, altered

Diagnostic Division: Social Interaction

Ability to establish and maintain relationships

Diagnoses

Caregiver Role Strain
Caregiver Role Strain, risk for
Communication, impaired verbal
Community Coping, ineffective
Community Coping, potential for enhanced
Family Coping, ineffective: compromised
Family Coping, ineffective: disabling
Family Coping: potential for growth
Family Processes, altered
Family Processes, altered: alcoholism
Loneliness, risk for
Parent/Infant/Child Attachment, risk for altered
Parental Role conflict
Parenting, altered
Parenting, risk for altered
Role Performance, altered
Social Interaction, impaired
Social Isolation

Diagnostic Division: Teaching/Learning

Ability to incorporate and use information to achieve healthy lifestyle/optimal wellness

Diagnoses

Development, risk for altered
Growth, risk for altered
Growth and Development, altered
Health-Seeking Behaviors (specify)
Knowledge Deficit [Learning Need] (specify)
Noncompliance [Compliance, altered] (specify)
Therapeutic Regimen: Community, ineffective management
Therapeutic Regimen: Families, ineffective management
Therapeutic Regimen: Individual, effective management
Therapeutic Regimen: Individuals, ineffective management

FOR EXAMPLE: When using the Diagnostic Divisions format, body temperature is recorded in the Safety section. When the patient temperature rises, the nurse reviews the diagnostic labels under Safety to find a possible fit, such as *Hyperthermia* or *Infection, risk for.* At the same time, cues are noted in other sections of the database that may be combined with fever or be totally unrelated. In fact, cues may have relevance in more than one section, as you can see in Box 3–2.

BOX 3–2

WALKING THROUGH THE USE OF DIAGNOSTIC DIVISIONS

During the Assessment phase, the following data were obtained from Robert.

Activity/Rest

Reports (Subjective)

Occupation: Retired truck driver
Usual Activities/Hobbies: Used to like to hunt
Leisure Time Activities: Mostly watch baseball on TV, take short walks—one to two blocks
Feelings of Boredom/Dissatisfaction: "Wish I could do more; just getting too old"
Limitations Imposed by Condition: "I get short of breath; stay at home mostly"
Sleep: Hours: 5   **Naps:** After lunch   **Aids:** None
Insomnia: Only if short of breath (1 or 2 ×/wk) or needs to void (1 ×/night)
Rested on Awakening: Not always; "feel weak most of the time"
Other: "Sometimes it feels like there isn't enough air

Exhibits (Objective)

Observed Response to Activity: Cardiovascular: BP 178/102, P 100 after walking half length of corridor from floor scale
   Respiratory: 32, rapid, leaning forward ("to catch breath")
Mental Status (i.e., withdrawn/lethargic): Alert, responding to all questions
Neuromuscular Assessment: Muscle mass/tone: Decreased/Bilaterally equal/diminished   **Posture:** Leans forward to breathe
Tremors: No   **ROM:** Movement in all extremities   **Strength:** Moderate
Deformity: No

Having previously noted respiratory cues of dyspnea with activity when you reviewed the Respiratory data in Box 2–5, you return to the Activity/Rest section of the Diagnostic Divisions, where the effects/limitations of this condition on both activity and sleep would also be considered. You are referred to the following nursing diagnoses Activity Intolerance [specify level]; Activity Intolerance, risk for; Mobility, impaired bed; Disuse Syndrome, risk for; Diversional Activity deficit; Fatigue; Sleep Deprivation; Sleep Pattern disturbance; Walking, impaired; Mobility, impaired, wheelchair; and Transfer Ability, impaired as possible choices to describe or label Robert's problem.

Step 2: Rule-Out Process

Alternative explanations are considered for the identified cues to determine which nursing diagnosis label may be the most appropriate. This step is crucial to establish an adequate list of diagnostic statements. As you compare and contrast the relationships among and between data, etiologic factors are identified within or between categories based on an understanding of the biologic, physical, and behavioral sciences.

> **FOR EXAMPLE:** Although *Hyperthermia* or *Infection, risk for,* were suggested during the first step of diagnostic reasoning, another consideration might be *Fluid Volume deficit*. In another example, cues of increased tension, restlessness, elevated pulse rate, and reported apprehension may initially be thought to indicate *Anxiety [specify level]*. However, a similar diagnosis of *Fear* should be considered, as well as the possibility that these cues may be physiologically based, needing medical treatment and nursing interventions related to learning needs/monitoring.

If you encounter difficulty in choosing a nursing diagnosis label, the questions in Box 3–3 may provide additional guidance.

Step 3: Synthesizing the Data

Looking at all the data as a whole (including information collected by other members of the healthcare team) can provide a comprehensive picture of the patient in relation to the past, present, and future health status. This is called **SYNTHESIZING**

SYNTHESIZING: viewing all data as a whole to provide a comprehensive picture of the patient.

BOX 3–3

QUESTIONS TO ASK YOURSELF WHEN THE NURSING DIAGNOSIS LABEL IS UNCLEAR

When the nursing diagnosis label is unclear, you can ask yourself these questions:

1. What are my concerns about this patient?
2. Can I/am I doing something about it?
3. Can the overall risk be reduced by nursing intervention?
   For example, in the pediatric patient, fever is often a major concern. Questions to ask might be:

- What are the concerns about the fever?
  The patient may convulse.
- Can I do something about it?
  Try to bring the temperature down and make the environment safe.
- Can the overall risk be reduced by nursing interventions?
  Yes, the risk of convulsions can be reduced if the temperature is lowered; or if convulsions do occur, measures can be taken to protect the patient from injury.

Conclusion: The Nursing Diagnosis would be Risk for Injury; and, the patient diagnostic statement would be Risk for Injury: seizure activity risk factor of prolonged high fever.

the data. The suggested nursing diagnosis label is combined with the identified related factor(s) and cues to create a hypothesis.

> **FOR EXAMPLE:** Sally had a period of bleeding during delivery of the placenta following the unexpected delivery of twins. Blood loss was estimated to be approximately 600 ml. In addition, she experienced several episodes of vomiting before delivery and reduced oral intake because of nausea. The nursing diagnosis label *Fluid Volume deficit* [isotonic]; related factor, hemorrhage, vomiting, poor PO intake; cues of dark urine, dry mouth/lips, low blood pressure.

Step 4: Evaluating or Confirming the Hypothesis

Test the hypothesis for appropriate fit; that is, review the NANDA nursing diagnosis and definition. Then, compare the assessed possible **ETIOLOGY** with NANDA's **RELATED FACTORS** or **RISK FACTORS.** Next, compare the assessed patient cues with NANDA's Defining Characteristics, which are used to support and provide an increased level of confidence in your selected nursing diagnosis. Appendix A provides a complete listing of NANDA nursing diagnostic labels, definitions, defining characteristics, and related factors. This listing will be helpful as you work through the Practice Activities and Work Pages contained in each chapter. Take a moment to review Box 3–4. The information contained within the box provides a beginning effort in assessing the appropriateness of a specific nursing diagnosis label.

Lunney (1989, 1990) addressed the self-monitoring task of accuracy determination and has defined characteristics of accuracy and an ordinal scale for measurement. The scale ranges from a high assigned accuracy point value describing a diagnosis that is consistent with all of the cues, to the lowest point value describing a diagnosis indicated by more than one cue but recommended for rejection based

ETIOLOGY: identified causes and/or contributing factors responsible for the presence of a specific patient problem/need.

RELATED FACTOR: the conditions/circumstances that contribute to the development/maintenance of a nursing diagnosis; forms the "related to" component of the patient diagnostic statement.

RISK FACTOR: environmental factors and physiological, psychological, genetic, or chemical elements that increase the vulnerability of an individual, family, or community to an unhealthy event.

BOX 3–4

ELEMENTS OF NANDA NURSING DIAGNOSTIC LABELS

Appendix A supplies a complete listing of NANDA nursing diagnosis labels, which will be helpful to you as you work through the exercises in this chapter and throughout the book. It is important to become familiar with this list, so that you can find information quickly in the clinical setting. Take a moment to identify the key elements of the diagnostic label, "Fluid Volume deficit," as excerpted below.

Fluid Volume Deficit [isotonic]

Definition: The state in which an individual experiences decreased intravascular, interstitial, and/or intracellular fluid. This refers to dehydration, water loss alone without changes in sodium.

Related Factors: Active fluid volume loss, failure of regulatory mechanisms.

Defining Characteristics: Decreased urine output; increased urine concentration; weakness; sudden weight loss (except in third-spacing); decreased venous filling; increased body temperature; change in mental state; elevated hematocrit; decreased skin/tongue turgor; dry skin/mucous membranes; thirst; increased pulse rate; decreased blood pressure.

PRACTICE ACTIVITY 3–1

Record the cues from Box 3–2 that are relevant to the problem of Activity Intolerance, identified for Robert, in the appropriate spaces on this worksheet.

INTERACTIVE CARE PLAN WORKSHEET

Student Name:

Patient's Medical Diagnosis:

ACTIVITY INTOLERANCE

DEFINITION: A state in which an individual has insufficient physiological or psychological energy to endure or complete required or desired daily activities.

DEFINING CHARACTERISTICS: Verbal report of fatigue or weakness; abnormal heart rate or blood pressure response to activity; exertional discomfort or dyspnea; ECG changes reflecting dysrhythmias or ischemia.

RELATED FACTORS: Bedrest and/or immobility; generalized weakness; sedentary life-style; imbalance between oxygen supply and/or demand.

STUDENT INSTRUCTIONS: In the space below enter the subjective and objective data gathered during your patient assessment.

ASSESSMENT

Subjective Data Entry

Objective Data Entry

TIME OUT! **Student Instructions:** To be sure your patient diagnostic statement written below is accurate, you need to re-view the defining characteristics and related factors associated with the nursing diagnosis, **Activity Intoler-ance**, and how your patient data matches. Do you have an accurate match or is additional data required or does another nursing diagnosis need to be investigated?

DIAGNOSIS

PATIENT DIAGNOSTIC STATEMENT:

Activity intolerance (specify) _____

Related to _____

on the presence of at least two disconfirming cues (see Appendix E). Additionally, Appendix F, Lunney's Integrated Model for Self-Monitoring of Accuracy of the Diagnostic Process, is an excellent self-evaluation of your progress in diagnostic efforts. Also, a separate section in the Suggested Readings is dedicated to the topic of accuracy of nursing diagnoses. The completed evaluation provides feedback of your diagnostic abilities. Reflection and self-monitoring are tools to assist you in developing your *critical thinking* skills. The attention you give to measuring the accuracy of your suggested nursing diagnosis is time well spent. Comparing the subjective and objective data gathered from the patient with the defining characteristics of the possible nursing diagnoses that are listed not only helps ensure the accuracy of your statement, but also stresses the importance of objectivity in this diagnostic process.

Now return to Box 3–2. In reviewing Robert's database, you *sense* he may have a problem with activity. After reviewing the NANDA nursing diagnosis labels and their definitions, relevant to the Activity/Rest Diagnostic Division, you choose the Activity Intolerance, risk for. Next, to confirm your hypothesis, compare the cues from the database with the related factors and defining characteristics noted in Appendix A. Practice Activity 3–1 presents an Interactive Care Plan Worksheet for the patient problem of Activity Intolerance, on which you can document the identified cues.

BOX 3–5

COMPONENTS OF THE PATIENT DIAGNOSTIC STATEMENT: PROBLEM, ETIOLOGY, AND SIGNS AND SYMPTOMS (PES)

P = Problem/Need is the name or diagnostic label identified from the NANDA list. The key to accurate nursing diagnosis is problem/need identification that focuses attention on a current risk or potential physical or behavioral response to health or illness that may interfere with the patient's quality of life. It deals with concerns of the patient/significant other(s) and the nurse that require nursing intervention and management.

E = Etiology is the suspected cause or reason for the response that has been identified from the assessment (patient database). The nurse makes inferences based on knowledge and expertise, such as understanding of pathophysiology, and situational or developmental factors. The etiology is stated as "related to." Note: One problem may have several suspected causes, such as Self-Esteem disturbance, related to lack of positive feedback and dysfunctional family system.

S = Signs and Symptoms are the manifestations (or cues) identified in the assessment that substantiate the nursing diagnosis. They are stated as "evidenced by" followed by a list of subjective and objective data. It is important to note that *risk* diagnoses are not accompanied by signs and symptoms because the problem has not yet actually occurred. In this instance, the "S" component of the diagnostic statement is omitted and the "E" component would be replaced by an itemization of the identified risk factors that suggest that the diagnosis could occur (e.g., Infection, risk for, risk factors of malnutrition, and invasive procedures).

Step 5: List the Patient's Problems/Needs

Based on the data obtained from steps 3 and 4, the accurate nursing diagnosis label is combined with the assessed etiology and signs/symptoms, if present, to finalize the patient diagnostic statement.

> FOR EXAMPLE, Sally is diagnosed with a Fluid Volume deficit [isotonic] related to hemorrhage, vomiting, reduced intake as evidenced by dark urine, dry mucous membranes, hypotension, and hemoconcentration. This individualized diagnosis reflects the PES format for a three-part diagnostic statement, as described in Box 3–5. A diagnostic statement is needed for *each* problem/need you identify. Take a moment here to complete Practice Activity 3–2.

PRACTICE ACTIVITY 3–2

Identifying the PES Components of the Patient Diagnostic Statement

Instructions (questions 1–5): Identify the "PES" components of each of these diagnostic statements:

1. Anxiety, severe, related to changes in health status of fetus/self and threat of death as evidenced by restlessness, tremors, focus on self/fetus.

   P = _____   E = _____   S = _____

2. Thought Processes, altered, related to pharmacological stimulation of the nervous system as evidenced by altered attention span, disorientation, and hallucinations.

   P = _____   E = _____   S = _____

3. Coping, Individual, ineffective, related to maturational crisis as evidenced by inability to meet role expectations and alcohol abuse.

   P = _____   E = _____   S = _____

4. Hyperthermia related to increased metabolic rate and dehydration as evidenced by elevated temperature, flushed skin, tachycardia, and tachypnea.

   P = _____   E = _____   S = _____

5. Pain, acute, related to tissue distention and edema as evidenced by verbal reports, guarding behavior, and changes in vital signs.

   P = _____   E = _____   S = _____

6. Explain the difference between actual and risk diagnoses: _____
   _____

7. Give an example of an actual and a risk problem for a patient with second-degree burns of the hand. _____
   _____
   _____

Step 6: Reevaluate the Problem List

Be sure all areas of concern are noted. Once all nursing diagnoses are identified, list them according to priority and classify them according to status: an actual problem/need; a risk problem/need; or a resolved problem/need. Box 3–6 explains this status classification.

- **Actual Diagnoses:** describe human responses to health conditions/life processes that exist in an individual, family, or community. It is supported by defining characteristics (manifestations/signs and symptoms) that cluster in patterns of related cues or inferences (NANDA, 1999).

FOR EXAMPLE: A patient is admitted for a medical workup for problems with bladder function related to her diagnosis of multiple sclerosis. an actual problem might be Urinary Retention.

- **Wellness Diagnoses:** reflect human responses to levels of wellness in an individual, family, or community that have potential for enhancement to a higher state (NANDA, 1999) (Note: See special section in Suggested Readings on wellness and health promotion.)

FOR EXAMPLE: The family of a patient with multiple sclerosis (MS) has been very supportive during periods of exacerbated symptoms. However, they want to learn to optimize health status and enrich lifestyle. A wellness diagnosis of Family Coping: potential for growth [enhanced] is appropriate.

- **Risk Diagnoses:** refer to human responses to health conditions/life processes that may develop in a vulnerable individual, family, or commu-

---

BOX 3–6

STATUS CLASSIFICATION OF PATIENT PROBLEMS/NEEDS

- **Actual:** A problem/need that is currently present and manifested by signs and symptoms. In recording the problem/need, you use a three-part PES statement. Urinary Elimination, altered, related to sensory motor impairment evidenced by dribbling, 250 ml residual urine.

  Another form of an actual diagnosis has a wellness focus that is more of an opportunity than a problem. In such cases, patients have an assessed opportunity to improve an aspect of their health or well-being. (Note: See Allen, 1989; Carpenito, 1997; Kelly et al., 1995; and Popkess-Vawter, 1991 in Suggested Readings.) The diagnostic statement would be written as potential for enhanced. For example, Spiritual Well-being, potential for enhanced could be used to label a patient's need to improve his or her sense of harmony with others (i.e., family members).

- **Risk:** A problem/need that you believe could develop, but because it has not yet occurred, there are no signs or symptoms, only "risk factors." The problem/need would be written as a two-part statement. Mobility, risk for impaired physical, risk factors of neuromuscular impairment, decreased strength, and pain with movement.

- **Resolved:** A problem/need that no longer requires intervention. Because the problem no longer exists, no diagnostic statement is needed.

nity. It is supported by risk factors that contribute to increased vulnerability (NANDA, 1999).

FOR EXAMPLE: The patient's MS has been in remission; however, she has had difficulty in the past with physical mobility. This past problem must be considered when planning this patient's care to minimize the possibility of recurrence. A potential problem would then be identified as Mobility, risk for impaired physical.

- **Resolved Diagnoses:** are those that no longer need action.

FOR EXAMPLE: Your patient once suffered a decubitus ulcer (Skin Integrity, impaired); however, she has learned techniques to prevent recurrence of this problem, and her skin is in good condition. Therefore, as long as she is able to participate in or direct her own care, this is of no significant concern to you at this time.

Finally, validate the diagnostic conclusions/impressions with the patient and/or a colleague. This helps reduce the possibility of **DIAGNOSTIC ERRORS** and/or omissions as discussed in Box 3–7. Inclusion of the patient/significant others promotes understanding and participation in the planning of individualized care.

DIAGNOSTIC ERROR: a mistaken assumption leading to a wrong conclusion.

As you can see, the process of problem/need identification is more complex than simply attaching a label to your patient. In reviewing the definition of nursing, "the human responses to health and illness" are complex and the process of accurately diagnosing these human responses attests to the complexity of nursing.

BOX 3–7

POTENTIAL ERRORS IN CHOOSING A NURSING DIAGNOSIS

- **Overlooking Cues** resulting in a missed diagnosis can lead to worsening of the problem.

FOR EXAMPLE: A patient reports discomfort at the insertion site of an intravenous (IV) catheter. You notice the area is slightly reddened but fail to consider the risk for infection. As a result, the patient develops sepsis or a blood infection requiring emergency intervention.

- **Making a Diagnosis with an Insufficient Database** can lead in the wrong direction, wasting valuable time and resources.

FOR EXAMPLE: The patient displays signs of anxiety. Without additional assessment, you administer a tranquilizer on the belief that the signs and symptoms are psychologically based. Later, when checking the patient, you find signs of cyanosis, suggesting inadequate oxygenation. Thus, the anxiety probably was at least in part physiologically based and needed other nursing interventions.

- **Stereotyping** leads to treating all patients in the same way and negates individualization.

FOR EXAMPLE: In a medical-surgical setting, the assumption is often made that a patient with a psychiatric diagnosis is apt to become violent.

OTHER CONSIDERATIONS FOR PROBLEM/NEED IDENTIFICATION

The medical/psychiatric diagnosis can provide a starting point for identifying associated patient problems (problem sensing). Review Box 3–8 for several medical/psychiatric diagnoses with examples of associated nursing diagnoses. Although they can suggest several nursing diagnoses, these nursing diagnoses must be supported by cues in the patient database.

FOR EXAMPLE: In the presence of a myocardial infarction, the patient often suffers pain, anxiety, and activity intolerance and requires teaching activities. In addition, the patient may be at risk for alteration of cardiac output, tissue perfusion, and fluid volume excess. These problems and needs are not necessarily present in each patient with this condition. One patient may actually be pain free, whereas another could demonstrate a sleep disturbance or report spiritual distress. Therefore, a medical diagnosis can be an initial point for problem-sensing, but the validity of a nursing diagnosis depends on the presence of individually appropriate supporting data.

The patient's or family member's understanding of normal body function, individual (including cultural) expectations, or mistaken perceptions may result in the belief that a problem or need exists, even in the absence of diagnostically appropriate supporting data. Even though the problem seems to exist only in the mind of the patient/significant other, it needs to be addressed and resolved in order to promote optimal wellness.

FOR EXAMPLE:

1. The parent of a child with cancer may believe that the child is incapable of self-care activities even though the child's level of function and development would indicate otherwise. This then is not a patient problem with self-care but rather the parent's problem—possibly, Family Coping, ineffective: compromised.
2. A female patient may believe that sexual desire normally disappears after menopause/hysterectomy, and the fact that it is not indicates to her that something is wrong. Although sexual dysfunction may have occurred, the assessment reveals inadequate information and misconceptions. Therefore, the nursing diagnosis is Knowledge deficit: normal sexual functioning.
3. An elderly, confused patient, with a diagnosis of Alzheimer's disease, is found wandering in the day room. She has soiled herself and is smearing feces on the walls and couch. The problem would not be one of bowel elimination but of Thought Processes, altered. Interventions would be addressed to the solution of behavioral management rather than only to a bowel control program.

As noted in the previous examples, it is important to "reduce" the problem to its basic component in order to focus interventions on the "roots" of the human response. It is also important to take the related factors and the defining characteristics to the lowest "denominator" possible so the patient and nurse are better able to formulate individually specific goals/outcomes and to identify more clearly the appropriate interventions/actions to be taken to correct or alleviate the problem.

FOR EXAMPLE: Social Interaction, impaired: related to neurological impairment and the resulting sequelae (i.e., cognitive, behavioral, and emotional changes) is better stated, "related to skill deficit about ways to enhance mutuality, com-

BOX 3–8

APPLICABLE NURSING DIAGNOSES ASSOCIATED WITH SELECTED MEDICAL/PSYCHIATRIC DISORDERS

Certain nursing diagnoses may be linked to specific health problems (e.g., medical disorders). This linkage is often presented as choices in a diagnostic database, in various types of clinical pocket manuals, or on preprinted or computerized care planning forms. The purpose is to assist in rapidly identifying other applicable nursing diagnoses, based on the changing needs of the patient; and to develop a decisive plan of care.

Because the nursing process is cyclical and ongoing, other nursing diagnoses may become appropriate, as the individual patient situation changes. Therefore, you must continually assess, identify, and validate new problems and evaluate the effectiveness of subsequent care. Keep in mind that the patient may have problems/needs unrelated to the medical diagnosis.

AIDS (Acquired Immunodeficiency Syndrome)

Infection, risk for progression to sepsis/opportunistic overgrowth: risk factors may include depressed immune system, inadequate primary defenses, use of antimicrobial agents, broken skin, malnutrition, and chronic disease processes.

Fluid Volume deficit, risk for: risk factors may include excessive losses: copious diarrhea, profuse sweating, vomiting, hypermetabolic state, and fever; impaired intake (nausea, anorexia; lethargy).

Fatigue may be related to disease state, malnutrition, anemia, negative life events, stress/anxiety possibly evidenced by inability to maintain usual routines, decreased performance, lethargy/listlessness, and disinterest in surroundings.

Labor Stage I (Active Phase)

Pain [acute/Discomfort], may be related to contraction-related hypoxia, dilation of tissues, and pressure on adjacent structures combined with stimulation of both parasympathetic and sympathetic nerve endings, possibly evidenced by verbal reports, guarding/distraction behaviors (restlessness), muscle tension, and narrowed focus.

Urinary Elimination, altered may be related to retention of fluid in the prenatal period, increased glomerular filtration rate, decreased adrenal stimulation, dehydration, pressure of the presenting part, and regional anesthesia, possibly evidenced by increased/decreased output, decreased circulating blood volume, spasms of glomeruli and albuminuria, and reduced sensation.

Coping, Individual/[Couple], ineffective, risk for: risk factors may include stressors accompanying labor, personal vulnerability, use of ineffective coping mechanisms, inadequate support systems, and pain.

Continued

APPLICABLE NURSING DIAGNOSES ASSOCIATED WITH SELECTED MEDICAL/PSYCHIATRIC DISORDERS (Continued)

Fractures

Pain [acute] may be related to movement of bone fragments, muscle spasms, tissue trauma/edema, traction/immobility device, stress, and anxiety, possibly evidenced by verbal reports, distraction behaviors, self-focusing/narrowed focus, facial mask of pain, guarding/protective behavior, alteration in muscle tone, and autonomic responses (changes in vital signs).

Knowledge Deficit [Learning Need] regarding healing process, therapy requirements, potential complications, and self care needs may be related to lack of information, possibly evidenced by statements of concern, questions, and misconceptions.

Mobility, impaired physical may be related to neuromuscular/skeletal impairment, pain/discomfort, restrictive therapies (bedrest, extremity immobilization), and psychological immobility, possibly evidenced by inability to purposefully move within the physical environment, imposed restrictions, reluctance to attempt movement, limited range of motion, and decreased muscle strength/control.

Depressive Disorders (Mood Disorders)

Major Depression/Dysthymia

Violence, risk for directed at self/others: risk factors may include depressed mood and feelings of worthlessness and hopelessness.

Anxiety (moderate to severe)/Thought Processes, altered may be related to psychological conflicts, unconscious conflict about essential values/goals of life, unmet needs, threat to self concept, sleep deprivation, interpersonal transmission/contagion, possibly evidenced by reports of nervousness or fearfulness, feelings of inadequacy, agitation, angry/tearful outbursts, rambling/discoordinated speech, restlessness, hand rubbing or wringing, tremulousness; poor memory/concentration, decreased ability to grasp ideas, inability to follow/impaired ability to make decisions, numerous/repetitious physical complaints without organic cause, ideas of reference, hallucinations/delusions.

Sleep Pattern disturbance may be related to biochemical alterations (decreased serotonin levels), unresolved fears and anxieties, and inactivity possibly evidenced by difficulty in falling/remaining asleep, early morning awakening/awakening later than desired (hypersomnia), reports of not feeling well rested, and physical signs (e.g., dark circles under eyes, excessive yawning).

*A risk diagnosis is not evidenced by signs and symptoms because the problem has not occurred and nursing interventions are directed at prevention.

Extracted from Doenges, M. E., and Moorhouse, M. F. (1998). *Nurse's Pocket Guide, Nursing Diagnoses with Interventions*, ed 6. Philadelphia: F.A. Davis.

munication barriers, limited physical mobility as evidenced by family report of change in pattern of interacting, dysfunctional interactions with peers and family, observed discomfort in social situations." This simplifies care and increases the likelihood of a timely and satisfactory resolution.

Neurological impairment is a broad umbrella that reflects general pathophysiology and lacks the specificity that is necessary to guide nursing actions/interventions. By identifying specific responses, you focus attention directly on issues that can be corrected or altered by nursing interventions.

For beginners, it is advisable to use the NANDA list in Appendix A when choosing a diagnostic label. Because the list is still evolving, "holes" may exist. With practice and experience, you may very well identify a problem or need that is treatable with nursing interventions but for which there is no appropriate NANDA label. In this situation, the diagnosis should be stated clearly using the PES format and then reviewed with other nursing colleagues to verify that the meaning and intent are accurately communicated. Finally, the work should be documented and submitted to NANDA for consideration.

Nursing knowledge is both objective and subjective, and it is the combination of intuition and analysis that is nursing's methodology. Experienced nurses may use **INTUITION** to arrive at a conclusion as an integral part of critical thinking. This skill is difficult to teach, and may not develop in all nurses; however, it needs to be respected, valued, and encouraged. Intuition is grounded in both knowledge and experience and is involved in making nursing judgments. Paying attention to the feelings or sense of something for which there is no visible data can add an important dimension to the diagnostic reasoning process. Intuition, responsibly applied by checking, rechecking, and validating these impressions (to avoid errors in judgment) can lead to insights not available in any other way.

INTUITION: a sense of something that is not clearly evidenced by known facts.

Finally, problem identification may be assisted by entering the patient database into a computer. On-line diagnostic software programs are available that contain lists of frequently used nursing diagnoses correlated to specific medical diagnoses. Other programs may suggest possible nursing diagnoses based on cues that the program identifies. Such programs are support tools and do not eliminate your need to use the diagnostic reasoning process to identify and formulate appropriate patient diagnostic statements *independently* of the computer recommendations.

Writing a Patient Diagnostic Statement: Using PES

As NANDA's list of nursing diagnosis labels increases, and issues of **WELLNESS** are addressed, the focus of a nursing diagnosis no longer is limited solely to problems but may also include the patient's needs and strength areas for potential enhancement. For this reason, although we use the PES format, we have chosen to identify the outcome of the diagnostic reasoning process as the Patient Diagnostic Statement instead of the commonly used term *Patient Problem*.

WELLNESS: a state of optimal health, physical and psychosocial.

Using the PES format as previously outlined, the problem/need, etiology, and signs and symptoms (or risk factors) are combined into a "neutral" statement avoiding value-laden or judgmental language. The use of ambiguous or judgmental terms such as "too often," "uncooperative," or "manipulative" can lead to misunderstandings on the part of the reader. Patients may become defensive or other readers may be influenced to make an inaccurate or biased decision, resulting in a negative treatment outcome.

The *problem* (or need) and *etiology* sections of the diagnostic statement are joined by the phrase "related to." Phrases such as "due to" or "caused by" indicate a specific/limited causal link that should therefore be avoided. "Related to" suggests a connection between the nursing diagnosis and the identified factors, leaving open the possibility that there may be other contributing factors not yet recognized.

When writing a diagnostic statement, remember to include qualifiers or quantifiers as indicated in the NANDA list (e.g., Anxiety, severe . . .). If the term "specify" is noted with a diagnostic label, it is important that the correct information be provided to make the communication clear (see Box 3–9).

FOR EXAMPLE: Tissue perfusion, altered: *cerebral;* or Knowledge deficit regarding *care of the newborn.*

BOX 3–9

QUALIFIERS FOR DIAGNOSTIC LABELS

(Suggested/not limited to the following)

Acute—Severe but of short duration.

Altered—A change from baseline.

Chronic—Lasting a long time, recurring, habitual, constant.

Decreased—Lessened; lesser in size, amount, or degree.

Deficient—Inadequate in amount, quality, or degree; defective; not sufficient; incomplete.

Depleted—Emptied wholly or in part; exhausted of.

Disturbed—Agitated, interrupted, interfered with.

Dysfunctional—Abnormal, incomplete functioning.

Excessive—Characterized by an amount or quantity that is greater than necessary, desirable, or useful.

Increased—Greater in size, amount, or degree.

Impaired—Made worse, weakened, damaged, reduced, deteriorated.

Ineffective—Not producing the desired effect.

Intermittent—Stopping and starting again at intervals, periodic, cyclic.

Potential for Enhanced (for use with wellness diagnoses)—Made greater, to increase in quality or more desired.

Types of Diagnostic Concepts

Actual—Describes human responses to health condition/life processes that exist in an individual, family, or community. It is supported by defining characteristics (manifestations, signs, and symptoms) that cluster in patterns of related cues or inferences.

Risk—Describes human responses to health conditions/life processes that may develop in a vulnerable individual, family, or community. It is supported by risk factors that contribute to increased vulnerability.

Wellness—describes human responses to levels of wellness in an individual, family, or community that have a potential for enhancement to a higher state.

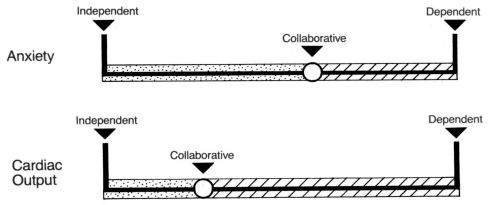

FIGURE 3–1. Representative comparison of the degree of independent nursing function in two nursing diagnoses. Nursing diagnoses have a varying degree of independent function, and nursing actions can be identified for any patient situation. As shown in this diagram, the nursing diagnosis *Anxiety* has a high degree of independent nursing actions, whereas *Cardiac Output* has a lower degree.

By definition, nursing diagnoses identify patient problems/needs that can be positively affected, or possibly prevented, by nursing actions. Some diagnoses permit greater independent function, whereas others are more collaborative. This may be visualized as a continuum without a fixed midpoint differentiating independent from dependent actions (Fig. 3–1). Furthermore, the extent of independent function is influenced by the individual nurse's experience, level of expertise, and work setting and the presence of established **PROTOCOLS** or standards of care. For this reason, the authors recommend that nurses identify the nursing component and appropriate interventions for any patient problem, instead of labeling independent versus **COLLABORATIVE PROBLEMS** or potential complications.

PROTOCOL: written guidelines of steps to be taken for providing patient care in a particular situation/condition.

COLLABORATIVE PROBLEM: a need identified by another discipline that contains a nursing component requiring nursing intervention and/or monitoring and therefore is an element of the interdisciplinary plan of care.

FOR EXAMPLE:

• During and following Sally's bleeding episode, the nursing component would be *Fluid Volume deficit* [isotonic] and the nurse would not only monitor the problem, but take action to control/prevent further blood loss (e.g., fundal massage) and would provide assurance to the patient.

• A low serum potassium level may result in dysrhythmias that can be addressed in *Cardiac Output, risk for decreased* requiring electrocardiographic

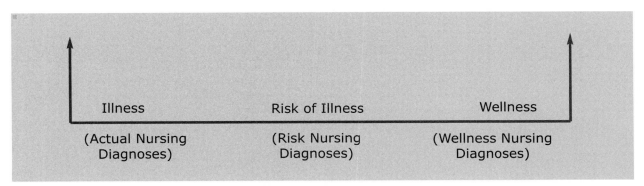

FIGURE 3–2. Trifocal model for client assessment. Adapted from Kelly, Frisch, & Avant, 1995.

interpretation, possible limiting activities, provision of potassium-containing foods/fluids as appropriate, and other interventions based on protocols.

- Michelle has a subclavian intravenous catheter. You might be concerned with *Infection, risk for,* with implications for sterile dressing changes and observation of the site.

Debate concerning the amount of independent function associated with nursing diagnoses and the interpretation of the definition of nursing diagnoses has been ongoing. These debates attest to the perceived and actual importance that nursing diagnoses have had and continue to have in the structuring of both the education and the practice of nursing. A bifocal model of nursing diagnosis and collaborative problems has existed for many years (Carpenito, 1997; Wallace et al., 1989). Also, a trifocal model of nursing diagnosis (Kelly et al., 1995) reinforcing the wellness diagnoses has been proposed since the publication of our last edition (Fig. 3–2).

Box 3–10 summarizes some common errors in creating and writing the patient diagnostic statement. Review this box and In a Nutshell before proceeding to Practice Activity 3–3 (see page 65).

BOX 3–10

COMMON ERRORS IN CREATING AND WRITING THE PATIENT DIAGNOSTIC STATEMENT

Identifying an incorrect nursing diagnosis or misstatement of problems/needs can lead to incorrect goals/outcomes and inappropriate nursing interventions. This can result in inappropriate/inadequate treatment of the patient that may not resolve the problem and that may occasionally place the nurse at risk for legal liability.

- **Using the Medical Diagnosis:** Self Care deficit related to stroke.
  Correct: Self Care deficit related to neuromuscular impairment.
- **Relating the Problem to an Unchangeable Situation:** Injury, risk for, related to blindness.
  Correct: Injury, risk for, related to unfamiliarity with surroundings.
- **Confusing the Etiology or Signs/Symptoms for the Problem:** Postoperative lung congestion related to bedrest.
  Correct: Airway Clearance, ineffective, related to general weakness and immobility.
- **Use of a Procedure Instead of the "Human Response":** Catheterization related to urinary retention.
  Correct: Urinary Retention related to perineal swelling.
- **Lack of Specificity:** Constipation related to nutritional intake.
  Correct: Constipation related to inadequate dietary bulk and fluid intake.
- **Combining Two Nursing Diagnoses:** Anxiety and Fear related to separation from parents.
  Correct: Fear related to separation from parents, or Anxiety, moderate, related to change in environment and unmet needs.
- **Relating One Nursing Diagnosis to Another:** Coping, Individual ineffective, related to anxiety.

Continued

COMMON ERRORS IN CREATING AND WRITING THE PATIENT DIAGNOSTIC STATEMENT (Continued)

Correct: Anxiety, severe, related to change in role functioning and socioeconomic status.

- **Use of Judgmental/Value-Laden Language:** Pain, chronic, related to secondary/monetary gain.

  Correct: Pain, chronic, related to recurrent muscle spasms.

  Note: The patient's report is valid, but the issue of secondary gain may require additional assessment to choose other appropriate nursing diagnoses and interventions.

- **Making Assumptions:** Parenting risk for altered, related to inexperience (new mother).

  Correct: Knowledge deficit regarding child care issues related to lack of previous experience, unfamiliarity with resources. **Note:** The label "Knowledge deficit" can have negative connotations for the patient and may result in defensive responses. The authors support the use of a substitute label "Learning Need."

- **Writing a Legally Inadvisable Statement:** Skin Integrity impaired, related to not being turned every 2 hours.

  Correct: Skin Integrity impaired, related to pressure and altered circulation. **Note:** If a patient complication occurs as a result of poor care/failure to meet standards of care, an incident report would be completed to document what happened.

IN A NUTSHELL . . .

How to Write a Patient Diagnostic Statement

1. Using physical assessment and history-taking interview techniques, collect both subjective and objective data from the patient, significant other, family members, other healthcare professionals, and patient records. A nursing framework is recommended such as Diagnostic Divisions (Doenges and Moorhouse), Functional Health Patterns (Gordon), or Human Response Patterns (NANDA).

2. Organize the collected data using a nursing framework (see item 1, above), a body systems approach (cardiovascular, gastrointestinal, and so on), a head-to-toe review (head, neck, thorax, and so on), or a combination of these. Your institution may use its own clustering model. If you have used a nursing framework, however, you will discover that information in the patient database is already conveniently structured for ease in identifying applicable nursing diagnoses.

3. Using diagnostic reasoning skills, review and analyze the database to identify cues (signs and symptoms) suggesting problems or needs that can be described by nursing diagnostic labels. Check the NANDA definitions of

Continued

IN A NUTSHELL . . . (Continued)

specific diagnoses for further assistance in distinguishing between two or more potentially applicable labels (see Appendix A).

4. Consider alternative rationales for the identified cues by comparing and contrasting the relationships among and between data, and isolating etiologic factors. This will allow you to determine which nursing diagnostic labels may be most appropriate, while ruling out those that are not.

5. Test your selection of nursing diagnostic label(s) and associated etiology(ies) for appropriate "fit" by:
   - Confirming the NANDA nursing diagnosis and definition for your choice of diagnostic label [P]
   - Comparing your proposed etiology with the NANDA "Related Factors" or "Risk Factors" associated with that particular diagnosis [E]
   - Comparing your identified signs and symptoms (cues) with the NANDA "Defining Characteristics" for the selected diagnosis, taking special note of the major/critical cues [S]

6. Re-evaluate your list of selected diagnoses to be sure that all patient problems/needs are accounted for. Then, order your list according to a needs priority model (the Maslow or Kalish models are usually used) and classify each diagnosis as actual (signs and symptoms supporting it are already present), risk for (risk factors are present, but the problem has not yet occurred), potential for enhanced (there is a desire to move to a higher state), or resolved (problem no longer requires nursing action).

7. Write the patient diagnostic statement for each diagnosis on your list. A three-part statement using the PES format is needed for actual or wellness diagnoses, and an adaptation of the PES format is used to create the two-part statement needed for risk diagnoses. Resolved diagnoses do not require diagnostic statements.

Three-Part Patient Diagnostic Statement

To write the patient diagnostic statement for actual/wellness diagnoses, combine (1) the confirmed nursing diagnosis label [P], (2) related factors [E], and (3) defining characteristics [S]. These elements are linked together by the phrases "related to" and "as evidenced by":

PROBLEM: [nursing diagnostic label]
ETIOLOGY: Related to [etiologic factors]
SIGNS AND SYMPTOMS: As evidenced by [defining characteristics]

Two-Part Diagnostic Statement

To write the diagnostic statement for risk diagnoses, combine (1) the confirmed risk nursing diagnosis label [P] and (2) the associated risk factors [E]. These elements are linked together by the phrase "risk factors of."

PROBLEM: [risk nursing diagnosis label]
ETIOLOGY: Risk factors of [associated risk factors]

PRACTICE ACTIVITY 3–3

Identifying Correct and Incorrect Patient Diagnostic Statements

Label each patient diagnostic statement as correct or incorrect. Identify why a statement is incorrect:

____ 1. Airway Clearance, ineffective, related to increased pulmonary secretions and bronchospasm evidenced by wheezing, tachypnea, and ineffective cough. _____

____ 2. Thought Processes, altered, related to delusional thinking or reality base evidenced by persecutory thoughts of "I am victim," and interference with ability to think clearly and logically. _____

____ 3. Gas Exchange, impaired, related to bronchitis evidenced by rhonchi, dyspnea, and cyanosis. _____

____ 4. Knowledge Deficit, diabetic care, related to inaccurate follow-through of instructions evidenced by information misinterpretation and lack of recall. _____

____ 5. Pain, related to tissue distension and edema evidenced by reports of severe colicky pain in right flank, elevated pulse and respirations, and restlessness. _____

Finally, although the PES format is a commonly recognized way of structuring the patient diagnostic statement, other formats may be appropriate when a different standardized language is used. For example, the Omaha System identifies four levels of a diagnostic statement: Level 1—Domain, Level 2—Problem Classification, Level 3—Modifier, Level 4—Signs/Symptoms (Box 3–11).

Summary

Although identifying an accurate nursing diagnosis requires time to analyze the gathered data and to validate the diagnosis, this process is critical and essential because it is the pivotal part of the nursing process. The time you take to formulate an accurate patient diagnostic statement and to plan the required care results in increased nursing efficiency, better use of time for all nursing staff, and the delivery of appropriate patient care, with the end result of better patient outcomes.

Some nurses still organize care directly around medical diagnoses, spending most of their time following medical orders. Medical diagnoses have a narrower focus than nursing diagnoses because they are based on pathology. A nursing diagnosis takes into account the psychological, social, spiritual, and physiological responses of the patient and family. NANDA diagnostic labels listed in Appendix A are used in formulating diagnostic statements that are structured in a three-part Problem, Etiology, and Signs/Symptoms (PES) format. Two-part statements may be used for risk diagnoses.

At times, something that appears easy to do in theory may seem difficult to achieve in practice. Nurses often have visionary ideas for the delivery of quality care to all patients. All too frequently, turning those ideas into actions can seem to

---

BOX 3–11

OMAHA SYSTEM EXAMPLE

In Box 3–2, Robert is assessed using the Activity/Rest diagnostic division revealing a range of possible NANDA nursing diagnosis labels:

Activity Intolerance
Disuse Syndrome, risk for
Diversional Activity deficit
Fatigue
Mobility, impaired bed
Sleep Deprivation
Sleep Pattern disturbance
Walking, impaired

These lead to a patient diagnostic statement of: Activity intolerance related to imbalance between oxygen supply/demand as evidenced by dyspnea and tachycardia with exertion, weakness, and limitation of desired activities. If we apply the Omaha System to the assessment data for Robert's level of physical activity, his problem would be documented as:

Level 1—Domain IV, Health-Related Behaviors
Level 2—Problem Classification, No. 37. Physical activity
Level 3—Modifier, Individual Impairment
Level 4—Signs/Symptoms, No. 3. Inappropriate type/physical condition

You are encouraged to read the articles and texts included in the Omaha System section of the Suggested Readings at the end of this chapter.

---

be a frustrating exercise in futility. However, as you work with and become more familiar with nursing diagnoses, the patient goals, related outcomes, and nursing interventions for attaining these goals and outcomes become more readily apparent. As you can see, an accurate and complete nursing diagnosis serves as the basis for the activities of the *Planning* step of the nursing process, discussed in Chapter 4.

Before continuing, let us return to the second ANA Standard of Clinical Nursing Practice and review the measurement criteria necessary to achieve and ensure compliance with the standard as discussed in this chapter (Box 3–12).

BOX 3–12

MEASUREMENT CRITERIA FOR ANA STANDARD II

ANA Standard II: Diagnosis: The nurse analyzes the assessment data in determining diagnoses.

1. Diagnoses are derived from the assessment data.
2. Diagnoses are validated with the patient, family, and healthcare providers, when possible and appropriate.
3. Diagnoses are documented in a manner that facilitates the determination of expected outcomes and plan of care.

1. What is the definition of Problem/Need Identification? _____

_____

2. What two factors influenced the development and acceptance of nursing diagnosis as the language
   of nursing? _____

_____

_____

3. List three reasons for using nursing diagnosis:

   a. _____

   b. _____

   c. _____

4. List the six steps of diagnostic reasoning:

   a. _____

   b. _____

   c. _____

   d. _____

   e. _____

   f. _____

5. Name the components of the Patient Diagnostic Statement:

   a. _____

   b. _____

   c. _____

6. If a risk diagnosis is identified, how is the Patient Diagnostic Statement altered?

_____

_____

7. What is the difference between a medical and a nursing diagnosis?

_____

_____

8. Which of these patient diagnostic statements are stated correctly? Indicate by placing a *C* before correct,
   or an *I* before incorrect statements. Then, differentiate actual (*A*) from risk (*R*) problems by placing an *A*
   or *R* by each statement.

   _____ a. Knowledge deficit, drug therapy related to misinterpretation and unfamiliarity with resources as
   evidenced by request for information and statement of misconception.

   _____ b. Risk for infection, risk factors of altered lung expansion, decreased ciliary action, decreased hemoglobin, and invasive procedures.

67

_____ c. Urinary Elimination, altered, related to indwelling catheter evidenced by inability to void.

_____ d. Anxiety [moderate], related to change in health status, role functioning, and socioeconomic status evidenced by apprehension, insomnia, and feelings of inadequacy.

9. Underline the cues in the patient database below that indicate that a problem may exist, and write a Patient Diagnostic Statement based on your findings.

VIGNETTE: Sally is 2 days postdelivery. She reports that her bowels have not moved but says she has been drinking plenty of fluids, including fruit juices, and has been eating a balanced diet.

ELIMINATION (EXCERPT FROM THE PATIENT DATABASE)

Subjective

Usual bowel patterns: every morning
Laxative use: rare/MOM PM
Character of stool: brown, formed
Last BM: 4 days ago
History of bleeding: No
Hemorrhoids: last 5 weeks
Constipation: since delivery
Diarrhea: No
Usual voiding pattern: 3–4 ×/day
Incontinence: No
Urgency: No
Character of urine: Yellow
Pain/burning/difficulty voiding: No
History of kidney/bladder disease: several bladder infections, last one 6 years ago
Associated complaints: pain with stool, nausea, "I just can't go no matter what I do."

Objective

Abdomen tender: Yes
Soft/firm: somewhat firm
Palpable mass: No
Size/girth: enlarged/postpartal
Bowel sounds: present all four quadrants, hypoactive every 1 to 2 minutes
Hemorrhoids: Visual examination not done.
Now, write the Patient Diagnostic Statement. Refer to the listing of Nursing Diagnoses in Appendix A to compare diagnostic labels addressing bowel elimination.

_____

_____

_____

BIBLIOGRAPHY

American Nurses' Association. (1980). *Nursing: A Social Policy Statement.* Kansas City, MO: Author.

American Nurses' Association. (1995). *Nursing's Social Policy Statement.* Washington, DC: Author.

Carpenito, L. J. (1997). *Nursing Diagnosis: Application to Clinical Practice,* ed 7. Philadelphia: J.B. Lippincott.

Fry, V. S. (1953). The creative approach to nursing. *Am J Nurs, 53:*301–302.

Gebbie, K. M., & Lavin, M. A. (1975). *Classification of Nursing Diagnoses: Proceedings from the First National Conference.* St. Louis: Mosby.

Gordon, M. (1976). Nursing diagnosis and the diagnostic process. *American Journal of Nursing, 76*(8):1298–1300.

Kelly, J., Frisch, N., & Avant, K. (1995). A trifocal model of nursing diagnosis: Wellness reinforced. *Nursing Diagnosis, 6*(3):123–128.

Lunney, M. (1989). Self-monitoring of accuracy using an integrated model of diagnostic process. *J Adv Med Surg Nurs, 1*(3):43–52.

Lunney, M. (1990). Accuracy of nursing diagnosis: Concept development. *Nursing Diagnosis, 1*(1):12–17.

North American Nursing Diagnosis Association. (1999). *Nursing Diagnoses: Definition & Classification.* Philadelphia: Author.

Wallace, D., & Ivey, J. (1989). The Bifocal Clinical Nursing Model: Descriptions and Applications to Patient's Receiving Thrombolytic or Anticoagulant Therapy. *Journal of Cardiovascular Nursing, 4*(1): 33–45.

SUGGESTED READINGS

Nursing Language, Classification, Theory, and Taxonomy

Advant, K. C. (1990). The art and science in nursing diagnosis development. *Nursing Diagnosis, 1*(1):51–56.

Dobryzn, J. (1995). Components of written nursing diagnostic statements. *Nursing Diagnosis, 6*(1):29–38.

Kerr, M. (1991). Validation of taxonomy. In R. M. Carroll-Johnson (Ed.). *Classification of Nursing Diagnoses: Proceedings of the Ninth Conference North American Nursing Diagnosis Association.* Philadelphia: J.B. Lippincott.

Kerr, M., et al. (1992). Development of definitions for taxonomy II. *Nursing Diagnosis, 3*(2):65–71.

Kerr, M., et al. (1993). Taxonomic validation: An overview. *Nursing Diagnosis, 4*(1):6–14.

Loomis, M. E., & Conco, D. (1991). Patients perception of health, chronic illness, and nursing diagnosis. *Nursing Diagnosis, 2*(4):162–170.

Miers, L. J. (1991). NANDA's definition of nursing diagnosis: A plea for conceptual clarity. *Nursing Diagnosis, 2*(1):9–18.

Mills, W. C. (1991). Nursing diagnosis: The importance of a definition. *Nursing Diagnosis, 2*(1):3–8.

Shoemaker, J. (1984). Essential features of a nursing diagnosis. In M. Kim, G. K. McFarland, & A. M. McLane (Eds.). *Classification of Nursing Diagnoses: Proceedings of the Fifth Conference North American Nursing Diagnosis Association.* St. Louis: Mosby.

Warren, J. J., & Hoskins, L. M. (1990). The development of NANDA's nursing diagnosis taxonomy. *Nursing Diagnosis, 1*(4):162–168.

Whitley, G. G., & Gulanick, M. (1995). Barriers to use of nursing diagnosis in clinical settings. *Nursing Diagnosis, (5):*25–32.

Texts

Carpenito, L. J. (1997). *Nursing Diagnosis: Application to Clinical Practice,* ed 7. Philadelphia: J.B. Lippincott.

Cox, H., et al. (1997). *Clinical Applications of Nursing Diagnosis: Adult, Child, Women's, Psychiatric, Gerontic, and Home Health Considerations,* ed 3. Philadelphia: F.A. Davis.

Doenges, M. E., Moorhouse, M. F., & Geissler, A. C. (2000). *Nursing Care Plans: Guidelines for Individualizing Patient Care,* ed 5. Philadelphia: F.A. Davis.

Leuner, J. D., Manton, A. K., Kelliher, D., Sullivan, S. D., & Doherty, M. (1990). *Mastering the Nursing Process: A Case Study Approach*. Philadelphia: F.A. Davis.

Maas, M., Buckwalter, K. C., & Hardy, M. (1991). *Nursing Diagnosis and Interventions for the Elderly*. Menlo Park, CA: Addison-Wesley.

Validation of Nursing Diagnoses

Brukwitzki, G., Holmgen, C., & Maibusch, R. M. (1996). Validation of the defining characteristics of the nursing diagnosis Ineffective Airway Clearance. *Nursing Diagnosis, 7*:63–69.

Chiang, L., Ku, N., & Lo, C. K. (1994). Clinical validation of the etiologies and defining characteristics of Altered Nutrition: Less than body requirements in patients with cancer. In R. M. Carroll-Johnson & M. Paquette (Eds.). *Classification of Nursing Diagnoses: Proceedings of the Tenth Conference North American Nursing Diagnosis Association*. Philadelphia: J.B. Lippincott.

Chung, L. (1997). The clinical validation of defining characteristics and related factors of fatigue in hemodialysis patients. In M. J. Rantz & P. Lemone (Eds.). *Classification of Nursing Diagnoses: Proceedings of the Twelfth Conference North American Nursing Diagnosis Association*. Glendale, CA: Cinahl.

Dougherty, C. (1997). Reconceptualization of the nursing diagnosis decreased cardiac output. *Nursing Diagnosis the Journal of Nursing Language and Classification, 8*:29–36.

Ennen, K. A., Komorita, N. I., & Pogue, N. (1997). Validation of defining characteristics of the nursing diagnosis: Fluid volume excess. In M. J. Rantz & P. Lemone (Eds.). *Classification of Nursing Diagnoses: Proceedings of the Twelfth Conference North American Nursing Diagnosis Association*. Glendale, CA: Cinahl.

Fowler, S. B. (1997). Impaired verbal communication: During short-term oral intubation. *Nursing Diagnosis the Journal of Nursing Language and Classification, 8*:93–98.

Hensley, L. D. (1994). Spiritual Distress: A validation study. In R. M. Carroll-Johnson & M. Paquette (Eds.). *Classification of Nursing Diagnoses: Proceedings of the Tenth Conference North American Nursing Diagnosis Association*. Philadelphia: J.B. Lippincott.

Kerr, M., et al. (1993). Development of definitions for taxonomy II. *Nursing Diagnosis, 3*(2):65–71.

Kraft, L. A., Maas, M., & Hardy, M. A. (1994). Diagnostic content validity of impaired physical mobility in the older adult. In R. M. Carroll-Johnson & M. Paquette (Eds.). *Classification of Nursing Diagnoses: Proceedings of the Tenth Conference North American Nursing Diagnosis Association*. Philadelphia: J.B. Lippincott.

Lemone, P. (1993). Validation of the defining characteristics of altered sexuality. *Nursing Diagnosis, 4*(2):56–62.

Lemone, P., & Weber, J. (1995). Validating gender specific defining characteristics. *Nursing Diagnosis, 6*(2):64–72.

Lemone, P., & James, D. (1997). Nursing assessment of altered sexuality: A review of salient factors and objective measures. *Nursing Diagnosis the Journal of Nursing Language and Classification, 8*:120–128.

Levin, R. F., Krainovich, B. C., Bahrenburg, E., & Mitchell, C. A. (1988). Diagnostic content validity of nursing diagnosis. *Image J Nurs Schol, 21*(1):40–44.

Morton, N. (1997). Validation of the nursing diagnosis decreased cardiac output in a population without cardiac disease. In M. J. Rantz & P. Lemone (Eds.). *Classification of Nursing Diagnoses: Proceedings of the Twelfth Conference North American Nursing Diagnosis Association*. Glendale, CA: Cinahl.

Sidani, S., & Woodtli, M. A. (1994). Testing and validating an instrument to assess the defining characteristics of stress and urge incontinence. In R. M. Carroll-Johnson & M. Paquette (Eds.). *Classification of Nursing Diagnoses: Proceedings of the Tenth Conference North American Nursing Diagnosis Association*. Philadelphia: J.B. Lippincott.

Simon, J., Baumann, M. A., & Nolan, L. (1995). Differential diagnostic validation: Acute and chronic pain. *Nursing Diagnosis, 6*(2):73–79.

Smith, J. E., et al. (1997). Risk for suicide and risk for violence: A case study approach for separating the current violence diagnoses. *Nursing Diagnosis the Journal of Nursing Language and Classification, 8*:67–77.

Tiesinga, L. J., Dassen, T. W. N., & Halfens, R. J. G. (1997). Validation of the nursing diagnosis fatigue among patients with chronic heart failure. In M. J. Rantz & P. Lemone (Eds.). *Classification of Nursing Diagnoses: Proceedings of the Twelfth Conference North American Nursing Diagnosis Association*. Glendale, CA: Cinahl.

Wall, B., Howard, J., & Perry-Phillips, J. (1995). Validation of two nursing diagnoses: Increases intracranial pressure and High risk for increased intracranial pressure. In M. J. Rantz & P. Lemone (Eds.). *Clas-*

sification of Nursing Diagnoses: Proceedings of the Eleventh Conference North American Nursing Diagnosis Association. Glendale, CA: Cinahl.

Whitley, G. G. (1992). Concept analysis of anxiety. *Nursing Diagnosis, 3*(3):107–116.

Whitley, G. G. (1992). Concept analysis of fear. *Nursing Diagnosis, 3*(4):155–161.

Specific Nursing Diagnoses

Bakker, R. H., Kastermans, M. C., & Dassen, T. W. N. (1997). Noncompliance and ineffective management of therapeutic regimen: Use in practice and theoretical implications. In M. J. Rantz & P. Lemone (Eds.). *Classification of Nursing Diagnoses: Proceedings of the Twelfth Conference North American Nursing Diagnosis Association.* Glendale, CA: Cinahl.

Bakker, R. H., Kastermans, M.C., & Dassen, T. W. N. (1995). An analysis of the nursing diagnosis Ineffective Management of Therapeutic Regimen compared to Noncompliance and Orem's Self-Care Deficit theory. *Nursing Diagnosis, 6:*161–168.

Harness-DoGloria, D., & Pye, C. G. (1995). Risk for impaired skin integrity: Incorporation of the risk factors from AHCPR guidelines. In M. J. Rantz & P. Lemone (Eds.). *Classification of Nursing Diagnoses: Proceedings of the Eleventh Conference North American Nursing Diagnosis Association.* Glendale, CA: Cinahl.

Heliker, D. (1992). Reevaluation of the nursing diagnosis: Spiritual distress. *Nurs Forum, 27*(4):15–20.

Mahon, S. M. (1994). Concept analysis of pain: Implications related to nursing diagnoses. *Nursing Diagnosis, 1*(5):15–25.

Minton, J. A., & Creason, N. S. (1991). Evaluation of admission nursing diagnoses. *Nursing Diagnosis, 2*(1):119–125.

Schmelz, J. O. (1997). Ineffective airway clearance: State of the science. In M. J. Rantz & P. Lemone (Eds.). *Classification of Nursing Diagnoses: Proceedings of the Twelfth Conference North American Nursing Diagnosis Association.* Glendale, CA: Cinahl.

Smucker, C. (1995). A phenomenological description of the experience of spiritual distress. In M. J. Rantz & P. Lemone (Eds.). *Classification of Nursing Diagnoses: Proceedings of the Eleventh Conference North American Nursing Diagnosis Association.* Glendale, CA: Cinahl.

Tiesinga, L. J., Dassen, T. W. N., & Halfens, R. J. G. (1995). Fatigue: A summary of definitions, dimensions, and indicators. *Nursing Diagnosis, 7:*51–62.

Whitley, G. G. (1997). A comparison of two methods of clinical validation of nursing diagnosis. In M. J. Rantz & P. Lemone (Eds.). *Classification of Nursing Diagnoses: Proceedings of the Twelfth Conference North American Nursing Diagnosis Association.* Glendale, CA: Cinahl.

Whitley, G. G., & Tousman, S. A. (1996). A multivariate approach for the validation of anxiety and fear. *Nursing Diagnosis, 7:*116–124.

Woodtli, M. A., & Yocum, K. (1994). Urge incontinence: Identification and clinical validation of defining characteristics. In R. M. Carroll-Johnson and M. Paquette (Eds.). *Classification of Nursing Diagnoses: Proceedings of the Tenth Conference North American Nursing Diagnosis Association.* Philadelphia: J.B. Lippincott.

Woodtli, A. (1995). Stress incontinence: Clinical identification and validation of defining characteristics. *Nursing Diagnosis, 6:*115–122.

Woolridge, J., et al. (1998). A validation study using the case-control method of the nursing diagnosis Risk for Aspiration. *Nursing Diagnosis the Journal of Nursing Language and Classification, 9:*5–14.

Accuracy of Nursing Diagnoses

Lunney, M. (1992). Divergent productive thinking factors and accuracy of nursing diagnoses. *Res Nurs Health, 15*(3):303–311.

Lunney, M. (1994). Measurement of accuracy of nursing diagnosis. In R. M. Carroll-Johnson & M. Paquette (Eds.). *Classification of Nursing Diagnoses: Proceedings of the Tenth Conference North American Nursing Diagnosis Association.* Philadelphia: J.B. Lippincott.

Lunney, M., & Paradiso, C. (1995). Accuracy of interpreting human responses. *Nursing Management, 26*(10):48H–48K.

Lunney, M., Karlik, B. A., Kiss, M., & Murphy, P. (1995). Accuracy of nursing diagnosis in clinical settings. In M. J. Rantz & P. Lemone (Eds.). *Classification of Nursing Diagnoses: Proceedings of the Eleventh Conference North American Nursing Diagnosis Association.* Glendale, CA: Cinahl.

Lunney, M., Karlik, B. A., Kiss, M., & Murphy, P. (1997). Accuracy of nursing diagnosis of psychosocial responses. *Nursing Diagnosis the Journal of Nursing Language and Classification, 8:*157–66.

Wellness (Health Promotion)

Allen, C. (1989). Incorporating a wellness perspective for nursing diagnosis in practice. In R. M. Carroll-Johnson (Ed.). *Classification of Nursing Diagnoses: Proceedings of the Eighth Conference North American Nursing Diagnosis Association*. Philadelphia: J.B. Lippincott.

Appling, S. E. (1997). Wellness issues. Sleep: Linking research to improved outcomes. *MEDSURG Nursing, 6*(3):159–161.

Armentrout, G. (1993). A comparison of the medical model and the wellness model: The importance of knowing the difference. *Holistic Nursing Practice, 7*(4):57–62.

Carpenito, L. J. (1997). *Nursing Diagnosis: Application to Clinical Practice*, ed 7. Philadelphia: J.B. Lippincott.

Fleury, J. (1991). Empowering potential: A theory of wellness motivation. *Nursing Research, 40*:286–291.

Fleury, J. (1991). Wellness motivation in cardiac rehabilitation. *Heart & Lung: Journal of Critical Care, 20*(1):3–8.

Fleury, J. (1996). Wellness motivation theory: An exploration of theoretical relevance. *Nurs Res, 45*:277–283.

Kelly, J., Frisch, N., & Avant, K. (1995). A trifocal model of nursing diagnosis: Wellness reinforced. *Nursing Diagnosis, 6*(3):123–128.

Moch, S. (1989). Health within illness: Conceptual evolution and practice possibilities. *Advances in Nursing Science, 11*:230–31.

Murdaugh, C. L., & Vanderboom, C. (1997). Individual and community models for promoting wellness. *J Cardiovasc Nurs, 11*(3):1–14.

Pender, N. (1987). *Health Promotion in Nursing Practice*, ed 2. Norwalk, CT: Appleton-Century.

Popkess-Vawter, S. (1991). Wellness nursing diagnoses: To be or not to be? *Nursing Diagnosis, 2*(1):19–25.

Ryan, J. P. (1993). Wellness and health promotion of the elderly. *Nurs Outlook, 41*(3):143.

Stolte, K. M. (1994). Health-oriented nursing diagnoses: Development and use. In R. M. Carroll-Johnson & M. Paquette (Eds.). *Classification of Nursing Diagnoses: Proceedings of the Tenth Conference North American Nursing Diagnosis Association*. Philadelphia: J.B. Lippincott.

Stolte, K. M. (1996). *Wellness Nursing Diagnosis for Health Promotion*. Philadelphia: Lippincott-Raven.

Omaha System

Elfrink, V. L., Martin, K. S., & Davis, L. S. (1997). The nightingale tracker: information technology for community nursing education. In U. Gerdin, M. Tallberg, & P. Wainright (Eds.). *Nursing Informatics: The Impact of Nursing Knowledge on Health Care Informatics*. Amsterdam, The Netherlands: IOS Press, pp 364–368.

Elfrink, V. L., & Martin, K. S. (1996). Educating for community nursing practice: Point of care technology. *Healthcare Information Management, 10*(2):81–89.

Lang, N. et al. (1997). *Nursing practice and outcomes measurement*. Oakbrook Terrace, IL: Joint Commission on Accreditation of Healthcare Organizations, pp 17–34.

Martin, K. S. (1989). The Omaha System and NANDA: A review of similarities and differences: In R. M. Carroll-Johnson (Ed.). *Classification of Nursing Diagnoses: Proceedings of the Eighth Conference*. Philadelphia: J.B. Lippincott, pp 171–172.

Martin, K. S. (1997). The Omaha System: In M. J. Rantz & P. Lemone (Eds.), *Classification of Nursing Diagnoses: Proceedings of the Twelfth Conference*. Glendale, CA: Cinahl Information Systems, pp 16–21.

Martin, K. S., Leak, G. K., & Aden, C. A. (1992). The Omaha System: A research based model for decision making. *J Nurs Adm, 22*:44–52.

Martin, K. S., & Martin, D. L. (1997). How can the quality of nursing practice be measured? In J. C. McCloskey & H. K. Grace (Eds.). *Current Issues in Nursing*, ed 5. St. Louis: Mosby, pp 315–321.

Martin, K. S., & Norris, J. (1996). The Omaha System: A model for describing practice. *Holistic Nursing Practice, 11*(1):75–83.

Martin, K. S., & Scheet, N. J. (1992). *The Omaha System: Applications for Community Health Nursing*. Philadelphia: W.B. Saunders.

Martin, K. S., & Scheet, N. J. (1992). *The Omaha System: A Pocket Guide for Community Health Nursing*. Philadelphia: W.B. Saunders.

Martin, K. S., Scheet, N. J., & Stegman, M. R. (1993). Home health care clients: Characteristics, outcomes of care, and nursing interventions. *Am J Public Health* 83:1730–1734.

Merrill, A. S., Hiebert, V., Moran, M., & Weatherby, F. (1998). Curriculum restructuring using the practice-based Omaha System. *Nurse Educator, 23*(3):41–44.

Westra, B. (1995). Implementing nursing diagnoses in community settings. In M. J. Rantz & P. Lemone (Eds.). *Classification of Nursing Diagnoses: Proceedings of the Eleventh Conference.* Glendale, CA: Cinahl Information Systems, pp 47–51.

Home Healthcare Classification

Saba, V. K. (1997). An innovative Home Health Care Classification (HHCC) System. In M. J. Rantz & P. Lemone (Eds.). *Classification of Nursing Diagnoses: Proceedings of the Twelfth Conference North American Nursing Diagnosis Association.* Glendale, CA: Cinahl.

Saba, V. K. (1994). Home health care classification (HHCC) of nursing diagnoses and interventions. (Revised). Washington, DC: Author.

Saba, V. K. (1992). The classification of home health care nursing: Diagnoses and interventions. *Caring, 11*(3):5–57.

Saba, V. K. (1992). Home health care classification. *Caring, 11*(5):58–60.

Saba, V. K., & Zucherman, A. E. (1992). A new home health care classification method. *Caring, 11*(10):27–34.

Patient Care Data Set

Ozbolt, J. G. (1997). From minimum data to maximum impact: Using clinical data to strengthen patient care. *MD Computing,* 14:295–301. [Note: Adapted from *Advanced Practice Nursing Quarterly* (1996: 1:62–69)]

Ozbolt, J. G., Russo, M., & Schultz, M. P. (1995). Validity and reliability of standard terms and codes for patient care data. In R. M. Gardner (Ed.). *Proceedings of the Nineteenth Annual Symposium on Computer Applications in Medical Care,* pp 37–41.

Ozbolt, J. G., Fruchtnicht, J. N., & Hayden, J. R. (1994). Toward data standards for clinical nursing information. *J Am Med Inform Assoc* 1:175–185.

The Planning Step: Creating the Plan of Care

- **ANA Standard 3:** Outcome identification: The nurse identifies expected outcomes individualized to the client.
- **ANA Standard 4:** Planning: The nurse develops a plan of care that prescribes interventions to attain expected outcomes.

PLANNING: third step of the nursing process, during which goals/outcomes are determined and interventions chosen.

PLAN OF CARE: written evidence of the second and third steps of the nursing process that identifies the patient's problems/needs, goals/outcomes of care, and interventions to treat the problems/need and achieve the outcomes.

Once the etiology, signs, and symptoms previously identified are incorporated into a patient diagnostic statement, you can proceed to the **PLANNING** step of the nursing process. Now, attention is focused on the actions that are most appropriate to effectively address the patient's problems/needs. You begin to set priorities, establish goals, identify desired outcomes, and determine specific nursing interventions. These actions are documented as the **PLAN OF CARE,** which then serves to guide the activities of all healthcare workers who are involved in the patient's care. Whenever possible, the patient and/or significant others are included in the process of planning, so that they may contribute to, participate in, and take responsibility for their own care and the achievement of the desired outcomes and goals.

Setting Priorities for Patient Care

The starting point for planning care is generally to rank the patient's problems/needs, so that the nurse's attention and subsequent actions are properly focused. Although there are many ways of prioritizing patient needs, a useful framework is one developed by Abraham Maslow (Fig. 4–1). In 1943, Maslow theorized that human behavior is motivated by a hierarchy arranged from basic to progressively higher level needs (Maslow, 1970). According to Maslow, physiological needs are generally considered baseline survival needs because they must be met in order for life to continue. When these base-level needs (such as food, fluid, and oxygen) are not satisfied, it is difficult or impossible to focus on, or attempt to meet, higher-level needs (such as love, belonging, and self-esteem). Once base-level needs are satisfied, however, it becomes possible for higher-level needs to be addressed.

Richard Kalish (1983) expanded and further subdivided the structure of Maslow's hierarchy, resulting in a more comprehensive description of the specific need categories. This expanded hierarchy can help you, as a nurse, to identify and prioritize patient needs more precisely as well as desired outcomes and the associated nursing interventions (Fig. 4–2). Failure to meet human needs at any level can dramatically interfere with a patient's overall progress. Clearly, it is difficult to use Active-listening techniques (meeting a higher-level patient need for self-esteem) to teach a patient who is choking (a basic need of survival) about maintaining a patent airway.

Once you determine the priorities of care, the patient's care needs can also be ranked based on a system (such as Maslow's hierarchy; see Appendix C) that can help you identify basic to higher level actions/interventions. This is necessary because it is usually difficult to plan and provide care effectively when more than three to five nursing diagnoses exist at one time, depending on their complexity. By ranking the patient's problems/needs, you can proceed in a logical way to facilitate your patient's recovery.

FOR EXAMPLE:

- Basic survival needs (i.e., air, water, and food) must be met before other needs can be considered. Sample diagnostic labels involving basic survival needs include Airway Clearance, ineffective, and Nutrition, altered, less than body requirements.

FIGURE 4–1. Maslow's hierarchy of needs. The pyramid of Maslow's hierarchy is a model that allows us to look at human behavior in a structured way to determine physiological and psychological needs. Physiological needs appear at the bottom or base of the pyramid. Maslow's theory tells us that these lower-level needs must be met before higher-level needs (such as self-esteem) can be addressed. This knowledge of the needs that must be met first can help the nurse determine the priorities of patient care.

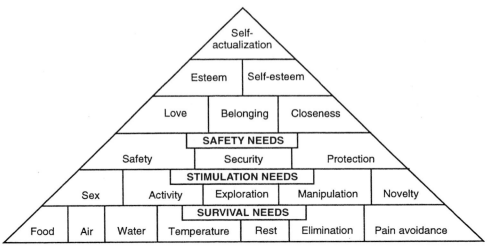

FIGURE 4–2. Kalish's expanded hierarchy. In an expansion of Maslow's model, Kalish restructured the first two levels of Maslow's pyramid (physiological and safety/security needs) into three levels and identified more-specific subcategories. The base level is labeled *survival,* the second level *stimulation,* and the third level *safety.* The refinement of these subcategories can further assist the nurse to identify the priorities for planning patient care.

- Safety needs are next in order of importance. Nursing diagnostic labels relating to safety needs include Violence, risk for, self-directed; Injury, risk for; Health Maintenance, altered.
- Once these categories of patient care needs are met, concerns regarding needs in the social, self-esteem, and self-actualization categories can be considered. Examples of nursing diagnostic labels relating to these categories of needs are: Social Interaction, impaired (a need for relationships with others); Self-Esteem disturbance (the need to feel good about oneself); and Family Coping: potential for growth (a need for family and belonging).

Setting priorities for patient care is a complex and dynamic challenge. What you may perceive as the number one patient care need or appropriate nursing intervention today could change tomorrow or, for that matter, within minutes. Practice Activity 4–1 gives you some experience in prioritizing patient problems based on levels of need.

ESTABLISHING PATIENT GOALS

Once you have prioritized patient problems, establish the **GOALS** for treatment/discharge. The patient care goal(s) is a broad description of the general direction in which your patient is expected to progress in response to treatment.

Goals may be either long term or short term. **LONG-TERM GOALS** indicate the overall direction or end result of care and may very well *not* be achieved before discharge. Examples of long-term goals might be "Maintains control of blood glucose level" or "Uses resources/supports to prevent rehospitalization." **SHORT-TERM GOALS** are more specific guides for care and must usually be met before discharge or transfer to a less acute level of care, supervision, or support. Short-term goals may be building blocks for attaining the long-term goals. Nursing care can then be

GOALS: broad guidelines indicating the overall direction for movement as a result of the interventions of the healthcare team; divided into long-term goals and short-term goals.

LONG-TERM GOALS: those goals that may not be achieved before discharge from care but may require continued attention by patient and/or others.

SHORT-TERM GOALS: those goals that usually must be met before discharge or movement to a less acute level of care.

PRACTICE ACTIVITY 4–1

Prioritizing Nursing Diagnoses

Instructions: Prioritize the nursing diagnoses listed in each separate set by using the Maslow and Kalish models. Rank the four diagnoses by using 1 to designate the most basic or more immediate patient need and continuing to 4, which designates the highest-level need (but least in priority). Review Appendix A as needed to compare definitions of these nursing diagnoses.

a. _____ [Urinary] Incontinence, stress

_____ Sexuality Patterns, altered

_____ Airway Clearance, ineffective

_____ Skin Integrity, risk for impaired

b. _____ Gas Exchange, impaired

_____ Knowledge deficit

_____ Hypothermia

_____ Infection, risk for

c. _____ Pain, acute

_____ Self-Esteem, chronic low

_____ Mobility, impaired physical

_____ Social Isolation

planned more accurately when the focus is directed to the short-term goals. Depending on the patient's anticipated length of stay/care, a short-term goal may be evaluated within a few hours or over the period of several therapeutic sessions. This period of time could reflect as much as several calendar weeks if the patient is seen for counseling/therapy on a weekly, or even monthly, basis. Examples of short-term goals might be "Learns to use blood glucose monitoring system" or "Using three support agencies within the community appropriately."

If the short-term goal is to be met within the nursing shift or visit during which it is identified, it is not necessary to write the goal on the plan of care; it can be noted in the progress note. If the goal is not accomplished by the end of the shift/visit, it is added to the plan of care, with a new timeframe, so that those involved in the care can continue to work toward it.

IDENTIFYING DESIRED OUTCOMES

OUTCOMES: measurable steps to achieve the goals of treatment and to meet discharge criteria; the result of actions undertaken to achieve a broader goal.

The next step in developing the plan of care is to form specific **OUTCOMES,** which are defined as patient responses that are achievable and desired by the patient and that can be attained within a defined time period given the present situation and resources. These *desired outcomes* are the measurable steps toward achieving the patient goals that were established earlier. Because they must be measurable, outcome statements need to:

- Be specific
- Be realistic
- Consider the patient's circumstances and desires
- Indicate a definite timeframe
- Provide measurable evaluation criteria for determining success or failure

Desired outcomes are written by listing items/behaviors that can be observed and monitored to determine whether or not a positive/acceptable outcome has been achieved within the indicated timeframe. For example, "Verbalizes understanding of disease process and potential complications. . . ." This itemized listing of outcomes then serves as the evaluation tool, which is discussed more fully in Chapter 6. Take a moment to look over Box 4–1 to give you a better idea of how to make the distinction between goals and outcomes.

Measurable action verbs are used to describe outcomes. Some examples of this type of verb are: discusses, states, identifies, administers, explains, and reports. For instance, "Patient will: *Ambulate* with use of cane." Refer to Box 4–2 for additional examples. Passive words are generally avoided. The use of specific time elements in outcome statements also provide measurable criteria, such as: "Patient will: Ambulate with cane without assistance *within 3 days.*" On occasion, some outcomes may be ongoing because they do not have a specific timeframe short of discharge from care. Examples of these ongoing outcomes are statements such as "Patient will: Maintain a patent airway" or "Patient will: Be free of skin breakdown." It is your job to monitor each of these situations and document regularly any patient findings. However, the situations may not be *resolved* until the patient's condition/status changes or discharge has occurred.

When outcomes are properly written, they provide direction for planning and validating the choice of appropriate nursing interventions.

FOR EXAMPLE:

- Patient will: Identify individual nutritional needs within 30 hours.
- Patient will: Formulate a dietary plan based on these needs within 48 hours.

From these desired outcomes, you know that the patient's level of dietary knowledge should be assessed, individual patient needs identified, and patient teaching

NURSING-SENSITIVE OUTCOMES: neutral concepts reflecting a patient's status influenced by nursing care and measured as a continuum rather than as discrete goals that are met/not met. Useful in monitoring nursing practice, advancing standards of care, and documenting nursing's contribution to healthcare. (Johnson & Maas, 1997)

BOX 4–1

DISTINGUISHING BETWEEN GOALS AND OUTCOMES

Goals are overall, broad directions to guide the plan of care. A broad goal for a patient with chronic obstructive pulmonary disease (COPD) might be:

- Ventilation/oxygenation adequate to allow a functional lifestyle.

Outcomes are the desired results of actions undertaken to achieve the broader goal and are the measurable steps to achieving the goals of treatment/discharge criteria. Often there is more than one outcome for each goal. The integral outcomes to achieve the above goal could include:

- Maintains patent airway with breath sounds clear.
- Demonstrates techniques to improve airway clearance (i.e., use of pursed-lip breathing, liquefying secretions, and/or nebulizer therapy).
- Initiates necessary lifestyle changes and participates in treatment regimen.

> **BOX 4–2**
>
> ## ACTION VERBS USEFUL IN WRITING MEASURABLE OUTCOMES
>
> Using action rather than passive verbs provides a clearer method for determining patient progress. The following are examples of action verbs that can be measured or observed:
>
> List, Record, Name, State
> Describe, Explain, Identify
> Demonstrate, Use, Schedule
> Differentiate, Compare, Relate
> Design, Prepare, Formulate, Calculate
> Select, Choose, Compare
> Increase/Decrease, Stand, Walk, Participate
>
> **FOR EXAMPLE:** The patient will: *List* three things he understands about his diagnosis. The patient will: *Walk* to the end of the hall and back three times today.
>
> Below are a few samples of "passive" verbs. Notice that the "actions" described by the verbs are not measurable:
>
> Understand, Feel, Learn, Know, Accept
>
> **FOR EXAMPLE:** The patient will: *Understand* his treatment plan. How will the nurse measure achievement and *know* that the patient understands?

information presented to provide the patient with the tools necessary to formulate a dietary plan.

Remember, though, that interventions can be wide ranging. The outcome statement "Patient will: Verbalize acceptance of actual body image within 2 weeks" may call for interventions ranging from learning to recognize and express own feelings about body changes, to developing a program of diet and exercise to promote weight loss, to instruction in the use of makeup, hairstyles, and ways of dressing that maximize figure assets/minimize perceived faults.

All outcomes should tell the readers specifically what the patient is working on or doing. If the outcome does not seem to logically relate to the goals for treatment/discharge, it should be questioned. Is the outcome, in fact, a valid component of the plan of care? With this in mind, there is a simple and straightforward method of determining whether or not an outcome is correctly written: Ask yourself if you could observe the patient in the performance of the behavior indicated. If the answer is no, the desired, measurable outcome you have written should be modified. Below are several pairs of correctly and incorrectly written outcomes with notations to identify the desired elements. When you have finished looking them over, work through the exercises in Practice Activity 4–2.

1. **Incorrect:** "Understands insulin therapy within 48 hours."
   Rationale: This patient outcome states a clear time line, but can you measure a patient's "understanding"? This outcome needs a measurable action verb.

   Correct: "Demonstrates correct insulin administration techniques within 48 hours."

PRACTICE ACTIVITY 4–2

Identifying Correctly Stated Outcomes

Instructions: Identify which of the following outcome statements are written correctly, or if written incorrectly, state why it is incorrect. Modify those statements that are not correct.

1. Patient will: List individual risk factors and appropriate interventions. _____

   _____

2. Patient will: Identify four adaptive/protective measures for individual situation by discharge.

   _____

   _____

3. Patient will: Understand behaviors, lifestyle changes necessary to promote physical safety within 72 hours. _____

   _____

4. Airway patent, aspiration prevented, ongoing. _____

   _____

5. Patient will: Assume responsibility for own learning by participating in group discussions twice a day no later than 10/29/99. _____

   _____

or

"Explains reasons for the steps of insulin administration within 48 hours."

   Rationale: These are well-written outcomes that are observable, measurable, and time limited.

2. **Incorrect:** "Requires no reminders from staff regarding dietary restrictions within 3 days."

   Rationale: This outcome tells what the staff will do, not what the patient will do.

   Correct: "Lists individual dietary restrictions and makes appropriate choices from daily menu within 3 days."

   Rationale: This outcome is observable and easy to document.

3. **Incorrect:** "Receives fewer restrictions for defying staff instructions during the next 2 weeks."

   Rationale: What exactly is the definition of "fewer"? A specific number is clearer. What constitutes "defiance," and what is the patient doing? According to this outcome, the patient "receives" fewer restrictions, which places the patient in an essentially passive role. Good measurable outcomes state what the patient actively does.

   Correct: "Follows rules so that infractions decrease from the current rate of one per day to no more than two per week within 7 days."

   Rationale: Incidents of violation of unit rules are events that are observable, well documented, and easy to track. This outcome is also time limited.

As mentioned in Chapter 1, a classification of outcomes associated with both nursing diagnoses and nursing interventions has been researched and developed. The Nursing Outcomes Classification (NOC) was developed by a research team at the University of Iowa's College of Nursing. The current edited work including the 190 nursing outcomes is titled *Iowa Outcomes Project: Nursing Outcomes Classification (NOC)*. A sample of NOC labels includes Abuse Cessation, Bone Healing, Cardiac Pump Effectiveness, Child Adaptation to Hospitalization, Dignified Dying, Hope, Leisure Participation, Oral Health, Quality of Life, Social Support, Will to Live.

The Outcomes Classification is designed to describe the patient state following the implementation of nursing interventions. Whereas the nursing diagnosis Activity Intolerance is defined by NANDA as "A state in which an individual has insufficient physiological or psychological energy to endure or complete required or desired daily activities," the nursing outcome of "Endurance: Extent that energy enables a person's activity" describes the state (or status) the patient would achieve after the implementation of selected nursing interventions (Box 4–3).

Each outcome then has an associated list of indicators that are measured by a variety of specific Likert-scales (see Appendix J). Thus, the outcome is a variable state with indicators used to measure the patient response to the care provided. For example, Robert, with questioned Sleep Pattern disturbance as possibly diagnosed in the last chapter, can have an outcome state of "Sleep," and indicators of "sleep quality" and "hours of sleep," which, measured on a 1–5 scale, assesses the degree of compromise.

Now that we have introduced you to NOC, let's go back and revisit your patient Robert and review how another language of nursing, the Omaha System, will assist in goal development. See Box 4–4 for the application of the Omaha System to Robert's NANDA Activity Intolerance nursing diagnosis and the Omaha System Problem: No. 37, Physical Activity.

BOX 4–3

PAIRING NANDA WITH NOC OUTCOMES

In the last chapter your patient, Robert, had the possible nursing diagnosis of either Activity Intolerance or Sleep Pattern disturbance. Possible nursing outcomes included in NOC associated with these diagnoses include:

Nursing Diagnosis: Activity Intolerance
Outcomes: Endurance
                        Mobility level
                        Pain: Disruptive effect
Nursing Diagnosis: Sleep Pattern disturbance
Outcomes: Comfort Level
                        Rest
                        Sleep

Source: Johnson, M., & Mass, M. (Eds.). (1997). *Iowa Outcomes Project: Nursing Outcomes Classification (NOC)*. St. Louis: Mosby.

BOX 4–4

APPLICATION OF THE OMAHA SYSTEM: GOAL DEVELOPMENT—PART I

NANDA Nursing Diagnosis: Activity Intolerance
Omaha System Problem: No. 37, Physical Activity

The Omaha System has a Problem Rating Scale for Outcomes. This scale rates three conceptual components: knowledge, behavior, and status. Each scale has a Likert-scale ranging from 1–5. As with NOC, each concept has an associated scale. For example, Robert's knowledge of his level of physical activity can range from the following:

1—No knowledge
2—Minimal knowledge
3—Basic knowledge
4—Adequate knowledge
5—Superior knowledge

When Robert is questioned about his current medical condition and its effect on cardiac activity, we may find that Robert's knowledge of his physical activity is rated at 1, no knowledge.

Robert's behavior is also rated using the following:

1—Not appropriate
2—Rarely appropriate
3—Inconsistently appropriate
4—Usually appropriate
5—Consistently appropriate

Robert's behavior toward physical activity is assessed at 3, inconsistently appropriate. The assessed data indicate Robert does try to complete some activities, but data do not confirm that he participates in a routine exercise program.

Robert's status is rated as follows:

1—Extreme signs/symptoms
2—Severe signs/symptoms
3—Moderate signs/symptoms
4—Minimal signs/symptoms
5—No signs/symptoms

Further assessment data would be required to assess his level of independence. For this example, however, we could assign a rating of 3, moderate signs/symptoms, based on the decrease of physical activity due to current medical condition and past health history of limited physical activity and no routine exercise program.

Selecting Appropriate Nursing Interventions

NURSING INTERVENTIONS:
any direct care treatment that a nurse performs on behalf of a patient, including nurse- and physician-initiated treatments (resulting from nursing and medical diagnoses), and provision of essential daily functions for the patient who cannot do them (Bulechek & McCloskey, 1989).

NURSING INTERVENTIONS are prescriptions for behaviors, treatments, activities, or actions that assist the patient in achieving the expected outcomes. Nursing interventions, like nursing diagnoses, are key elements of the knowledge of nursing; in fact, the scientific body of knowledge of nursing interventions like that of nursing diagnoses continues to grow as research supports the connection between actions and outcomes (McCloskey & Bulechek, 1992). In Chapter 3 we discussed the need to select the right nursing diagnosis. Selecting the appropriate nursing intervention so that your patient can achieve the desired outcomes is as important as accuracy in diagnosing. It also is another method of individualizing your patient's care.

Naturally your expectation is that the interventions you select will benefit the patient and/or family/significant other in a predictable way. You need to base your nursing interventions on the patient's nursing diagnosis; the established goals and desired outcomes; the ability of the nurse to successfully implement the intervention; and the ability, appropriateness, and willingness of the patient to undergo the intervention. Interventions need to be age/situation appropriate and promote identified patient strengths, when possible.

FOR EXAMPLE:

- Discussion of fears may help to reduce the adult patient's level of anxiety, whereas an infant will respond more positively to *holding and cuddling*.
- Although a walk down the hall to take a shower or bath may be desired by many new mothers, cultural beliefs may dictate the new mother remain on bedrest for 7 days, or refrain from a full shower for 2 to 4 weeks.
- Orange juice is a good choice for fluid replacement unless the patient has open lesions on the oral mucosa, in which case, mild fruit nectars would be preferred because acidic juices will cause pain.
- Visualization to assist with stress or pain management may be the appropriate intervention for the patient assessed as having creative abilities.

You are accountable for being current and accurate when identifying nursing interventions. Therefore, you need to be familiar with the body of scientific knowledge (rationale) that supports these interventions (in addition to respecting your patient's personal preferences and cultural/religious beliefs).

NURSING STANDARD:
identified criterion against which nursing care is compared and evaluated; generally reflects the minimum level of nursing care.

NURSING STANDARDS and agency policy must also be considered when choosing specific interventions. For example, one nursing standard describes the minimum level for nursing care related to urinary catheterization. The standard also contains the policies and procedures required to meet the standard. The policy identifies the level of educational preparation that is required to perform the procedure while the procedural section provides the needed equipment and suggested method of performing the procedure. The interventions must be deliberate and purposeful and include independent nursing activities (such as frequency of monitoring activities/focused assessments, counseling, teaching, suctioning an airway), as well as any collaborative activities necessary to carry out orders from other healthcare providers (including consultation by and referral to other providers).

To be communicated accurately, nursing interventions, like nursing diagnoses and patient care goals and outcomes, need to be developed in the correct format and be specifically and clearly stated. The following criteria should be included in creating and documenting the intervention in the patient's plan of care:

- The date when the intervention is written
- An action verb describing the activity to be performed
- Qualifiers of how, when (time/frequency), where, and amount
- Signature and/or initials of originating nurse

FOR EXAMPLE:

- 1/27 Assist as needed with self-care activities each AM. *AG*
- 6/12 Record respiratory and pulse rates before, during, and after activity. *BB*
- 3/13 Inspect wound during each dressing change. *MR*
- 10/12 Measure intake and output hourly. *SP*

Note: Depending on agency policy, when the original plan of care is written, a single date and signature is sufficient. As subsequent interventions are added, the entry should be individually dated and initialed or signed. Now take a moment to complete Practice Activity 4–3 before proceeding to Box 4–5, which walks you through the first three steps of the nursing process. Patient data are presented, and a patient problem is identified. Then a goal, outcomes, and appropriate interventions are chosen to treat the problem.

Having completed that activity, consider how you would identify appropriate interventions using the Omaha System. You recall that in Robert's case the Omaha System first presented a problem based on the assessed signs/symptoms. To begin planning care for Robert, the Outcome Rating Scales were used to assess knowledge, behavior, and status. The next portion of the Omaha System, the Intervention Scheme, is used to complete the plan of care (Box 4–6).

PRACTICE ACTIVITY 4–3

Identifying Correctly Stated Interventions

Instructions: Identify which of the following interventions are correctly stated, and rewrite those that are not.

1. Walk length of hall 2 ×/day with assistance from two staff members. _____
   _____

2. Force fluids. _____
   _____

3. Pericare after each BM. _____
   _____

4. Encourage deep-breathing exercises and cough q 2 h. _____
   _____

5. Reduce environmental stimuli. _____
   _____

6. Provide written handout for side effects of medications before discharge. _____
   _____

BOX 4–5

APPLICATION OF THE NURSING PROCESS THROUGH THE PLANNING STEP

Step I: Assessment

On 6/11/99 at 5:30 PM, Michelle, a 14-year-old female (DOB 3/2/85), is admitted with a compound multiple fracture of the right tibia and fibula and a mild concussion following a mountain bike accident.

Assessment Data

Pain/Discomfort

Subjective

Location: R lower leg, as well as general muscle aches and right-sided headache.
Intensity (1–10): 9
Frequency: Since accident
Quality: Sharp ache R leg (headache dull, throbs)
Duration: Constant
Radiation: Toes to knee
Precipitating factors: Movement
How relieved: Morphine sulfate in ED
Associated symptoms: Muscle spasms

Objective

Facial grimacing: Yes
Guarding affected area: Yes
Emotional response: Tearful
Narrowed focus: Yes

Step II: Problem Identification

Based on this assessment (and additional data recorded in other sections of the Assessment Tool), using the diagnostic reasoning process and working with Appendix A, you choose the nursing diagnosis label "Pain [acute]," and write the plan of care.

6/11/99   6 PM

Patient Diagnostic Statement: Pain [acute] related to movement of bone fragments R lower leg, soft tissue injury/edema, and use of external fixator as evidenced by verbal reports, guarding, muscle tension, narrowed focus, and tachycardia.

Step III: Planning

Goal: Pain-free or controlled.
Outcomes:

　　Patient will:

* Verbalize relief of pain within 30 minutes of administration of medication.
* Use relaxation skills to reduce level of pain by 6/12, 9 AM.

Continued

APPLICATION OF THE NURSING PROCESS THROUGH THE PLANNING STEP (Continued)

- Identify methods that provide relief by 6/12, 4 PM.

Interventions:

- Maintain limb rest of R leg × 24 hours.
- Elevate lower leg with folded blanket.
- Apply ice to area 20 minutes on/20 minutes off, as tolerated × 48 hours.
- Place cradle over foot of bed.
- Document reports and characteristics of pain.
- Medicate with Demerol 75 mg and Phenergan 25 mg IM q4h, prn, *or* Vicodin 5 mg PO q4h, prn.
- Demonstrate/encourage use of progressive relaxation techniques, deep breathing exercises, and visualization.
- Provide alternate comfort measures, position change, backrub. *BB*

(Note: Michelle has reported a dull headache associated with the concussion, but it is not a major problem for her at this time; some of the interventions noted above will be effective in relieving this pain.)

BOX 4–6

APPLICATION OF THE OMAHA SYSTEM: GOAL DEVELOPMENT—PART 2

NANDA Nursing Diagnosis: Activity Intolerance
Omaha System Problem: No. 37, Physical Activity

Knowledge Rating Scale = 1
Behavior Rating Scale = 3
Status Rating Scale = 3

The Omaha System also has an Intervention Scheme. The scheme has 62 specific targets or objects of nursing actions. For example, Behavioral modification No. 2 may be selected to assist Robert in his lack of an exercise program.

The scheme has four categories of intervention application:

1. Health teaching, guidance, and counseling.
2. Treatments and procedures
3. Case management
4. Surveillance

Based on the assessed data and the outcome ratings on Robert's physical activity, the selection of the category, health teaching, guidance, and counseling, would be appropriate. The actual target for the nursing actions could be No. 2, Behavioral modification, or No. 19, Exercises.

Authors' Note: This is just an example of one possible application of the Omaha System. The Omaha System is a comprehensive nursing language system and different problems, ratings, intervention categories, and targets could apply to Robert's case and would attest to your critical thinking skills. Our purpose is to introduce you to the Omaha System.

> ## BOX 4–7
>
> ### PAIRING NANDA WITH NIC INTERVENTIONS
>
> To continue the process of planning care for Robert, you have chosen the NANDA diagnosis of Activity Intolerance and the NOC outcome of Endurance with the following indicators as measured by the 1–5 scale of "extremely compromised" to "not compromised."
>
> **1.** Performance of usual routine.
> **2.** Activity
> **3.** Exhaustion not present
> **4.** Blood oxygen level within normal limits (WNL)
>
> Reviewing NIC, you choose Activity Therapy (Definition: Prescription of and assistance with specific, physical, cognitive, social, and spiritual activities to increase the range, frequency, or duration of an individual's activity) and the following nursing activities:
>
> Assist with regular physical activities (e.g., ambulation, transfers, turning, and personal care), as needed.
> Assist patient to identify deficits in activity level.
> Assist to focus on what patient can do rather than on deficits.
> Assist patient to identify meaningful activities.
> Assist to choose activities consistent with physical, psychological, and social capabilities.
> Assist to identify and obtain resources required for the desired activity.
> Refer to community centers or activity programs.
> Assist to obtain transportation to activities, as appropriate.

Another approved standardized nursing language complements the NOC presented previously in this chapter. The Iowa Interventions Project (University of Iowa) has also developed Nursing Interventions Classification (NIC). Having chosen the NANDA diagnosis of Activity Intolerance and the NOC of Endurance for your patient Robert, you next determine the appropriate nursing intervention (NIC) to address Robert's problem (Box 4–7).

The Patient Plan of Care

Planning care can save valuable time when the goals of care, patient outcomes, and nursing interventions to achieve them are clearly identified, and then recorded, for all to see. The documentation of the planning process is the patient's plan of care, which some nurses refer to as the "care plan." This plan of care is written to:

- *Provide continuity of care* from nurse to nurse, from one nursing shift to the next, or from one unit/care setting to another.
- *Enhance communication* as the written plan becomes a permanent part of the patient record and supplies consistent information for each person who reads it.
- *Assist with determining agency or unit staffing needs,* setting priorities for the work schedule and individual patient assignments.

- *Document the nursing process* by providing reminders of what needs to be charted and when evaluations should be done.
- *Serve as a teaching tool* that supports the sharing of nurses' expertise and fosters professional growth as nurses learn what interventions are successful.
- *Coordinate care among disciplines,* maximizing effort and use of resources to enhance quality of care and patient outcomes.

The term *healthcare* is not synonymous with medicine or nursing, but includes many professional disciplines, each of which has its own definite characteristics and independent, but overlapping, functions. Thus, the fields of nursing and medicine are closely related. The relationship includes the exchange of data, the sharing of ideas/thinking, and the development of a plan of care that includes all data pertinent to the individual patient/family/significant others. The same type of relationship also extends to all healthcare disciplines that have contact with the patient.

The implication of this relationship is seen in what is contained in the plan of care, which is more than simply the actions initiated by medical orders (collaborative actions). It also includes a combination of nursing orders (independent actions) and is the written coordination of care given by all health-related disciplines. The nurse becomes the person responsible for seeing to it that all of the different activities are coordinated. This is essential to the delivery of holistic, cost-effective healthcare that promotes optimal patient recovery in a timely manner.

Exercises in "care planning" are assigned to students to increase their mastery of the nursing process and application of related knowledge from other scientific disciplines. The need to identify and prepare for every possible patient problem in a given situation results in the creation of a *case study,* instead of the more abbreviated and succinct plan of care that is usually found in the nursing unit Kardex in most hospitals or case plans in community-based and/or home health agencies. However, the length of time and degree of detail required to complete these "case studies" often causes nursing students to develop a negative attitude toward planning care. It is important to keep this activity in perspective, because as a professional nurse, you will need to plan care for your patients sometimes on a daily basis for the inpatient and for weeks, months, or even years for community-based and/or home health patients. Mastery of the skills of planning care will allow you to complete this activity in a timely fashion as you gain experience.

The plan of care is primarily a communication tool that directs the patient's care. However, newly formulated requirements of outside agencies (for example, **JCAHO,** Medicare, private insurance companies) stipulate that the nurse is responsible for the planning of patient care and that the plan is to be documented in the patient's record. For these reasons, the plan of care is now a permanent part of the patient's record because it contains the *outline* for the care provided.

JCAHO: Joint Commission on Accreditation of Healthcare Organizations; surveying body that certifies clinical and organizational performance of an institution following established guidelines.

Discharge Planning

As you plan for the patient's current needs, you must also consider future needs, especially eventual discharge from the healthcare facility/setting. Discharge planning begins when the patient enters the healthcare setting. It is crucial to ensure continuity of care as appropriate, and to take into account the anticipated discharge destination (e.g., home or skilled nursing facility). You are responsible for planning continuity of care between nursing personnel, between services within the care setting, and between the care setting and the community. You may also be responsible for initiating/cooperating in referrals to other community services and providing needed direction for patient/family who are learning to facilitate recovery and promote wellness.

Documenting the Plan of Care

The plan of care may be recorded on a single page or in a multiple-page format, such as one page for each diagnostic statement for a particular patient. The page (or pages) may be kept in a folder (Kardex) at the nursing station, in the patient's chart, or at the bedside to communicate and provide direction on a daily basis.

The format for documenting the plan of care is determined by agency policy. Student plans of care (case studies) are individually generated, and very detailed. As a practicing professional, you might use a computer with a plan of care database, standardized care plan forms or **CLINICAL PATHWAYS** (e.g., Critical Pathway, Care Map, etc.). Whichever you use, the plan of care needs to reflect the basic nursing standards of care, to which personal patient data, nonroutine care, and qualifiers such as time or amount are added, as appropriate.

> **CLINICAL PATHWAYS:** are a type of abbreviated plan of care, providing outcome-based guidelines for goal achievement within a designated length of stay (see Appendix G).

FOR EXAMPLE:

Measure intake and output [insert frequency]
Increase oral fluids [insert amount and frequency]
Medicate with [insert name of medication, dose, and frequency] for pain
Weigh with bedscale [insert time, frequency]

Some computerized systems for plans of care generate an updated plan at the beginning of each shift. The care provided during the new shift is then recorded directly to the online plan of care throughout that shift. This format serves two purposes: It documents the planning and implementation steps of the nursing process, and it continuously updates the plan of care and the patient's record. Other formats require the nurse to document updates to the plan of care through a notation on the Kardex or in the progress or nursing notes.

As previously noted, the plan of care is the visualization of the nursing process. As such, it is preserved as part of the patient's permanent record. Therefore, all entries need to be dated and initialed or signed. Use key words instead of complete sentences and only agency-approved abbreviations/symbols (see Appendix H).

FOR EXAMPLE:

- 8/15 Routine urinary catheter care q (every) shift. *RE*
- 9/2 NPO (nothing by mouth) after 6 AM, 9/13. *PR*
- 3/7 Maintain subarachnoid bolt per protocol. *MT*

Regardless of the format used, the plan of care contains identifying patient data (including medical diagnosis), patient diagnostic statements, goals/outcomes, and interventions, as well as providing space to record the status of the outcomes (i.e., achieved, revised, or deleted) as shown in Figure 4–3. After reviewing the figure, take a moment to complete Practice Activity 4–4.

Validating the Plan of Care

Before the plan of care is implemented, it should be reviewed to ensure that:

- It is based on accepted nursing practice reflecting knowledge of scientific principles, nursing standards of care, and agency policies.

Patient: Donald   Age: 46   DOB: 2/4/53   Gender: M   Admission 11/12/99 - 3:40 Dx: Acute Alcoholism/Depression

Date	Patient Diagnostic Statement	Goal	Intervention	Outcomes	Status
11/12	Ineffective Individual Coping related to situational crisis of unemployment, recent divorce, personal vulnerability evidenced by reported inability to cope, use of alcohol, insomnia, and diminished problem-solving ability.	Short term: Dealing with current situation without reliance on alcohol Long term: Expresses sense of self-worth. Maintains sobriety.	1. Assess level of anxiety and Donald's perception of situation 2. Note verbal/nonverbal behaviors of anxiety 3. Look in q 2 h and prn at irregular intervals 4. Encourage verbalization, expression of feelings of denial, depression/anger 5. Discuss normalcy of these feelings 6. Identify current coping mechanisms 7. Note effectiveness/ need for change 8. Discuss/refer to resources: social worker, alcohol counselor, support group, AA	Verbalize awareness of sources of anxiety (1000 11/14) Demonstrate congruency between feelings/ behavior (1000 11/15) Demonstrate initial problem-solving skills as evidenced by participation in planning for future and setting realistic goals (1000 11/15) Identify options and resources available for assistance (1000 11/16) R. Smith, RN	Achieved 11/14 1030 R.S. Achieved 11/15 1000 P.D. Achieved 11/15 1000 P.D.

FIGURE 4–3. Sample documentation of a plan of care.

- It provides for the safety of the patient by ensuring that the care provided will do no harm.
- The patient diagnostic statements are supported by the patient data.
- The goals and outcomes are measurable/observable and can be achieved.
- The interventions can benefit the patient/family/significant others in a predictable way to achieve the identified outcomes and are arranged in a logical sequence.

Documenting the Plan of Care

Instructions: Record the plan of care information from Box 4–5 on pages 86–87 using the following documentation format.

DATE	PATIENT DIAGNOSTIC STATEMENT	GOAL	INTERVENTIONS	OUTCOMES	STATUS

- It demonstrates individualized patient care by including the concerns of the patient and significant others as well as their physical, psychosocial, and cultural needs and capabilities.

Professional Concerns Related to the Plan of Care

Professional concerns associated with the identification of patient problems/needs in the construction of the plan of care are:

- What is the nurse's responsibility once a nursing diagnosis is made if the patient is discharged from care before all short-term outcomes are met or problems are resolved?
- Who is responsible for follow-through in providing and evaluating care once the patient has been discharged?
- Who is responsible for monitoring patient progress toward long-term outcomes?
- Should this information be shared with the patient's admitting/primary physician or office nurse?
- Is the nurse who has made a nursing diagnosis responsible for follow-through to its resolution?

Nationally, these questions are unresolved, and patient outcomes may remain unmet. Ethically, it is up to the nursing community and the healthcare industry to formulate policies that promote optimal patient recovery and health maintenance. As a healthcare professional, you need to consider these issues because they affect the care you provide and the way you develop the plan of care for your patient.

Putting It All Together

Practice Activity 4–5 presents the back page of the interactive plan of care worksheet described and used in Chapter 3. The information included on the worksheet and in the TIME OUT sections should give you another view of the steps of the nursing process described in this chapter. Return to Practice Activity 3–1 in Chapter 3 and see what portion of the information you can include based on the subjective and objective data of your patient Robert, who, as you remember, was diagnosed with Activity Intolerance. What desired outcome would you identify for Robert? The TIME OUT sections will give you evaluation criteria to ensure Robert's outcome statement is correctly written. Once again, the TIME OUT sections give you guidance in correctly writing your nursing interventions.

Summary

Healthcare providers have a responsibility to plan care with the patient and family whether the desired outcome is an optimal state of wellness or a dignified death. Planning care by setting goals, determining outcomes, and choosing appropriate interventions are essential to the delivery of quality nursing care. These nursing activities comprise the Planning step of the Nursing Process, and are documented in the plan of care for a particular patient. As a part of the patient's permanent record, the plan of care not only provides a means for the nurse who is actively caring

PRACTICE ACTIVITY 4–5

PLANNING

Desired Outcome and Patient Criteria: The Patient will:

TIME OUT! The desired outcome must meet criteria to be accurate. The outcome must be specific, realistic, measurable, and include a time frame for completion. Does the action verb describe the patient's behavior to be evaluated? Can the outcome be used in the evaluation step of the nursing process to measure the patient's response to the nursing interventions listed below?

Interventions | **Rationale for Selected Intervention and References**

EVALUATION

TIME OUT! Do your interventions assist in achieving outcome? Do your interventions address further monitoring of the patient's response to your interventions and to the achievement of the desired outcome? Are qualifiers: **when, how, amount, time,** and **frequency** used? Is the focus of the action's verb on the nurse's actions and not on the patient? Do your rationales provide sufficient reason and directions?

What was your patient's response to the interventions?

Was the desired outcome achieved?   If no, what revisions to either the desired outcome or interventions would you make?
☐ Yes ☐ No

DOCUMENTATION

Documentation Focus: Now that you have completed the evaluation, the next step is to document your care and the patient's response. Use the areas below to enter your progress note information.

Reassessment Data:

Interventions Implemented:

Patient's Response:

INSTRUCTOR'S COMMENTS:

BOX 4–8

MEASUREMENT CRITERIA FOR ANA STANDARDS III AND IV

ANA Standard III: Outcome identification: The nurse identifies expected outcomes individualized to the client.

1. Outcomes are derived from the diagnoses.
2. Outcomes are mutually formulated with the client and healthcare providers, when possible and appropriate.
3. Outcomes are culturally appropriate and realistic in relation to the client's present and potential capabilities.
4. Outcomes are attainable in relation to resources available to the client.
5. Outcomes include a time estimate for attainment.
6. Outcomes provide direction for continuity of care.
7. Outcomes are documented as measurable goals.

ANA Standard IV: Planning: The nurse develops a plan of care that prescribes interventions to attain expected outcomes.

1. The plan is individualized to the client (e.g., age-appropriate, culturally sensitive) and the client's condition or needs.
2. The plan is developed with the client, family and other healthcare providers, as appropriate.
3. The plan reflects current nursing practice.
4. The plan provides for continuity of care.
5. Priorities for care are established.
6. The plan is documented.

for the patient to be aware of the problems/needs (nursing diagnoses), goals, and actions to be taken, but it also substantiates the plan of care for third-party payors, accreditation, and legal review.

This chapter introduced you to how the work of the Iowa Outcomes and Interventions Projects as well as the Omaha System can be used to assist you in providing a research-based approach to designing a plan of care. Both systems provide the structure, terms, and definitions to assist you in planning patient care in any healthcare environment. In Chapter 6, The Evaluation Step, you will see how helpful the standardized languages and accompanying rating and measurement scale are in evaluating the effectiveness of your plan of care.

Now, return to the third and fourth standards of the ANA Standard of Clinical Nursing Practice and review the measurement criteria necessary to achieve and ensure compliance with each standard. The knowledge and skill required to meet the criteria listed in Box 4–8 were described in this chapter.

The next chapter provides information on the fourth step of the nursing process, **IMPLEMENTATION.** You will have an opportunity to see how the plan of care can be implemented. To achieve the desired outcomes, you will learn what mechanisms help prioritize the nursing interventions that were selected during the Planning step. Finally, you will practice effective communication methods to help ensure the required continuity of care described in the patient plan of care.

1. List three reasons why the plan of care is important:

   a. _____

   b. _____

   c. _____

2. Briefly explain why setting priorities is necessary: _____

   _____

   _____

3. What is the difference between a goal and an outcome? _____

   _____

   _____

   _____

4. Identify five important components of patient outcomes:

   a. _____

   b. _____

   c. _____

   d. _____

   e. _____

5. List four types of information that nursing interventions need to contain:

   a. _____

   b. _____

   c. _____

   d. _____

6. Explain the difference between a measurable and a nonmeasurable verb and give an example of each:

   _____

   _____

   _____

7. When does discharge planning begin?

   _____

8. How is the plan of care documented?

   _____

9. In the following vignette, identify two additional problems facing Michelle; then set a goal with one outcome and two interventions for each problem.

VIGNETTE: Michelle, the 14-year-old female with compound fractures of the right lower leg and a mild concussion, has other problems in addition to Pain [acute], as previously discussed. Her wound was contaminated by dirt and she had significant blood loss before paramedics arrived. Although the wound was flushed with sterile saline and antibiotic solution before being packed and dressed, a cast was not applied because of tissue swelling and concerns about the wound and bone. Instead, an external fixation device [a metal frame with pins extending through the skin and bone] is currently being used for immobilization of the tibia and fibula. The device is heavy and awkward for Michelle to move without causing increased pain, and she is to remain on bedrest for 24 hours. In addition, IV antibiotics are to be administered every 4 hours.

1. Problem/Need: _____

_____

Goal: _____

Outcome: _____

Interventions: _____

1. _____

2. _____

2. Problem/Need: _____

_____

Goal: _____

Outcome: _____

Interventions: _____

1. _____

2. _____

BIBLIOGRAPHY

Bulechek, G. M., & McCloskey, J. C. (1989). *Nursing Interventions: Treatments for Potential Diagnoses.* In Carrol-Johnson, R. M. (Ed.). *Proceedings of Eighth Conference, NANDA.* Philadelphia: J.B. Lippincott.

Johnson, M., & Mass, M. (Eds.). (1997). *Iowa Outcomes Project: Nursing Outcomes Classification (NOC).* St. Louis: Mosby.

Kalish, R. (1983). *The Psychology of Human Behavior,* ed 5. Monterey, CA: Brooks/Cole.

Maslow, A. H. (1970). *Motivation and Personality,* ed 2. New York: Harper & Row.

McCloskey, J. C., & Bulecheck, G. M. (Eds.). (1992). *Nursing Interventions Classification (NIC).* St. Louis: Mosby.

SUGGESTED READINGS

Nursing Outcomes

Booten, D., & Naylor, M. D. (1995). Nurse's effect on changing patient outcomes. *Image J Nurs Schol, 27*:95–99.

Cox, R. A. (1998). Implementing nursing sensitive outcomes into care planning at a long-term facility. *J Nurs Care Qual, 12*(5):41–51.

Denehey, J. (1998). Integrating Nursing Outcomes Classification into education. *J Nurs Care Qual, 12*(5):73–83.

Head, B., et al. (1997). Outcomes for home and community nursing in integrated delivery systems. *Caring, 16*(1):50–56.

Hajewski, C., Maupin, J. M., Rapp, D. A., & Pappas, J. (1998). Implementation and evaluation of Nursing Outcomes Classification in a patient education plan. *J Nurs Care Qual, 12*(5):30–40.

Johnson, M., & Mass, M. (1998). The Nursing Outcomes Classification. *J Nurs Care Qual, 12*(5):9–20.

Lang, N. M., & Marek, K. D. (1990). The classification of patient outcomes. *J Prof Nurs, 6*(3):158–163.

Maas, M., et al. (1996). Classifying nursing-sensitive outcomes. *Image J Nurs Schol, 28*:295–301.

Moorhead, S., Clarke, M., Willitis, M., & Tomsha, K. A. (1998). Nursing Outcomes Classification implementation projects across care continuum. *J Nurs Care Qual, 12*(5):51–63.

Pierce, S. L. (1997). Nurse-sensitive health care outcomes in acute care settings: An integrative analysis of the literature. *J Nurs Care Qual, 11*(4):60–72.

Prophet, C. M., & Delaney, C. W. (1998). Nursing Outcomes Classification: Implications for nursing information systems and the computer-based patient record. *J Nurs Care Qual, 12*(5):21–29.

Timm, J. A., & Behrenbech, J. G. (1998). Implementing the Nursing Outcomes Classification in clinical information system in a tertiary care setting. *J Nurs Care Qual, 12*(5):65–72.

Nursing Interventions

Daley, J., et al. (1995). Use of standardized nursing diagnoses and interventions in long-term care. *Journal of Gerontological Nursing, 21*(8):29–36.

McCloskey, J. C., & Bulechek, G. M. (1993). The NIC Taxonomy structure: Iowa Intervention Project. *Image J Nurs Schol, 25*:178–192.

McCloskey, J. C., & Bulechek, G. M. (1994). Standardizing the language of nursing treatments: An overview of the issues. *Nurs Outlook, 42*(10):56–63.

Wakefield, B., et al. (1995). Nursing Interventions Classification: A standardized language for nursing care. *Journal of Health Care Quality, 17*:26–33.

Authors' Note: For an extensive listing of NIC-related publications, see Appendix D in McCloskey, J. C., & Bulechek, G. M. (Eds.). (1996). *Iowa Interventions Project: Nursing Interventions Classification (NIC),* ed 2.

Nursing Language

Delaney, C., et al. (1992). Standardized nursing language for health care information systems. *J Med Syst, 16*:145–159.

McCloskey, J. C., & Bulechek, G. M. (1994). Standardizing the language of nursing treatments: An overview of the issues. *Nurs Outlook, 42*(10):56–63.

Werley, H., & Lang, N. (Eds.). (1988). *Identification of Nursing Minimum Data Set.* New York: Springer.

CHAPTER 5

The Implementation Step: Putting the Plan of Care into Action

■ **ANA Standard 5:** Implementation: The nurse implements the interventions identified in the plan of care.

At this point of the nursing process, you are ready to perform the interventions and activities recorded in the patient's plan of care. In order to **IMPLEMENT** this plan in a timely and cost-effective manner, you first identify the priorities for providing patient care. Then, as care is provided, you monitor and document the patient's response to each of the interventions and communicate this information to other healthcare providers as appropriate. Then, using the data, you evaluate and revise the plan of care in the following step of the nursing process (see Chapter 6).

IMPLEMENT/IMPLEMENTATION:
fourth step of nursing process, in which the plan of care is put into action; performing identified interventions/activities.

Identifying Caregiving Priorities

Regardless of how well a plan of care has been constructed, it cannot predict everything that will occur with a particular patient on a daily basis. Your individual knowledge base, expertise, and recognition of agency routines allows you to exhibit the flexibility necessary to adapt to the changing needs of the patient. While listening

Pt.	7	8	9	10	11	12	1	2	3	Comments
Rbt		Vital signs Chair	Med	Bed bath	IV	V.S. Chair	Med	I & O		

FIGURE 5–1. Sample worksheet for the 7:00 AM to 3:00 PM shift. While listening to the change-of-shift report, you review the plan of care and begin to plan how you will implement specific interventions. You notice that Robert is to eat meals sitting up in a chair; therefore, he should be helped out of bed before the meal trays arrive on the unit. You identify times for medications, time for expected change of the IV bottle, and the routine time for calculating the intake and output for the shift. In addition, you are aware that Robert's family usually visits at lunch time, so you schedule hygiene needs appropriately while allowing Robert rest periods between activities.

closely to the change-of-shift report, you will get the first clues about where to begin. On a worksheet such as the one shown in Figure 5–1 or a form supplied by the agency/facility, you record specific information, interventions, or activities that are sequential or time related. Also, you review the plan of care for outcomes that are to be evaluated during the shift and for routine procedures/treatments and medication administration. Complete Practice Activity 5–1 at this time.

After completion of the shift report, performing a baseline assessment of each patient can provide clues about general physical status, equipment/supply needs, and safety concerns (e.g., patency of invasive lines [catheters/tubes] and intravenous [IV] flow rate). At this time you may recognize a change in the significance or severity of a patient problem which could affect the plan of care.

FOR EXAMPLE: Robert, who is being treated for pneumonia, appears dyspneic at 7:30 AM. You will need to do a more thorough focused assessment now to determine his immediate needs. This could include obtaining arterial blood gases (ABGs) and restarting supplemental oxygen. In addition, you may decide against getting Robert up in a chair to eat his breakfast. Thus, interventions previously identified are not appropriate at this time, and new or alternate interventions are needed.

Ethical and Legal Concerns

This is also the time to review the plan of care with the patient/significant other to schedule activities and verify the patient's responsibilities.

FOR EXAMPLE: Donald, admitted 48 hours ago for depression and alcohol withdrawal, displays coarse tremors of his hands and an unsteady gait and requires assistance with self-care. It is 7:30 AM and breakfast trays have just arrived. Donald is required to attend the Community Meeting at 8:15 AM before proceeding to individually prescribed activities. Donald is ambivalent about his morning care, but in reviewing the scheduled activities, he decides that he will postpone his shower until his 10:30 AM break.

Legal and ethical concerns related to the interventions also need to be considered. The wishes of the patient and family/significant others regarding what is being done need to be discussed and respected.

PRACTICE ACTIVITY 5–1

Setting Your Work Schedule for Implementing the Plan of Care

VIGNETTE: Michelle incurred a compound fracture of the right lower leg 2 days ago. In reviewing the plan of care, you take note of the following:

- Assist with bed bath
- Calculate input and output (I&O) every 8 hours (2 PM)
- Change dressing twice a day and prn (9 AM)
- Assess vital signs every 4 hours (8 AM, 12 noon)
- Monitor circulation/nerve function R lower leg every hour × 24 hours, then every 4 hours and prn (8 AM, 12 noon)
- IV medications (8 AM, 2 PM)
- Up in chair with meals (7:30 AM, 12 noon)
- Walk in halls three times a day after instructed in crutch walking

1. Organize the above interventions and activities on the worksheet below:

Worksheet

Pt.	7	8	9	10	11	12	1	2	3	Comments

2. During nursing rounds, just after the change-of-shift report on 6/13, you find that Michelle is crying and she reports sudden throbbing pain in her right lower leg. How will this affect your work plan? _____

_____

FOR EXAMPLE: Robert has decided that if he should suffer respiratory failure, he is not to be placed on a mechanical ventilator. This does not negate the need for intervention when you notice that he is developing problems. You still need to act promptly to prevent or limit further deterioration. Therefore, in addition to providing oxygen and assessing breath sounds and airway patency, you elevate the head of Robert's bed, encourage Robert to deep-breathe and cough regularly, and notify other healthcare providers (e.g., physician and respiratory therapist) as appropriate, as well as the identified family member or contact person.

Take a few minutes to consider the legal and ethical concerns of Robert's decision and work through Practice Activity 5–2 before continuing with the next section.

PRACTICE ACTIVITY 5–2

Legal and Ethical Concerns of Care

As noted, Robert had completed a form directing healthcare providers to withhold advanced life-support measures including the use of a mechanical ventilator.

1. Have you and your family members completed Advance Directives stating specific healthcare

desires? _____

   If not, why: _____

   _____

2. As a nurse, how do you feel about adhering to Advance Directives as stipulated by an elderly

   patient? _____

   _____

   for a premature infant as stipulated by the parents? _____

   _____

3. Review the Code for Nurses [see Appendix D] and choose two principles you believe may address
   your responsibility to patient's/guardian's in regard to their decisions limiting care.

   _____

   _____

It is beyond the scope of this text to discuss these critical issues in detail. To assist you in your studies, an extensive bibliography on advance directives, ethics, and legal issues is included in the Suggested Readings. Also see Appendix D, ANA's Code for Nurses.

Delivering Nursing Care

Interventions may be composed of many activities ranging from simple tasks to complex procedures. These activities may require direct "hands-on" care (such as a complete bed bath) or may merely require assisting a patient by setting up a basin of water and washing his back. Other frequent activities include instructing a patient and/or significant other regarding the management of care and then supervising these efforts. The patient and/or significant others may need to be counseled regarding psychosocial concerns, treatment regimens, or alternative ways to manage healthcare needs. Throughout these activities, you also monitor the patient and such resources as diagnostic studies and/or progress reports from other healthcare providers for changes in health status/development of complications.

Before implementing the interventions listed in the plan of care, you need to be sure that you:

* **Understand the reason for doing the intervention, its expected effect, and any potential hazards that can occur.** Without this knowledge, the

nurse cannot be sure that the intervention will be beneficial. In addition, it will be difficult to determine if the desired effect is being achieved or if adaptations are required to provide for specific patient needs/safety concerns.

FOR EXAMPLE: You realize that an ABG study will provide information about Robert's current oxygenation status/needs, and also that he requires supplemental oxygen to increase his oxygen level. That means you will implement these interventions in a slightly different sequence; that is, the diagnostic study (ABG) should be obtained *before* the supplemental oxygen is begun, so that test results are not affected by the additional oxygen.

- **Provide an environment or milieu conducive to carrying out the planned interventions.** What is happening in the patient's environment is known to affect the person's physical and psychological self (e.g., noise, temperature, activities).

FOR EXAMPLE: Exposing Robert for a bed bath when the room is cold can cause him physical discomfort and affect his psychological response. Michelle has difficulty focusing on your instructions for administering medications when the volume of her roommate's TV is turned up and visitors are talking loudly.

- **Consider which interventions can be combined so you can accomplish the activities within your time constraints.** In some cases, shortcuts may be chosen or activities combined as long as consideration is given to the successful accomplishment of the outcome.

FOR EXAMPLE: While administering Librium to Donald at 8:00 AM, you can review the drug's actions, side-effects, and adverse reactions. Or while assisting Sally with her sitz bath, you may choose to discuss her concerns about caring for herself and the new babies once she is discharged.

As noted in Box 5–1, one "simple" intervention such as providing a bedpan for a patient actually encompasses multiple nursing activities that, when listed individually, may appear to take considerable time and energy to perform. However, by carefully prioritizing interventions and sequencing related activities you can accomplish these tasks quickly.

BOX 5–1

THE TRUTH ABOUT BEDPANS

Even the simplest of nursing tasks is really a complex series of actions and judgments, requiring professional knowledge and experience in order to provide optimal patient care. Read through the short article reprinted below.* You will be surprised to see just how complicated supplying a patient with a bedpan can be.

There are many nursing activities interwoven in the "simple" act of providing a bedpan. As a nurse, you assess the patient's:

Level of consciousness and mood, including self-image while dependent with these bodily functions.

Skin color, temperature, and suppleness.

Continued

THE TRUTH ABOUT BEDPANS (Continued)

Respiratory pattern and rate, breath sounds, and dyspnea with or without activity.

Comfort level with voiding or with stool.

Range of motion, strength, and any pain with movement.

Urine for color, amount, odor, and by-products such as mucus or blood.

Stool for color, consistency, amount, and by-products such as mucus, undigested food, or blood.

You also determine:

If urine assessment relates to medications (Lasix, Pyridium, aminoglycosides), fluid intake, disease process (diabetes, dehydration, renal failure), or infection.

If stool assessment relates to medication (antibiotics, barium enema, narcotics), food or fluid intake, disease process (cholelithiasis, Crohn's disease, bleeding ulcers), infection, activity or inactivity.

If assessment demands any action and whether the doctor needs to be notified.

You then go on to teach:

Symptoms to watch for, comfort measures, and ways to maintain or achieve normal functioning.

Disease process and how it affects the individual.

On top of all that you:

Promote self-esteem by using proper technique, including disposal of waste material.

Obtain necessary specimens using correct procedure and send to lab.

Make sure patient is clean and dry to promote good skin integrity.

Model good handwashing technique on completion.

*"The Truth about Bedpans" by Karen Tolin, RN, Joplin, MO, printed by RN Magazine.

Ongoing Data Collection

Once you have formulated the plan of care and put it into action, monitor the patient to collect additional data. As you talk to the patient, note changes in tone of voice and expression, or when providing a back rub, be aware of such abnormalities as a reddened area on the coccyx. All of these data need to be noted, and their meaning validated. This information will be used to make decisions regarding the need for new goals, outcomes, interventions, and reprioritizing the plan of care during the evaluation process.

DOCUMENTATION

It is legally required that all healthcare settings document nursing observations, the care provided, and the patient's response. This record serves as a communication tool and a resource to aid in determining the effectiveness of care and to assist in setting priorities for ongoing care. In order to simplify record-keeping and to promote timely and accurate charting, many agencies use flow sheets to document routine activities, monitoring, and patient care (Fig. 5–2). Flow sheets reduce the need to write detailed progress notes. Instead, only variations from the recorded baseline and any exceptions requiring more explanation are written in the progress note. Additional discussion about documentation and the use of progress notes will be presented in Chapter 7.

VERBAL COMMUNICATION WITH THE HEALTHCARE TEAM

In addition to the written record, patient information is shared verbally with other healthcare providers. Whether reporting to another nurse, reviewing with a physician, or discussing with other resources (e.g., social worker, dietitian, or physical therapist), the manner in which information is conveyed, as well as the content itself, can affect the way in which this information is heard. This, in turn, can have an impact on the quality of the healthcare provided. For this reason, it is important to avoid judgmental language, tone of voice, or body language. Presenting information in an objective and accurate manner reduces the likelihood of being misunderstood or of negatively influencing the patient's care.

> **FOR EXAMPLE:** When Sally talked to the nurse, she tearfully expressed concern about going home. The nurse reported this information to the oncoming shift personnel and to the doctor by saying: "I think Sally is trying to manipulate us. She says she's not ready to go home, and she thinks if she 'acts weak,' she won't have to leave the hospital."

After listening to this judgmental report, the oncoming nurse's response might be one of defensiveness and the nurse might be inclined to *show* Sally that she is indeed ready to go home. The nurse may also subconsciously stop listening and is likely to be less receptive to what Sally *is* saying. Contrast the above example with the one which appears below.

> **FOR EXAMPLE:** If the nurse reports: "Sally has expressed concern about her ability to manage at home. She was weak when we got her up this morning, requiring assistance with walking. Then she spent the afternoon talking on the telephone, at one point ignoring the cries of Baby B until I responded to the room. We need information about her situation at home and her need for assistance with newborn care of twins."

In this report, the nurse expresses a problem in terms that challenge colleagues to find a solution. This problem is approached with an open mind, as additional data are gathered and appropriate resources are identified. Maintaining an open mind and actively problem-solving provides opportunities for creating solutions instead of additional problems, thus promoting a positive patient/nurse experience.

The primary format for communicating the patient's current situation and needs is the nursing change-of-shift report. This type of report may be done either in person or via tape recorder. Because time for this activity is usually limited, it is necessary to be brief and organized while still providing pertinent data. After supplying basic patient data (e.g., room number, name, age, diagnosis, and physician), reporting may be done "by exception." This means that only occurrences that are out of the ordinary are reported. You report:

Patient Care Flow Sheet

Page 1		2300 – 0700	0700 – 1500	1500 – 2300
Date:				

Page 1 (left portion)

		2300 – 0700	0700 – 1500	1500 – 2300
CNS ASSESSMENT	Alert/Oriented			
	Confused/Disoriented			
	Sleeping			
	Unable to Arouse			
	Vital Signs			
CARDIOVASCULAR ASSESSMENT	Heart — Rate			
	Heart — Rhythm			
	Heart — Intensity			
	Heart — Abnormal Sounds			
	Pulses			
	Telemetry/Lead			
PULMONARY ASSESSMENT	Breath Sounds			
	Cough/Deep-Breathe			
O_2				
GI & GU ASSESSMENT	Nausea/Emesis			
	Bowel Sounds			
	Voiding frequency			
	Diet			
SKIN ASSESSMENT	Color			
	Warm-Cool			
	Edema			

Page 2

		2300 – 0700	0700 – 1500
PAIN ASSESSMENT	Site		
	Onset/Duration		
	Relief		
WOUND ASSESSMENT	Type		
	Incision Care		
	Appearance		
	Draining		
TUBES PRESENT	Nasogastric		
	Chest		
	IV/Site		
	Color/Consistency of Drainage		
ACTIVITY	Type		
	Toleration		
	Repositioned		
	Range of Motion		
HYGIENE	Bath		
	Oral Care		
	Back Care		
	H. S. Care		
	Remove/Reapply Elastic Stockings		
	PERI/CATH Care		
EQUIPMENT	IV Pump		
	Flotation Mattress		
	Traction		
M.D. Contact			
COMMENTS			
Signature & Initials			

FIGURE 5–2. Sample flow sheet.

- **Abnormalities/changes in assessment findings**

    "Robert became short of breath during AM rounds and required supplemental oxygen at 2 L/min by nasal cannula." Or "Michelle's right lower leg edema is resolving."

- **Diagnostic procedures and results**

    "Robert's oxygen saturation is 92% on 2 L of oxygen; chest x-ray report is pending."

- **Variations from usual routine**

    "Robert was not out of bed this AM but was up for lunch and tolerated sitting up in a chair for 45 minutes without difficulty."

- **Activities not completed on your shift**

    "The crutches are in Michelle's room, a physical therapist will return at 4 PM to instruct her in their use; then we can begin getting her out of bed."

- **Status of invasive treatments**

    "Sally's IV of lactated Ringer's with 2 amps of Pitocin is infusing in the left forearm at 60 ml/hr with 300 ml remaining."

- **Additions or changes to the plan of care** (this includes evaluation of outcomes and the status of patient problems)

    "Robert's Airway Clearance problem has recurred, requiring aggressive pulmonary toilet every 2 hours and use of incentive spirometer."

Change-of-shift reports may include nursing rounds, with each patient being visited by the offgoing and oncoming nurse together. Nursing rounds are beneficial in verifying the status of invasive treatments, appearance of wounds/dressings, and the current condition of the patient (e.g., degree of jaundice, level of coolness of an extremity, etc.). It is imperative to maintain the confidentiality of patient information, and usually it is preferable to review the change-of-shift information before going to the patient's bedside.

Patient confidentiality is an ethical/moral concern that must be respected by each professional at all times. These concerns are extended to conversations at the nursing station, on the telephone, or wherever patient information is discussed. This includes refraining from discussions with those not directly involved in the patient's care (e.g., staff on other units, your own family, friends and acquaintances of the patient).

Before concluding this chapter, take a moment to complete Practice Activity 5–3.

Summary

In putting the plan of care into action and providing effective patient care, you review resources to determine priorities, consulting with and considering the desires of the patient during this Implementation step of the nursing process. You identify who is responsible for the actions to be taken and set realistic timeframes for carrying out actions. Changes in the patient's needs must be continually monitored because patient care takes place in a dynamic environment. The relevance of new data collected in each interaction with the patient is determined according to what is already known. This newly gathered information is documented and shared with

PRACTICE ACTIVITY 5–3

Communicating Nursing Information to Other Caregivers

Work through the questions below.

1. Two methods of communicating your observations about patient care and activities to other nurses are by:

   a. _____

   b. _____

2. Discuss the benefits of nursing rounds: _____

   _____

3. Underline the information listed below that you would include in your change-of-shift report:

   Sally   Ate well   Age 30   Dr. Jefferson
   Weak and unsteady while up in hall
   Episiotomy reddened, slight edema, no drainage second day postpartum
   Scheduled for discharge tomorrow
   Received oral pain medication at 11 AM with reported relief
   Does not want to go home
   Sister in to visit at lunchtime
   Coordination for home care services in progress with the Discharge Planner
   Spent afternoon talking on phone
   Has not named Baby B and at times has ignored infant cues

4. The wife of a prominent local politician is admitted for treatment of alcoholism. You could discuss her admission and course of therapy with which of the following people?

   _____ attending/primary physician

   _____ the nursing supervisor

   _____ a pediatric nurse (her best friend)

   _____ your husband

   _____ the patient's son

   _____ an interested newspaper reporter

   _____ other nurses on your unit

other healthcare providers as appropriate. Throughout these activities, flexibility is important to allow for changed circumstances, interruptions, and so forth.

Before we begin the next chapter, let us return to the fifth standard of the ANA Standard of Clinical Nursing Practice and review the measurement criteria necessary to achieve and ensure compliance with the standard. The knowledge and skill required to meet the criteria listed in Box 5–2 were described in this chapter on the **IMPLEMENTATION** step of the nursing process.

BOX 5–2

MEASUREMENT CRITERIA FOR ANA STANDARD V

ANA Standard V: Implementation: The nurse implements the interventions identified in the plan of care.

1. Interventions are consistent with the established plan of care.
2. Interventions are implemented in a safe and appropriate manner.
3. Interventions are documented.

Chapter 6 will help you see how continuous evaluation of nursing actions helps you determine whether or not the interventions are leading to achievement of the desired outcomes. In addition, evaluation of patient plans of care serves as a mechanism for review of the care provided on a unit or within an agency. This review process addresses professional issues of overall quality of care and also provides a means by which outside agencies can evaluate the institution.

1. Identify three activities involved in implementing the plan of care:

   a. _____

   b. _____

   c. _____

2. Discuss the importance of understanding the expected effect and potential hazards of the interventions you will implement: _____

   _____

3. Explain the purpose for ongoing data collection throughout the Implementation step of the nursing process: _____

   _____

4. List two reasons why documentation of the care provided is important:

   a. _____

   b. _____

5. Name three activities you might use to carry out interventions for planned patient care:

   a. _____ b. _____ c. _____

6. What is the advantage of reporting "by exception"? _____

   _____

7. When and where is patient confidentiality important? _____

   _____

8. Flexibility in providing patient care is important because: _____

   _____

9.

   > **VIGNETTE:** Robert signed Advanced Directives asking that no extraordinary means (e.g., intubation and mechanical ventilation) be used to prolong his life. When his condition changed, his daughter was notified as required. While visiting with her father, she is surprised to learn of his decision. She is very upset and a confrontation develops. Robert tells her "it is none of your business" and refuses to enter into further conversation.

   a. What can you do now? _____

   _____

SUGGESTED READINGS

Doenges, M. E., & Moorhouse, M. F. (2000). *Nurse's Pocket Guide: Nursing Diagnoses with Interventions,* ed. 4. Philadelphia: F.A. Davis.

McCloskey, J. C., & Grace, H. L. (Eds.). (1994). *Current Issues in Nursing.* St. Louis: Mosby.

Advanced Directives, Ethics, and Legal Aspects

Aiken, T. D., & Catalano, J. T. (1994). *Legal, Ethical, and Political Issues in Nursing.* Philadelphia: F.A. Davis

American Nurses' Association. (1998). *Legal Aspects of Standards and Guidelines for Clinical Nursing Practice.* Washington, DC: American Nurses' Association.

Arras, J. D. (1995). (Ed.). *Bringing the Hospital Home: Ethical and Social Implications of High-tech Home Care.* Baltimore: Johns Hopkins University.

Bandman, E. L., & Bandman, B. (1995). *Nursing Ethics Through the Life Span,* ed 3. Norwalk, CT: Appleton & Lange.

Beckmann, J. P. (1996). *Nursing Negligence: Analyzing Malpractice in the Hospital Setting.* Thousand Oaks, CA: Sage Publications.

Benner, P. A., Tanner, C. A., & Chesla, C. A. (1996). *Expertise in Nursing Practice: Caring, Clinical Judgment, and Ethics.* New York: Springer.

Berger, A. S. (1995). *When Life Ends: Legal Overviews, Medicolegal Forms, and Hospital Policies.* Westport, CN: Praeger.

Bishop, A. H., & Scudder, J. R. (1996). *Nursing Ethics: Therapeutic Caring.* Boston: Jones & Bartlett.

Brent, N. J. (1997). *Nurses and the Law: A Guide to Principles and Applications.* Philadelphia: Saunders.

Burkhardt, M. A., & Nathaniel, A. K. (1998). *Ethics & Issues in Contemporary Nursing.* Albany, NY: Delmar.

Cantor, N. L. (1993). *Advance Directives and the Pursuit of Death with Dignity.* Bloomington: Indiana University Press.

Catalano, J. T. (1995). *Ethical and Legal Aspects of Nursing,* ed 2. Springhouse, PA: Springhouse.

Concern for Dying. (1991). *Advance Directive Protocols and the Patient Self-Determination Act.* New York: Author.

Davis, A. J., Arosker, M. A., & Liaschinko, J. (1997). *Ethical Dilemmas and Nursing Practice,* ed 4. Stamford, CT: Prentice Hall.

Dougas, D. J., & McCullough, L. B. (1991). The values history: The evaluation of the patient's values and advanced directives. *J Fam Prac, 32:*145–153.

Doukas, D. J., & Reichel, W. (1993). *Planning for Uncertainty: A Guide to Living Wills and Other Advance Directives for Health Care.* Baltimore: Johns Hopkins University.

English, D. D. (1994). *Bioethics: A Clinical Guide for Medical Students.* New York: W.W. Norton.

Fiesta, J. (1997). *Legal Implications in Long-term Care.* Albany: Delmar.

Guido, G. W. (1997). *Legal Issues in Nursing,* ed 2. Stamford, CT: Appleton & Lange.

Hall, J. K. (1996). *Nursing Ethics and Law.* Philadelphia: W.B. Saunders.

Husted, G. L., & Husted, J. H. (1995). Ethical Decision Making in Nursing, ed 2. St. Louis: Mosby.

Kapp, M. B. (1994). (Ed.). *Patient Self-determination in Long-term Care: Implementing the PSDA in Medical Decisions.* New York: Springer.

Kikuchi, H., & Simmons, D. R. (1996). (Eds.). *Truth in Nursing Inquiry.* Thousand Oaks, CA: Sage Publications.

King, N. M. P. (1996). *Making Sense of Advance Directives.* Washington, DC: Georgetown University Press.

Lashley, F. R. (Ed.). (1997). *The Genetics Revolution: Implications for Nursing.* Washington, DC: American Academy of Nursing.

Martin, S., & Vitello, J. M. (1992). Making a critical decision before it becomes critical. *Heart Lung, 21:*15A–18A.

Reigle, J. (1992). Preserving patient self-determination through advance directives. *Heart Lung, 21:*196–198.

Salipante, D. M. (1998). Cultural diversity. Refusal of blood by a critically ill patient: A healthcare challenge. *Critical Care Nurse, 18*(2):68–76.

Scanlon, C., & Fibison, W. (1995). *Managing Genetic Information: Implications of Nursing Practice.* Washington, DC: American Nurses Publishing.

Silverman, H. J., Fry, S. T., & Armistead, N. (1994). Nurses' perspective on implementation of the Patient Self-Determination Act. *J Clin Ethics, 5:*30–37.

Silverman, H. J., Vinicky, J. K., & Gasner, M. R. (1992). Advance directives: Implications for critical care. *Crit Care Med, 20:*1027–1031.

Singleton, K. A., Dever, R., & Donner, T. A. (1992). Durable power of attorney: Nursing implications. *Dimensions of Critical Care Nursing, 11:*41–46.

Snider, G. L. (1995). Withholding and withdrawing life-sustaining therapy: All systems are not yet "go." *Am J Crit Care Med, 151:*279–281.

Sullivan, G. H., & Mattera, M. D. (1997). *RN's Legally Speaking: How to Protect Your Patients and Your License.* Montvale, NJ: Medical Economics.

Trandel-Korenchuk, D. M., & Trandel-Korenchuk, K. M. (1997). *Nursing and the Law,* ed 5. Gaithersburg, MD: Aspen.

Veins, D. C. (1989). A history of nursing's code of ethics. *Nursing Outlook, 37*(1): 43–49.

White, G. B. (1992). *Ethical Dilemmas in Contemporary Nursing Practice.* Washington, DC: American Nurses Publishing.

White, P. D. (1997). The role of the critical care nurse in counseling families about advance directives. *Critical Care Nursing Clinics of North America, 9:*53–61.

Zucker, M. B., & Zucker, H. D. (1997). (Eds.). *Medical Futility and the Evaluation of Life-sustaining Interventions.* Cambridge, NY: Cambridge University Press.

Change of Shift Report

Barbera, M. L. (1994). Giving report: How to sidestep common pitfalls. *Nursing, 24*(9):41.

Bosek, M. S. D., & Fugate, K. (1994). Intershift report: a quality improvement project. *MEDSURG Nursing, 3*(2):128–132.

Coleman, S., & Henneman, E. A. (1991). Comprehensive patient care and documentation through unit-based nursing rounds. *Clinical Nurse Specialist, 5*(2): 117–120.

Copp, L. A. (1998). Change of shift report. *J Prof Nurs, 14*(2):63–64.

Cox, S. S. (1994). Taping report tips to record by. *Nursing, 24*(3):64.

Fraser, L. E., O'Brien, K., Tobar, I., & Waller, D. M. (1991). Patient care plans for intershift report. *Journal of Pediatric Nursing: Nursing Care of Children and Families, 6*(5):310–316.

Guido, G. W. (1988). Legal commentary: Shift reports. *Dimensions Critical Care Nursing* Nov–Dec; 7:380.

Howell, M. (1994). Confidentiality during staff reports at the bedside. *Nursing Times, 90*(34):44–45.

Liukkonen, A. (1993). The content of nurses' oral shift reports in homes for elderly people. *J Adv Nurs, 18*(7):1095–1100.

McMahon, R. (1990). What are we saying? *Nursing Times, 86*(30):38–40.

Monahan, M. L., et al. (1998). Change of shift report: A time for communication with patients. *Nursing Management, 19*(2):80.

Mosher, C., & Bontomasi, R. (1996). How to improve your shift report. *Am J Nurs, 96*(8):32–43.

Patterson, P. K., Blehm, R., Foster, J., Fuglee, K., & Moore, J. (1995). Nurse information needs for efficient care continuity across patient units. *J Nurs Adm, 25*(10):28–36.

Reiley, P. J., & Stengrevics, S. S. (1989). Change-of-shift report: Put it in writing! *Nursing Management, 20*(9):54–56.

Taylor, C. (1993). Intershift report: Oral communication using a quality assurance approach. *J Clin Nurs, 2*(5):266–267.

Wolf, Z. R. Learning the professional jargon of nursing during change of shift report. *Holistic Nursing Practice, 4*(1):78–83.

CHAPTER 6

The Evaluation Step: Determining Whether Desired Outcomes Have Been Met

---

REASSESSMENT

MODIFICATION OF THE PLAN OF CARE

TERMINATION OF SERVICES

ENHANCING DELIVERY OF QUALITY CARE

SUMMARY

- **ANA Standard 6:** Evaluation: The nurse evaluates the client's progress toward attainment of outcomes.

The final step of the nursing process is evaluating the patient's response to the care delivered to make sure the desired outcomes developed in the **PLANNING** step and documented in the plan of care have been achieved. **EVALUATION,** which is an ongoing process, is necessary for determining how well the plan of care is working. As the patient's condition changes, information is added to the patient database, requiring revision and updating of the plan of care, which is an essential component of the **EVALUATION** step.

Although the process of evaluation may seem similar to the activity of assessment, there are important differences. Instead of identifying the patient's general status and problems/needs, the evaluation focuses on the *appropriateness* of the care provided and the patient's progress or lack of progress toward the desired outcomes. Evaluation is an interactive, continuous process. As each nursing action is performed, the patient's response is noted and *evaluated* in relation to the identified

EVALUATION: final step of the nursing process. A continuous process essential to assuring the quality and appropriateness of the care provided that is done by reviewing patient responses to determine effectiveness of the plan of care in meeting patient needs.

outcomes. Then, based on the patient's response, appropriate revisions of nursing interventions and/or patient outcomes may be necessary.

Although it is frequently viewed simplistically as a pass-or-fail judgment, evaluation should actually be seen as a constructive opportunity to provide positive feedback to both the patient and caregivers for their efforts, and encouragement to continue to strive for a higher level of functioning or wellness. It is an opportunity for problem solving and personal growth. The EVALUATION step has three components: reassessment, modification of the plan of care, and finally, termination of services. The first two components form a continuous loop of recurring assessment and reaction, which eventually leads to the third component. This "termination of services" may sound rather abrupt, but this final part of the EVALUATION step is in reality the next step for the patient in looking toward the future and "moving on." Termination in part includes completion of discharge planning and addresses those patient nursing diagnoses or patient needs that were not fully attained during the time frame when nursing care was provided. Further description of this part of the EVALUATION step is presented later in this chapter.

Reassessment

Reassessment is a constant "measuring and monitoring" of the patient's status that looks at the patient's response to nursing interventions and progress toward attaining the desired outcome. This evaluation process is ongoing; it does not occur only when an outcome is to be reviewed or a determination of the patient's readiness for discharge is to be made. Data collected as the plan of care was implemented in step 4 of the nursing process are now evaluated or reassessed. Evaluation of the data determines:

- **The appropriateness of the nursing actions**

  FOR EXAMPLE: Robert's dyspnea has resolved with the provision of oxygen and attention to pulmonary toilet (i.e., periodic deep-breathing exercises, effective cough, position changes, and use of the incentive spirometer). Or Donald's tremors have lessened since receiving his AM dose of Librium.

- **The need to revise the interventions**

  FOR EXAMPLE: Robert was kept in bed for breakfast but should be able to be out of bed for lunch. Or while you were assisting Michelle to walk the length of the hall, you noted that she is unsteady on her crutches and will initially require the assistance of two individuals to provide for patient and employee safety.

- **The development of new patient problems/needs**

  FOR EXAMPLE: Sally is scheduled for discharge tomorrow. Her current weakness and lack of attention to her infant's cues raise concerns about her current coping abilities and the potential for parenting/attachment problems as well as issues of self-care.

- **The need for referral to other resources**

  FOR EXAMPLE: Sally's physician is notified of your observations, and possible solutions are discussed. A family meeting may be requested, to clarify roles/responsibilities and availability of assistance. The home health nurse is to be contacted to arrange self-care and homemaker assistance and to supervise Sally's situation after discharge. Referrals to community support groups (such as Mothers of Twins) may be made to provide additional assistance and problem-solving options.

- **The need to rearrange priorities to meet the changing demands of care**

  FOR EXAMPLE: You had planned to get Robert up in the chair for breakfast, but the focused assessment revealed a change in his respiratory status requiring new interventions and revision of the plan. Or external factors may occur, such as the emergency department calling to say that they have a new patient requiring admission. You need to review and reschedule the activities planned for Robert in order to accommodate these additional and unplanned responsibilities.

While evaluating the patient's response to care, you also note progress toward the specified outcomes. In addition, as each outcome has an identified timeframe, achievement of the outcomes is periodically reviewed. You must now determine whether the outcomes have been met completely, partially, or not at all; and whether or not the plan of care needs to be revised. Outcome(s) may be evaluated by:

- **Direct observation**

  FOR EXAMPLE: Did the patient ambulate the length of the hall without developing dyspnea? Did the patient demonstrate proper technique for the administration of insulin? Is the patient free of skin breakdown?

- **Patient interview**

  FOR EXAMPLE: Does the patient report decreased level of pain after administration of oral pain medication? Can the patient list available community resources? Is the patient able to verbalize the signs/symptoms that require medical evaluation or follow-up?

- **Review of records:** (e.g., progress notes, flow sheets, medication record)

  FOR EXAMPLE: Has the patient's temperature remained within normal range? Are the intake and output balanced? Has the patient gained weight? Has a laxative been required for constipation?

An important aspect of this process is the involvement of the patient. How does the patient believe she or he is doing? Inclusion of the patient's point of view

---

BOX 6–1

OMAHA PROBLEM RATING SCALE FOR OUTCOMES

CONCEPT	1	2	3	4	5
Knowledge	No knowledge	Minimal knowledge	Basic knowledge	Adequate knowledge	Superior knowledge
Behavior	Not appropriate	Rarely appropriate	Inconsistently appropriate	Usually appropriate	Consistently appropriate
Status	Extreme signs/ symptoms	Severe signs/ symptoms	Moderate signs/ symptoms	Minimal signs/ symptoms	No signs/ symptoms

Source: Martin, K. S., & Scheet, N. J. (1992). The Omaha System: A Pocket Guide for Community Health Nursing. Philadelphia: W.B. Saunders.

BOX 6–2

UNMET OUTCOMES—QUESTIONS TO ASK

If the outcomes have not been met completely, questions to be considered are:

- Were the outcomes realistic and appropriate?
- Was the patient involved in setting the outcomes?
- Does the patient believe the outcomes were important?
- Does the patient know why the outcomes have not been met?
- Have all the interventions that were identified been carried out and in the timeframe specified?
  If not, why not? Were they too vague or misinterpreted?
- What variables may have affected achievement of the outcomes?
- Were new problems/adverse patient responses detected early enough to make appropriate changes in the plan of care?

---

can provide important insights that may provide additional data for evaluating and revising the plan of care.

As mentioned in Chapter 4, the Omaha System's Problem Rating Scale for Outcomes provides three levels of evaluation. Box 6–1 lists the three System concepts of knowledge, behavior, and status. Also review Appendix J to see an example of one of the many evaluation tools available in the Nursing Outcomes Classification. (Similar five-point scales are also used by NOC to evaluate the outcome indicators.)

If the outcome were completely met, ask yourself the following questions: "Which interventions can be terminated?" "How easily were the outcomes achieved?" "Can timeliness be shortened?" To determine why an outcome was not met, questions such as those noted in Box 6–2 may help provide clarification.

In addition, you review the orders and progress notes of all healthcare providers and identify factors that helped or hindered achievement of outcomes. The findings are then documented on the plan of care and/or progress notes as appropriate and shared with the patient.

Modification of the Plan of Care

When you have completed evaluating the outcomes and the plan of care, you may find the patient's condition has changed in a direction that was or was not anticipated regardless of your nursing interventions and the patient's desire to achieve the stated outcomes. At this point, a change in treatment approach is indicated and the plan of care must be modified to reflect these changes.

As basic physiological needs such as air, water, food, and safety are met, nursing care can progress to such higher level concerns as self-esteem. Alternatively, when dealing with higher level needs they may be put "on hold" while those associated with *newly* emerging basic needs are addressed. At any time, the nurse may identify or activate additional patient diagnostic statements, goals, and/or desired outcomes and corresponding interventions. An earlier chapter discussed the difficulty dealing with more than three to five patient problems at one time. The actual number varies from patient to patient and the complexity of the nursing diagnoses present, but the point is, there may simply be too many patient needs to address in the initial plan of care. Priority setting is required when this situation exists, with progression to higher-level needs as the patient's condition permits.

When the desired outcomes are evaluated and found to be unmet, the reasons need to be identified and documented, and the outcomes then revised or new ones written. When revising patient outcomes, keep in mind that they may simply need to be restated, or their time frames lengthened so that the patient can successfully achieve them.

FOR EXAMPLE: When Donald was first admitted for acute alcoholism and depression, the initial concerns focused on issues of patient safety/potential for injury, changes in sensory interpretation, anxiety, and general nutrition. When Donald completed his initial withdrawal from alcohol and his physical condition stabilized, nursing attention became focused on previously identified problems concerning individual coping and role performance.

As the plan of care is modified, remember to address the changing needs of the patient/significant others, the changes in the patient's health status, environment, and therapeutic regimen. To assist in this process, a patient care conference may be scheduled or a consultation with a colleague or other resource people with special knowledge may be necessary to provide additional insight and to problem-solve solutions.

Practice Activity 6–1 provides an opportunity to review and evaluate the plan of care for Michelle. Read the narrative accompanying Michelle's plan of care and follow the directions for evaluating whether Michelle had attained the stated outcomes. Write your evaluations in the STATUS column of the plan of care. Once you have completed Practice Activity 6–1, turn to Practice Activity 6–2 (p. 125) and add your modifications to Michelle's plan of care in the provided space.

Termination of Services

When the desired outcomes have been achieved and the broader goals met, termination of care is planned. You now focus on how the patient will manage on his or her own. Although termination of care occurs when all goals/outcomes are met, it is possible that some will not be met before discharge. The goals/outcomes that have not been met need to be reviewed, and the reasons why documented. Some nursing diagnoses, such as Anxiety or Altered Nutrition, may require many months or years to be completely resolved. Because the hospitalization is only one point along the patient's health continuum, it is realistic that not all outcomes will be achieved or all nursing diagnoses resolved.

The discharge plans that began at the time of admission and were periodically updated are finalized and put into action. Verify that the patient/significant other have received written and verbal instructions regarding treatments, medications, and activities to be followed/referred to at home. Signs and symptoms indicating the need for continued contact with the healthcare providers are reviewed. When necessary, referral/contact phone numbers and other information about resources are given to the patient/significant other. You also determine whether contact has been made with appropriate providers for follow-up care as indicated (e.g., social worker, home health nurse, or equipment suppliers).

PRACTICE ACTIVITY 6–1

Evaluating Patient Outcomes

Read over the case study information below. It has been used to develop a plan of care for Michelle.

When Michelle was admitted to the hospital the evening of 6/11, a physiological (Maslow's) or survival (Kalish) need of pain avoidance was identified (i.e., Pain [acute]). A higher-level problem of safety or stimulation was noted (i.e., Impaired Physical Mobility), as was a safety need of protection (i.e., Risk for Infection).

The following morning (6/12) during the 8 AM assessment, Michelle indicates she was successful in obtaining relief of pain after periodic injection of analgesics. Michelle also found that deep-breathing exercises and focusing her attention on the scenic picture at the foot of her bed helped minimize the severity of recurrent muscle spasms in her right leg. In addition, frequent weight shifts using the overhead trapeze and range of motion exercises reduced general aches and joint stiffness and meditation enhanced general relaxation.

The nurse noticed that most of Michelle's breakfast tray was untouched. Michelle reported she wasn't very hungry but did want fruit juice and other fluids. After the morning bed bath, the dressings were changed and the right leg wound was evaluated. Skin edges were pink and serous drainage was odorless. Pin sites were also cleaned and no signs of inflammation noted. At lunch, Michelle's intake was poor. She indicated that she was having difficulty opening her mouth and chewing, and had an aching sensation located in her right temple and ear.

During the afternoon assessment at 4:30 PM, Michelle's nurse verified that Michelle understood and was using infection control techniques of proper handwashing and avoidance of contact with wound and pin sites.

When Michelle was set up on the side of the bed before her dinner, she reported dizziness and sharp pain in her right leg, and she became pale and diaphoretic. She was returned to the supine position and a focused assessment was performed, revealing a blood pressure of 92/60. Within 20 minutes, Michelle's color had improved, the dizziness was gone, and the pain relieved with medication.

In reviewing the excerpts from Michelle's plan of care, complete the status column denoting whether the outcomes have been met (m), partially met (pm), or not met (nm) appropriately for the timeframes indicated.

Concerns regarding unmet needs, the need for follow-up monitoring, and progress toward long-term goals after discharge were discussed in Chapter 4. Depending on how your facility or agency has decided to deal with these issues, you may choose to document your findings and patient instructions in a discharge summary, which also identifies additional activities for the patient and family to resolve unmet needs and achieve long-range outcomes/goals. A copy of this nursing discharge summary may then be given to the patient. Table 6–1 shows how patient teaching information can be organized and conveyed to the patient.

Even though the patient has been discharged, it is important for the patient and family to know what has been accomplished and how they can continue to enhance the patient's future health status. In addition, the discharge summary may be shared with the home care nurse/nurse practitioner and possibly sent to the primary/involved physician for inclusion in the office record to promote continuity of care with continued work toward goals and monitoring of progress/changing needs.

PLAN OF CARE: MICHELLE

Patient: Michelle   Age: 14—3/2/85   Gender: F   Admission: 6/11/99 5:30 PM   Dx: Compound Fx R tibia/fibula, closed head injury/mild concussion

Date	Patient Diagnostic Statement	Goal	Interventions	Outcomes	Status
6/11/99	Pain [acute]: related to movement of bone fragments. soft tissue injury/edema, and use of external fixator as evidenced by verbal reports, guarding, muscle tension, narrowed focus, and tachycardia.	Pain-free or controlled by discharge.	1. Maintain limb rest R leg × 24 hr to 5 PM 6/12. 2. Elevate lower leg with folded blanket. 3. Apply ice to area as tolerated × 48 hr to 5 PM 6/13. 4. Place cradle over foot of bed. 5. Document reports and characteristics of pain. 6. Medicate with Demerol 75 mg and Phenergan 25 mg IM, q4h prn or Vicodin 5 mg PO q4h prn. 7. Demonstrate/encourage use of progressive relaxation techniques, deep-breathing exercises, visualization. 8. Provide alternate comfort measures. position change, backrub. 9. Encourage use of diversional activities.	Verbalizes relief of pain within 30–60 min of administration of medication. Identifies methods that provide relief by 9 AM, 6/12. Uses relaxation skills to reduce level of pain by 9 AM, 6/12.	
6/11/99	Risk for Infection: risk factors of broken skin, traumatized tissues,	Free of infection.	1. Monitor temp, VS q4h. 2. Aseptic dressing change bid 9 AM, 9 PM, and prn.	Identifies and practices interventions to reduce risk of infection by	

Continued

PLAN OF CARE: MICHELLE (Continued)

Patient: Michelle   Age: 14—3/2/85   Gender: F   Admission: 6/11/99 5:30 PM   Dx: Compound Fx R tibia/fibula, closed head injury/mild concussion

Date	Patient Diagnostic Statement	Goal	Interventions	Outcomes	Status
	decreased hemoglobin levels, invasive procedures, environmental exposure.		3. Pin care per protocol bid 9 AM, 9 PM. 4. Routine IV site care daily. 5. Document condition of wound, IV, and pin sites q4h. 6. Review ways patient can reduce risk of infection. 7. Administer cefoxitin 2 g IV piggyback q8h (8 AM, 4 PM, 12 AM).	5 PM, 6/12. Identifies signs/ symptoms requiring medical evaluation by 9 AM, 6/13. Displays initial wound healing free of purulent drainage/signs of infection by discharge.	
6/11/99	Impaired Physical Mobility: related to musculoskeletal impairment and pain, and restrictive therapy (external fixator) as evidenced by reluctance to attempt movement and imposed restrictions of movement.	Ambulates safely with assistive device.	1. Monitor circulation/nerve function R leg q1h × 24 hr to 5 PM, 6/12, then q4h and prn. 2. Support R leg fixator during movement. 3. Support feet with footboard. 4. Encourage use of side rails/overhead trapeze for position change. 5. Demonstrate/assist with ROM exercises to unaffected limbs 2qh. 6. Assist out of bed, non–weight-bearing R leg 6 PM, 6/12. 7. Instruct in/monitor use of crutches 6/13.	Participates in activities to maintain muscle strength by 9 AM, 6/12. Increases level of activity beginning 6 PM, 6/12 and ongoing. Demonstrates techniques/behaviors that enable resumption of activities by 6 PM, 6/13. Maintains position of function R leg, free of foot drop—ongoing.	

PRACTICE ACTIVITY 6–2

Modification of the Plan of Care

Based on your evaluation, how would you alter Michelle's plan of care from Practice Activity 6–1?

_____

_____

_____

_____

Enhancing Delivery of Quality Care

Evaluation is an important step for determining the success of the plan of care because it involves a review of all the steps of the nursing process. Although patient care is evaluated on an individual basis, unit and/or general agency-based nursing audit committees focus attention on selected groups of patients, such as those receiving chemotherapy or those with longer than normal lengths of stay. Comparing

TABLE 6–1. Example of Patient Teaching Information for Patient Going Home on Antidysrhythmic Medication

Dear Patient:
   This drug has been prescribed for you. This is what you should know about your drug to get the most from your therapy.

1. Antidysrhythmics are taken to regulate your heart rhythm.
2. Antidysrhythmic drugs may have to be taken for the rest of your life.
3. Quinidine, procainamide hydrochloride (Pronestyl), propranolol (Inderal), and phenytoin (Dilantin) are taken with meals.
4. Do not take your antidysrhythmics concurrently with [fill in appropriate drugs].
5. Always check with your doctor or pharmacist before taking other drugs because interactions may occur. Drugs known to cause interactions include over-the-counter products for nasal congestion, allergy, pain, or obesity. Drugs of abuse such as marijuana may raise blood pressure and stimulate heart activity and thus increase abnormal heart rhythm.
6. If you forget to take your antidysrhythmic, do not take the forgotten dose. **Do not** try to catch up by taking two doses at the same time.
7. Do not stop taking your drug unless directed by your doctor.
8. If you have any side effects from your drug, call your doctor. Side effects from taking antidysrhythmics include low blood pressure, light-headedness, gastrointestinal distress, changes in rate or rhythm of the heart, and often blurred vision. Keep a written log of the effects that are noted and the time of day, such as in the morning upon awaking, with meals, or with activity.
9. Weigh yourself weekly. A gain of 1–2 lb a week may be a sign of increased water. Call your doctor if this occurs.
10. Check your feet and ankles for swelling. If this occurs, call your doctor.
11. Limit your coffee, tea, or cola drinks because caffeine may cause an increase in abnormal heart rhythm.
12. Store these drugs in a tight, light-resistant bottle to prevent breakdown of drug.

Source: Mathewson-Kuhn, M. A. (1994). Pharmacotherapeutics: A Nursing Process Approach, ed 3. Philadelphia: FA Davis.

overall outcomes and noting the effectiveness of specific interventions are the clinical components of evaluation that can become the bases of research for validating the nursing process. This external evaluation process is the key for refining standards of care and determining the protocols, policies, and procedures necessary for the provision of quality nursing care in a particular agency.

Summary

The **EVALUATION** step of the nursing process monitors and reports on the current status of the identified patient problems/needs and is based on the outcomes that were developed in the **PLANNING** step. The evaluation process includes the patient, significant others, and whoever else is involved in the care of the patient. This process is a positive one in which the patient's responses to the nursing interventions are evaluated to determine whether or not the desired outcomes were achieved. When the findings are analyzed and it is determined that the outcomes have been met, termination of services is begun and discharge planning is completed. However, if the outcomes have not been met (all or in part), reassessment is required to determine why this is the case. Consider factors, like new information, unexpected complications, or the choice of the wrong nursing diagnosis as possibilities when a desired patient outcome is not achieved. At this point, you would reinitiate the nursing process and modify the plan of care to include the newly identified nursing diagnoses, outcomes, and/or interventions. This modification, in turn, will be re-evaluated at an appropriate time.

The evaluation process can also be more broadly applied at an institutional level to measure the overall quality of care. It is increasingly used to set standards and to supply patient information about many facets of the care provided by healthcare agencies. The **EVALUATION** step needs to be viewed positively as an opportunity for growth, both for individuals and for the profession as a whole. It is essential for the effective delivery of patient care, and therefore a process to be valued rather than avoided and/or glossed over quickly.

BOX 6–3

MEASUREMENT CRITERIA FOR ANA STANDARD VI

ANA STANDARD VI EVALUATION: The nurse evaluates the client's progress toward attainment of outcomes.

Measurement Criteria

1. Evaluation is systematic, ongoing, and criterion-based.
2. The client, family, and other healthcare providers are involved in the evaluation process, as appropriate.
3. Ongoing assessment data are used to revise diagnoses, outcomes, and the plan of care, as needed.
4. Revisions in diagnoses, outcomes, and the plan of care are documented.
5. The effectiveness of interventions is evaluated in relation to outcomes.
6. The patient's responses to interventions are documented.

Now, let us return to the sixth and last standard of the ANA Standard of Clinical Nursing Practice and review the measurement criteria necessary to achieve and ensure compliance. The knowledge and skill required to meet the criteria listed in Box 6–3 were described in this chapter. The measurement criteria for this standard, combined with the previous standards, provide a valuable tool for evaluating your understanding and application of the nursing process.

Accurate documentation of the findings of the EVALUATION step is essential for ensuring the continuity of care described in the plan of care. This topic is discussed in Chapter 7.

1. What is the difference between assessment and evaluation? _____

_____

_____

2. What is the primary purpose of the evaluation process? _____

_____

3. The evaluation process provides what three opportunities for the patient and nurse:

   a. _____

   b. _____

   c. _____

4. List the three methods in which patient outcomes may be evaluated, and give an example for each:

   Method of Evaluation   **Example**

   a. _____   _____

   b. _____   _____

   c. _____   _____

5. Because it is advisable to deal with only three to five nursing diagnoses at a time, how are needs

   prioritized? _____

   _____

6. When is consideration of discharge planning begun? _____

   _____

7.

> **VIGNETTE:** Today is Donald's fifth hospital day. At the start of the shift, you have completed a focused assessment to evaluate progress/changes in status of the identified patient problems. Donald's initial nausea has resolved and his intake yesterday was approximately 3000 calories. During rounds you notice he has eaten all of the food on his breakfast tray. He fills out the next day's menu, neglecting to include any vegetables and selecting only one fruit.
>
> Later, during group, Donald talks about his options for employment and says he knows an employment agency and a business where he can check about possible jobs. He also mentions a friend who he believes might be willing to help him. He says he is realizing that he is really OK, even though the loss of his job was a devastating event for him following so soon after his divorce. He acknowledges that his feelings of anxiety led to an increase in his drinking. He further says he still has feelings of sadness and occasionally feels a sense of despair but believes he will feel better as he begins to get his life back together again. He seems tentative about accepting his need to be involved in AA, saying he doesn't know "where they meet, or anyone who attends the meetings."

   a. **Evaluation:** Based on the above information, evaluate Donald's progress regarding his problems of Altered Nutrition: less than body requirements, Ineffective Individual Coping, and Altered Role Performance, as outlined in the Plan of Care.

b. **Modification:** How would you change Donald's plan of care? _____

_____

_____

c. **Termination:** How might new concerns regarding the patient affect your discharge plans? _____

_____

BIBLIOGRAPHY

Martin, K. S., & Scheet, N. J. (1992). *The Omaha System: A Pocket Guide for Community Health Nursing.* Philadelphia: W.B. Saunders.

Mathewson-Kuhn, M. A. (1994). *Pharmacotherapeutics: A Nursing Process Approach,* ed 3. Philadelphia: F.A. Davis.

SUGGESTED READINGS

Carpenito, L. J. (1995). *Nursing Care Plans and Documentation,* ed 2. Philadelphia: J.B. Lippincott.

Cox, H., et al. (1997). *Clinical Applications of Nursing Diagnosis: Adult, Child, Women's, Psychiatric, and Home Health Considerations,* ed 3. Philadelphia: F.A. Davis.

Craft, M. J., & Denehy, J. A. (1990). *Nursing Interventions for Infants and Children.* Philadelphia: W.B. Saunders.

Doenges, M. E., & Moorhouse, M. F. (2000). *Nurse's Pocket Guide: Nursing Diagnoses with Interventions,* ed 7. Philadelphia: F.A. Davis.

Doenges, M. E., Moorhouse, M. F., & Geissler, A. C. (2000). *Nursing Care Plans: Guidelines for Planning and Documenting Patient Care,* ed 5. Philadelphia: F.A. Davis.

Holloway, N. M. (1993). *Medical-Surgical Care Planning,* ed 2. Springhouse, PA: Springhouse.

Joint Commission on Accreditation of Healthcare Organizations. (1997). *Nursing Practice and Nursing Outcomes Measurement.* Oakbrook Terrace, IL: Author.

Leuner, J. D., Manton, A. K., Kelliher, D. B., Sullivan, S. P., & Doherty, M. (1990). *Mastering the Nursing Process: A Case Study Approach.* Philadelphia: F.A. Davis.

Maas, M., Buckwalter, K. C., & Hardy, M. (1991). *Nursing Diagnosis and Interventions for the Elderly.* Menlo Park, CA: Addison-Wesley.

CHAPTER 7

Documenting the Nursing Process

ROLE OF DOCUMENTATION

PROGRESS NOTES
Staff Communication
Evaluation
Relationship Monitoring
Reimbursement
Legal Documentation
Accreditation
Training and Supervision

TECHNIQUES FOR DESCRIPTIVE NOTE WRITING
Judgmental Language
Undefined Periods of Time
Undefined Quantities
Qualities
Objective Basis for Judgments
Descriptive Language
Content of Note/Entry
Format of Note/Entry

SUMMARY

■ **JCAHO Standard:** Patient-Specific Data/Information
IM.7.1. A medical record is initiated and maintained for every individual assessed or treated. The medical record incorporates information from subsequent contacts between the patient and the organization.
IM.7.2. The medical record contains sufficient information to identify the patient, support the diagnosis, justify the treatment, document the course and results accurately, and facilitate continuity of care among healthcare providers.

Role of Documentation

Documentation is not only a requirement for accreditation but is also a legal requirement in any healthcare setting. From a nursing focus, documentation provides a record of the use of the nursing process for the delivery of individualized patient care. The initial **ASSESSMENT** is recorded in the patient history or database.

Remember, for legal purposes, if an event/activity is not documented, it did not occur or was not done.

131

The **IDENTIFICATION** of patient problems/needs, and the **PLANNING** of patient care are recorded in the plan of care. The **IMPLEMENTATION** of the plan is recorded in the progress notes and/or flow sheets. Finally, the **EVALUATION** of care may be documented in the progress notes and/or plan of care.

The goals of the documentation system are to:

- Facilitate the delivery of quality patient care.
- Ensure documentation of progress with regard to patient-focused outcomes.
- Facilitate interdisciplinary consistency and the communication of treatment goals and progress.

Progress Notes

The plan of care that has been developed for a particular patient serves as a framework or outline for the charting of administered care. As noted, this information may be recorded on flow sheets and/or progress notes. Progress notes are an integral component of the overall medical record and should include all significant events that occur during the patient's hospitalization/treatment program. The notes should be written in a clear and objective fashion and in a manner that reflects progress towards desired measurable outcomes with the use of planned staff interventions. Progress notes have seven major functions, as noted in Box 7–1.

STAFF COMMUNICATION

Clearly, staff arriving for the next and subsequent shifts need to know what has occurred with the patient during the current shift to make appropriate judgments regarding patient management. Colleague-to-colleague communication is the most obvious function of the progress note, yet it is only a piece of the communication picture. Nursing staff are in the unique position of being in contact with the patient for extended periods of time and in a variety of situations. As a nurse, your observations of your patient's behavior and response to therapy provide invaluable information to the physician or other providers who may only see the patient for a few minutes each day. Whether or not the patient's current desired measurable out-

---

BOX 7–1

SEVEN FUNCTIONS OF PROGRESS NOTES

Progress notes serve multiple functions, and any given note may be written to address one function more than the others. Thus it is important to recognize the seven major functions of progress notes:

1. Staff documentation
2. Evaluation
3. Relationship monitoring
4. Reimbursement
5. Legal documentation
6. Accreditation
7. Training and supervision

comes and interventions are discontinued or revised, or new ones developed, depends on the information gathered.

EVALUATION

Periodic review of the patient's progress and the effectiveness of the treatment plan is completed by the nurse and/or the treatment team. An evaluation of the patient's progress may be documented on the plan of care and/or in the progress notes.

For the purpose of review (e.g., nursing audit committees and state, federal, and private agencies such as the Board of Health, Medicare, Joint Committee on the Accreditation of Healthcare Organizations [JCAHO]), the medical record should be written to facilitate an assessment of the care given the patient. Progress notes need to be written to reflect the patient's progress toward measurable outcomes and the interventions used. Someone not associated with the healthcare facility should be able to read the notes, determine if the plan of care is being implemented, and whether progress is being made toward the measurable outcomes. The medical record should serve as a method of tracking the patient's response to treatment and, consequently, as a means for evaluating the quality of care provided.

RELATIONSHIP MONITORING

The therapeutic relationship existing between staff and patient is an important aspect of treatment in any setting. The **NURSE-PATIENT RELATIONSHIP** is the tool used by the nurse to help the patient make the most of his or her own abilities. In the psychiatric setting, many of the patient's pathologies are manifested in these relationships, and indications of progress are first identified through the patient's ability to relate more positively and openly with staff, as well as peers and family. Therefore, monitoring the patient's relationships is essential, and notes detailing observations of these relationships (how the patient interacts in group situations, competitive situations, in one-to-one situations, etc.) have important clinical implications in any setting.

NURSE/PATIENT RELATIONSHIP: a therapeutic relationship built on a series of interactions, developing over time and meeting the needs of the patient.

REIMBURSEMENT

Third-party payors are insistent that the *why, when, where, how, what,* and *who* of services be clearly documented. An absence of such documentation may result in termination of funding for individual patients and, therefore, termination of treatment. The medical record is a primary source for maintaining the revenues and information about the patient's treatment, providing proof of services. Therefore, progress notes must document any significant observations about what is happening to the patient during illness, treatment, and recovery. Data about medications, equipment used, and any other pertinent information also need to be recorded.

LEGAL DOCUMENTATION

Nurses have a legal and moral duty to do no harm to patients. Harm can result from a nurse's action *or* inaction. Careful attention to all the steps of the nursing process reduces the possibility that harm will result from errors of omission (failing to take appropriate action as a result of missing an actual nursing diagnosis) or errors of commission (taking inappropriate action because of incorrect or overdiagnosing).

In our litigious society, with the threat of malpractice lawsuits, all aspects of the medical record (including the information contained in daily progress notes) may be important for legal documentation. Both the implementation of interventions and progress toward the measurable outcomes should be documented in the progress notes of the patient's medical record. Progress notes and flow sheets need to document that appropriate actions have been carried out and precautions taken as required to implement the treatment plan. These notations need to be specific about date and time and be signed by the person making the entry. In addition, the time an entry is written needs to be noted, along with the time the activity *actually* occurred when charting is delayed. Errors in the document must be crossed out with one line so that it is still legible, identified by the author as an "error," and then initialed. White-outs or cross-outs that make the information unreadable are not acceptable because they could be construed to mean that the individual or facility is trying to alter the facts.

ACCREDITATION

One of the most essential requirements for healthcare facilities (as determined by JCAHO and/or other accreditation and licensing agencies) is to maintain a medical record. JCAHO standards state that the medical record be documented accurately and in a timely manner. Therefore, the importance of completing notes on schedule and in a manner that facilitates retrieval of data should be emphasized. In addition, the JCAHO standards specify that "Nursing care data related to patient assessments, nursing diagnoses and/or patient needs, nursing interventions, and patient outcomes are permanently integrated into the medical record."

TRAINING AND SUPERVISION

An often underestimated aspect of note writing is their value for training and supervision purposes. An experienced nurse's description of how a complicated situation was handled, a supervisor's analysis of the problems presented by a new admission, and a description of patterns noted in another patient's response to care are all examples of notes that provide models for the remainder of the staff. Supervisors also gain an insight into the employee's abilities through reading progress notes and may be able to isolate areas in which additional supervision or training/education would be beneficial.

Finally, regardless of the setting, the patient's relationship with significant other(s) can have an impact on general well-being, progress toward recovery, independence in self-care, and (ultimately) a successful transition to the home setting. Thus, observation and monitoring of these interactions are important components of nursing care. At this point, complete Practice Activity 7–1 before proceeding to the next section.

Techniques for Descriptive Note Writing

Potential readership for notes written in the medical record might include coworkers, clinical specialist nurses, nurse practitioners, physicians, therapists, psychiatrists, psychologists, social workers, nurse reviewers, lawyers, judges, utilization re-

PRACTICE ACTIVITY 7–1

Elements of Progress Notes

Give a brief explanation of how progress notes provide for the following elements of the nurse/patient relationship.

1. Staff communication: _____

_____

_____

2. Evaluation: _____

_____

_____

3. Relationship monitoring: _____

_____

_____

4. Reimbursement: _____

_____

_____

5. Legal documentation: _____

_____

_____

6. Accreditation: _____

_____

_____

7. Training/Supervision: _____

_____

_____

_____

viewers, insurance personnel, surveyors, agency representatives, and parents or guardians, as well as the patient. Because of the number of possible readers, the need for clarity and accuracy in the progress notes is a priority.

From the notes, the reader should be able to form a clear picture of what occurred with the patient. The best way to ensure the clarity of progress notes is through the use of descriptive (or observational) statements. The following guideline for writing observation-based notes compares and contrasts judgmental and descriptive language.

JUDGMENTAL LANGUAGE

We are all aware of the possibilities for miscommunication that exist in ordinary conversations. The dangers of miscommunication may be even greater when information is written, and the opportunities for clarification present in face-to-face communication are absent. We are accustomed to speaking and writing in a judgmental (and therefore ambiguous) manner without even being aware of it. Examples are noted in Box 7–2. Types of judgmental statements include phrases that:

- Make reference to undefined periods of time
- Refer to undefined quantities
- Refer to qualities
- Fail to specify any objective basis for the judgment made

UNDEFINED PERIODS OF TIME

Statements that refer to undefined periods of time may contain words or phrases such as the following:

often	almost always	most of the time
rarely	frequently	now and then
seldom	occasionally	every so often

Use of these and similar phrases without clarification may leave the statement unclear and judgmental. How often, for example, is "every so often"? Is it every 5 minutes, once an hour, or three times per shift? This is not to say that the staff member must time each and every interaction or occurrence. Rather, be aware of the *potential* for confusion in these words. Ask yourself: Do I need to be more specific about the time of the event mentioned in this note? If you are documenting for potential legal purposes (an injury, for example), specificity is essential; however,

---

BOX 7–2

EXAMPLES OF JUDGMENTAL LANGUAGE

Consider the following statements:

"S/he asks for pain medication *too often*."

"He is *uncooperative* today."

"She did a *good job* on her incentive spirometer today."

"He is a *manipulative* patient."

"The new patient is really *difficult*."

"He has a *poor* outlook."

"She had a *bad attitude* about doing her physical therapy this morning."

The highlighted words in each of the above statements represent judgments (or conclusions), not facts. Without any elaboration or basis for comparison, each of the statements is a statement of opinion, open to varying interpretations. Contrast these with the statements in Box 7–3.

for routine communication purposes, this may not be the case. For example, if you note "The patient was quiet for most of the shift today," the exact number of minutes during which he or she was quiet or not quiet is not necessary for reasonably accurate communication to occur.

UNDEFINED QUANTITIES

Statements that refer to undefined quantities may use such words or phrases as the following:

some	enough	a great deal	too much
a lot	many	very little	large amount

As with the previous statements, each of these terms is open to interpretation. "A lot" of complaints to one person, for example, might mean 5; to another it might mean 20. Or, "a moderate amount of bloody drainage" could be 200 ml or only 50 ml of fluid. It is generally advisable to avoid undefined quantities.

QUALITIES

All descriptive adjectives applied to patients have the potential to fall under this category because they may involve making subjective definitions beforehand. Of most concern, however, are words that could be called "semitechnical" in nature.

passive	irritating	incompetent
nervous	manipulative	overprotective
demanding	alcoholic	disturbed

Because these kinds of words have connotations in the health field beyond the scope of their ordinary definitions, more common adjectives may pose less of a problem because there is less potential for misunderstanding. However, observed behaviors may call for conclusions that are influenced by your own biases and cultural background. It is best to verify the connotations of the following terms with others and particularly with the patient before using them:

friendly	unhappy	enthusiastic	proud
attentive	excited	bored	observant
aloof	apathetic	cheerful	happy

Finally, slang words, which are used informally and mostly by small subcultural groups, are unclear and should not be contained in a professionally written note in any case. For example:

hyped-up	spaced-out	bummed	crazy
loose	pushy	cool	tanked-up

OBJECTIVE BASIS FOR JUDGMENTS

Some statements are clearly a judgment on the part of the observer and are offered without any objective basis. Such statements may cause the reader to ask "How do you *know* this patient . . ."

- is improving?
- has a good attitude?
- enjoys reading?
- hates his roommate?

Recording your observations and providing an objective basis for your judgment (as in Box 7–3) reduces the possibility of miscommunication or misinterpretation, and the reader will not have to look elsewhere for clarification.

DESCRIPTIVE LANGUAGE

As noted previously, descriptive language contains observations only and avoids statements that are evaluative or judgmental unless observational evidence can be presented to back up the judgment. You will remember that being able to actually observe the patient doing something was the criterion of a well-written outcome. The situation is similar for observation-based progress notes; properly written objective statements refer to specific observable or measurable events. Descriptive statements:

- **Contain measurable periods of time**

FOR EXAMPLE:

10 times in 1 hour	every half hour	15 minutes
48 hours	four times a day	once

- **Contain measurable quantities**

FOR EXAMPLE:

20 percent of the diet	all of the patients
six out of eight	completely saturated
none	5 ml

- **Provide a basis or rationale for qualities named in the note**

FOR EXAMPLE:

Sally's lochia flow is moderate to heavy, saturating one peripad in approximately 1 hour on two separate occasions.

Donald's intake at lunch was poor, consisting of 1/2 cup of soup, 2 bites of sandwich, and 1/2 glass of milk.

BOX 7–3

PROVIDING AN OBJECTIVE BASIS FOR YOUR JUDGMENTS

Consider the following statements. Although the highlighted words represent a judgment or conclusion, objective facts or behavioral observations are provided to support or substantiate the judgment.

Michelle *is improving;* she walked the length of the hall using her crutches unassisted.

Robert *has a good attitude,* expressing optimism that he will be able to prevent a recurrence of pneumonia.

Sally *enjoys reading,* spending 1 to 2 hours a day in this activity.

Donald *expresses anger* toward his roommate's smoking, loud conversations with visitors, and commandeering of the TV. (Note: Making the inference that Donald *hates his roommate* from his expression of anger results in an unclear or unsupported judgment.)

You may have gotten the impression in the preceding section that you can never use adjectives in your notes. This is far from the case. In fact, you should give your impressions of the patient.

Statements in which you note that the patient "seemed" or "appeared" to be exhibiting a certain physical/emotional state are inferential statements. These are a subset of descriptive statements in which you infer the patient's state based on your observations of the patient's behavior and interactions, your knowledge of the patient's patterns, and the connections you make between behavior/affect and what has been happening during the illness. Such statements are often of great value.

However, you do not allow your subjective impressions to stand alone, particularly if your observation involves some of the more "semitechnical" qualities noted earlier. You also need to provide some reasons why you believed the patient was "improving," "demanding," "manipulative," or whatever.

FOR EXAMPLE:

> Robert was upset by his daughter's objections to his Advance Directive choices, cutting off the discussion and instructing her to "mind her own business."
>
> Donald is passive, responding to the nurse's questions regarding scheduling of his care by replying "whatever you want to do."
>
> Sally appears distressed, expressing concern about how she will manage two newborns when she already has two children at home, needs to return to work, and has no energy to do anything.
>
> Michelle's mother is oversolicitous, refusing to leave her daughter's bedside and performing all care activities that Michelle is capable of doing herself.

When comparisons or judgments are made, a descriptive statement should state the source or basis of judgment.

FOR EXAMPLE:

> According to the patient's laboratory reports . . .
> Psychological testing showed that . . .
> The other patient stated that . . .
> Judging by the fact that . . .

Also note that whenever the source of a judgment is specified, the statement becomes a behavioral report. Because such a report can be observed, this type of statement is an observation and is therefore descriptive. Consider the differences between the following two statements.

FOR EXAMPLE:

> The patient is stronger today.
> The physical therapist reports, "Michelle is stronger today."

The first statement is clearly judgmental because of the undefined phrase "stronger today." The second, however, is an observable event. Obviously (although the physical therapist may be wrong), it is an objective fact that the physical therapist said that the patient is stronger today. It may help to think of such statements as quotations. What the physical therapist said does not influence our ability to observe him or her saying it, and then objectively reporting that observation. However, physical therapy notes should reflect measurable descriptions of the patient situation.

> ### BOX 7–4
>
> ## COMPARISON OF JUDGMENTAL AND BEHAVIORAL NOTES
>
> The important thing to know about judgmental statements is that they can be translated into more precise terms. For example:
>
> **Judgmental:** The patient did pretty well today.
> **Behavioral:** The patient followed directions for drawing up and administering his insulin without any mistakes.
> **Judgmental:** The meeting with the physical therapist did not go very well.
> **Behavioral:** The patient stated she "could not do the exercises which were to be started today."
> **Judgmental:** The patient had a bad attitude all day.
> **Behavioral:** The patient argued with staff five times during the shift.
> **Judgmental:** The patient became aggressive.
> **Behavioral:** The patient clenched his fists and yelled at the nurse, "I'd like to hit you." He then hit the wall twice with his right fist.
> **Judgmental:** The patient would not follow directions.
> **Behavioral:** The patient drank a glass of water 30 minutes before his scheduled surgery in spite of reminders to remain NPO.
> **Judgmental:** The patient ate poorly.
> **Behavioral:** The patient ate one third of her lunch (all of the broccoli and corn, no meat, potatoes, or bread) and drank 50 ml of apple juice.
>
> As you can see from the above examples, it often takes a bit more thought to write a note that is objectively descriptive. However, the benefits in clarity of communication make the effort essential for the many purposes of progress notes.

Finally, you can chart observations in a nonjudgmental manner. "Michelle displayed increased endurance, walked the length of hall without assistance, appeared more confident with crutch use." In Box 7–4, additional examples further illustrate how judgmental statements may be interpreted and restated more objectively. To further assist you in your understanding of documenting descriptive progress notes, take a moment to complete Practice Activity 7–2.

CONTENT OF NOTE/ENTRY

The term *progress note* indicates that the patient's progress is to be documented along with the implementation of the treatment plan. Contents should be as specific and accurate as possible.

For communication purposes, it is important to record in the progress notes any information that is of importance to oncoming shifts as well as observations you have made that may be significant for other healthcare providers. Box 7–5 profiles the information that should be included. Remember, you are actually charting for the future. You know what is happening today. However, the reader of tomor-

PRACTICE ACTIVITY 7–2

Writing Nonjudgmental Statements

*Circle either the **J** or **O/B** for each of the following statements to identify either judgmental (**J**) or observational/behavioral (**O/B**) documented statements. If the statement is judgmental rewrite to reflect observational/behavioral language.*

1. Mrs. Jewel has a poor body image since undergoing a mastectomy. **J** **O/B** _____

   _____

2. Mr. Dunn needs to be evaluated regarding his competence to manage his household affairs because of his left-sided weakness since his stroke. **J** **O/B** _____

   _____

3. Miss Janus does a good job of breast self-examination. **J** **O/B** _____

   _____

4. Mary Bird does not eat enough for her current level of activity. **J** **O/B** _____

   _____

5. Mr. Lambert stops taking his medication; then when he has a seizure, he presents at the doctor's office for treatment. **J** **O/B** _____

   _____

6. It has been a long time since Mr. Babbitt has had his medication evaluated. **J** **O/B** _____

   _____

   _____

row, next week, or next year must rely on your written words to share your understanding of the patient's situation at a given moment.

For example, when applying restraints, which constitutes a *major event with both therapeutic and legal ramifications*, you need to document the exact time the procedure was initiated, whether any injuries resulted, and so forth. It is also necessary to document what led up to the situation, how staff and other participants reacted, what less restrictive measures were tried, and any significant observations regarding the incident. An example of how to document a therapeutic event is presented in Box 7–6.

Other areas of concern that enhance accurate communication are the use of correct grammar and spelling, legible writing, and the use of nonerasable ink. To promote clarity, avoid repeating data when possible. Because this is "the patient's record," it is not necessary to use the term "the patient"; however, periodically using the patient's name can help to identify the proper chart and prevent problems of charting on the wrong record, especially when you chart on several patient's

BOX 7–5

CONTENT OF SUCCESSFUL PROGRESS NOTES

Examples of the kind of information important to record in the progress notes include:

- **Unsettled or unclear problems or "issues"** that need to be dealt with, including attempts to contact other healthcare providers
- **Noteworthy incidents or interviews** involving the patient that would benefit from a more detailed recording
- **Other pertinent data** such as notes on phone calls, home visits, and family interactions
- **Additional critical incident data** such as seemingly significant or revealing statements made by the patient, an insight you have into a patient's patterns of behavior, patient injuries, the use of any special treatment procedure, or other major events such as episodes of pain, respiratory distress, panic attacks, medication reactions, suicidal comments
- **Administered care activities or observations** if not recorded elsewhere on flow sheets (physician visits, completion of ordered tests, nonroutine medications, etc.)

BOX 7–6

DOCUMENTING A THERAPEUTIC EVENT

Twenty-four hours after Donald was admitted to the unit with a diagnosis of acute alcoholism, he became disoriented to time, place, and person; was extremely agitated; and was "picking in the air" saying he was trying to "catch the bugs." He was given medication and placed in restraints in a seclusion room with the door open. This was charted as follows:

4:00 PM: Suddenly became agitated. Medicated with Valium, reoriented to place/events in quiet tones as staff paced with him, and reinforced that he would be kept safe. Agitation escalated, unable to remain in one place for longer than 60 seconds, expressed fear of the "things" he was seeing. Agreed to use of restraints to help keep him safe until he could regain control and/or medication becomes effective.

4:15 PM: Procedure explained as Donald was put in seclusion room C and placed in 4-point wrist/ankle restraints without incident or injury. He was informed that door would remain open and a staff member would check on him every 10 minutes or more frequently as needed. Vital signs: B/P 150/90, P 120. Respirations 32.

4:20 PM: Dr. Carter notified of current events.

4:30 PM: Level of agitation reassessed. Donald reports feeling less anxious, but still "jumpy" inside. Remains restless. Restraints continued.

records at a time. Use abbreviations with caution or avoid them in most instances. Although some institutions provide a list of approved abbreviations that identifies the correct meaning (such as those included in Appendix H), abbreviations can be misleading or easily misinterpreted, resulting in misunderstandings and errors with serious consequences. For example, a patient reading his record might not realize that "SOB" stands for short of breath.

Last, but not least, remember to be brief. Entries need to be concise, short, succinct sentences or phrases that provide enough information to communicate your observations, thoughts, and plans. The entry needs to be consistent in style and format to avoid confusion and comply with agency policies. Avoid repetition/ redundancy. Do not rewrite what is already recorded on flow sheets, but do use the progress note to expand on the flow sheet as appropriate and to note the patient's response. For example: when documenting your repeat assessment of a wound, you may chart "no change" (if that is the case) if your baseline or previous observations are recorded.

FORMAT OF NOTE/ENTRY

Several charting formats have been used for documentation. These include: block notes, with a single entry covering an entire shift (e.g., 7 AM–3 PM); narrative timed notes (e.g., 8:30 AM, Ate all of breakfast); and the problem-oriented medical record system (**POMR** or **PORS**) using the **SOAP/SOAPIER** approach (Box 7–7), to name a few. The last format can provide thorough documentation, but it was designed by physicians for episodic care and requires that the entries be tied to a patient problem identified from a problem list.

A system format created by nurses for documentation of frequent/repetitive care is FOCUS CHARTING™. It was designed to encourage looking at the patient from a positive rather than a negative (or problem-oriented) perspective by using precise documentation to record the nursing process. Recording assessment, interventions, and evaluation information in a **DAR** (Data, Action, and Response) format (Box 7–8) facilitates tracking and following what is happening to the patient at any

POMR OR PORS: Problem Oriented Medical Record— a method of recording data about the health status of the patient by focusing on the patient's problems.

SOAP/SOAPIER: format for documentation— subjective, objective, analysis, plan; implementation, evaluation, revision.

DAR: format for documentation—data, action, response.

BOX 7-7

COMPONENTS OF THE SOAP/SOAPIER CHARTING FORMAT

The **SOAP** format is generally used for the initial assessment of the patient. Once the plan of care is implemented and the evaluation process begun, the **SOAPIER** format becomes more appropriate.

Subjective: statements from patient/others
Objective: measurable or observable data
Analysis: interpretations/conclusions based on the subjective and/or objective data
Plan: what is to be done about the identified problem(s)
Implementation: how plan is carried out
Evaluation: patient's response to the interventions
Revision: how the plan of care will be changed

BOX 7–8

COMPONENTS OF THE FOCUS CHARTING™ FORMAT

Focus: Nursing diagnosis, patient problem/concern, sign/symptom, event

Data: Subjective/objective information describing and/or supporting the focus

Action: immediate/future nursing actions based on assessment and consistent with/complimentary to the goals and nursing action recorded in the patient plan of care

Response: Describes the effects of interventions and whether or not the goal/outcome was met

---

given moment. Charting focuses on patient and nursing concerns. The focal point is patient status and the associated nursing care. The "Focus" is always stated to reflect the patient's concern/need rather than a nursing task or medical diagnosis. Box 7–9 highlights some of the distinguishing features of a Focus.

Whatever documentation system you use, an organized format is a method of identifying, working through, and solving the patient's problems. SOAP and DAR help organize your thinking and provide structure, which can promote creative problem solving. Structured communication facilitates consistency between various services and healthcare providers. Compare the charts in Tables 7–1 and 7–2 for a patient with type 2 diabetes (non–insulin-dependent diabetes mellitus) who has an ulceration of the left foot.

A copy of the back page of the interactive plan of care worksheet is included in Figure 7–1. It is an example of one method of documenting by focusing on certain aspects of the nursing process. The DOCUMENTATION section of the interactive plan of care worksheet is divided into three possible areas where documentation is appropriate and may be required in certain agencies. The first section is reassessment data. In this area you will review the patient's initial assessment data to note any changes. Also, data derived from MONITORING focused nursing interventions ("monitor vital signs every shift" or "monitor serum potassium level every 8 hours") are documented in this section. The second documentation area directs attention to the nursing interventions implemented to assist patients in attaining their stated desired outcomes. Examples may include "Assisted patient with ambulation bid" or "Instructed in proper use of a walker." Finally, the third section is the patient's response to your interventions: How well did the patient tolerate his assisted ambulation? Or, did the patient use the walker in the correct manner as demonstrated?

Summary

Documentation of patient care communicates and reflects the individualization of care you provide. Documentation promotes continuity of patient care among the varied healthcare providers and serves as a basis for the evaluation of the care provided. Finally, the documentation process continually reinforces your accountability and responsibility to implement and evaluate the nursing process. As your documentation skills improve, you will save time by consistently using a documentation

BOX 7–9

WHAT IS A FOCUS?

The nurse often speaks of "a focus" for her assessment, diagnosis, and planning of care.

- A patient problem/concern or nursing diagnosis,

FOR EXAMPLE:

> Airway   Nutrition   Fluid excess
> Knowledge deficit: wound care

The "stem" or diagnostic label is taken from the plan of care. You do not need to use time and space to repeat the entire diagnostic statement.

- Signs/symptoms of potential importance

FOR EXAMPLE:

> fever   confusion
> hypotension   nausea
> dysrhythmia   edema

These require monitoring or limited intervention, but if the signs and symptoms persist, a patient problem will be identified and added to the plan of care.

FOR EXAMPLE: Continued nausea can affect fluid volume; sustained dysrhythmias and hypotension may develop into a cardiac output concern.

- Significant event or change in status.

FOR EXAMPLE:

> admission/transfer   seizure activity
> fall out of bed   respiratory arrest

- A single incident may evolve into a patient problem for inclusion in the plan of care.

FOR EXAMPLE: A fall raises concerns about Risk for Injury, or possibly, Altered Thought Processes, if patient is disoriented; or a respiratory arrest may be related to Ineffective Airway Clearance or Ineffective Breathing Pattern.

- Specific standards of care/hospital policy

FOR EXAMPLE:

> admission/discharge   preoperative visit
>   summary   discharge planning
> routine shift assessment

system that focuses on specific issues. Accurate documentation can also help in meeting legal and accreditation requirements.

The last chapter in this text includes a patient case study to help you bring all the steps of the nursing process together. The case study includes information about a new patient, Mr. R. Simmons. His completed nursing database and the physician's admitting orders are provided to assist you in identifying possible nursing diagnoses,

TABLE 7–1. Sample SOAP/IER Charting Format for Richard

DATE	TIME	NUMBER/PROBLEM*	SOAP FORMAT†
6/30/99	1400	1 (Skin Integrity)	**S:** "That hurts" (when tissue surrounding wound palpated). **O:** Scant amount serous drainage on dressing. Wound borders pink. No odor present. **A:** Wound shows early signs of healing, free of infection. **P:** Continue skin care per plan of care.

In order to document more of the nursing process, some institutions have added the following: Implementation, Evaluation, and Review (if plan was altered)

DATE	TIME	NUMBER/PROBLEM*	SOAP FORMAT†
			I: NS irrigation as ordered. Applied wet sterile dressing with paper tape. **E:** Wound clean, no drainage present. Signed: *E. Moore RN*
6/28/99	2100	2 (Pain)	**S:** "Dull, throbbing pain (in left foot), no radiation to other areas." **O:** Muscles tense. Moving about bed, appears uncomfortable. **A:** Persistent pain. **P:** Foot cradle placed on bed. Darvon 65 mg given PO. Signed: *M. Liskin, L.P.N.*
	2130		**E:** Reports pain relieved. Appears relaxed. Signed: *B. Marsh RN*
6/30/99	1100	3 (Knowledge deficit, diabetic teaching)	**S:** Listed questions/concerns of self and wife. (Copy attached to teaching plan.) **O:** Attended group teaching session with wife and read *Understanding Your Diabetes.* **A:** Richard and wife need review of information and practice for insulin administration. **P:** Review questions/concerns and meet with dietitian. **I:** He demonstrated insulin administration technique for wife to observe. Procedure handout sheet for future reference provided to couple. Scheduled meeting for them with dietitian at 1300 today to discuss remaining questions. **E:** Richard more confident in demonstration, performed activity without hesitation, correctly and without hand tremors. Richard explained steps of procedure and reasons for actions to wife. Couple identified resources to contact if questions/problems arise. Signed: *B. Briner, RN*

*As noted on Plan of Care.
†S = Subjective: statements from patient/others.
O = Objective: measurable or observable data.
A = Analysis: interpretations/conclusions based on the subjective and/or objective data.
P = Plan: what is to be done about the identified problem(s).
I = Implementation: how plan is carried out.
E = Evaluation: patient's response to the interventions.
R = Revision: how the plan of care will be changed.

TABLE 7–2. Sample of DAR for Richard

DATE	TIME	FOCUS	DAR FORMAT*
6/30/99	1400	Skin integrity L foot	**D:** Scant amount serous drainage on dressing, wound borders pink, no odor present, denies discomfort except with direct palpation of surrounding tissue **A:** NS irrigation as ordered. Sterile wet dressing applied with paper tape **R:** Wound clean—no drainage present. Signed: *E. Moore RN*
6/28/99	2100	Pain L foot	**D:** Reports dull/throbbing ache L foot—no radiation. Muscles tense, restless in bed. **A:** Foot cradle placed on bed. Darvon 65 mg given PO. Signed: *M. Liskin L.P.N.*
	2200	Pain L foot	**R:** Reports pain relieved. Appears relaxed. Signed: *B. Marsh RN*
6/30/99	1100	Knowledge deficit, diabetic teaching	**D:** Attended group teaching session with wife. Both have read *Understanding Your Diabetes.* **A:** Reviewed list of questions/concerns from Richard and wife. (Copy attached to teaching plan.) Richard demonstrated insulin administration technique for wife to observe. Procedure handout sheet for future reference provided to couple. Scheduled meeting for them with dietitian at 1300 today to discuss remaining questions. **R:** Richard more confident in demonstration, performed activity without hesitation, correctly and without hand tremors. He explained steps of procedure and reasons for actions to wife. Couple identified resources to contact if questions/problems arise. Signed: *B. Briner, RN*

The following is an example of documentation of a patient need/concern that currently does not require identification as a patient problem (nursing diagnosis) or inclusion in the plan of care and therefore not easily documented in the SOAP format:

6/29/99	2020	Gastric distress	**D:** Awakened, from light sleep by "indigestion/burning sensation." Places hand over epigastric area. Skin warm/dry, color pink, vital signs unchanged. **A:** Given Mylanta 30 ml PO. Head of bed elevated approximately 15 degrees. **R:** Reports pain relieved. Appears relaxed, resting quietly. Signed: *E Moore, RN*

*D = Data: subjective/objective information describing and/or supporting the focus.
A = Action: immediate or future nursing actions that address the focus, any changes required for the plan of care.
R = Response: description of patient responses to care provided and whether goals/outcomes are met.
Source: Lampe, S. S. (1997). Focus Charting™. Minneapolis: Creative Nursing Management.

Desired Outcome and Patient Criteria: The Patient will:

PLANNING

TIME OUT! The desired outcome must meet criteria to be accurate. The outcome must be specific, realistic, measurable, and include a time frame for completion. Does the action verb describe the patient's behavior to be evaluated? Can the outcome be used in the evaluation step of the nursing process to measure the patient's response to the nursing interventions listed below?

Interventions	Rationale for Selected Intervention and References

EVALUATION

TIME OUT! Do your interventions assist in achieving the desired outcome? Do your interventions address further monitoring of the patient's response to your interventions and to the achievement of the desired outcome? Are qualifiers: **when, how, amount, time,** and **frequency** used? Is the focus of the action's verb on the nurse's actions and not on the patient? Do your rationales provide sufficient reason and directions?

What was your patient's response to the interventions?

Was the desired outcome achieved?   If no, what revisions to either the desired outcome or interventions would you make?
☐ Yes   ☐ No

DOCUMENTATION

Documentation Focus: Now that you have completed the evaluation, the next step is to document your care and the patient's response. Use the areas below to enter your progress note information.

Reassessment Data:

Interventions Implemented:

Patient's Response:

INSTRUCTOR'S COMMENTS:

FIGURE 7–1. Reverse side of the interaction plan worksheet previously introduced, providing documentation of the nursing process.

developing appropriate desired outcomes for Mr. Simmons, and selecting nursing interventions that will assist him in attaining the desired outcomes.

The final chapter also presents an evaluation checklist that was developed to include the important aspects of all of the American Nurses' Association's Standards of Clinical Nursing Practice detailed throughout this text. This comprehensive evaluation checklist serves as a helpful tool for your self-evaluation and ensures that your assigned written care-planning efforts are correctly accomplished.

1. You are writing a paper regarding documentation. Identify three goals of the documentation process you will include:

   a. _____

   b. _____

   c. _____

2. Steps of the nursing process are documented on which form:

   Steps

   _____ Assessment

   _____ Problem identification

   _____ Planning

   _____ Implementation

   _____ Evaluation

   Form

   a. Plan of care

   b. Progress notes

   c. Patient database

   d. Flow sheets

3. List five functions of progress notes:

   a. _____

   b. _____

   c. _____

   d. _____

   e. _____

4. Complete the following statements describing the JCAHO's standards for documentation.

   a. A medical record is _____ and _____ for every individual assessed or treated. The medical record incorporates information from subsequent contacts between the _____ and _____.

   b. The medical record contains _____ _____ to _____ the patient, support the _____, justify the _____, document the course and results accurately, and facilitate _____ of care among healthcare providers.

5. When documenting for reimbursement, five factors need to be included. These are: _____

   _____

   _____

6. Two ways in which the plan of care can be used for supervision are: _____

   _____

7. The best way to ensure clarity of the progress notes is: _____

   _____

8. Rewrite the following judgmental statements to make them nonjudgmental:

   a. He is uncooperative today. _____

   _____

   b. He is a manipulative patient. _____

   _____

   c. She had a bad attitude about taking her medication this morning. _____

   _____

   d. The new patient is really difficult. _____

   _____

9. List three types of judgmental statements:

   a. _____

   b. _____

   c. _____

10. Name three types of data that are important to record in the progress notes:

    a. _____

    b. _____

    c. _____

11. List five additional factors that can enhance accurate communication:

    a. _____

    b. _____

    c. _____

    d. _____

    e. _____

12. What actions can be taken to correct an error in charting? _____

    _____

13. Name three charting formats:

    a. _____ b. _____ c. _____

14. Read the following Vignette and record the patient data using the SOAP and DAR formats, and the format used in your facility/agency, if different.

VIGNETTE: Sally was discharged home with the twins on the evening of her third postpartal day. On the morning of day 5, she is visited by the public health nurse specializing in maternal/newborn care.

Sally is dressed in a robe and slippers, her hair is uncombed, her color is pale, and she has dark circles under her eyes. She is sitting in a recliner, bottle-feeding Baby A. Her mother is sitting on the couch feeding Baby B. Living area is noted to be clean and neat with comfortable ambient temperature. The two older children are reported to be at preschool from 9:00 AM to 2:30 PM daily.

Postpartal assessment form is completed with physical findings within normal limits. Sally reports that her bowels are working "slowly" (small, firm BM this AM) with fluid intake approximately 2 liters per day and moderate appetite—"just too tired to really eat or do anything else." Sally's mother indicates she is providing household assistance—cooking, cleaning, and child care. Sally and her mother agree fatigue is a major concern for Sally. Both Sally and her mother are up twice during the night to feed the twins. Sally does take short naps during the day. Sally is observed to display usual attachment behaviors toward Baby A (Laura); however, her interaction with Baby B (unnamed) is of short duration, appears to lack warmth, and is restricted to caretaking activities.

You provide Sally with a teaching sheet describing postpartal fatigue and discussing dietary needs/supplements, energy conservation techniques, and the importance of balanced activity/exercise and rest. You suggest Sally's husband might get up for one feeding during the night to allow her a longer period of uninterrupted sleep and provide him with additional opportunity for interaction with his daughters.

Next, you ask Sally how she feels about being the mother of twins. Sally becomes tearful and states, "I just don't know what I'm going to do when Mom goes home." You ask if she would like to have a visit from a member of the Mothers of Multiples group. You also suggest having a family meeting to problem-solve her concerns. You then discuss your observation that Sally appears more comfortable with Laura than with her twin, asking Sally to describe her perceptions of and feelings for Baby B. After reflecting on the question, Sally says she has felt so overwhelmed that she hasn't truly accepted the reality of having twins. She is visibly upset, berating herself for being a "poor mother." You tell her that it is not unusual to be overwhelmed by the reality of a multiple birth, even when planned for in advance of delivery.

You ask Sally to think about what she needs to help her resolve this situation. Sally decides she needs to spend more time getting to know Baby B, allowing other family members to care for and interact with Laura. Following a discussion about the individual characteristics of her other children, Sally says Baby B is unique in her level of alertness and her "acceptance" of anyone who cares for her. "She deserves a name reflecting family ties and thanksgiving for the special gift of twins." You encourage Sally to read the literature about twins provided before her discharge and to apply techniques she has found successful in dealing with previous stressful situations. You schedule a follow-up visit for 1 week and leave a contact number if Sally has any questions or needs assistance before your next visit. When you depart, Sally appears focused on ways to improve her current situation—smiling, displaying a lighter mood, and giving a firm handshake.

POMR/SOAP FORMAT: Problem: _____

S: _____

_____

O: _____

_____

A: _____

P: _____

I: _____

E: _____

R: _____

DAR FORMAT: Focus: _____

D: _____

_____

_____

_____

A: _____

_____

_____

_____

R: _____

_____

_____

_____

FORMAT USED IN YOUR INSTITUTION/AGENCY, if different: _____

_____

_____

_____

BIBLIOGRAPHY

Lampe, S. S. (1997). *Focus Charting™*. Minneapolis: Creative Nursing Management.

SUGGESTED READINGS

Burke, L. J. (1995). *Charting by Exception Applications: Making It Work in Clinical Settings*. Albany: Delmar.
Burke, L. J. (1998). *Charting Made Incredibly Easy*. Springhouse, PA: Springhouse.

Eggland, E. T., & Eggland, N. H. (1999). *Nursing Documentation: Charting, Recording, and Reporting.* Philadelphia: J.B. Lippincott, Williams & Wilkins.

Fischbach, F. T. (1991). *Documenting Care: Communication, the Nursing Process and Documentation Standards.* Philadelphia: F.A. Davis.

Iyer, P. W., & Camp, N. H. (1999). *Nursing Documentation: A Nursing Process Approach,* ed 3. St. Louis: Mosby.

Kerr, S. D. (1992). A comparison of four nursing documentation systems. *Journal of Nursing Staff Development, 8*(1):26–31.

(1999). *Mastering Documentation,* ed 2. Springhouse, PA: Springhouse.

Meiner, S. (1999). *Nursing Documentation: Legal Focus Across Practice Settings.* Corwin.

Yocum, F. (1993). *Documentation Skills for Quality Patient Care.* Tipp City, OH: Awareness Productions.

CHAPTER 8

Interactive Care Planning: From Assessment to Patient Response

This final chapter provides you the opportunity to apply and evaluate the steps of the nursing process presented in the previous chapters. A case study based on simulated assessment data gathered on your patient, Mr. Simmons, and the inclusion of physician admission orders add to the realism of this nursing process exercise. The objective and subjective data are organized within the Doenges and Moorhouse 13 diagnostic divisions assessment tool, which was described earlier in Chapter 2. (A copy of the complete assessment tool is available for your future use in Appendix B.)

Instructions for Case Study

First, read over the admitting physician's orders and reflect on how your implementation of these orders will assist you in structuring Mr. Simmons' plan of care. After reviewing the physician's orders, review the extensive patient database gathered on

Mr. Simmons. As you study the database, start to record or highlight those subjective and objective cues that suggest a problem or need and may be similar to the defining characteristics of possible nursing diagnoses for Mr. Simmons.

One purpose of this exercise is for you to identify two accurate nursing diagnoses. The accuracy of your nursing diagnoses depends on the availability of the subjective and objective data gathered during the admission history and physical examination and the subsequent matching of these data with the defining characteristics of the nursing diagnoses described by NANDA. Remember, all the NANDA nursing diagnoses, their related/risk factors, and their defining characteristics are included in Appendix A.

To further assist you in comparing Mr. Simmons' assessment data with the defining characteristics of possible nursing diagnoses, Table 8–1 presents the 13 diagnostic divisions with selected associated NANDA nursing diagnoses. By reviewing this information, you will be able to better visualize the relationship between the varied nursing diagnoses and the focused assessments of the different diagnostic divisions.

For example, when analysing the patient's assessment data gathered in the **ELIMINATION** diagnostic division, if abnormal subjective and/or objective data are present, your next step would be to direct your attention to Table 8–1. Review the

TABLE 8–1. Nursing Diagnoses Organized According to Diagnostic Divisions

After data have been collected and areas of concern/need have been identified, consult the Diagnostic Divisions framework to review the list of nursing diagnoses that fall within the individual categories. This will assist you with the choice of the specific diagnostic labels to accurately describe the data from the patient database. Then, with the addition of etiology (when known) and signs and symptoms, the patient diagnostic statement emerges.

Diagnostic Division: Activity/Rest: Ability to engage in necessary/desired activities of life (work and leisure) and to obtain adequate sleep/rest

Diagnoses
Activity intolerance [specify level]
Activity intolerance, risk for
Disuse Syndrome, risk for
Diversional Activity deficit
Fatigue
Mobility, impaired bed
Mobility, impaired wheelchair
Sleep Deprivation
Sleep Pattern disturbance
Transfer Ability, impaired
Walking, impaired

Diagnostic Division Circulation: Ability to transport oxygen and nutrients necessary to meet cellular needs

Diagnoses
Adaptive Capacity: Intracranial, decreased
[Autonomic] Dysreflexia
Autonomic Dysreflexia, risk for
Cardiac Output, decreased
Tissue Perfusion, altered [specify]; cerebral, cardiopulmonary, renal, gastrointestinal, peripheral

Continued

TABLE 8–1. Nursing Diagnoses Organized According to
Diagnostic Divisions (Continued)

Diagnostic Division: Ego Integrity: Ability to develop and use skills and behaviors to integrate and manage life experiences

Diagnoses
Adjustment, impaired
Anxiety [specify level]
Anxiety, death
Body Image disturbance
Coping, defensive
Coping, Individual, ineffective
Decisional Conflict (specify)
Denial, ineffective
Energy Field, disturbance
Fear
Grieving, anticipatory
Grieving, dysfunctional
Hopelessness
Loneliness, risk for
Personal Identity disturbance
Post-Trauma Syndrome
Post-Trauma Syndrome, risk for
Powerlessness
Rape-Trauma Syndrome
Rape-Trauma Syndrome: compound reaction
Rape-Trauma Syndrome: silent reaction
Relocation Stress syndrome
Self-Esteem, chronic low
Self-Esteem, disturbance
Self-Esteem, situational low
Sorrow, chronic
Spiritual Distress
Spiritual Distress, risk for
Spiritual Well-Being, potential for enhanced

Diagnostic Division: Elimination: Ability to excrete waste products

Diagnoses
Bowel Incontinence
Constipation
Constipation, perceived
Constipation, risk for
Diarrhea
Urinary Elimination, altered patterns
Urinary Incontinence, functional
Urinary Incontinence, reflex
Urinary Incontinence, risk for urge
[Urinary] Incontinence, stress
[Urinary] Incontinence, total
[Urinary] Incontinence, urge
Urinary Retention [acute/chronic]

Diagnostic Division: Food/Fluid: Ability to maintain intake of and utilize nutrients and liquids to meet physiological needs

Diagnoses
Breastfeeding, effective
Breastfeeding, ineffective

Continued

TABLE 8–1. Nursing Diagnoses Organized According to Diagnostic Divisions (Continued)

Breastfeeding, interrupted
Dentition, altered
Failure to Thrive, adult
Fluid Volume deficit [hypo/hypertonic]
Fluid Volume deficit [isotonic]
Fluid Volume, risk for deficit
Fluid Volume excess
Fluid Volume, risk for imbalance
Infant Feeding Pattern, ineffective
Nausea
Nutrition: altered, less than body requirements
Nutrition: altered, more than body requirements
Nutrition: altered, risk for more than body requirements
Oral Mucous Membrane, altered
Swallowing, impaired

Diagnostic Division: Hygiene: Ability to perform activities of daily living

Diagnoses
Self-Care deficit (specify): feeding, bathing/hygiene, dressing/grooming, toileting

Diagnostic Division: Neurosensory: Ability to perceive, integrate, and respond to internal and external cues

Diagnoses
Confusion, acute
Confusion, chronic
Infant Behavior: disorganized
Infant Behavior: risk for disorganized
Infant Behavior: organized potential for enhanced
Memory, impaired
Peripheral Neurovascular, risk for dysfunction
Sensory-Perceptual alterations (specify): visual, auditory, kinesthetic, gustatory, tactile, olfactory
Thought Processes, altered
Unilateral Neglect

Diagnostic Division: Pain/Discomfort: Ability to control internal/external environment to maintain comfort

Diagnoses
Pain [acute]
Pain, chronic

Diagnostic Division: Respiration: Ability to provide and use oxygen to meet physiologic needs

Diagnoses
Airway Clearance, ineffective
Aspiration, risk for
Breathing Pattern, ineffective
Gas Exchange, impaired
Spontaneous Ventilation, inability to sustain
Ventilatory Weaning Response, dysfunctional (DVWR)

Diagnostic Division: Safety: Ability to provide safe, growth-promoting environment

Diagnoses
Body Temperature, risk for altered
Environmental Interpretation Syndrome, impaired

Continued

TABLE 8–1. Nursing Diagnoses Organized According to Diagnostic Divisions (Continued)

Health Maintenance, altered
Home Maintenance Management, impaired
Hyperthermia
Hypothermia
Infection, risk for
Injury, risk for
Latex Allergy
Latex Allergy, risk for
Mobility, impaired physical
Perioperative Positioning Injury, risk for
Poisoning, risk for
Protection, altered
Self-Mutilation, risk for
Skin Integrity, impaired
Skin Integrity, risk for impaired
Suffocation, risk for
Surgical Recovery, delayed
Thermoregulation, ineffective
Tissue Integrity, impaired
Trauma, risk for
Violence, [actual]/risk for directed at others
Violence, [actual]/risk for self-directed

Diagnostic Division: Sexuality: [Component of Ego Integrity and Social Interaction] Ability to meet requirement/characteristics of male/female role

Diagnoses
Sexual Dysfunction
Sexuality Patterns, altered

Diagnostic Division: Social Interaction: Ability to establish and maintain relationships

Diagnoses
Caregiver Role Strain
Caregiver Role Strain, risk for
Communication, impaired verbal
Community Coping, ineffective
Community Coping, potential for enhanced
Family Coping, ineffective: compromised
Family Coping, ineffective: disabling
Family Coping: potential for growth
Family Processes, altered
Family Processes, altered: alcoholism
Parent/Infant/Child Attachment, risk for altered
Parental Role conflict
Parenting, altered
Parenting, risk for altered
Role Performance, altered
Social Interaction, impaired
Social Isolation

Diagnostic Division: Teaching/Learning: Ability to incorporate and use information to achieve healthy lifestyle/optimal wellness

Diagnoses
Development, risk for altered
Growth and Development, altered

Continued

TABLE 8–1. Nursing Diagnoses Organized According to Diagnostic Divisions (Continued)

Growth, risk for altered
Health-Seeking Behaviors (specify)
Knowledge Deficit [Learning need] (specify)
Noncompliance [Compliance, altered] (specify)
Therapeutic Regimen: Community, ineffective management
Therapeutic Regimen: Families, ineffective management
Therapeutic Regimen: Individual, effective management
Therapeutic Regimen: Individual, ineffective management

12 NANDA nursing diagnoses associated with the Elimination diagnostic division. To help you in this analysis, Box 8–1 displays the diagnostic division of Elimination and the 12 associated nursing diagnoses. Once you have identified a possible nursing diagnosis from the Elimination division, your next task is to review the defining characteristics of that nursing diagnosis (Appendix A) and determine if there is an accurate match with your data. Box 8–2 provides an abbreviated checklist to assist you as you begin diagnosing and constructing plans of care.

Case Study Care Planning Worksheet

Use the case study care planning worksheets on pages 175–182 to enter your two patient diagnostic statements (NANDA nursing diagnosis label, the related factors [etiologies], and evidence of signs/symptoms you used in making the diagnosis) for Mr. Simmons. Then use the worksheets to list two outcome statements for each of

---

BOX 8–1

ELIMINATION DIAGNOSTIC DIVISION AND NURSING DIAGNOSES

Elimination: ability to excrete waste products

Associated Nursing Diagnoses

Bowel Incontinence
Constipation
Constipation, perceived
Constipation, risk for
Diarrhea
Urinary Elimination, altered
Urinary Incontinence, functional
Urinary Incontinence, reflex
Urinary Incontinence, risk for urge
[Urinary] Incontinence, stress
[Urinary] Incontinence, total
[Urinary] Incontinence, urge
Urinary Retention [acute/chronic]

BOX 8–2

DIAGNOSTIC DECISION MAKING

1. Read the physician's admitting orders.
2. Review all of the data included in the 13 diagnostic divisions. Pay particular attention to Mr. Simmons' subjective data, which describe his perception of his illness and his responses to the various healthcare problems described.
3. Review the discharge considerations section at the end of the assessment tool. Can this information assist you in accurately identifying his nursing diagnoses?
4. Record or highlight any abnormal responses or observations identified while reviewing Mr. Simmons' assessment data.
5. Review the assessment tool's individual diagnostic divisions where you recorded or highlighted abnormal data.
6. In those divisions where abnormal data were highlighted, review the nursing diagnoses associated with the Diagnostic Division (see Table 8–1).
7. Select a possible nursing diagnosis from the diagnostic division.
8. Review the defining characteristics of your selected possible nursing diagnosis (see Appendix A).
9. Compare the recorded or highlighted data with the selected nursing diagnosis' defining characteristics. Is there sufficient match? _____ (refer to Appendix E, Lunney's Scale.) "Yes": move to step 10. "No": return to the assessment tool and ensure you have reviewed all the appropriate data. If your review is sufficient, then return to step 6 because another possible nursing diagnosis may be appropriate for consideration.
10. Once you have decided on an accurate nursing diagnosis, complete the patient diagnostic statement by adding the related factor(s) specific to Mr. Simmons' situation (refer again to Appendix A).
11. Now develop a patient outcome statement for Mr. Simmons' identified nursing diagnosis. Two options are available for this step.
    a. Look at the nursing diagnosis and define how Mr. Simmons could resolve this identified response to his healthcare problem. For example, if his nursing diagnosis is Anxiety, an appropriate path in the development of an outcome statement would include "a reduction or elimination of his identified anxiety."
    b. A second strategy in outcome statement development is to review the *related factor(s)* and develop an outcome reflecting either elimination or reduction of the related factor(s). For example, if the Anxiety is determined to be related to a change in health status, then his outcome statement could reflect a correction in health status or return to premorbid state, or in this case, more appropriately, an increase in Mr. Simmons' control of his condition.

Continued

> ## DIAGNOSTIC DECISION MAKING (Continued)
>
> **12.** Once you have developed the outcome statements for Mr. Simmons, your attention must now turn to selecting appropriate nursing interventions to assist him in achieving the desired outcome. Several methods can be employed to assist you in selecting nursing interventions.
>
> **FOR EXAMPLE:** Your assigned medical-surgical or fundamentals texts are excellent resources for nursing interventions and their rationales. Other resources include care planning guides (such as Doenges, Moorhouse, and Geissler's *Nursing Care Plans,* ed 5, 2000) or nursing diagnoses handbooks (such as Doenges and Moorhouse's *Nurse's Pocket Guide,* ed 7, 2000) that provide outcome statements and nursing interventions for each NANDA nursing diagnosis.
>
> **13.** Repeat steps 6–12 for your second nursing diagnosis.

the diagnostic statements you have identified for Mr. Simmons. Next, select at least three nursing interventions that will assist Mr. Simmons in achieving the two measurable outcome statements you have listed and record them in the space provided on the worksheets.

The two-page Interactive Care Plan Worksheet described can also assist you during this care planning and evaluation exercise. Review the TIME OUT sections to further assist you in accurately complying with the criteria required for developing accurate diagnostic statements, constructing patient outcome statements, and selecting appropriate nursing interventions.

Care Planning Evaluation Checklist

The evaluation checklist (Fig. 8–1) is included in this chapter to provide a workable guide for constructing Mr. Simmons' plan of care as well as future care planning assignments. The evaluation checklist was designed to include the criteria presented in the TIME OUT sections of the Interactive Care Plan Worksheets, the requirements of the ANA's Standards of Clinical Nursing Practice presented in the previous chapters, and the current standards for JCAHO Management of Information. An additional copy of the checklist is included so that you'll be able to take it with you to your assigned nursing unit and use it to help construct plans of care and evaluate your implementation of the steps of the nursing process.

Use the evaluation checklist after you have documented your first attempts at identifying Mr. Simmons' two nursing diagnoses, his two measurable outcome statements, and the appropriate nursing interventions for each outcome statement. Review the checklist's criteria against your completed case study care plan worksheet for feedback on how well your plan of care for Mr. Simmons is being accomplished.

Conclusion

The nursing process steps described in this text are an integral part of the day-to-day science and practice of nursing. Regardless of the nursing practice setting you choose, the steps of the nursing process are universal in their application.

CRITERIA	Yes	No	Instructor's Comments

1. Patient assessment data include areas of biophysical, psychosocial, environmental, self-care, and/or discharge planning.
2. Appropriate assessment techniques used (interviewing, questioning).
3. Assessment data are documented in appropriate manner (nursing history form, progress note, flow sheet).
4. Patient diagnostic statement is accurately derived from assessment data.
5. Patient diagnostic statement is verified against NANDA defining characteristics and related factors.
6. Patient diagnostic statement is verified with patient, significant other(s), and/or other healthcare providers.
7. Patient's desired outcome is derived from the identified diagnostic statement.
8. Outcome is specific to the identified diagnostic statement.
9. Outcome is realistic in relation to the patient's current and potential resources and capabilities.
10. Outcome is attainable in relation to the patient's current and potential resources and capabilities.
11. Outcome includes a realistic time frame for attainment.
12. Outcome is mutually formulated with patient and/or significant other(s).
13. Plan of care includes nursing interventions based on the identified patient diagnostic statement and the desired outcome.
14. Selected nursing interventions assist the patient in attaining the desired outcome.
15. Interventions include monitoring the patient's response to the implemented nursing interventions.
16. Interventions include monitoring the patient's response toward the attainment of the outcome.
17. Interventions include the qualifiers of who, what, how, amount, time, and frequency.
18. The action verb describing the nursing intervention focuses on the nurse's behavior, not the patient's.

FIGURE 8–1. Evaluation checklist for Interactive Care Plan Worksheets. (Adapted in part from ANA Standards of Clinical Nursing Practice and the Joint Commission Standards for Management of Information.)

CRITERIA	Yes	No	Instructor's Comments

19. Interventions are implemented in a safe manner.
20. Rationale included for a selected nursing intervention thoroughly explains the reason for selection and the desired effect of implementation.
21. Reassessment is used to revise patient diagnostic statements, desired outcomes, and/or nursing interventions.
22. Evaluation includes the patient's response to implemented nursing interventions.
23. Evaluation includes the patient's progress toward desired outcome attainment.
24. Documentation of patient care includes reassessment data.
25. Documentation of patient care includes reference to nursing interventions implemented.
26. Documentation of patient care includes reference to the patient's response to nursing interventions.

FIGURE 8–1. (Continued)

It is our hope that this interactive approach was helpful in learning and using the steps of the nursing process. The several interactive approaches were all designed to assist in your development of the necessary cognitive, affective, and psychomotor learning skills required to successfully apply the decision-making steps used in the nursing process. We extend our best wishes to you as you begin your nursing career.

Putting Together What You Have Learned About the Nursing Process

Review the following vignette and nursing history. Then, create a plan of care for your patient, Mr. Simmons. Identify two patient problems/needs and write the patient diagnostic statement and two outcomes. Choose three interventions for each patient diagnostic statement.

VIGNETTE: Mr. R. Simmons, who has had type 2 diabetes for 5 years, presented to his physician's office with a nonhealing ulcer on his left foot, of 3 weeks' duration. Laboratory studies at that time revealed blood glucose of 356 per fingerstick and Chemstix of 2%. Because of distance from medical provider and lack of local community services, he is admitted to the hospital.

ADMITTING PHYSICIAN'S ORDERS

Culture/sensitivity and Gram stain of foot ulcer
Random blood glucose on admission and finger stick BG qid
CBC, electrolytes, glycosylated Hb in AM
Chest x-ray and ECG in AM
Diabeta 10 mg PO bid
Glucophage 500 mg PO qd to start, will increase gradually
Humulin N insulin 10 U q AM and hs. Begin insulin instruction for postdis-
  charge self-care if necessary
Dicloxacillin 500 mg PO q6h; start after culture obtained
Darvocet-N 100 mg q4h prn for pain
Diet—2400 calories ADA/three meals with two snacks
Up in chair ad lib with feet elevated
Foot cradle for bed
Irrigate lesion L foot with NS tid, then cover with wet-to-dry sterile dressing
Vital signs bid

PATIENT ASSESSMENT DATABASE

Name: R. Simmons   **Informant:** Patient
Reliability (Scale 1–4): 3
Age: 67   **DOB:** 5/3/31   **Race:** Caucasian   **Gender:** M
Adm. date: 6/28/98   **Time:** 7 PM   **From:** Home

ACTIVITY/REST

Reports (Subjective)

Occupation: Farmer
Usual activities/hobbies: reading, playing cards. "Don't have time to do much. Anyway, I'm too tired
  most of the time to do anything after the chores."
Limitations imposed by illness: "I have to watch what I order if I eat out."
Sleep: Hours: 6–8 hr/night   **Naps:** no   **Aids:** no
Insomnia: "not unless I drink coffee after supper." Usually feels rested when awakens at 4:30 AM; has
  been feeling fatigued last several weeks. Up 1 or 2 times at night to void.

Exhibits (Objective)

Observed response to activity: limps, favors L foot when walking
Mental status: alert/active
Neuro/muscular assessment: muscle mass/tone: bilaterally equal/firm
  Posture: erect   **ROM:** full all extremities
  Strength: equal three extremities/favors L foot currently

CIRCULATION

Reports (Subjective)

Slow healing: lesion L foot, 3 weeks' duration
Extremities: numbness/tingling: "My feet feel cold and tingling like sharp pins poking the bottom of my feet when I walk the quarter mile to the mailbox."
Cough/character of sputum: occ./white
Change in frequency/amount of urine: yes/voiding more lately

Exhibits (Objective)

Peripheral pulses: radials 3 + ; popliteal, dorsalis, postibial/pedal, all 1 +
B/P: R: Lying: 146/90   **Sit:** 140/86   **Stand:** 138/90
      L: Lying: 142/88   **Sit:** 138/88   **Stand:** 138/84
Pulse: Apical: 86   **Radial:** 86   **Quality:** strong   **Rhythm:** regular
Chest auscultations: few wheezes clear with cough, no murmurs/rubs
Jugular vein distention: -0-
Extremities:
   Temperature: feet cool bilat./legs warm
   Color: skin: legs pale
   Capillary refill: slow both feet (approx 5 sec)
   Homan's sign: -0-   **Varicosities:** few enlarged superficial veins both calves
   Nails: toenails thickened, yellow, brittle
   Distribution and quality of hair: coarse hair to midcalf, none on ankles/toes
Color: General: ruddy face/arms   **Mucous membranes/lips:** pink
   Nailbeds: blanch well   **Conjunctiva and sclera:** white

EGO INTEGRITY

Reports (Subjective)

Stress factors: "normal farmer's problems: weather, pests, bankers, etc."
Ways of handling stress: "I get busy with the chores and talk things over with my livestock, they listen pretty good."
Financial concerns: no insurance, needs to hire someone to do chores while here.
Relationship status: married
Cultural factors: rural/agrarian, eastern European descent "American, no ethnic ties."
Religion: Protestant/practicing
Lifestyle: middle class/self-sufficient farmer
Recent changes: no
Feelings: "I'm in control of most things, except the weather and this diabetes." Concerned re possible therapy change "from pills to shots."

Exhibits (Objective)

Emotional status: generally calm; appears frustrated
Observed physiological response(s): occasionally sighs deeply/frowns, shrugs shoulders/throws up hands, shoulders tense, fidgeting with coin

ELIMINATION

Reports (Subjective)

Usual bowel pattern: most every PM
Last BM: last night   **Character of stool:** firm/brown
Bleeding: -0-   **Hemorrhoids:** -0-   **Constipation:** occ.
Laxative used: hot prune juice
Urinary: no problems, has been voiding more frequently/gets up 1 or 2 times to void during night
   Character of urine: pale yellow

Exhibits (Objective)

Abd. tender: no   **Soft/firm:** soft   **Palpable mass:** none
Bowel sounds: active all four quads

FOOD/FLUID

Reports (Subjective)

Usual diet (type): 2400 ADA (occ. "cheats" with dessert, "My wife watches it pretty closely.")
No. of meals daily: 3/1 snack
Dietary pattern:
   B: fruit juice/toast/ham/decaf coffee
   L: meat/potatoes/veg/fruit/milk
   D: meat sandwich/soup/fruit/decaf coffee
   Snack: milk/crackers at hs.   **Usual beverage:** skim milk, 2–3 cups decaf coffee, and drinks lots of water
Last meal/intake: Dinner: roast beef sandwich, vegetable soup, pear with cheese, decaf coffee
Loss of appetite: "Never, but lately I don't feel as hungry as usual."
Nausea/vomiting: -0-   **Food allergies:** none
Heartburn/food intolerance: cabbage causes gas, coffee after supper causes heartburn
Mastication/swallowing probs: no   **Dentures:** partial upper plate
Usual weight: 175   **Recent changes:** has lost about 4 lbs this month.
Diuretic therapy: no

Exhibits (Objective)

Wt: 171 lb   **Ht:** 5'10"   **Build:** stocky   **Skin turgor:** good/leathery
Appearance of tongue: midline, pink   **Mucous membranes:** pink, intact
Condition of teeth/gums: good, no irritation/bleeding noted
Breath sounds: few wheezes cleared with cough
Bowel sounds: active all four quads
Urine Chemstix 2%/**Fingerstick** 356 (Dr office) random BG drawn on adm.

HYGIENE

Reports (Subjective)

Activities of daily living: independent in all areas
Preferred time of bath: PM

Exhibits (Objective)

General appearance: clean, shaven, short cut hair, hands rough and dry, skin on feet dry, cracked and scaly, no body odor
Scalp & eyebrows: scaly white patches

NEUROSENSORY

Reports (Subjective)

Headache: "Occasionally behind my eyes when I worry too much."
Tingling/Numbness: feet, once or twice a week (as noted)
Eyes: vision loss; far-sighted, seems a little blurry   **Exam:** 2 yr ago
Ears: Hearing loss   **R:** "some"   **L:** no (has not been tested)
Nose: Epistaxis: -0-   **Sense of smell:** states no problem

Exhibits (Objective)

Mental status: alert; oriented to time, place, person, situation
  Affect: concerned   **Memory: Remote/Recent:** clear and intact
Speech: clear/coherent, appropriate
Pupil reaction: PERLA/small   **Glasses:** reading   **Hearing Aid:** no
Handgrip/release: strong/equal

PAIN/DISCOMFORT

Reports (Subjective)

Location: medial aspect, heel of L foot   **Intensity (0–10):** 4–5   **Quality:** dull ache with occ. sharp stabbing sensation
Frequency/duration: "Seems like all the time."   **Radiation:** no
Precipitating factors: shoes, walking   **How relieved:** ASA, not helping
Other complaints: sometimes has back pain following chores/heavy lifting, relieved by ASA/liniment rubdown.

Exhibits (Objective)

Facial grimacing: when lesion border palpated
Guarding affected area: pulls foot away   **Narrowed focus:** no
Emotional response: tense, irritated

RESPIRATION

Reports (Subjective)

Dyspnea: -0-   **Cough:** occ. morning cough, white sputum
Emphysema: -0-   **Bronchitis:** -0-   **Asthma:** -0-   **Tuberculosis:** -0-
Smoker: filters   **Pack/day:** 1/2   **No. of pack years:** 25 +
Use of respiratory aids: -0-

Exhibits (Objective)

Respiratory rate: 22   **Depth:** good   **Symmetry:** equal, bilateral
Auscultation: few wheezes, clear with cough
Cyanosis: -0-   **Clubbing of fingers:** -0-
Sputum characteristics: none to observe
Mentation/restlessness: alert/oriented/relaxed

SAFETY

Reports (Subjective)

Allergies: -0-   **Blood transfusions:** -0-
Sexually transmitted disease: none
Fractures/dislocations: L clavicle, 1962, fell getting off tractor
Arthritis/unstable joints: "I think I've got some in my knees."
Back problems: occ. lower back pain
Vision impaired: requires glasses for reading
Hearing impaired: slightly (R), compensates by turning "good ear" toward speaker

Exhibits (Objective)

Temperature: 99.4°F tympanic
Skin integrity: impaired L foot   **Scars:** R inguinal, surgical
Rashes: -0-   **Bruises:** -0-   **Lacerations:** -0-   **Blisters:** -0-
  Ulcerations: medial aspect L foot, 2.5 cm diameter, approx. 3 mm deep, draining sm. amt. cream
    color/pink-tinged matter, no odor noted
Strength (general): equal all extremities   **Muscle tone:** firm
ROM: good   **Gait:** favors L foot   **Paresthesia/Paralysis:** -0-

SEXUALITY: MALE

Reports (Subjective)

Sexually active: yes   **Use of condoms:** no (monogamous)
Recent changes in frequency/interest: "I've been too tired lately."
Penile discharge: -0-   **Prostate disorder:** -0-   **Vasectomy:** -0-
Last proctoscopic exam: 2 yr ago   **Prostate exam:** 1 yr ago
Practice self-exam: Breast/testicles: No
Problems/complaints: "I don't have any problems, but you'd have to ask my wife if there are any
  complaints."

Exhibits (Objective)

Exam: Breast: no masses   **Testicles:** deferred   **Prostate:** deferred

SOCIAL INTERACTIONS

Reports (Subjective)

Marital status: married 43 yr   **Living with:** wife
Report of problems: none
Extended family: one daughter lives in town (30 miles away); one daughter married/grandson, living
    out of state
Other: several couples, he and wife play cards/socialize 2–3 times/month
Role: works farm alone; husband/father/grandfather
Report of problems related to illness/condition: none until now
Coping behaviors: "My wife and I have always talked things out. You know the 11th commandment is
    `Thou shalt not go to bed angry.' "

Exhibits (Objective)

Speech: clear, intelligible
Verbal/nonverbal communication with family/SO(s): speaks quietly with wife, looking her in the
    eye; relaxed posture
Family interaction patterns: wife sitting at bedside, relaxed, both reading paper, making occasional
    comments to each other

TEACHING/LEARNING

Reports (Subjective)

Dominant language: English   **Second language:** no   **Literate:** yes
Education level: 2 yr college
Health and illness beliefs/practices/customs: "I take care of the minor problems and only see the
    doctor when something's broken."
Familial risk factors/relationship:
   Diabetes: Uncle   **Tuberculosis:** brother died, age 27
   Heart Disease: f. died, age 78, heart attack
   Strokes: mo. died, age 81   **High B/P:** mo.
Prescribed medications: Drug: Diabeta   **Dose:** 10 mg   **Schedule:** 8 AM/6 PM. Last dose 6 PM today
   Purpose: control diabetes
   Does patient take medications regularly? yes
Home glucose monitoring: "Stopped several months ago when I ran out of TesTape. It was always
    negative anyway."
Nonprescription (OTC) drugs: occ. ASA
   Use of alcohol (amount/frequency): socially, occ. beer
   Tobacco: 1/2 pack/day
Admitting diagnosis (physician): hyperglycemia and nonhealing lesion L foot
Reason for hospitalization (patient): "Sore on foot and the doctor is concerned about my blood
    sugar, and says I'm supposed to learn this fingerstick test now."
History of current complaint: "Three weeks ago I got a blister on my foot from breaking in my new
    boots. It got sore so I lanced it, but it isn't getting any better."
Patient's expectations of this hospitalization: "Clear up this infection and control my diabetes."
Other relevant illness and/or previous hospitalizations/surgeries: 1969 R inguinal hernia repair
Evidence of failure to improve: lesion L foot, 3 wk
Last physical exam: complete 1 yr ago, office follow-up 3 mo ago

DISCHARGE CONSIDERATIONS (AS OF 6/28)

Anticipated discharge: 7/1/98 (3 days)

Resources: self; wife   **Financial:** "If this doesn't take too long to heal, we got some savings to cover things."   **Community supports:** Diabetic Support Group (has not participated)

Anticipated lifestyle changes: become more involved in management of condition

Assistance needed: may require farm help for several days

Teaching: learn new medication regimen and wound care; review diet, encourage smoking cessation

Referral: Supplies: Downtown Pharmacy or AARP

Equipment: Glucometer—AARP

Follow-up: primary care provider 1 wk after discharge to evaluate wound healing and potential need for additional changes in diabetic regimen.

Worksheets for Students' Future Use

INTERACTIVE CARE PLAN WORKSHEET

Student Name:

Patient's Medical Diagnosis:

NURSING DIAGNOSIS		
DEFINITION:		
DEFINING CHARACTERISTICS:		
RELATED FACTORS:		
STUDENT INSTRUCTIONS:	In the space below enter the subjective and objective data gathered during your patient assessment.	

A S S E S S M E N T

Subjective Data Entry

Objective Data Entry

TIME OUT!

Student Instructions: To be sure your patient diagnostic statement written below is accurate, you need to review the defining characteristics and related factors associated with the nursing diagnosis and see how your patient data match. Do you have an accurate match or are additional data required or does another nursing diagnosis need to be investigated?

D I A G N O S I S

PATIENT DIAGNOSTIC STATEMENT:	Nursing Diagnosis (specify) _____
	_____
	Related to _____
	_____

175

Desired Outcome and Patient Criteria:	The Patient will:
TIME OUT!	The desired outcome must meet criteria to be accurate. The outcome must be specific, realistic, measurable, and include a time frame for completion. Does the action verb describe the patient's behavior to be evaluated? Can the outcome be used in the evaluation step of the nursing process to measure the patient's response to the nursing interventions listed below?

PLANNING

Interventions	Rationale for Selected Intervention and References

EVALUATION

TIME OUT!	Do your interventions assist in achieving the desired outcome? Do your interventions address further monitoring of the patient's response to your interventions and to the achievement of the desired outcome? Are qualifiers: **when, how, amount, time,** and **frequency** used? Is the focus of the action's verb on the nurse's actions and not on the patient? Do your rationales provide sufficient reason and directions?

What was your patient's response to the interventions?

Was the desired outcome achieved?   If no, what revisions to either the desired outcome or interventions would you make?
☐ Yes ☐ No

Documentation Focus: Now that you have completed the evaluation, the next step is to document your care and the patient's response. Use the areas below to enter your progress note information.

Reassessment Data:

Interventions Implemented:

Patient's Response:

DOCUMENTATION

INSTRUCTOR'S COMMENTS:

Worksheets for Students' Future Use

INTERACTIVE CARE PLAN WORKSHEET

Student Name:

NURSING DIAGNOSIS

Patient's Medical Diagnosis:

DEFINITION:

DEFINING CHARACTERISTICS:

RELATED FACTORS:

STUDENT INSTRUCTIONS: In the space below enter the subjective and objective data gathered during your patient assessment.

ASSESSMENT

Subjective Data Entry	Objective Data Entry

TIME OUT!

Student Instructions: To be sure your patient diagnostic statement written below is accurate, you need to review the defining characteristics and related factors associated with the nursing diagnosis and see how your patient data match. Do you have an accurate match or are additional data required or does another nursing diagnosis need to be investigated?

PATIENT DIAGNOSTIC STATEMENT:

DIAGNOSIS

Nursing Diagnosis (specify) _____

Related to _____

Desired Outcome and Patient Criteria: The Patient will:

PLANNING

TIME OUT!

The desired outcome must meet criteria to be accurate. The outcome must be specific, realistic, measurable, and include a time frame for completion. Does the action verb describe the patient's behavior to be evaluated? Can the outcome be used in the evaluation step of the nursing process to measure the patient's response to the nursing interventions listed below?

Interventions	Rationale for Selected Intervention and References

EVALUATION

TIME OUT!

Do your interventions assist in achieving the desired outcome? Do your interventions address further monitoring of the patient's response to your interventions and to the achievement of the desired outcome? Are qualifiers: **when, how, amount, time,** and **frequency** used? Is the focus of the action's verb on the nurse's actions and not on the patient? Do your rationales provide sufficient reason and directions?

What was your patient's response to the interventions?

Was the desired outcome achieved? If no, what revisions to either the desired outcome or interventions would you make?
☐ Yes ☐ No

DOCUMENTATION

Documentation Focus: Now that you have completed the evaluation, the next step is to document your care and the patient's response. Use the areas below to enter your progress note information.

Reassessment Data:

Interventions Implemented:

Patient's Response:

INSTRUCTOR'S COMMENTS:

Worksheets for Students' Future Use

Student Name: _____

INTERACTIVE CARE PLAN WORKSHEET

Patient's Medical Diagnosis: _____

NURSING DIAGNOSIS

DEFINITION:

DEFINING CHARACTERISTICS:

RELATED FACTORS:

STUDENT INSTRUCTIONS: In the space below enter the subjective and objective data gathered during your patient assessment.

A S S E S S M E N T

Subjective Data Entry

Objective Data Entry

TIME OUT!

Student Instructions: To be sure your patient diagnostic statement written below is accurate, you need to review the defining characteristics and related factors associated with the nursing diagnosis and see how your patient data match. Do you have an accurate match or are additional data required or does another nursing diagnosis need to be investigated?

D I A G N O S I S

PATIENT DIAGNOSTIC STATEMENT:

Nursing Diagnosis (specify) _____

_____

Related to _____

_____

Desired Outcome and Patient Criteria: The Patient will:

TIME OUT! The desired outcome must meet criteria to be accurate. The outcome must be specific, realistic, measurable, and include a time frame for completion. Does the action verb describe the patient's behavior to be evaluated? Can the outcome be used in the evaluation step of the nursing process to measure the patient's response to the nursing interventions listed below?

Interventions	Rationale for Selected Intervention and References

P L A N N I N G

TIME OUT! Do your interventions assist in achieving the desired outcome? Do your interventions address further monitoring of the patient's response to your interventions and to the achievement of the desired outcome? Are qualifiers: **when, how, amount, time,** and **frequency** used? Is the focus of the action's verb on the nurse's actions and not on the patient? Do your rationales provide sufficient reason and directions?

What was your patient's response to the interventions?

Was the desired outcome achieved?   If no, what revisions to either the desired outcome or interventions would you make?
☐ Yes ☐ No

E V A L U A T I O N

Documentation Focus: Now that you have completed the evaluation, the next step is to document your care and the patient's response. Use the areas below to enter your progress note information.

Reassessment Data:

Interventions Implemented:

Patient's Response:

D O C U M E N T A T I O N

INSTRUCTOR'S COMMENTS:

Worksheets for Students' Future Use

INTERACTIVE CARE PLAN WORKSHEET

Patient's Medical Diagnosis:

NURSING DIAGNOSIS	
DEFINITION:	
DEFINING CHARACTERISTICS:	
RELATED FACTORS:	
STUDENT INSTRUCTIONS:	In the space below enter the subjective and objective data gathered during your patient assessment.

A S S E S S M E N T

Subjective Data Entry

Objective Data Entry

TIME OUT!

Student Instructions: To be sure your patient diagnostic statement written below is accurate, you need to review the defining characteristics and related factors associated with the nursing diagnosis and see how your patient data match. Do you have an accurate match or are additional data required or does another nursing diagnosis need to be investigated?

D I A G N O S I S

PATIENT DIAGNOSTIC STATEMENT:

Nursing Diagnosis (specify) _____

Related to _____

181

Desired Outcome and Patient Criteria: The Patient will:

TIME OUT! The desired outcome must meet criteria to be accurate. The outcome must be specific, realistic, measurable, and include a time frame for completion. Does the action verb describe the patient's behavior to be evaluated? Can the outcome be used in the evaluation step of the nursing process to measure the patient's response to the nursing interventions listed below?

Interventions	Rationale for Selected Intervention and References

PLANNING

TIME OUT! Do your interventions assist in achieving the desired outcome? Do your interventions address further monitoring of the patient's response to your interventions and to the achievement of the desired outcome? Are qualifiers: **when, how, amount, time,** and **frequency** used? Is the focus of the action's verb on the nurse's actions and not on the patient? Do your rationales provide sufficient reason and directions?

What was your patient's response to the interventions?

Was the desired outcome achieved? ☐ Yes ☐ No   If no, what revisions to either the desired outcome or interventions would you make?

EVALUATION

Documentation Focus: Now that you have completed the evaluation, the next step is to document your care and the patient's response. Use the areas below to enter your progress note information.

Reassessment Data:

Interventions Implemented:

Patient's Response:

DOCUMENTATION

INSTRUCTOR'S COMMENTS:

North American Nursing Diagnosis Association (NANDA) Nursing Diagnoses with Definitions, Related/Risk Factors, and Defining Characteristics

Activity Intolerance [specify level]

DEFINITION: A state in which an individual has insufficient physiological or psychological energy to endure or complete required or desired daily activities.

RELATED FACTORS: ○ Generalized weakness ○ Sedentary lifestyle ○ Bedrest or immobility ○ Imbalance between oxygen supply and demand ○ [Cognitive deficits/emotional status; underlying disease process/depression]

DEFINING CHARACTERISTICS

Subjective: ○ Verbal report of fatigue or weakness ○ Exertional discomfort or dyspnea ○ [Pain]

○ [Verbalizes no desire for and/or lack of interest in activity]

Objective: ○ Abnormal heart rate or blood pressure response to activity ○ Electrocardiographic changes reflecting arrhythmias or ischemia ○ [Pallor] ○ [Cyanosis]

Suggested levels for determining degree of impairment (Gordon, 1993):

Level I: Walk, regular pace, on level indefinitely; one flight or more but more short of breath than normally

Level II: Walk one city block 500 feet on level; climb one flight slowly without stopping

Gordon, M. (1993). Manual of Nursing Diagnosis 1993–1994. St. Louis: Mosby.
NOTE: Information appearing in [ ] has been added by the authors to clarify and facilitate the use of nursing diagnoses.

Level III: Walk no more than 50 feet on level without stopping; unable to climb one flight of stairs without stopping

Level IV: Dyspnea and fatigue at rest

Activity Intolerance, risk for*

DEFINITION: A state in which an individual is at risk of experiencing insufficient physiological or psychological energy to endure or complete required or desired daily activities.

RISK FACTORS: ○ History of previous intolerance ○ Presence of circulatory/respiratory problems ○ Deconditioned status ○ Inexperience with the activity ○ [Early diagnosis of progressive disease state such as cancer, multiple sclerosis; extensive surgical procedures] ○ [Verbalized reluctance/inability to perform expected activity]

Adaptive Capacity: Intracranial, decreased

DEFINITION: A clinical state in which intracranial fluid dynamic mechanisms that normally compensate for increases in intracranial volumes are compromised, resulting in repeated disproportionate increases in intracranial pressure (ICP) in response to a variety of noxious and non-noxious stimuli.

RELATED FACTORS: ○ Brain injuries ○ Sustained increase in ICP greater than or equal to 10–15 mm Hg ○ Decreased cerebral perfusion pressure less than or equal to 50–60 mm Hg ○ Systemic hypotension with intracranial hypertension

DEFINING CHARACTERISTICS

Objective: ○ Repeated increases in ICP of greater than 10 mm Hg for more than 5 minutes following a variety of external stimuli ○ Disproportionate increase in ICP following single environmental or nursing maneuver stimulus ○ Elevated P2-ICP waveform ○ Volume pressure response test variation (Volume-pressure ratio greater than 2, Pressure-volume index less than 10) ○ Baseline ICP equal to or greater than 10 mm Hg ○ Wide amplitude ICP waveform

Adjustment, impaired

DEFINITION: Inability to modify lifestyle/behavior in a manner consistent with a change in health status.

RELATED FACTORS: ○ Disability or health status change requiring change in lifestyle ○ Inadequate support systems ○ Impaired cognition, sensory overload ○ Assault to self-esteem, altered locus of control ○ Incomplete grieving [severe emotional loss] ○ [Physical and/or learning disability] ○ [Life-threatening condition or disease]

DEFINING CHARACTERISTICS

Subjective: ○ Verbalization of nonacceptance of health status change

Objective: ○ Nonexistent or unsuccessful ability to be involved in problem solving or goal setting ○ Lack of movement toward independence ○ Extended period of shock, disbelief, or anger regarding health status change ○ Lack of future-oriented thinking ○ [Lack of ability to limit expectations of self]

Airway Clearance, ineffective

DEFINITION: Inability to clear secretions or obstructions from the respiratory tract to maintain a clear airway.

RELATED FACTORS

Environmental: ○ Smoking ○ Second-hand smoke ○ Smoke inhalation

Obstructed Airway: ○ Retained secretions ○ Secretions in the bronchi ○ Exudate in the alveoli ○ Excessive mucus ○ Airway spasm ○ Foreign body in airway ○ Presence of artificial airway

Physiological: ○ Chronic obstructive pulmonary disease ○ Asthma ○ Allergic airways ○ Hyperplasia of the bronchial walls ○ Neuromuscular dysfunction ○ Infection

DEFINING CHARACTERISTICS

Subjective: ○ [Statement of difficulty breathing]

Objective: ○ Diminished/adventitious breath sounds (rales, crackles, rhonchi, wheezes) ○ Changes in respiratory rate and rhythm ○ Orthopnea ○ Cough, ineffective or absent ○ Spu-

---

NOTE: Information appearing in [ ] has been added by the authors to clarify and facilitate the use of nursing diagnoses.

*[Note: A risk diagnosis is not evidenced by signs and symptoms because the problem has not yet occurred, and nursing interventions are directed at prevention. Therefore, risk factors present are noted instead.]

tum ○ Cyanosis ○ Dyspnea ○ Difficulty vocalizing ○ Wide-eyed appearance ○ Restlessness ○ [Use of accessory muscles for breathing] ○ [Choking or noisy respirations] ○ [Apnea]

Anxiety [mild, moderate, severe, panic]

DEFINITION: A vague uneasy feeling of discomfort or dread accompanied by an autonomic response; the source often nonspecific or unknown to the individual; a feeling of apprehension caused by anticipation of danger. It is an altering signal that warns of impending danger and enables the individual to take measures to deal with threat.

RELATED FACTORS: ○ Unconscious conflict about essential values, [beliefs], and goals of life ○ Situational/maturational crises ○ Stress ○ Familial association/heredity ○ Interpersonal transmission/contagion ○ Threat to self-concept [perceived or actual], [unconscious conflict] ○ Threat of death [perceived or actual] ○ Threat to or change in health status [terminal illness], role function, environment [safety], interaction patterns, economic status ○ Unmet needs ○ Exposure to toxins ○ Substance abuse ○ [Physiological factors such as hyperthyroidism, pheochromocytoma, use of steroids]

DEFINING CHARACTERISTICS

Subjective: Behavioral: ○ Expressed concerns due to change in life events

Objective: Behavioral: ○ Poor eye contact ○ Glancing about ○ Scanning and vigilance ○ Extraneous movement (e.g., foot shuffling, hand/arm movements) ○ Fidgeting ○ Restlessness ○ Diminished productivity

Subjective: Affective: ○ Regretful ○ Scared ○ Rattled ○ Distressed ○ Apprehensive ○ Uncertain ○ Fearful ○ Having feelings of inadequacy ○ Anxious ○ Jittery ○ [Having sense of impending doom]

Objective: Affective: ○ Increased wariness ○ Focus on self ○ Irritability ○ Overexcitement ○ Anguish ○ Painful and persistent feelings of increased helplessness

Subjective: Physiological: ○ Shakiness ○ Worried ○ Regretful ○ Dry mouth (s)† ○ Tingling in extremities (p)† ○ Heart pounding (s) ○ Nausea (p) ○ Abdominal pain (p) ○ Diarrhea (p) ○ Urinary hesitancy (p) ○ Urinary frequency (p) ○ Faintness (p) ○ Weakness (s) Decreased pulse (p) ○ Respiratory difficulties (s) ○ Fatigue (p) ○ Sleep disturbance (p)

Objective: Physiological: ○ Voice quivering ○ Trembling/hand tremors increased tension ○ Facial tension ○ Increased pulse ○ Increased perspiration ○ Cardiovascular excitation (s) ○ Facial flushing (s) ○ Superficial vasoconstriction (s) ○ Increased blood pressure (s) ○ Twitching (s) ○ Increased reflexes (s) ○ Urinary urgency (p) ○ Decreased blood pressure (p)) ○ Insomnia ○ Anorexia (s) ○ Increased respiration (s)

Subjective: Cognitive: ○ Fear of unspecific consequences ○ Awareness of physiological symptoms

Objective: Cognitive: ○ Preoccupation ○ Impaired attention ○ Difficulty concentrating ○ Forgetfulness ○ Diminished ability to problem solve ○ Diminished learning ability ○ Rumination ○ Tendency to blame others ○ Blocking of thought ○ Confusion ○ Decreased perceptual field

Anxiety, Death

DEFINITION: The apprehension, worry, or fear related to death or dying.

RELATED FACTORS: To be developed

DEFINING CHARACTERISTICS

Subjective: ○ Fear of developing a terminal illness, process of dying, loss of physical and/or mental abilities when dying, premature death because it prevents the accomplishment of important life goals, delayed demise, leaving family alone after death ○ Worrying about the impact of one's own death on significant others, being the cause of other's grief and suffering ○ Concerns of overworking the caregiver as terminal illness incapacitates self ○ Deep sadness ○ Negative death images or unpleasant thoughts about any event related to death or dying ○ Concern about meeting one's cre-

---

(s) = sympathetic; (p) = parasympathetic

NOTE: Information appearing in [ ] has been added by the authors to clarify and facilitate the use of nursing diagnoses.

*[**Note:** A risk diagnosis is not evidenced by signs and symptoms because the problem has not yet occurred, and nursing interventions are directed at prevention. Therefore, risk factors present are noted instead.]

ator or feeling doubtful about the existence of a god or higher being ○ Anticipated pain related to dying ○ Powerless over issues related to dying ○ Total loss of control over an aspect of one's own death ○ Denial of one's own mortality or impending death

Aspiration, risk for*

DEFINITION: The state in which an individual is at risk for entry of gastric secretions, oropharyngeal secretions, or [exogenous food] solids or fluids into tracheobronchial passages [due to dysfunction or absence of normal protective mechanisms].

RISK FACTORS: ○ Reduced level of consciousness ○ Depressed cough and gag reflexes ○ Impaired swallowing [because of inability of the epiglottis and true vocal cords to move to close off trachea] ○ Facial/oral/neck surgery or trauma; wired jaws ○ Situation hindering elevation of upper body ○ Delayed gastric emptying; decreased gastrointestinal motility; increased intragastric pressure; increased gastric residual ○ Presence of tracheostomy or endotracheal tube; [over- or inadequate inflation of tracheostomy/endotracheal tube cuff] ○ Gastrointestinal tubes; bolus tube feedings/medication administration

[Autonomic] Dysreflexia

DEFINITION: The state in which an individual with a spinal cord injury at T7 or above experiences a life-threatening uninhibited sympathetic response of the nervous system to a noxious stimulus.

RELATED FACTORS: ○ Bladder or bowel distention ○ Skin irritation ○ Lack of patient and caregiver knowledge ○ [Sexual excitation]

DEFINING CHARACTERISTICS: ○ Individual with spinal cord injury (T7 or above) with:

Subjective: ○ Headache (a diffuse pain in different portions of the head and not confined to any nerve distribution area) ○ Paresthesia ○ Chilling ○ Blurred vision ○ Chest pain ○ Metallic taste in mouth ○ Nasal congestion

Objective: ○ Paroxysmal hypertension (sudden periodic elevated BP where systolic pressure is over 140 mm Hg and diastolic is above 90 mm Hg) ○ Bradycardia or tachycardia (pulse rate of less than 60 or over 100 bpm) ○ Diaphoresis (above the injury); red splotches on skin (above the injury); pallor (below the injury) ○ Pilomotor reflex (gooseflesh formation when skin is cooled) ○ Horner's syndrome (contraction of the pupil, partial ptosis of the eyelid, enophthalmos and sometimes loss of sweating over the affected side of the face) ○ Conjunctival congestion

Autonomic Dysreflexia, risk for

DEFINITION: A lifelong, threatening uninhibited response of the sympathetic nervous system for an individual with a spinal cord injury or lesion at T8 or above and having recovered from spinal shock.

RISK FACTORS

Cardiac/Pulmonary Problems: ○ Pulmonary emboli

Gastrointestinal Problems: ○ Constipation ○ Distention ○ Stimulation (e.g., digital, instrumentation, surgery) ○ Enemas ○ Gastrointestinal system pathology, esophageal reflux, gastric ulcers

Neurological Problems: ○ Painful or irritating stimuli below the level of injury

Regulatory Problems: ○ Temperature fluctuations

Reproductive Problems: ○ Menstruation ○ Sexual intercourse, ejaculation

Integumentary Problems: ○ Cutaneous stimulations (e.g., pressure ulcer, ingrown toenail, dressing, burns, rash) ○ Heterotrophic bone

Situational Problems: ○ Positioning ○ Range-of-motion exercises ○ Constrictive clothing ○ Drug reactions (e.g., decongestants, sympathomimetics, vasoconstrictors, narcotic withdrawal) ○ Deep vein thrombosis ○ Pregnancy ○ Labor and delivery ○ Ovarian cyst ○ Surgical procedures ○ Fractures

Urological Problems: ○ Bladder distention ○ Spasm ○ Instrumentation ○ Infection ○ Urethritis ○ Epididymitis

NOTE: Information appearing in [ ] has been added by the authors to clarify and facilitate the use of nursing diagnoses.

*[**Note:** A risk diagnosis is not evidenced by signs and symptoms because the problem has not yet occurred, and nursing interventions are directed at prevention. Therefore, risk factors present are noted instead.]

Body Image disturbance

DEFINITION: Confusion in mental picture of one's physical self.

RELATED FACTORS: ○ Biophysical ○ Trauma or injury ○ Illness ○ Illness treatment ○ Surgery ○ Developmental [maturational] changes, [pregnancy, physical change caused by biochemical agents (drugs), dependence on machine] ○ Psychosocial ○ Cultural or spiritual ○ Cognitive/perceptual ○ [Significance of body part or functioning with regard to age, sex, developmental level, or basic human needs]

DEFINING CHARACTERISTICS

Subjective: ○ Verbalization of feelings/perceptions that reflect an altered view of one's body in appearance, structure, or function ○ Verbalization of change in lifestyle ○ Fear of rejection or of reaction by others ○ Focus on past strength, function, or appearance ○ Negative feelings about body (e.g., feelings of helplessness, hopelessness, or powerlessness) ○ Preoccupation with change or loss ○ [Feelings of depersonalization/grandiosity] ○ Refusal to verify actual change ○ Emphasis on remaining strengths, heightened achievement ○ Personalization of part or loss by name ○ Depersonalization of part or loss by impersonal pronouns ○ Extension of body boundary to incorporate environmental objects

Objective: ○ Missing body part ○ Actual change in structure and/or function ○ Nonverbal response to actual or perceived change in structure/function ○ Behaviors of avoidance, monitoring, or acknowledgment of one's body ○ Not looking at/not touching body part ○ Trauma to nonfunctioning part ○ Change in ability to estimate spatial relationship of body to environment ○ Hiding or overexposing body part (intentional or unintentional) ○ Change in social involvement ○ [Inability to differentiate internal/external stimuli/loss of ego boundaries]

Body Temperature, risk for altered*

DEFINITION: The state in which the individual is at risk for failure to maintain body temperature within normal range.

RISK FACTORS: ○ Extremes of age, weight ○ Exposure to cold/cool or warm/hot environments ○ Dehydration ○ Inactivity or vigorous activity ○ Medications causing vasoconstriction/vasodilation, altered metabolic rate, sedation, [use or overdose of certain drugs or exposure to anesthesia] ○ Inappropriate clothing for environmental temperature ○ Illness or trauma affecting temperature regulation, [Infections, systemic or localized, neoplasms, tumors, collagen/vascular disease]

Bowel Incontinence

DEFINITION: Change in normal bowel habits characterized by involuntary passage of stool.

RELATED FACTORS: ○ Environmental factors, e.g. (inaccessible bathroom) ○ Dietary habits ○ Stress ○ Immobility ○ Self-care deficit—toileting ○ Medications ○ Laxative abuse ○ Impaired cognition ○ Colorectal lesions ○ Incomplete emptying of bowel ○ Impaction ○ Chronic diarrhea ○ General decline in muscle tone ○ Abnormally high abdominal or intestinal pressure ○ Impaired reservoir capacity ○ Rectal sphincter abnormality ○ Loss of rectal sphincter control ○ Lower/upper motor nerve damage

DEFINING CHARACTERISTICS

Subjective: ○ Recognizes rectal fullness but reports inability to expel formed stool ○ Urgency ○ Inability to delay defecation ○ Self-report of inability to feel rectal fullness ○ Inability to recognize/inattention to urge to defecate

Objective: ○ Constant dribbling of soft stool ○ Fecal staining of clothing and/or bedding ○ Red perianal skin ○ Fecal odor

Breastfeeding, effective

DEFINITION: The state in which a mother-infant dyad/family exhibits adequate proficiency and satisfaction with breastfeeding process.

RELATED FACTORS: ○ Basic breastfeeding knowledge ○ Normal breast structure ○ Normal infant oral structure ○ Infant gestational age greater than

NOTE: Information appearing in [ ] has been added by the authors to clarify and facilitate the use of nursing diagnoses.

*[**Note:** A risk diagnosis is not evidenced by signs and symptoms because the problem has not yet occurred, and nursing interventions are directed at prevention. Therefore, risk factors present are noted instead.]

34 weeks ○ Support sources [available] ○ Maternal confidence

DEFINING CHARACTERISTICS

Subjective: ○ Maternal verbalization of satisfaction with the breastfeeding process

Objective: ○ Mother able to position infant at breast to promote a successful latch-on response ○ Infant is content after feeding ○ Regular and sustained sucking/swallowing at the breast ○ Appropriate infant weight patterns [gain] for age ○ Effective mother/infant communication pattern (infant cues, maternal interpretation and response) ○ Signs and/or symptoms of oxytocin release (let down or milk ejection reflex) ○ Adequate infant elimination patterns for age [e.g., soft stools; over six wet diapers per day of unconcentrated urine]; eagerness of infant to nurse

Breastfeeding, ineffective

DEFINITION: The state in which a mother, infant, or child experiences dissatisfaction or difficulty with the breastfeeding process.

RELATED FACTORS: ○ Prematurity; infant anomaly; poor infant sucking reflex ○ Infant receiving [numerous or repeated] supplemental feedings with artificial nipple ○ Maternal anxiety or ambivalence ○ Knowledge deficit ○ Previous history of breastfeeding failure ○ Interruption in breastfeeding ○ Nonsupportive partner/family ○ Maternal breast anomaly; previous breast surgery; painful nipples/breast engorgement

DEFINING CHARACTERISTICS

Subjective: ○ Unsatisfactory breastfeeding process ○ Persistence of sore nipples beyond the first week of breastfeeding ○ Insufficient emptying of each breast per feeding ○ Actual or perceived inadequate milk supply

Objective: ○ Observable signs of inadequate infant intake [inappropriate weight loss/or inadequate gain, decreased urinary output] ○ Nonsustained suckling, or insufficient opportunity for suckling, at the breast ○ Infant inability [failure] to attach on to maternal breast correctly ○ Infant arching and crying at the breast; resisting latching on ○ Infant exhibiting fussiness and crying within the first hour after breastfeeding; unresponsive to other comfort measures ○ No observable signs of oxytocin release

Breastfeeding, interrupted

DEFINITION: A break in the continuity of the breastfeeding process as a result of inability or inadvisability to put baby to breast for feeding.

RELATED FACTORS: ○ Maternal or infant illness ○ Prematurity ○ Maternal employment ○ Contraindications to breastfeeding (e.g., drugs, true breast-milk jaundice) ○ Need to abruptly wean infant

DEFINING CHARACTERISTICS

Subjective: ○ Infant does not receive nourishment at the breast for some or all of feedings ○ Maternal desire to maintain lactation and provide (or eventually provide) her breastmilk for her infant's nutritional needs ○ Lack of knowledge regarding expression and storage of breastmilk

Objective: ○ Separation of mother and infant

Breathing Pattern, ineffective

DEFINITION: Inspiration and/or expiration that does not provide adequate ventilation.

RELATED FACTORS:

○ Anxiety ○ Pain ○ Hyperventilation ○ Bony/chest wall deformity ○ Body position ○ Obesity ○ Decreased energy/fatigue ○ Respiratory muscle fatigue ○ Hypoventilation syndrome ○ Musculoskeletal impairment ○ Neuromuscular dysfunction ○ Spinal cord injury ○ Neurological immaturity ○ Perception/cognitive impairment

DEFINING CHARACTERISTICS

Subjective: ○ Shortness of breath

Objective: ○ Dyspnea ○ Orthopnea ○ Nasal flaring ○ Use of accessory muscles ○ Pursed-lip breathing/prolonged expiratory phase ○ Assumption of three-point position ○ Cyanosis; abnormal arterial blood gas ○ Increased anterior-posterior diameter ○ Decreased vital capacity ○ Decreased minute ventilation ○ Timing ratio ○ Decreased inspiratory/expiratory pressure ○ Respiratory rate (adults [ages 14 or greater], 11 or 24; infants, 25 or 60; ages 1–4, 20

NOTE: Information appearing in [ ] has been added by the authors to clarify and facilitate the use of nursing diagnoses.

or 30; ages 5–14, 15 or 25 ∘ Depth of breathing (adults VT500 ml at rest, infants 6–8 ml/kgo)

∘ Use of accessory muscles ∘ Dyspnea ∘ Cough ∘ [Liver engorgement/ascites]

Cardiac Output, decreased

DEFINITION: A state in which the blood pumped by the heart is inadequate to meet the metabolic demands of the body.

[**Note:** In a hypermetabolic state, although cardiac output may be within normal range, it may still be inadequate to meet the needs of the body's tissues. Cardiac output and tissue perfusion are interrelated although there are differences. When cardiac output is decreased, tissue perfusion problems will develop; however, tissue perfusion problems can exist without decreased cardiac output.]

RELATED FACTORS: To be developed by NANDA ∘ (Mechanical: alteration in preload [e.g., decreased venous return, altered myocardial contractility]; afterload [e.g., alteration in systemic vascular resistance]; inotropic changes in heart) ∘ (Electrical: alterations in rate; rhythm; conduction) ∘ (Structural [e.g., ventricular-septal defect, ventricular aneurysm, papillary muscle rupture, valvular disease])

Note: These factors were identified when the diagnosis was originally accepted and have been retained here to assist the user until NANDA completes its work.

DEFINING CHARACTERISTICS

Subjective: ∘ Fatigue ∘ Chest pain ∘ [Syncope] ∘ [Weakness]

Objective: ∘ Variations in blood pressure readings ∘ Elevated pulmonary artery pressures ∘ Decreased cardiac output by thermodilution method ∘ Ejection fraction less than 40% ∘ Skin color changes, skin and mucous membranes [cyanosis] ∘ Cold, clammy skin ∘ Orthopnea/paroxysmal nocturnal dyspnea ∘ Arrhythmias ∘ ECG changes ∘ Jugular vein distention ∘ Oliguria ∘ Decreased peripheral pulses ∘ Rales [crackles] ∘ Wheezing ∘ Restlessness ∘ Increased heart rate ∘ S_3 or S_4 ∘ Abnormal cardiac enzymes ∘ Abnormal chest x-ray (pulmonary vascular congestion) ∘ Mixed venous oxygen SaO_2 ∘ Weight gain ∘ Edema ∘ Altered mental status ∘ Increased respiratory rate

Caregiver Role Strain

DEFINITION: A caregiver's felt difficulty in performing the family caregiver role.

RELATED FACTORS

Physiological: ∘ Increasing care needs/dependency ∘ Illness severity of the care receiver ∘ Premature birth/congenital defect ∘ Addiction or codependency ∘ Discharge of family member with significant home care needs ∘ Caregiver health impairment ∘ Unpredictable illness course or instability in the care receiver's health

Resources: ∘ Insufficient information, finances ∘ Inadequate transportation, equipment for providing care, community services ∘ Lack of support from significant others, respite resources, recreational resources ∘ Caregiver is not developmentally ready for caregiver role

Roles and Relationships: ∘ Unrealistic expectations of caregiver by care receiver ∘ Change in relationship ∘ History of marginal family coping, family dysfunction

Social: ∘ Alienation from family, friends, and co-workers ∘ Insufficient recreation

Individual: ∘ Illness chronicity ∘ Instability of care receiver's health ∘ Problem behaviors ∘ Psychological or cognitive problems in care receiver

Caregiver: ∘ Ongoing changes in activities ∘ Amount of activities ∘ Unpredictability of care situation ∘ 24-hour care responsibility ∘ Inability to fulfill one's own or other's expectations ∘ Unrealistic expectations of self ∘ Marginal caregiver's coping patterns ∘ Addiction or codependency ∘ Psychological or cognitive problems

Situational: ∘ Presence of abuse or violence ∘ Inadequate physical environment for providing care, e.g., housing, transportation, community services, equipment ∘ Family/caregiver isolation ∘ Inexperience with caregiving ∘ Caregiver's competing role commitments ∘ Complexity/amount of caregiving tasks

[**Note:** The presence of this problem may encompass numerous problems/high-risk concerns. Careful attention to data gathering will identify and clar-

NOTE: Information appearing in [ ] has been added by the authors to clarify and facilitate the use of nursing diagnoses.

ify the client's specific needs, which can then be co-ordinated under this single diagnostic label.]

DEFINING CHARACTERISTICS

Subjective: ○ Apprehension about possible institutionalization of care receiver/the future regarding care receiver's health and caregiver's ability to provide care/care receiver's care when caregiver is ill or deceased ○ Altered caregiving activities ○ Altered caregiver health status (e.g., hypertension, cardiovascular disease, diabetes, headaches, gastrointestinal upset, weight change, rash) ○ [Care receiver reports problems with care]

Objective: ○ Difficulty performing required activities ○ Inability to complete caregiving tasks ○ Preoccupation with care routine ○ [Disorderly surroundings]

Caregiver Role Strain, risk for*

DEFINITION: A caregiver is vulnerable for felt difficulty in performing the family caregiver role.

RELATED FACTORS:

Pathophysiological/Physiological: ○ Illness severity of the care receiver ○ Addiction or codependency ○ Premature birth/congenital defect ○ Discharge of family member with significant home care needs ○ Caregiver health impairment ○ Unpredictable illness course or instability in the care receiver's health ○ Caregiver is female

Developmental: ○ Caregiver is not developmentally ready for caregiver role, e.g., young adult needing to provide care for a middle-aged parent ○ Developmental delay or retardation of the care receiver or caregiver

Psychosocial: ○ Psychosocial or cognitive problems in care receiver ○ Marginal family adaptation or dysfunction before the caregiving situation ○ Marginal caregiver's coping patterns ○ Past history of poor relationship between caregiver and care receiver ○ Caregiver is spouse ○ Care receiver exhibits deviant, bizarre behavior

Situational: ○ Presence of abuse or violence ○ Presence of situational stressors that normally affect families, such as significant loss, disaster or cri-

sis, poverty or economic vulnerability, or major life events, e.g., birth, hospitalization, leaving home, returning home, marriage, divorce, employment, retirement, death ○ Duration of caregiving required ○ Inadequate physical environment for providing care (e.g., housing, transportation, community services, equipment) ○ Family/caregiver isolation ○ Lack of respite and recreation for caregiver ○ Inexperience with caregiving ○ Caregiver's competing role commitments ○ Complexity/amount of caregiving tasks

Communication, impaired verbal

DEFINITION: The state in which an individual experiences a decreased, delayed, or absent ability to receive, process, transmit, and use a system of symbols; anything that has meaning (i.e., transmits meaning).

RELATED FACTORS: ○ Decrease in circulation to brain; brain tumor ○ Anatomic deficit (e.g., cleft palate, alteration of the neuromuscular visual/auditory system, or phonatory apparatus) ○ Physical barrier (tracheostomy, intubation) ○ Psychological barriers (e.g., psychosis, lack of stimuli, [depression, panic, anger]) ○ Cultural difference ○ Lack of information ○ Difference related to developmental age ○ Physiological conditions [e.g., dyspnea] ○ Alteration of central nervous system ○ Weakening of the musculoskeletal system ○ Side effects of medication ○ Environmental barriers ○ Stress ○ Emotional conditions ○ Alteration of self-esteem or self-concept ○ Altered perceptions ○ Absence of significant others

DEFINING CHARACTERISTICS

Subjective: ○ [Reports of difficulty expressing self]

Objective: ○ Unable to speak dominant language ○ Speaks or verbalizes with difficulty ○ Does not or cannot speak ○ Willful refusal to speak ○ Disorientation in the three spheres of time, space, person ○ Stuttering ○ Slurring ○ Dyspnea ○ Difficulty forming words or sentences (e.g., aphonia, dyslalia, dysarthria) ○ Difficulty expressing thought verbally (e.g., aphasia, dysphasia, apraxia, dyslexia) ○ Inap-

---

NOTE: Information appearing in [ ] has been added by the authors to clarify and facilitate the use of nursing diagnoses.
*[**Note:** A risk diagnosis is not evidenced by signs and symptoms because the problem has not yet occurred, and nursing interventions are directed at prevention. Therefore, risk factors present are noted instead.]

propriate verbalization [incessant, loose association of ideas, flight of ideas] ○ Absence of eye contact or difficulty in selective attending ○ Difficulty in comprehending and maintaining the usual communicating pattern, partial or total visual deficit ○ Inability or difficulty in use of facial or body expressions ○ [Inability to modulate speech] ○ [Message inappropriate to content] ○ [Frustration, anger, hostility]

Community Coping, potential for enhanced

DEFINITION: A pattern of community activities for adaptation and problem solving that is satisfactory for meeting the demands or needs of the community but can be improved for management of current and future problems/stressors.

RELATED FACTORS: ○ Social supports available ○ Resources available for problem solving ○ Community has a sense of power to manage stressors

DEFINING CHARACTERISTICS

Subjective: ○ Agreement that community is responsible for stress management

Objective: ○ Deficits in one or more characteristics that indicate effective coping ○ Active planning by community for predicted stressors ○ Active problem solving by community when faced with issues ○ Positive communication among community members ○ Positive communication between community/aggregates and larger community ○ Programs available for recreation and relaxation ○ Resources sufficient for managing stressors

Community Coping, ineffective

DEFINITION: A pattern of community activities for adaptation and problem solving that is unsatisfactory for meeting the demands or needs of the community.

RELATED FACTORS: ○ Deficits in community social support services and resources ○ Inadequate resources for problem solving ○ Ineffective or nonexistent community systems (e.g., lack of emer-

gency medical system, transportation system, or disaster planning systems) ○ Natural or man-made disasters

DEFINING CHARACTERISTICS

Subjective: ○ Community does not meet its own expectations ○ Expressed community powerlessness ○ Expressed vulnerability ○ Stressors perceived as excessive

Objective: ○ Deficits of community participation ○ Excessive community conflicts ○ High illness rates ○ Increased social problems (e.g., homicides, vandalism, arson, terrorism, robbery, infanticide, abuse, divorce, unemployment, poverty, militancy, mental illness)

Confusion, acute

DEFINITION: The abrupt onset of a cluster of global, transient changes and disturbances in attention, cognition, psychomotor activity, level of consciousness, and/or sleep/wake cycle.

RELATED FACTORS: ○ Older than 60 years of age ○ Dementia ○ Alcohol abuse ○ Drug abuse ○ Delirium

DEFINING CHARACTERISTICS

Objective: ○ Fluctuation in cognition ○ Fluctuation in sleep-wake cycle ○ Fluctuation in level of consciousness ○ Fluctuation in psychomotor activity ○ Increased agitation or restlessness ○ Misperceptions ○ Lack of motivation to initiate and/or follow through with goal-directed or purposeful behavior ○ Hallucinations

Confusion, chronic

DEFINITION: An irreversible, long-standing, and/or progressive deterioration of intellect and personality characterized by decreased ability to interpret environmental stimuli, decreased capacity for intellectual thought processes and manifested by disturbances of memory, orientation, and behavior.

RELATED FACTORS: ○ Alzheimer's disease ○ Korsakoff's psychosis ○ Multi-infarct dementia ○ Cerebral vascular accident ○ Head injury

NOTE: Information appearing in [ ] has been added by the authors to clarify and facilitate the use of nursing diagnoses.

DEFINING CHARACTERISTICS

Objective: ○ Clinical evidence of organic impairment ○ Altered interpretation/response to stimuli ○ Progressive/long-standing cognitive impairment ○ No change in level of consciousness ○ Impaired socialization ○ Impaired memory (short-term, long-term) ○ Altered personality

Constipation

DEFINITION: A decrease in a person's normal frequency of defecation accompanied by difficult or incomplete passage of stool and/or passage of excessively hard, dry stool.

RELATED FACTORS:

Functional: ○ Irregular defecation habits ○ Insufficient physical activity ○ Recent environmental changes ○ Inadequate toileting (e.g., timeliness, positioning for defecation, privacy) ○ Abdominal muscle weakness ○ Habitual denial/ignoring of urge to defecate

Psychological: ○ Emotional stress ○ Depression ○ Mental confusion

Pharmacological: ○ Antilipemic agents ○ Laxative overdose ○ Calcium carbonate ○ Aluminum-containing antacids ○ Nonsteroidal anti-inflammatory agents ○ Opiates ○ Anticholinergics ○ Diuretics ○ Iron salts ○ Phenothiazides ○ Sedatives ○ Sympathomimetics ○ Bismuth salts ○ Antidepressants ○ Calcium channel blockers

Mechanical: ○ Hemorrhoids ○ Pregnancy ○ Obesity ○ Rectal abscess or ulcer, anal fissures, prolapse; anal strictures; rectocele ○ Prostate enlargement ○ Postsurgical obstruction ○ Electrolyte imbalance ○ Neurological impairment ○ Megacolon (Hirschsprung's disease) ○ Tumors

Physiological: ○ Poor eating habits ○ Insufficient fiber intake ○ Insufficient fluid intake, dehydration ○ Inadequate dentition or oral hygiene ○ Change in usual foods and eating patterns ○ Decreased motility of gastrointestinal tract

DEFINING CHARACTERISTICS

Subjective: ○ Change in bowel pattern ○ Decreased frequency ○ Decreased volume of stool ○ Increased abdominal pressure ○ Feeling of rectal fullness or pressure ○ Abdominal pain ○ Pain with defecation ○ Unable to pass stool ○ Nausea and/or vomiting ○ Headache ○ Indigestion ○ Generalized fatigue

Objective: ○ Dry, hard, formed stool ○ Straining with defecation ○ Palpable rectal/abdominal mass ○ Distended abdomen ○ Hypoactive or hyperactive bowel sounds ○ Change in abdominal growling (borborygmi) ○ Percussed abdominal dullness ○ Abdominal tenderness with or without palpable muscle resistance ○ Presence of soft paste-like stool in rectum ○ Oozing liquid stool ○ Bright red blood with stool ○ Dark, black, or tarry stool ○ Severe flatus ○ Anorexia ○ Atypical presentations in older adults (e.g., change in mental status, urinary incontinence, unexplained falls, elevated body temperature)

Constipation, perceived

DEFINITION: The state in which an individual makes a self-diagnosis of constipation and ensures a daily bowel movement through use of laxatives, enemas, and suppositories.

RELATED FACTORS: ○ Cultural/family health benefits ○ Faulty appraisal ○ Impaired thought processes

DEFINING CHARACTERISTICS

Subjective: ○ Expectation of a daily bowel movement with the resulting overuse of laxatives, enemas, and suppositories ○ Expected passage of stool at same time every day

Constipation, risk for

DEFINITION: At risk for a decrease in a person's normal frequency of defecation accompanied by difficult or incomplete passage of stool and/or passage of excessively hard, dry stool.

RISK FACTORS

Functional: ○ Irregular defecation habits ○ Insufficient physical activity ○ Recent environmental changes ○ Inadequate toileting (e.g., timeliness, positioning for defecation, privacy) ○ Abdominal muscle weakness ○ Habitual denial/ignoring of urge to defecate

NOTE: Information appearing in [ ] has been added by the authors to clarify and facilitate the use of nursing diagnoses.

Psychological: ○ Emotional stress ○ Depression ○ Mental confusion

Physiological: ○ Change in usual foods and eating patterns ○ Insufficient fiber/fluid intake, dehydration ○ Poor eating habits ○ Inadequate dentition or oral hygiene ○ Decreased motility of gastrointestinal tract

Pharmacological: ○ Phenothiazides ○ Nonsteroidal anti-inflammatory agents ○ Sedatives ○ Aluminum-containing antacids ○ Laxative overuse ○ Iron salts ○ Anticholinergics ○ Antidepressants ○ Anticonvulsants ○ Antilipemic agents ○ Calcium channel blockers ○ Calcium carbonate ○ Diuretics ○ Sympathomimetics ○ Opiates ○ Bismuth salts

Mechanical: ○ Hemorrhoids ○ Pregnancy ○ Obesity ○ Rectal abscess or ulcer; anal stricture; anal fissures; prolapse; rectocele ○ Prostate enlargement ○ Postsurgical obstruction ○ Electrolyte imbalance ○ Neurological impairment ○ Megacolon (Hirschsprung's disease) ○ Tumors

Coping, defensive

DEFINITION: The state in which an individual repeatedly projects falsely positive self-evaluation based on a self-protective pattern that defends against underlying perceived threats to positive self-regard.

RELATED FACTORS: Refer to ND Coping, Individual, ineffective.

DEFINING CHARACTERISTICS

Subjective: ○ Denial of obvious problems/weaknesses ○ Projection of blame/responsibility ○ Hypersensitive to slight/criticism ○ Grandiosity ○ Rationalizes failures ○ [Refuses or rejects assistance]

Objective: ○ Superior attitude toward others ○ Difficulty establishing/maintaining relationships ○ Hostile laughter or ridicule of others ○ Difficulty in reality testing perceptions ○ Lack of follow-through or participation in treatment or therapy

Coping, Individual, ineffective

DEFINITION: Inability to form a valid appraisal of the stressors, inadequate choices of practiced responses, and/or inability to use available resources.

RELATED FACTORS: ○ Situational/maturational crises ○ High degree of threat ○ Inadequate opportunity to prepare for stressor ○ Disturbance in pattern of appraisal of threat ○ Inadequate level of confidence in ability to cope ○ Uncertainty ○ Inadequate resources available ○ Inadequate social support created by characteristics of relationships ○ Inadequate level of perception of control ○ Disturbance in pattern of tension release ○ Inability to conserve adaptive energies ○ Gender differences in coping strategies ○ [Multiple stressors, repeated over period of time] ○ [Multiple life changes; conflict] ○ [Inadequate relaxation, little or no exercise] ○ [Unmet expectations] ○ [Impairment of nervous system] ○ [Memory loss] ○ [Severe pain]

DEFINING CHARACTERISTICS

Subjective: ○ Verbalization of inability to cope or inability to ask for help ○ Fatigue ○ Sleep disturbance ○ Poor concentration ○ Abuse of chemical agents ○ [Reports of chronic worry/anxiety/depression]

Objective: ○ Inadequate problem-solving ○ Inability to meet role expectations/basic needs ○ Lack of goal-directed behavior/resolution of problem including: inability to attend, difficulty with organizing information [lack of assertive behavior] ○ Use of forms of coping that impede adaptive behavior [including inappropriate use of defense mechanisms, verbal manipulation] ○ Decreased use of social support ○ Poor concentration ○ Change in usual communication patterns ○ High illness rate [including high blood pressure, ulcers, irritable bowel, frequent headaches/neckaches] ○ Risk taking ○ [High rate of accidents] ○ Destructive behavior toward self or others [including overeating, excessive smoking/drinking, overuse of prescribed medications]

Decisional Conflict (specify)

DEFINITION: The state of uncertainty about course of action to be taken when choice among competing actions involves risk, loss, or challenge to personal life values.

NOTE: Information appearing in [ ] has been added by the authors to clarify and facilitate the use of nursing diagnoses.

RELATED FACTORS: ○ Unclear personal values/beliefs; perceived threat to value system ○ Lack of experience or interference with decision-making ○ Lack of relevant information; multiple or divergent sources of information ○ Support system deficit

DEFINING CHARACTERISTICS

Subjective: Verbalized: ○ Uncertainty about choices ○ Undesired consequences of alternative actions being considered ○ Feelings of distress or questioning personal values and beliefs while attempting a decision

Objective: ○ Vacillation between alternative choices; delayed decision-making ○ Self-focusing ○ Physical signs of distress or tension (increased heart rate; increased muscle tension; restlessness)

Denial, ineffective

DEFINITION: The state of a conscious or unconscious attempt to disavow the knowledge or meaning of an event to reduce anxiety/fear to the detriment of health.

RELATED FACTORS: To be developed by NANDA ○ [Personal vulnerability; unmet self-needs] ○ [Presence of overwhelming anxiety-producing feelings/situation; reality factors that are consciously intolerable]

DEFINING CHARACTERISTICS

Subjective: ○ Minimizes symptoms; displaces source of symptoms to other organs ○ Unable to admit impact of disease on life pattern ○ Displaces fear of impact of the condition ○ Does not admit fear of death or invalidism

Objective: ○ Delays seeking or refuses healthcare attention to the detriment of health ○ Does not perceive personal relevance of symptoms or danger ○ Makes dismissive gestures or comments when speaking of distressing events ○ Displays inappropriate affect ○ Uses home remedies (self-treatment) to relieve symptoms

Dentition, altered

DEFINITION: Disruption in tooth development/eruption patterns or structural integrity of individual teeth.

RELATED FACTORS: ○ Dietary habits ○ Nutritional deficits ○ Selected prescription medications ○ Chronic vomiting ○ Chronic use of tobacco, coffee or tea, red wine ○ Ineffective oral hygiene, sensitivity to heat or cold ○ Barriers to self-care ○ Lack of knowledge regarding dental health ○ Excessive use of abrasive cleaning agents ○ Excessive intake of fluorides ○ Access or economic barriers to professional care ○ Genetic predisposition ○ Premature loss of primary teeth ○ Bruxism

DEFINING CHARACTERISTICS

Subjective: ○ Toothache

Objective: ○ Halitosis ○ Tooth enamel discoloration ○ Excessive plaque ○ Erosion of enamel ○ Worn down or abraded teeth ○ Crown or root caries ○ Tooth fracture(s) ○ Loose teeth ○ Missing teeth or complete absence ○ Premature loss of primary teeth ○ Incomplete eruption for age (may be primary or permanent teeth) ○ Excessive calculus ○ Malocclusion or tooth misalignment ○ Asymmetrical facial expression

Development, risk for altered

DEFINITION: At risk for delay of 25% or more in one or more of the areas of social or self-regulatory behavior, or cognitive, language, gross or fine motor skills.

RISK FACTORS

Prenatal: ○ Maternal age less than 15 or [greater than] 35 years ○ Unplanned or unwanted pregnancy ○ Lack of, late, or poor prenatal care ○ Inadequate nutrition ○ Substance abuse ○ Infections ○ Genetic or endocrine disorders ○ Poverty ○ Illiteracy

Individual: ○ Prematurity ○ Positive drug screening test ○ Congenital or genetic disorders ○ Brain damage (e.g., hemorrhage in postnatal period, shaken baby, abuse, accident) ○ Seizures ○ Vision/hearing impairment or frequent otitis media ○ Failure to thrive, inadequate nutrition ○ Chronic illness ○ Technology-dependent ○ Foster or adopted child ○ Lead poisoning ○ Chemotherapy ○ Radiation therapy ○ Behavior disorders ○ Substance abuse ○ Natural disaster

NOTE: Information appearing in [ ] has been added by the authors to clarify and facilitate the use of nursing diagnoses.

Environmental: ○ Poverty ○ Violence

Caregiver: ○ Abuse ○ Mental retardation or severe learning disability ○ Mental illness

Diarrhea

DEFINITION: Passage of loose, unformed stools.

RELATED FACTORS

Psychological: ○ High stress levels and anxiety

Situational: ○ Laxative abuse ○ Alcohol abuse ○ Toxins ○ Contaminants ○ Adverse effects of medications ○ Tube feedings ○ Travel ○ Radiation

Physiological: ○ Inflammation ○ Irritation ○ Infectious processes ○ Parasites ○ Malabsorption

DEFINING CHARACTERISTICS

Subjective: ○ Abdominal pain ○ Urgency; cramping

Objective: ○ At least three loose liquid stools per day ○ Hyperactive bowel sounds

OTHER POSSIBLE CHARACTERISTICS

Objective: ○ Change in color

Disuse Syndrome, risk for*

DEFINITION: A state in which an individual is at risk for deterioration of body systems as the result of prescribed or unavoidable musculoskeletal inactivity.

(**Note:** NANDA-identified complications from immobility can include pressure ulcer, constipation, stasis of pulmonary secretions, thrombosis, urinary tract infection/retention, decreased strength/endurance, orthostatic hypotension, decreased range of joint motion, disorientation, body image disturbance, and powerlessness.)

RISK FACTORS: ○ Severe pain, [chronic pain] ○ Paralysis, [other neuromuscular impairment] ○ Mechanical or prescribed immobilization ○ Altered level of consciousness ○ [Chronic physical or mental illness]

Diversional Activity deficit

DEFINITION: The state in which an individual experiences decreased stimulation from or interest or engagement in recreational or leisure activities.

[**Note:** Internal/external factors may or may not be beyond the individual's control.]

RELATED FACTORS: ○ Environmental lack of diversional activity (e.g., long-term hospitalization; frequent, lengthy treatments, [homebound]) ○ [Physical limitations, bedridden, fatigue, pain] ○ [Situational, developmental problem, lack of resources] ○ [Psychological condition, e.g., depression]

DEFINING CHARACTERISTICS

Subjective: Patient's statement regarding the following: ○ Boredom ○ Wish there were something to do, to read, etc. ○ Usual hobbies cannot be undertaken in hospital [or are restricted by physical limitations]

Objective: ○ [Flat affect; disinterested] ○ [Restless; crying] [Lethargy; withdrawal] ○ [Hostility] ○ [Overeating or lack of interest in eating] ○ [Weight loss or gain]

Energy Field disturbance

DEFINITION: A disruption of the flow of energy surrounding a person's being [aura] that results in a disharmony of the body, mind, and/or spirit.

RELATED FACTORS: [none listed]

DEFINING CHARACTERISTICS

Subjective: ○ Temperature change (warmth/coolness) ○ Visual changes (image/color) ○ Disruption of the field (vacant/hold/spike/bulge) ○ Movement (wave/spike/tingling/dense/flowing) ○ Sounds (tone/words)

Environmental Interpretation Syndrome, impaired

DEFINITION: Consistent lack of orientation to person, place, time, or circumstances over more than

---

NOTE: Information appearing in [ ] has been added by the authors to clarify and facilitate the use of nursing diagnoses.

*[Note: A risk diagnosis is not evidenced by signs and symptoms because the problem has not yet occurred, and nursing interventions are directed at prevention. Therefore, risk factors present are noted instead.]

3–6 months, necessitating a protective environment.

RELATED FACTORS: ○ Dementia (Alzheimer's disease, Multi-infarct dementia, Pick's disease, AIDS dementia) ○ Parkinson's disease ○ Huntington's disease ○ Depression ○ Alcoholism

DEFINING CHARACTERISTICS

Objective: ○ Consistent disorientation in known and unknown environments ○ Chronic, confusional states ○ Loss of occupation or social functioning from memory decline ○ Inability to follow simple directions, instructions ○ Inability to reason; concentrate ○ Slow in responding to questions

Failure to Thrive, adult

DEFINITION: A progressive functional deterioration of a physical and cognitive nature; the individual's ability to live with multisystem diseases, cope with ensuing problems, and manage his/her care are remarkably diminished.

RELATED FACTORS: ○ Depression ○ Apathy ○ Fatigue ○ [Chronic illness] ○ [Dementia]

DEFINING CHARACTERISTICS

Subjective: ○ States does not have an appetite, not hungry, or "I don't want to eat" ○ Expresses loss of interest in pleasurable outlets, such as food, sex, work, friends, family, hobbies, or entertainment ○ Difficulty performing simple self-care tasks ○ Altered mood state—expresses feelings of sadness, being low in spirit ○ Verbalizes desire for death

Objective: ○ Inadequate nutritional intake—eating less than body requirements ○ Consumes minimal to no food at most meals (i.e., consumes less than 75% of normal requirements at each or most meals) ○ Anorexia—does not eat meals when offered ○ Weight loss (decreased body mass from baseline weight)—5% unintentional weight loss in 1 month, 10% unintentional weight loss in 6 months ○ Physical decline (decline in bodily function)—evidence of fatigue, dehydration, incontinence of bowel and bladder ○ Frequent exacerbations of chronic health problems such as pneumonia or urinary tract infections ○ Cognitive decline (decline in mental processing)—as evidenced by problems with responding appropriately to environmental stimuli, demonstrates difficulty in reasoning, decision making, judgment, memory concentration, decreased perception ○ Apathy as evidenced by lack of observable feeling or emotion in terms of normal activities of daily living and environment ○ Decreased participation in activities of daily living that the older person once enjoyed ○ Self-care deficit—no longer looks after or takes charge of physical cleanliness or appearance ○ Neglects home environment and/or financial responsibilities ○ Decreased social skills/social withdrawal—noticeable decrease from usual past behavior in attempts to form or participate in cooperative and interdependent relationships (e.g., decreased verbal communication with staff, family, friends)

Family Coping, ineffective: compromised

DEFINITION: A usually supportive primary person (family member or close friend [significant other]) is providing insufficient, ineffective, or compromised support, comfort, assistance, or encouragement that may be needed by the client to manage or master adaptive tasks related to his/her health challenge.

RELATED FACTORS: ○ Inadequate or incorrect information or understanding by a primary person ○ Temporary preoccupation by a significant person who is trying to manage emotional conflicts and personal suffering and is unable to perceive or act effectively in regard to client's needs ○ Temporary family disorganization and role changes ○ Other situation or developmental crises or situations the significant person may be facing ○ Little support provided by client, in turn, for primary person ○ Prolonged disease or disability progression that exhausts the supportive capacity of significant people ○ [Unrealistic expectations of patient/SO of the other] ○ [Lack of mutual decision skills] ○ [Diverse coalitions of family members]

DEFINING CHARACTERISTICS

Subjective: ○ Client expresses or confirms a concern or complaint about significant other's re-

NOTE: Information appearing in [ ] has been added by the authors to clarify and facilitate the use of nursing diagnoses.

sponse to his or her health problem ○ Significant person describes preoccupation with personal reaction (e.g., fear, anticipatory grief, guilt, anxiety) to client's illness/disability, or to other situation or development crises ○ Significant person describes or confirms an inadequate understanding or knowledge base, which interferes with effective assistive or supportive behaviors

Objective: ○ Significant person attempts assistive or supportive behaviors with less than satisfactory results ○ Significant person withdraws or enters into limited or temporary personal communication with client at the time of need ○ Significant person displays protective behavior disproportionate (too little or too much) to client's abilities or need for autonomy ○ [Significant person displays sudden outbursts of emotions/shows emotional lability or interferes with necessary nursing/medical interventions]

Family Coping, ineffective: disabling

DEFINITION: Behavior of significant person (family member or other primary person) that disables his/her capacities and the client's capacities to effectively address tasks essential to either person's adaptation to the health challenge.

RELATED FACTORS: ○ Significant person with chronically unexpressed feelings of guilt, anxiety, hostility, despair ○ Dissonant discrepancy of coping styles for dealing with adaptive tasks by the significant person and client or among significant people ○ Highly ambivalent family relationships ○ Arbitrary handling of family's resistance to treatment, which tends to solidify defensiveness as it fails to deal adequately with underlying anxiety

DEFINING CHARACTERISTICS

Subjective: ○ [Expresses despair regarding family reactions/lack of involvement]

Objective: ○ Intolerance, abandonment, rejection, desertion ○ Psychosomaticism ○ Agitation, depression, aggression, hostility ○ Taking on illness signs of the client ○ Neglectful relationships with other family members ○ Carrying on usual routines, disregarding client's needs ○ Neglectful care

of the client in regard to basic human needs and/or illness treatment ○ Distortion of reality regarding the client's health problem, including extreme denial about its existence or severity ○ Decisions and actions by family which are detrimental to economic or social well-being ○ Impaired restructuring of a meaningful life for self ○ Impaired individualization, prolonged overconcern for client ○ Client's development of helpless, inactive dependence

Family Coping: potential for growth

DEFINITION: Effective managing of adaptive tasks by family member involved with the client's health challenge, who now is exhibiting desire and readiness for enhanced health and growth in regard to self and in relation to the client.

RELATED FACTORS: ○ Needs sufficiently gratified and adaptive tasks effectively addressed to enable goals of self-actualization to surface ○ [Developmental stage, situational crises/supports]

DEFINING CHARACTERISTICS

Subjective: ○ Family member attempting to describe growth impact of crisis on his/her own values, priorities, goals, or relationships ○ Individual expressing interest in making contact on a one-to-one basis or on a mutual-aid group basis with another person who has experienced a similar situation

Objective: ○ Family member moving in direction of health-promoting and enriching lifestyle that supports and monitors maturational process, audits and negotiates treatment programs, and generally chooses experiences that optimize wellness

Family Processes, altered

DEFINITION: A change in family relationships and/or functioning.

RELATED FACTORS: ○ Situational transition and/or crises [e.g., economic, change in roles, illness] ○ Developmental transition and/or crises [e.g., loss or gain of a family member] ○ Family roles shift ○ Power shift of family members ○ Modification in

NOTE: Information appearing in [ ] has been added by the authors to clarify and facilitate the use of nursing diagnoses.

family finances ○ Shift in health status of a family member ○ Modification in family social status/interaction with community ○ Informal or formal interaction with community

DEFINING CHARACTERISTICS

Subjective: ○ Changes in: power alliances, effectiveness in completing assigned tasks, satisfaction with family, stress-reduction behaviors, expressions of conflict with and/or isolation from community resources, somatic complaints, expressions of conflict within family

Objective: ○ Changes in: assigned tasks, mutual support, availability for affective responsiveness and intimacy, patterns and rituals, participation in problem solving, participation in decision making, communication patterns, availability for emotional support

Family Processes, altered: alcoholism

DEFINITION: The state in which the psychosocial, spiritual, and physiological functions of the family unit are chronically disorganized, leading to conflict, denial of problems, resistance to change, ineffective problem-solving, and a series of self-perpetuating crises.

RELATED FACTORS: ○ Abuse of alcohol ○ Family history of alcoholism ○ Resistance to treatment ○ Inadequate coping skills ○ Genetic predisposition ○ Addictive personality ○ Lack of problem-solving skills ○ Biochemical influences

DEFINING CHARACTERISTICS

Subjective: Feelings: ○ Decreased self-esteem/worthlessness ○ Anger/suppressed rage; frustration ○ Powerlessness ○ Anxiety/tension/distress ○ Insecurity ○ Repressed emotions ○ Responsibility for alcoholic's behavior ○ Lingering resentment ○ Shame/embarrassment; guilt ○ Hurt ○ Unhappiness ○ Emotional isolation/loneliness; vulnerability ○ Mistrust ○ Hopelessness ○ Rejection ○ Being different from other people ○ Depression ○ Hostility; fear ○ Emotional control by others ○ Confusion ○ Dissatisfaction ○ Loss ○ Misunderstood ○

Abandonment ○ Confused love and pity ○ Moodiness ○ Failure ○ Being unloved ○ Lack of identity

Roles and Relationships: ○ Deterioration in family relationships/disturbed family dynamics ○ Ineffective spouse communication/marital problems ○ Altered role function/disruption of family roles ○ Inconsistent parenting/low perception of parental support ○ Family denial ○ Intimacy dysfunction ○ Chronic family problems ○ Triangulating family relationships ○ Reduced ability of family members to relate to each other for mutual growth and maturation ○ Lack of skills necessary for relationships ○ Lack of cohesiveness ○ Disrupted family rituals ○ Family unable to meet security needs of its members ○ Pattern of rejection ○ Economic problems ○ Neglected obligations

Objective: Roles and Relationships: ○ Closed communication systems ○ Family does not demonstrate respect for individuality and autonomy of its members

Behaviors: ○ Expression of anger inappropriately ○ Difficulty with intimate relationships ○ Loss of control of drinking ○ Alcohol abuse ○ Impaired communication ○ Ineffective problem-solving skills ○ Enabling to maintain drinking ○ Inability to meet emotional needs of its members ○ Manipulation ○ Dependency ○ Criticizing, blaming ○ Broken promises ○ Rationalization/denial of problems ○ Refusal to get help/inability to accept and receive help appropriately ○ Inadequate understanding or knowledge of alcoholism ○ Inability to meet spiritual needs of its members ○ Inability to express or accept wide range of feelings ○ Orientation toward tension relief rather than achievement of goals ○ Family special occasions are centered on alcohol ○ Escalating conflict ○ Lying ○ Contradictory, paradoxical communication ○ Lack of dealing with conflict ○ Harsh self-judgment ○ Isolation○ Nicotine addiction ○ Difficulty having fun ○ Self-blaming ○ Unresolved grief ○ Controlling communication/power struggles ○ Inability to adapt to change ○ Immaturity ○ Stress-related physical illness ○ Inability to deal with traumatic experiences constructively ○ Seeking approval and affirmation ○ Lack of reliability ○ Disturbances in academic performance in children ○ Disturbances in concentration ○ Chaos ○ Abuse of substances other than alcohol ○ Failure

NOTE: Information appearing in [ ] has been added by the authors to clarify and facilitate the use of nursing diagnoses.

to accomplish current or past developmental tasks/difficulty with life cycle transitions ○ Verbal abuse of spouse or parent ○ Agitation ○ Diminished physical contact

Fatigue

DEFINITION: An overwhelming sustained sense of exhaustion and decreased capacity for physical and mental work at usual level.

RELATED FACTORS

Psychological: ○ Boring lifestyle ○ Stress ○ Anxiety ○ Depression

Environmental: ○ Noise ○ Lights ○ Humidity ○ Temperature ○ Anemia

Situational: ○ Occupation ○ Negative life events

Physiological: ○ Increased physical exertion ○ Poor physical condition ○ Disease states ○ Sleep deprivation ○ Pregnancy ○ Malnutrition

DEFINING CHARACTERISTICS

Subjective: ○ Verbalization of an unremitting and overwhelming lack of energy ○ Inability to maintain usual routines/level of physical activity ○ Perceived need for additional energy to accomplish routine tasks ○ Tired ○ Compromised concentration ○ Compromised libido ○ Feelings of guilt for not keeping up with responsibilities

Objective: ○ Increase in physical complaints ○ Emotionally labile or irritable ○ Lethargic or listless; disinterest in surroundings, introspection ○ Decreased performance ○ Increase in rest requirements ○ Inability to restore energy even after sleep ○ Drowsy

Fear [specify focus]

DEFINITION: Fear is anxiety caused by consciously recognized and realistic danger. It is a perceived threat, real or imagined. Operationally, fear is the presence of immediate feelings of apprehension and fright; source known and specific; subjective responses that act as energizers but cannot be observed; and objective signs that are the result of the transformation of energy into relief behaviors and responses.

RELATED FACTORS: ○ Phobic stimulus or phobia ○ Fear for others ○ Physical/social conditions ○ Separation from support system in potentially stressful situation ○ Natural/innate origins ○ Ideas ○ Knowledge deficit ○ Language barrier ○ Discrepancy ○ Environmental stimuli ○ Sensory impairment ○ Learned response ○ Classical conditioning ○ Innate releasers

DEFINING CHARACTERISTICS

Subjective: ○ Dread ○ Focus on "it" out there ○ Worry ○ Alarm ○ Afraid ○ Horror

Objective: ○ Fight behavior-aggression ○ Fight behavior-withdrawal ○ Increased alertness ○ Panicky ○ Bedwetting ○ Jittery ○ Impulsiveness ○ Ability to identify object of fear ○ Concentration on the source ○ Frightened ○ Apprehension ○ Immediate response to object of fear ○ Terrified ○ Increased heart rate ○ Decreased self-assurance ○ Scared ○ Wide-eyed ○ Attack behavior ○ Increased tension ○ Wariness

Fluid Volume deficit [isotonic]

DEFINITION: The state in which an individual experiences decreased intravascular, interstitial and intracellular fluid. This refers to dehydration, water loss alone without change in sodium.

RELATED FACTORS: ○ Active fluid volume loss [e.g., hemorrhage, diarrhea, wounds, burns, abdominal cancer, fistulas, ascites (third-spacing), use of hyperosmotic radiopaque contrast agents] ○ Failure of regulatory mechanisms [e.g., fever/thermo-regulatory response, renal tubule damage]

DEFINING CHARACTERISTICS

Subjective: ○ Thirst ○ Weakness

Objective: ○ Decreased urine output ○ Increased urine concentration ○ Decreased venous filling ○ Sudden weight loss (except in third-spacing) ○ Decreased blood pressure ○ Increased pulse rate ○ Decreased skin/tongue turgor ○ Decreased pulse volume/pressure ○ Change in mental state ○ Increased body temperature ○ Dry skin/mucous membranes ○ Elevated hematocrit

NOTE: Information appearing in [ ] has been added by the authors to clarify and facilitate the use of nursing diagnoses.

Fluid Volume deficit, [hypertonic/hypotonic]

DEFINITION: [The state in which an individual experiences decreased intravascular, interstitial and intracellular fluid. This refers to dehydration with changes in sodium.]

Note: NANDA has restricted Fluid Volume deficit to address only isotonic dehydration. For patient needs related to dehydration associated with alterations in sodium, the authors have provided this second diagnostic category.

RELATED FACTORS

[**Hypertonic:** ○ Uncontrolled diabetes mellitus/insipidus; hyperglycemic, hyperosmotic nonketotic coma (HHNC), increased intake of hypertonic fluids/IV therapy, inability to respond to thirst reflex/inadequate free water supplementation (high-osmolarity enteral feeding formulas), renal insufficiency/failure]

[**Hypotonic:** ○ Chronic illness/malnutrition, excessive use of hypotonic IV solutions (e.g., D_5W), renal insufficiency]

DEFINING CHARACTERISTICS

Subjective: ○ [Reports of fatigue, nervousness, exhaustion] ○ [Thirst]

Objective: ○ [Increased urine output ○ Dilute urine (initially) and/or decreased output/oliguria] ○ [Weight loss] ○ [Decreased venous filling] ○ [Hemoconcentration; altered serum sodium] ○ [Hypotension (postural)] ○ [Increased pulse rate; decreased pulse volume and pressure] ○ [Decreased skin turgor] ○ [Change in mental status (e.g., confusion)] ○ [Increased body temperature] ○ [Dry skin/mucous membranes]

Fluid Volume, risk for deficit*

DEFINITION: The state in which an individual is at risk of experiencing vascular, cellular, or intracellular dehydration [due to active or regulatory losses of body water in excess of needs or replacement capability].

RISK FACTORS: ○ Extremes of age and weight ○ Loss of fluid through abnormal routes (e.g., indwelling tubes) ○ Knowledge deficiency related to fluid volume ○ Factors influencing fluid needs (e.g., hypermetabolic states) ○ Medications (e.g., diuretics) ○ Excessive losses through normal routes (e.g., diarrhea) ○ Deviations affecting access to, intake of, or absorption of fluids (e.g., physical immobility)

Fluid Volume, excess

DEFINITION: The state in which an individual experiences increased isotonic fluid retention.

RELATED FACTORS: ○ Compromised regulatory mechanisms [e.g., heart/renal failure, cirrhosis, steroid excess or decreased plasma proteins (e.g., malnutrition, draining fistulas, burns)] ○ Excess fluid intake ○ Excess sodium intake ○ [Drug therapies: e.g., chlorpropamide, tolbutamide, vincristine, triptyline, carbamazepine]

DEFINING CHARACTERISTICS

Subjective: ○ Shortness of breath, orthopnea ○ Anxiety

Objective: ○ Dyspnea ○ Edema ○ Pleural effusion ○ Anasarca ○ Weight gain over short period ○ Intake exceeds output ○ S_3 heart sound ○ Pulmonary congestion ○ Abnormal breath sounds (rales or crackles) ○ Change in respiratory pattern ○ Change in mental status; restlessness ○ Blood pressure changes ○ Increased central venous pressure ○ Pulmonary artery pressure changes ○ Jugular venous distention ○ Positive hepatojugular reflex ○ Oliguria; specific gravity changes ○ Azotemia ○ Altered electrolytes ○ Decreased hemoglobin, hematocrit

Fluid Volume, risk for imbalance

DEFINITION: A risk of a decrease, increase, or rapid shift from one to the other of intravascular, interstitial, and/or intracellular fluid. This refers to the loss or excess or to the other of intravascular, interstitial, and/or intracellular fluid. This refers to the loss or excess or both of body fluids or replacement fluids.

NOTE: Information appearing in [ ] has been added by the authors to clarify and facilitate the use of nursing diagnoses.

*[**Note:** A risk diagnosis is not evidenced by signs and symptoms because the problem has not yet occurred, and nursing interventions are directed at prevention. Therefore, risk factors present are noted instead.]

RISK FACTORS: ○ Scheduled for major invasive procedures ○ [Rapid/sustained loss (e.g., hemorrhage, burns, fistulas)] ○ [Rapid fluid replacement] ○ Other risk factors to be determined

Gas Exchange, impaired

DEFINITION: Excess or deficit in oxygenation and/or carbon dioxide elimination at the alveolar capillary membrane. [This may be an entity of its own but may also be an end result of other pathology with an interrelatedness between airway clearance and/or breathing pattern problems.]

RELATED FACTORS: ○ Ventilation perfusion imbalance: ○ [Altered blood flow, e.g., pulmonary embolus, increased vascular resistance] ○ Alveolar-capillary membrane changes [e.g., adult respiratory distress syndrome; chronic conditions, such as pneumonoconiosis, asbestosis/silicosis] ○ [Altered oxygen supply, e.g., altitude sickness] ○ [Altered oxygen-carrying capacity of blood, e.g., Sickle cell/other anemia, carbon monoxide poisoning]

DEFINING CHARACTERISTICS

Subjective: ○ Headache upon awakening ○ Visual disturbances ○ [Sense of impending doom]

Objective: ○ Restlessness ○ Irritability ○ Confusion ○ Somnolence ○ Abnormal rate, rhythm, depth of breathing ○ Nasal flaring ○ Dyspnea ○ Abnormal skin color (pale, dusky) ○ Cyanosis (in neonates only) ○ Diaphoresis ○ Tachycardia ○ Abnormal arterial blood gases/pH ○ Hypoxia/Hypoxemia ○ Hypercarbia ○ Decreased carbon dioxide ○ Hypercapnia

Grieving, anticipatory

DEFINITION: Intellectual and emotional responses and behaviors by which individuals, families, communities work through the process of modifying self-concept based on the perception of potential loss. [**Note:** May be a healthy response requiring interventions of support and information-giving.]

RELATED FACTORS: To be developed by NANDA ○ [Perceived potential loss of: significant other, physiopsychosocial well-being, personal possessions]

DEFINING CHARACTERISTICS

Subjective: ○ Sorrow; guilt; anger; [choked feelings] ○ Denial of potential loss/significance of the loss ○ Expression of distress at potential loss ○ Alteration in activity level; sleep/dream patterns, eating habits, libido ○ Bargaining ○ Resolution of grief before the reality of loss

Objective: ○ Potential loss of significant object ○ Altered communication patterns ○ Difficulty taking on new or different roles ○ [Altered affect] ○ [Crying] ○ [Social isolation, withdrawal]

Grieving, dysfunctional

DEFINITION: Extended, unsuccessful use of intellectual and emotional responses by which individuals, families, communities attempt to work through the process of modifying self-concept based on the perceptions of loss.

RELATED FACTORS: ○ Actual or perceived object loss (object loss is used in the broadest sense) and may include people, possessions, a job, status, home, ideals, parts and processes of the body [e.g., amputation, paralysis, chronic/fatal illness] ○ [Thwarted grieving response to a loss] ○ [Lack of resolution of previous grieving response] ○ [Absence of anticipatory grieving]

DEFINING CHARACTERISTICS

Subjective: ○ Verbal expression of distress at loss ○ Expression of unresolved issues ○ Idealization of lost object ○ Denial of loss ○ Anger; sadness ○ Alterations in: eating habits, sleep and dream patterns, activity levels, libido, concentration and/or pursuit of tasks ○ Reliving of past experiences with little or no reduction (diminishment) of intensity of the grief ○ Expression of guilt ○ [Hopelessness]

Objective: ○ Crying ○ Difficulty in expressing loss ○ Prolonged interference with life functioning ○ Alterations in concentration and/or pursuits of tasks ○ Labile affect ○ Developmental regression ○ Repetitive use of ineffectual behaviors associated with attempts to reinvest in relationships ○ Onset or exacerbation of somatic or psychosomatic responses ○ [Isolation]

NOTE: Information appearing in [ ] has been added by the authors to clarify and facilitate the use of nursing diagnoses.

Growth and Development, altered

DEFINITION: The state in which an individual demonstrates deviations in norms from his/her age group.

RELATED FACTORS: ○ Inadequate caretaking [physical/emotional neglect/abuse] ○ Indifference, inconsistent responsiveness, multiple caretakers ○ Separation from significant other(s) ○ Environmental and stimulation deficiencies ○ Effects of physical disability [handicapping condition] ○ Prescribed dependence ○ [Insufficient expectations for self-care] ○ [Prolonged/painful treatments; prolonged/repeated hospitalizations] ○ [Physical/emotional illness (chronic, traumatic)]

DEFINING CHARACTERISTICS

Subjective: ○ Inability to perform self-care or self-control activities appropriate for age ○ [Regression/loss of previously acquired skills; precocious or accelerated skill attainment]

Objective: ○ Delay or difficulty in performing skills (motor, social, or expressive) typical of age group ○ Altered physical growth ○ Flat affect ○ Listlessness, decreased responses ○ [Sleep disturbances, negative mood/responses]

Growth, risk for altered

DEFINITION: At risk for growth above the 97th percentile or below the third percentile for age, crossing two percentile channels; disproportionate growth.

RISK FACTORS

Prenatal: ○ Maternal nutrition ○ Multiple gestation ○ Substance use/abuse ○ Teratogen exposure ○ Congenital/genetic disorders

Individual: ○ Prematurity ○ Malnutrition ○ Caregiver and/or individual maladaptive feeding behaviors ○ Insatiable appetite ○ Anorexia ○ Infection ○ Chronic illness ○ Organic and inorganic factors ○ Substance abuse

Environmental: ○ Deprivation ○ Poverty ○ Violence ○ Teratogen ○ Lead poisoning ○ Natural disasters

Caregiver: ○ Abuse ○ Mental illness, mental retardation, severe learning disability

Health Maintenance, altered

DEFINITION: Inability to identify, manage, and/or seek out help to maintain health. [This diagnosis contains components of other nursing diagnoses. We recommend subsuming health maintenance interventions under the "basic" nursing diagnosis when a single causative factor is identified, e.g., Knowledge Deficit [Learning Need] (specify); Communication, impaired: verbal; Thought processes, altered; Individual/Family Coping, ineffective.]

RELATED FACTORS: ○ Lack of or significant alteration in communication skills (written, verbal, and/or gestural) ○ Unachieved development tasks ○ Lack of ability to make deliberate and thoughtful judgments ○ Perceptual or cognitive impairment ○ Complete or partial lack of gross and/or fine motor skills ○ Ineffective individual/family coping ○ Dysfunctional grieving; disabling spiritual distress ○ Lack of material resource

DEFINING CHARACTERISTICS

Subjective: ○ Expressed interest in improving health behaviors ○ Reported or observed lack of equipment, financial, and/or other resources ○ Reported or observed impairment of personal support system ○ [Reported or observed compulsive behaviors]

Objective: ○ Demonstrated lack of knowledge regarding basic health practices ○ Reported or observed inability to take the responsibility for meeting basic health practices in any or all functional pattern areas ○ Demonstrated lack of adaptive behaviors to internal/external environmental changes ○ History of lack of health-seeking behavior

Health Seeking Behaviors [specify]

DEFINITION: A state in which an individual in stable health is actively seeking ways to alter personal health habits and/or the environment to move toward higher level of health. (Stable health status is defined as age appropriate illness prevention measures achieved, client reports good or excellent health, and signs and symptoms of disease if present are controlled.)

NOTE: Information appearing in [ ] has been added by the authors to clarify and facilitate the use of nursing diagnoses.

RELATED FACTORS: ○ [Situational/maturational occurrence precipitating concern about current health status]

DEFINING CHARACTERISTICS

Subjective: ○ Expressed desire to seek a higher level of wellness ○ Expressed desire to modify codependent behaviors ○ Expressed desire for increased control of health practice ○ Expression of concern about current environmental conditions on health status ○ Stated (or observed) unfamiliarity with wellness community resources

Objective: ○ Observed desire to seek a higher level of wellness ○ Observed desire for increased control of health practice ○ Demonstrated or observed lack of knowledge in health promotion behaviors

Home Maintenance Management, impaired

DEFINITION: Inability to independently maintain a safe, growth-promoting immediate environment.

RELATED FACTORS: ○ Individual/family member disease or injury ○ Insufficient family organization or planning ○ Insufficient finances ○ Impaired cognitive or emotional functioning ○ Lack of role modeling ○ Unfamiliarity with neighborhood resources ○ Lack of knowledge ○ Inadequate support systems

DEFINING CHARACTERISTICS

Subjective: Household members: ○ Express difficulty in maintaining their home in a comfortable fashion ○ Request assistance with home maintenance ○ Describe outstanding debts or financial crises

Objective: ○ Accumulation of dirt, food, or hygienic wastes ○ Unwashed or unavailable cooking equipment, clothes, or linen ○ Overtaxed family members (e.g., exhausted, anxious) ○ Repeated hygienic disorders, infestations, or infections ○ Disorderly surroundings ○ Inappropriate household temperature ○ Lack of necessary equipment or aids ○ Presence of vermin or rodents ○ Offensive odors

Hopelessness

DEFINITION: A subjective state in which an individual sees limited or no alternatives or personal choices available and is unable to mobilize energy on own behalf.

RELATED FACTORS: ○ Prolonged activity restriction creating isolation ○ Failing or deteriorating physiological condition ○ Long-term stress; abandonment ○ Lost belief in transcendent values/God

DEFINING CHARACTERISTICS

Subjective: ○ Verbal cues (despondent content, "I can't," sighing)

Objective: ○ Passivity, decreased verbalization ○ Decreased affect ○ Lack of initiative ○ Decreased response to stimuli ○ Turning away from speaker ○ Closing eyes ○ Shrugging in response to speaker ○ Decreased appetite, increased/decreased sleep ○ Lack of involvement in care/passively allowing care ○ [Withdrawal from environs] ○ [Lack of involvement/interest in significant other(s) (children, spouse)] ○ [Angry outbursts]

Hyperthermia

DEFINITION: A state in which an individual's body temperature is elevated above his/her normal range.

RELATED FACTORS: ○ Exposure to hot environment; inappropriate clothing ○ Vigorous activity; dehydration ○ Inability or decreased ability to perspire ○ Medications/anesthesia ○ Increased metabolic rate; illness or trauma

DEFINING CHARACTERISTICS

Subjective: ○ [Headache]

Objective: ○ Increase in body temperature above normal range ○ Flushed skin, warm to touch ○ Increased respiratory rate, tachycardia ○ Seizures/convulsions ○ [Unstable blood pressure] ○ [Muscle rigidity/fasciculations] ○ [Confusion]

Hypothermia

DEFINITION: The state in which an individual's body temperature is reduced below normal range.

NOTE: Information appearing in [ ] has been added by the authors to clarify and facilitate the use of nursing diagnoses.

RELATED FACTORS: ○ Exposure to cool or cold environment, [prolonged exposure, immersion in cold water/near drowning, artificial hypothermia/cardiopulmonary bypass] ○ Inadequate clothing ○ Evaporation from skin in cool environment ○ Inability or decreased ability to shiver ○ Aging [or very young] ○ [Debilitating] illness or trauma, damage to hypothalamus ○ Malnutrition; decreased metabolic rate; inactivity ○ Consumption of alcohol; medications causing vasodilation ○ [Vasodilation, e.g., sepsis, drug overdose]

DEFINING CHARACTERISTICS

Subjective: ○ Reduction in body temperature below normal range ○ Shivering (mild) ○ Cool skin ○ Pallor (moderate) ○ Slow capillary refill ○ Cyanotic nail beds ○ Hypertension; tachycardia ○ Piloerection ○ [Core temperature 95°F: decreased pulse, increased respiration, poor judgment, memory loss] ○ [Core temperature 94°F–90.5°F: all vital signs decreased, myocardial irritability/dysrhythmias, muscle rigidity, no shivering, obtunded] ○ [Core temperature 85°F: no apparent vital signs, heart rate unresponsive to drug therapy, cyanotic, dilated pupils, appears dead]

Infant Behavior, disorganized

DEFINITION: Disintegrated physiological and neurobehavioral responses to the environment.

RELATED FACTORS:

Prenatal: ○ Congenital or genetic disorders ○ Teratogenic exposure ○ [Exposure to drugs]

Postnatal: ○ Prematurity ○ Oral/motor problems ○ Feeding intolerance ○ Malnutrition ○ Invasive/painful procedures ○ Pain

Individual: ○ Gestational/postconceptual age ○ Immature neurological system ○ Illness; [Infection]; [Hypoxia/birth asphyxia]

Environmental: ○ Physical environment inappropriateness ○ Sensory inappropriateness/overstimulation/deprivation ○ [Lack of containment/boundaries]

Caregiver: ○ Cue misreading/cue knowledge deficit ○ Environmental stimulation contribution

DEFINING CHARACTERISTICS

Regulatory Problems: ○ Inability to inhibit [e.g., "locking in"—inability to look away from stimulus] ○ Irritability

State-Organization System: ○ Active awake (fussy, worried gaze) ○ Quiet-awake (staring, gaze aversion) ○ Diffuse/unclear sleep, state oscillation ○ Irritable or panicky crying

Attention-Interaction System: ○ Abnormal response to sensory stimuli (e.g., difficult to soothe, inability to sustain alert status)

Motor System: ○ Increased, decreased, or limp tone ○ Finger splay, fisting or hands to face ○ Hyperextension of arms and legs ○ Tremors, startles, twitches ○ Jittery, jerky, uncoordinated movement ○ Altered primitive reflexes

Physiological: ○ Bradycardia, tachycardia, or arrhythmias ○ Bradypnea, tachypnea, apnea ○ Pale, cyanotic, mottled, or flushed color ○ "Time-out signals" (e.g., gaze, grasp, hiccough, cough, sneeze, sigh, slack jaw, open mouth, tongue thrust) ○ Oximeter desaturation ○ Feeding intolerances (aspiration or emesis)

Infant Behavior, risk for disorganized*

DEFINITION: Risk for alteration in integration and modulation of the physiological and behavioral systems of functioning (i.e., autonomic, motor, state, organizational, self-regulatory, and attentional-interactional systems).

RISK FACTORS: ○ Pain ○ Oral/motor problems ○ Environmental overstimulation ○ Lack of containment/boundaries ○ Prematurity ○ Invasive/painful procedures

Infant Behavior, organized, potential for enhanced

DEFINITION: A pattern of modulation of the physiological and behavioral systems of functioning of an infant (i.e., autonomic, motor, state, organizational, self-regulatory, and attentional-interactional sys-

NOTE: Information appearing in [ ] has been added by the authors to clarify and facilitate the use of nursing diagnoses.

*[**Note:** A risk diagnosis is not evidenced by signs and symptoms because the problem has not yet occurred, and nursing interventions are directed at prevention. Therefore, risk factors present are noted instead.]

tems) that is satisfactory but can be improved, resulting in higher levels of integration in response to environmental stimuli.

RELATED FACTORS: ○ Prematurity ○ Pain

DEFINING CHARACTERISTICS

Subjective: ○ Stable physiological measures ○ Definite sleep-wake states ○ Use of some self-regulatory behaviors ○ Response to visual/auditory stimuli

Infant Feeding Pattern, ineffective

DEFINITION: A state in which an infant demonstrates an impaired ability to suck or coordinate the suck-swallow response.

RELATED FACTORS: ○ Prematurity ○ Neurological impairment/delay ○ Oral hypersensitivity ○ Prolonged NPO ○ Anatomic abnormality

DEFINING CHARACTERISTICS

Subjective: ○ [Mother reports infant is unable to initiate or sustain an effective suck]

Objective: ○ Inability to initiate or sustain an effective suck ○ Inability to coordinate sucking, swallowing, and breathing

Infection, risk for*

DEFINITION: The state in which an individual is at increased risk for being invaded by pathogenic organisms.

RISK FACTORS: ○ Inadequate primary defenses (broken skin, traumatized tissue, decrease in ciliary action, stasis of body fluids, change in pH secretions, altered peristalsis) ○ Inadequate secondary defenses (e.g., decreased hemoglobin, leukopenia, suppressed inflammatory response) and immunosuppression ○ Inadequate acquired immunity; tissue destruction and increased environmental exposure ○ Chronic disease; malnutrition; trauma ○ Invasive procedures ○ Pharmaceutical agents [including antibiotic therapy] ○ Rupture of amniotic membranes ○ Insufficient knowledge to avoid exposure to pathogens

Injury, risk for*

DEFINITION: A state in which the individual is at risk of injury as a result of environmental conditions interacting with the individual's adaptive and defensive resources. [**Note:** The potential for injury differs from individual to individual and situation to situation. It is our belief that the environment is not safe, and there is no way to list everything that might present a danger to someone. Rather, we believe nurses have the responsibility to educate people throughout their life cycles to live safely in their environment.]

RISK FACTORS

Internal: ○ Biochemical, regulatory function: (sensory, integrative, effector dysfunction; tissue hypoxia); malnutrition; immune-autoimmune; abnormal blood profile, (leukocytosis/leukopenia; altered clotting factors, thrombocytopenia; sickle cell, thalassemia; decreased hemoglobin) ○ Physical: (broken skin, altered mobility); developmental age; (physiological, psychosocial) ○ Psychological: (affective, orientation)

External: ○ Biological (immunization level of community, microorganism) ○ Chemical: (pollutants, poisons, drugs, pharmaceutical agents, alcohol, caffeine, nicotine, preservatives, cosmetics and dyes), nutrients (vitamins, food types) ○ Physical: (design, structure, and arrangement of community, building, and/or equipment); mode of transport/transportation ○ People-provider: (nosocomial agent, staffing patterns; cognitive, affective, and psychomotor factors)

Knowledge Deficit [Learning Need] (specify)

DEFINITION: [Lack of specific information necessary for patient/SO to make informed choices regarding condition/therapies/treatment plan.]

RELATED FACTORS: ○ Lack of exposure ○ Information misinterpretation ○ Unfamiliarity with information resources ○ Lack of recall ○ Cognitive limitation ○ Lack of interest in learning ○ [Pa-

NOTE: Information appearing in [ ] has been added by the authors to clarify and facilitate the use of nursing diagnoses.

*[**Note:** A risk diagnosis is not evidenced by signs and symptoms because the problem has not yet occurred, and nursing interventions are directed at prevention. Therefore, risk factors present are noted instead.]

tient's request for no information] ○ [Inaccurate/incomplete information presented]

DEFINING CHARACTERISTICS

Subjective: ○ Verbalization of the problem ○ [Request for information] ○ [Statement of misconception]

Objective: ○ Inaccurate follow-through of instruction ○ Inadequate performance of test ○ Inappropriate or exaggerated behaviors (e.g., hysterical, hostile, agitated, apathetic) ○ [Development of preventable complication]

Latex Allergy Response

DEFINITION: An allergic response to natural latex rubber products.

RELATED FACTORS: No immune mechanism response

DEFINING CHARACTERISTICS

Type I Reactions: Immediate

Type IV Reactions: Eczema; irritation; reaction to additives causes discomfort (e.g., thiurams, carbamates); redness; delayed onset (hours)

Irritant Reactions: Erythema; chapped or cracked skin; blisters

Latex Allergy Response, risk for

DEFINITION: At risk for allergic response to natural latex rubber products.

RISK FACTORS: ○ History of reactions to latex (e.g., balloons, condoms, gloves); allergies to bananas, avocados, tropical fruits, kiwi, chestnuts, poinsettia plants; history of allergies and asthma ○ Professions with daily exposure to latex (e.g., medicine, nursing, dentistry) ○ Conditions needing continuous or intermittent catheterization ○ Multiple surgical procedures, especially from infancy (e.g., spina bifida)

Loneliness, risk for*

DEFINITION: A subjective state in which an individual is at risk of experiencing vague dysphoria.

RISK FACTORS: ○ Affectional deprivation ○ Physical isolation ○ Cathectic deprivation ○ Social isolation

Memory, impaired

DEFINITION: The state in which an individual experiences the inability to remember or recall bits of information or behavioral skills. Impaired memory may be attributed to physiopathological or situational causes that are either temporary or permanent.

RELATED FACTORS: ○ Acute or chronic hypoxia ○ Anemia ○ Decreased cardiac output ○ Fluid and electrolyte imbalance ○ Neurological disturbances ○ Excessive environmental disturbances

DEFINING CHARACTERISTICS

Subjective: ○ Reported experiences of forgetting ○ Inability to recall recent or past events

Objective: ○ Observed experiences of forgetting ○ Inability to determine if a behavior was performed ○ Inability to learn or retain new skills or information ○ Inability to perform a previously learned skill ○ Inability to recall factual information

Mobility, impaired bed

DEFINITION: Limitation of independent movement from one bed position to another.

RELATED FACTORS: To be developed

DEFINING CHARACTERISTICS

Subjective or objective: ○ Impaired ability to: Turn side to side ○ Move from supine to sitting or sitting to supine ○ "Scoot" or reposition self in bed ○ Move from supine to prone or prone to supine ○ Move supine to long sitting or long sitting to supine

Mobility, impaired physical [specify level]

DEFINITION: A limitation in independent, purposeful physical movement of the body or of one or more extremities.

NOTE: Information appearing in [ ] has been added by the authors to clarify and facilitate the use of nursing diagnoses.

*[**Note:** A risk diagnosis is not evidenced by signs and symptoms because the problem has not yet occurred, and nursing interventions are directed at prevention. Therefore, risk factors present are noted instead.]

RELATED FACTORS: ○ Intolerance to activity/ decreased strength and endurance ○ Pain/discomfort ○ Neuromuscular/musculoskeletal impairment ○ Sensoriperceptual/cognitive impairments ○ Depressive mood state or anxiety ○ Decreased muscle strength, control and/or mass ○ Joint stiffness or contracture ○ Loss of integrity of bone structures ○ Reluctance to initiate movement ○ Lack of knowledge regarding value of physical activity ○ Cultural beliefs regarding age appropriate activity ○ Lack of physical or social environmental supports ○ Sedentary lifestyle of disuse or deconditioning ○ Selective or generalized malnutrition ○ Altered cellular metabolism ○ Body mass index above 75th age-appropriate percentile ○ Limited cardiovascular endurance ○ Developmental delay ○ Prescribed movement restrictions ○ Medications

DEFINING CHARACTERISTICS

Subjective: ○ [Reports of pain/discomfort on movement]

Objective: ○ Limited range of motion ○ Limited ability to perform gross fine/motor skills ○ Uncoordinated or jerky movements ○ Gait changes (e.g., decreased walk, speed, difficulty initiating gait, small steps, shuffles feet, exaggerated lateral postural sway) ○ Postural instability during performance of routine activities of daily living ○ Slowed movement ○ Decreased [sic] reaction time ○ Difficulty turning ○ Movement-induced shortness of breath ○ Engages in substitutions for movement (e.g., increased attention to other's activity, controlling behavior, focus on pre-illness/disability activity) ○ Suggested Functional Level Classification

0 = Completely independent
1 = Requires use of equipment or device
2 = Requires help from another person for assistance, supervision, or teaching
3 = Requires help from another person and equipment device
4 = Dependent, does not participate in activity (Code adapted from E. Jones, et al. [November 1974]. Patient classification for long-term care: User's manual, HEW, Publication No. HRA-74-3107.)

Mobility, impaired wheelchair

DEFINITION: Limitation of independent operation of wheelchair within environment.

RELATED FACTORS: To be developed

DEFINING CHARACTERISTICS: ○ Impaired ability to operate manual or power wheelchair on even or uneven surface, on an incline or decline, on curbs

Nausea

DEFINITION: An unpleasant, wavelike sensation in the back of the throat, epigastrium, or throughout the abdomen that may or may not lead to vomiting.

RELATED FACTORS: ○ Postsurgical anesthesia ○ Stimulation of neuropharmacological mechanisms ○ Irritation to the gastrointestinal system ○ Chemotherapy

DEFINING CHARACTERISTICS

Subjective: ○ Reports "nausea" or "sick to stomach"

Objective: ○ Usually precedes vomiting, but may be experienced after vomiting or when vomiting does not occur ○ Accompanied by swallowing movement affected by skeletal muscles ○ Accompanied by pallor, cold and clammy skin, increased salivation, tachycardia, gastric stasis, and diarrhea

Noncompliance [Compliance, altered] (specify)

DEFINITION: The extent to which a person's and/or caregiver's behavior coincides or fails to coincide with a health-promoting or therapeutic plan agreed upon by the person (and/or family, and/or community) and health care professional. In the presence of an agreed-upon, health-promoting or therapeutic plan, person's or caregiver's behavior may be fully, partially, or nonadherent and may lead to clinically effective, partially effective, or ineffective outcomes. [Note: Noncompliance is a term that may create a negative situation for patient and caregiver that may foster difficulties in resolving the causative factors. Because patients have a right to refuse therapy, we see this as a situation in which the professional

NOTE: Information appearing in [ ] has been added by the authors to clarify and facilitate the use of nursing diagnoses.

need is to accept the patient's point of view/behavior/choice(s) and work together to find alternate means to meet original and/or revised goals.]

RELATED FACTORS

Health care plan: ○ Duration ○ Significant others; cost; intensity; complexity

Individual factors: ○ Personal and developmental abilities; knowledge and skill relevant to the regimen behavior; motivational forces ○ Individual's value system; health beliefs, cultural influences, spiritual values ○ [Altered thought processes such as depression, paranoia] ○ [Difficulty changing behavior, as in addictions] ○ [Issues of secondary gain]

Health System: ○ Individual health coverage; financial flexibility of plan ○ Credibility of provider; client-provider relationships; provider continuity and regular follow-up; provider reimbursement of teaching and follow-up; communication and teaching skills of the provider ○ Access and convenience of care; satisfaction with care

Network: ○ Involvement of members in health plan; social value regarding plan; perceived beliefs of significant others

DEFINING CHARACTERISTICS

Subjective: ○ Statements by patient or significant other(s) of failure to adhere ○ [Denial]

Objective: ○ Behavior indicative of failure to adhere (by direct observation) ○ Objective tests (physiological measures, detection of physiological markers) ○ Failure to progress ○ Evidence of development of complications; exacerbation of symptoms ○ Failure to keep appointments ○ [Inability to set or attain mutual goals]

Nutrition: altered, less than body requirements

DEFINITION: The state in which an individual experiences an intake of nutrients insufficient to meet metabolic needs.

RELATED FACTORS: ○ Inability to ingest or digest food or absorb nutrients due to biological, psychological, or economic factors ○ [Lack of information regarding individual needs] ○ [Intake insufficient to meet increased metabolic demands]

DEFINING CHARACTERISTICS

Subjective: ○ Reported inadequate food intake (less than RDA) ○ Reported or evidence of lack of food ○ Lack of interest in food ○ Aversion to eating ○ Reported altered taste sensation ○ Perceived inability to ingest food ○ Satiety immediately after ingesting food ○ Abdominal cramping ○ Abdominal pain with or without pathology ○ Lack of information, misinformation, misconceptions [authors view this as a Related Factor]

Objective: ○ Body weight 20% or more under ideal [for height and frame] ○ Loss of weight with adequate food intake ○ Poor muscle tone ○ Weakness of muscles required for swallowing or mastication ○ Sore, inflamed buccal cavity ○ Capillary fragility ○ Hyperactive bowel sounds ○ Diarrhea and/or steatorrhea ○ Pale conjunctiva and mucous membranes ○ Excessive loss of hair [or increased growth of hair on body (lanugo)] ○ [Decreased subcutaneous fat/muscle mass] ○ [Cessation of menses]

Nutrition: altered, more than body requirements

DEFINITION: The state in which an individual is experiencing an intake of nutrients that exceeds metabolic needs.

RELATED FACTORS: ○ Excessive intake in relationship to metabolic need [**Note:** Underlying cause is often complex and may be difficult to diagnose/treat]

DEFINING CHARACTERISTICS

Subjective: ○ Reported dysfunctional eating patterns:

Pairing food with other activities
Eating in response to external cues such as time of day, social situation
Concentrating food intake at end of day
Eating in response to internal cues other than hunger, for example, anxiety

○ Sedentary activity level

NOTE: Information appearing in [ ] has been added by the authors to clarify and facilitate the use of nursing diagnoses.

Objective: ○ Weight 10% over ideal for height and frame [overweight] ○ Weight 20% over ideal for height and frame [obese] ○ Triceps skinfold greater than 15 mm in men and 25 mm in women ○ Observed dysfunctional eating patterns [as noted in Subjective] ○ [Percentage of body fat greater than: 18%–20% for trim women; 10%–12% for trim men]

Nutrition: altered, risk for more than body requirements*

DEFINITION: The state in which an individual is at risk of experiencing an intake of nutrients that exceeds metabolic needs.

RISK FACTORS: ○ Reported/observed obesity in one or both parents [/spouse; hereditary predisposition] ○ Rapid transition across growth percentiles in infants or children, [adolescence] ○ Reported use of solid food as major food source before 5 months of age ○ Reported/observed higher baseline weight at beginning of each pregnancy ○ Dysfunctional eating patterns:

Pairing food with other activities

Eating in response to external cues such as time of day or social situation

Concentrating food intake at end of day

Eating in response to internal cues other than hunger, for example, anxiety

○ Observed use of food as reward or comfort measure ○ [Socially/culturally isolated; lacking other outlets] ○ [Alteration in usual activity patterns/sedentary lifestyle] ○ [Alteration in usual coping patterns] ○ [Majority of foods consumed are concentrated, high-calorie or fat sources] ○ [Significant/sudden decline in financial resources, lower socioeconomic status]

Oral Mucous Membrane, altered

DEFINITION: Disruptions of the lips and soft tissue of the oral cavity.

RELATED FACTORS: ○ Pathological conditions— oral cavity (radiation to head and/or neck)

○ Trauma (chemical, e.g., acidic foods, drugs, noxious agents, alcohol), mechanical (e.g., ill-fitting dentures, braces, tubes [endotracheal, nasogastric], surgery in oral cavity) ○ NPO for more than 24 hours ○ Lack of, decreased, impaired salivation ○ Mouth breathing ○ Ineffective oral hygiene ○ Infection ○ Medication side effects ○ Malnutrition or vitamin deficiency ○ Dehydration ○ Chemotherapy ○ Immunosuppression/compromised ○ Decreased platelets ○ Radiation therapy ○ Chemical (e.g., alcohol, tobacco, acidic foods, regular use of inhalers) ○ Diminished hormone levels (women) ○ Barriers to oral self-care/professional care ○ Aging-related loss of connective, adipose, or bone tissue ○ Stress ○ Depression ○ Loss of supportive structures ○ Cleft lip or palate

DEFINING CHARACTERISTICS

Subjective: ○ Xerostomia (dry mouth) ○ Oral pain/discomfort ○ Self-report of bad, diminished, or absent taste; difficulty eating or swallowing

Objective: ○ Purulent drainage or exudates ○ Gingival recession, pockets deeper than 4 mm ○ Enlarged tonsils beyond what is developmentally appropriate ○ Smooth, atrophic, sensitive tongue ○ Geographic tongue ○ Mucosal denudation ○ Presence of pathogens ○ Difficult speech ○ Gingival or mucosal pallor ○ Vesicles, nodules, or papules ○ White patches/plaques, spongy patches or white curdlike exudate ○ Oral lesions or ulcers ○ Halitosis ○ Edema ○ Hyperemia ○ Desquamation ○ Coated tongue ○ Stomatitis ○ Macroplasia ○ Bleeding ○ Gingival hyperplasia ○ Fissures ○ Chelitis ○ Red or bluish masses (e.g., hemangiomas)

Pain [acute]

DEFINITION: An unpleasant sensory and emotional experience arising from actual or potential tissue damage or described in terms of such damage (International Association for the Study of Pain); sudden or slow onset of any intensity from mild to severe with an anticipated or predictable end and a duration of less than 6 months.

NOTE: Information appearing in [ ] has been added by the authors to clarify and facilitate the use of nursing diagnoses.

*[**Note:** A risk diagnosis is not evidenced by signs and symptoms because the problem has not yet occurred, and nursing interventions are directed at prevention. Therefore, risk factors present are noted instead.]

RELATED FACTORS: ○ Injury agents (biologic, chemical, physical, psychological)

DEFINING CHARACTERISTICS

Subjective: ○ Verbal or coded report [expect less from under age 40, males, and some cultural groups] ○ [Pain unrelieved and/or increased beyond tolerance]

Objective: ○ Observed evidence ○ Protective behavior/guarding behavior ○ Antalgic position/gestures ○ Distraction behavior (e.g., pacing, seeking out other people and/or activities, repetitive activities) ○ Expressive behavior (e.g., restlessness, moaning, crying, vigilance, irritability, sighing) ○ Autonomic responses (e.g., diaphoresis, blood pressure, respiration, pulse change, pupillary dilation) ○ Autonomic alteration in muscle tone (may span from listless to rigid) ○ Facial mask ○ Self-focus ○ Sleep disturbance (eyes lack luster, "hecohe look," fixed or scattered movement, grimace) ○ Changes in appetite and eating ○ Narrowed focus (altered time perception, impaired thought processes, reduced interaction with people and environment)

Pain, chronic

DEFINITION: An unpleasant sensory and emotional experience arising from actual or potential tissue damage or described in terms of such damage (International Association for the Study of Pain); sudden or slow onset of any intensity from mild to severe, constant or recurring without an anticipated or predictable end and a duration of greater than 6 months. [Pain is a signal that something is wrong. Chronic pain can be recurrent and periodically disabling (e.g., migraine headaches), or may be unremitting. Although chronic pain syndrome includes various learned behaviors, psychological factors become the primary contribution to impairment. It is a complex, separate entity, combining elements from other NDs: Powerlessness; Diversional Activity, altered; Family Processes, altered, Self-Care deficit (specify): feeding, bathing/hygiene, dressing/grooming, toileting.]

RELATED FACTORS: ○ Chronic physical/psychosocial disability

DEFINING CHARACTERISTICS

Subjective: ○ Verbal or coded report ○ Fear of reinjury ○ Altered ability to continue previous activities ○ Anorexia, weight changes ○ Changes in sleep patterns ○ Fatigue ○ [Desperately seeks alternative solutions/therapies for relief/control of pain]

Objective: ○ Observed evidence of protective/guarding behavior; irritability; restlessness; self-focusing; facial mask; depression ○ Reduced interaction with people ○ Sympathetic mediated response (e.g., temperature, cold, changes of body position, hypersensitivity) ○ Atrophy of involved muscle group ○ [Preoccupation with pain]

Parent/Infant/Child Attachment, risk for altered*

DEFINITION: Disruption of the interactive process between parent/significant other and infant that fosters the development of a protective and nurturing reciprocal relationship.

RISK FACTORS: ○ Inability of parents to meet the personal needs ○ Anxiety associated with the parent role ○ Substance abuse ○ Premature infant ○ Ill infant/child who is unable to effectively initiate parental contact due to altered behavioral organization ○ Separation ○ Physical barriers ○ Lack of privacy

Parental Role Conflict

DEFINITION: The state in which a parent experiences role confusion and conflict in response to crisis.

RELATED FACTORS: ○ Separation from child due to chronic illness ○ Intimidation with invasive or restrictive modalities (e.g., isolation, intubation) specialized care centers, policies ○ Home care of a child with special needs (e.g., apnea monitoring, postural drainage, hyperalimentation) ○ Change in marital status ○ Interruptions of family life due to

NOTE: Information appearing in [ ] has been added by the authors to clarify and facilitate the use of nursing diagnoses.

*[**Note:** A risk diagnosis is not evidenced by signs and symptoms because the problem has not yet occurred, and nursing interventions are directed at prevention. Therefore, risk factors present are noted instead.]

home care regimen (treatments, caregivers, lack of respite)

DEFINING CHARACTERISTICS

Subjective: Parent(s): ○ Express concerns/feelings of inadequacy to provide for child's physical and emotional needs during hospitalization or in the home ○ Express concerns about changes in parental role, family functioning, family communication; family health ○ Express concern about perceived loss of control over decisions relating to their child ○ Verbalize feelings of guilt, anger, fear, anxiety, and/or frustrations about effect of child's illness on family process

Objective: ○ Demonstrated disruption in caretaking routines ○ Reluctant to participate in usual caretaking activities even with encouragement and support ○ Demonstrate feelings of guilt, anger, fear, anxiety, and/or frustrations about effect of child's illness on family process

Parenting, altered

DEFINITION: Inability of the primary caretaker to create an environment that promotes the optimum growth and development of the child. (It is important to state as a preface to this diagnosis that adjustment to parenting in general is a normal maturational process that elicits nursing behaviors of prevention of potential problems and health promotion.)

RELATED FACTORS

Social: ○ Lack of access to resources ○ Social isolation ○ Lack of resources ○ Poor home environments ○ Lack of family cohesiveness ○ Inadequate child care arrangements ○ Lack of transportation ○ Unemployment or job problems ○ Role strain or overload ○ Marital conflict, declining satisfaction ○ Lack of value of parenthood ○ Change in family unit ○ Low socioeconomic class ○ Unplanned or unwanted pregnancy ○ Presence of stress (e.g., financial, legal, recent crisis, cultural move) ○ Lack of, or poor, parental role model ○ Single parents ○ Lack of social support networks ○ Father of child not involved ○ History of being abusive/being abused ○ Financial difficulties ○ Maladaptive coping strategies ○ Poverty

○ Poor problem-solving skills ○ Inability to put child's needs before own ○ Low self-esteem ○ Relocations ○ Legal difficulties

Knowledge: ○ Lack of knowledge about child health maintenance ○ Lack of knowledge about parenting skills ○ Unrealistic expectation for self, infant, partner ○ Limited cognitive functioning ○ Lack of knowledge about child development ○ Inability to recognize and act on infant cues ○ Low educational level or attainment ○ Poor communication skills ○ Lack of cognitive readiness for parenthood ○ Preference for physical punishment

Physiological: ○ Physical illness

Infant or Child: ○ Premature birth ○ Multiple births ○ Illness ○ Prolonged separation from parent/separation at birth ○ Not gender desired ○ Attention deficit hyperactivity disorder ○ Difficult temperament ○ Lack of goodness of fit (temperament) with parental expectations ○ Unplanned or unwanted child ○ Handicapping condition or developmental delay ○ Altered perceptual abilities

Psychological: ○ History of substance abuse or dependencies ○ Disability ○ Depression ○ Difficult labor and/or delivery ○ Young age, especially adolescent ○ History of mental illness ○ High number or closely spaced pregnancies ○ Sleep deprivation or disruption ○ Lack of, or late, prenatal care ○ Separation from infant/child ○ Multiple births

DEFINING CHARACTERISTICS

Subjective: Parental: ○ Statements of inability to meet child's needs ○ Verbalization, cannot control child ○ Verbalization of role inadequacy frustration [inability to care for/discipline child]

Objective: Infant or child: ○ Frequent accidents/illness ○ Failure to thrive ○ Incidence of physical and psychological trauma or abuse ○ Poor academic performance ○ Poor cognitive development ○ Poor social competence ○ Behavioral disorders ○ Lack of attachment ○ Lack of separation anxiety ○ Runaway

Parental: ○ Negative statements about child ○ Inappropriate visual, tactile, auditory stimulation ○ Rejection or hostility to child ○ Inflexibility to meet needs of child, situation ○ Poor or inappropriate caretaking skills ○ High punitiveness ○ Inconsistent care ○ Child abuse ○ Inadequate child

NOTE: Information appearing in [ ] has been added by the authors to clarify and facilitate the use of nursing diagnoses.

health maintenance ○ Unsafe home environment ○ Inappropriate child care arrangements ○ Abandonment ○ Insecure or lack of attachment to infant ○ Inconsistent behavior management ○ Child neglect ○ Little cuddling ○ Maternal-child interaction deficit ○ Poor parent-child interaction

Parenting, risk for altered*

DEFINITION: Risk for inability of the primary caretaker to create, maintain, or regain an environment that promotes the optimum growth and development of the child. (It is important to state as a preface to this diagnosis that adjustment to parenting in general is a normal maturational process that elicits nursing behaviors of prevention of potential problems and health promotion.

RISK FACTORS

Social: ○ Marital conflict, declining satisfaction ○ History of being abused ○ Poor problem-solving skills ○ Role strain/overload ○ Social isolation ○ Lack of access to resources ○ Poor home environment ○ Lack of value of parenthood ○ Lack of or poor parental role model ○ Father of child not involved ○ History of being abusive ○ Lack of family cohesiveness ○ Inadequate child care arrangements ○ Lack of transportation ○ Unemployment or job problems ○ Change in family unit ○ Low socioeconomic class ○ Unplanned family unit ○ Low socioeconomic class ○ Unplanned or unwanted pregnancy ○ Single parent ○ Lack of social support network ○ Financial difficulties ○ Maladaptive coping strategies ○ Poverty ○ Poor problem-solving skills ○ Inability to put child's needs before own ○ Low self-esteem ○ Relocation ○ Legal difficulties ○ Stress

Knowledge: ○ Lack of knowledge about child health maintenance ○ Lack of knowledge about parenting skills ○ Unrealistic expectation of child ○ Low cognitive functioning ○ Lack of knowledge about child development ○ Inability to recognize and act on infant cues ○ Low educational level or attainment ○ Poor communication skills ○ Lack of cognitive readiness for parenthood ○ Preference for physical punishment

Physiological: ○ Physical illness

Infant or child: ○ Multiple births ○ Premature birth ○ Prolonged separation from parent/at birth ○ Illness ○ Not gender desired ○ Attention deficit hyperactivity disorder ○ Difficult temperament ○ Lack of goodness of fit (temperament) with parental expectations ○ Unplanned or unwanted child ○ Handicapping condition or developmental delay

Psychological: ○ History of substance abuse or dependencies ○ Disability ○ Depression ○ Difficult labor and/or delivery ○ Young age, especially adolescent ○ History of mental illness ○ High number or closely spaced children ○ Sleep deprivation or disruption ○ Lack of, or late, prenatal care ○ Separation from infant/child ○ Multiple births

Perioperative Positioning, risk for injury*

DEFINITION: A state in which the client is at risk for injury as a result of the environmental conditions found in the perioperative setting.

RISK FACTORS: ○ Disorientation ○ Immobilization, muscle weakness ○ Sensory/perceptual disturbances due to anesthesia ○ Obesity ○ Emaciation ○ Edema

Peripheral Neurovascular, risk for dysfunction*

DEFINITION: A state in which an individual is at risk of experiencing a disruption in circulation, sensation, or motion of an extremity.

RISK FACTORS: ○ Fractures ○ Mechanical compression (e.g., tourniquet, cast, brace, dressing, or restraint) ○ Orthopedic surgery ○ Trauma ○ Immobilization ○ Burns ○ Vascular obstruction

Personal Identity, disturbance

DEFINITION: Inability to distinguish between self and nonself.

NOTE: Information appearing in [ ] has been added by the authors to clarify and facilitate the use of nursing diagnoses.

*[**Note:** A risk diagnosis is not evidenced by signs and symptoms because the problem has not yet occurred, and nursing interventions are directed at prevention. Therefore, risk factors present are noted instead.]

RELATED FACTORS: To be developed by NANDA ○ [Organic brain syndrome] ○ [Poor ego differentiation, as in schizophrenia] ○ [Panic/dissociative states] ○ [Biochemical body change]

DEFINING CHARACTERISTICS: To be developed by NANDA

 Subjective: ○ [Confusion about sense of self, purpose or direction in life, sexual identification/preference]

 Objective: ○ [Difficulty in making decisions] ○ [Poorly differentiated ego boundaries] ○ [See ND Anxiety, panic state]

Poisoning, risk for*

DEFINITION: Accentuated risk of accidental exposure to or ingestion of drugs or dangerous products in dosages sufficient to cause poisoning. [Adverse effects of prescribed medication/drug use.]

RISK FACTORS

 Internal (Individual): ○ Reduced vision ○ Lack of safety or drug education ○ Lack of proper precaution ○ Insufficient finances ○ Verbalization of occupational setting without adequate safeguards ○ Cognitive or emotional difficulties ○ [Age, e.g., young child, elderly] ○ [Chronic disease state, disability] ○ [Careless behaviors, attitudes, habits, belief systems]

 External (Environmental): ○ Large supplies of drugs in house ○ Dangerous products placed or stored within the reach of children or confused persons ○ Flaking, peeling paint or plaster in presence of young children ○ Paint, lacquer, and so on, in poorly ventilated areas or without effective protection ○ [Unsafe stoves, heaters; lack of smoke detectors] ○ Medicines stored in unlocked cabinets accessible to children or confused persons ○ Availability of illicit drugs potentially contaminated by poisonous additives ○ Chemical contamination of food and water ○ Unprotected contact with heavy metals or chemicals ○ Presence of poisonous vegetation ○ Presence of atmospheric pollutants

Post-Trauma Syndrome [specify stage]

DEFINITION: A sustained maladaptive response to traumatic, overwhelming event.

RELATED FACTORS: ○ Events outside the range of usual human experience ○ Physical and psychosocial abuse ○ Rape ○ Natural disasters and/or man-made disasters ○ Sudden destruction of one's home or community ○ Serious threat or injury to self or loved ones ○ Serious accidents ○ Industrial and motor vehicle accidents ○ Epidemics ○ Witnessing mutilation, violent death, or other horrors ○ Tragic occurrence involving multiple deaths ○ Military combat ○ Being held prisoner of war or criminal victimization (torture) ○ Wars

DEFINING CHARACTERISTICS

 Subjective: ○ Anxiety ○ Fear ○ Horror ○ Flashbacks ○ Intrusive thoughts/dreams ○ Nightmares ○ Shame ○ Hopelessness ○ Gastric irritability ○ Palpitations ○ Guilt ○ Headaches

 Objective: ○ Repression ○ Denial ○ Numbing ○ Psychologic amnesia ○ Hypervigilant ○ Exaggerated startle response ○ Irritability ○ Aggression ○ Anger and/or rage ○ Panic attacks ○ Substance abuse ○ Compulsive behavior ○ Detachment ○ Depression ○ Altered mood states ○ Difficulty in concentrating ○ Grief ○ Avoidance ○ Alienation ○ Neurosensory irritability ○ Enuresis (in children) [Stages:

 Acute subtype: Begins within 6 months and does not last longer than 6 months
 Chronic subtype: Lasts more than 6 months
 Delayed subtype: Period of latency of 6 months or more before onset of symptoms]

Powerlessness [specify level]

DEFINITION: Perception that one's own action will not significantly affect an outcome; a perceived lack of control over a current situation or immediate happening.

RELATED FACTORS: ○ Healthcare environment [e.g., loss of privacy, personal possessions, control

---

NOTE: Information appearing in [ ] has been added by the authors to clarify and facilitate the use of nursing diagnoses.

*[**Note:** A risk diagnosis is not evidenced by signs and symptoms because the problem has not yet occurred, and nursing interventions are directed at prevention. Therefore, risk factors present are noted instead.]

over therapies] ○ Interpersonal interaction [e.g., misuse of power, force; abusive relationships] ○ Illness-related regimen [e.g., chronic/debilitating conditions] ○ Lifestyle of helplessness [e.g., repeated failures, dependency]

DEFINING CHARACTERISTICS

Subjective

Severe: ○ Verbal expressions of having no control or influence over situation, outcome, or self-care ○ Depression over physical deterioration that occurs despite patient compliance with regimens

Moderate: ○ Expressions of dissatisfaction and frustration over inability to perform previous tasks and/or activities ○ Expression of doubt regarding role performance ○ Reluctance to express true feelings; fearing alienation from caregivers

Low: ○ Expressions of uncertainty about fluctuating energy levels

Objective

Severe: ○ Apathy; [withdrawn, resigned, crying] ○ [Anger]

Moderate: ○ Does not monitor progress ○ Nonparticipation in care or decision-making when opportunities are provided ○ Dependence on others that may result in irritability, resentment, anger, and guilt ○ Inability to seek information regarding care ○ Does not defend self-care practices when challenged ○ Passivity

Low: ○ Passivity

Protection, altered

DEFINITION: The state in which an individual experiences a decrease in the ability to guard the self from internal or external threats such as illness or injury.

RELATED FACTORS: ○ Extremes of age ○ Inadequate nutrition ○ Alcohol abuse ○ Abnormal blood profiles (leukopenia, thrombocytopenia, anemia, coagulation) ○ Drug therapies (antineoplastic, corticosteroid, immune, anticoagulant, thrombolytic) ○ Treatments (surgery, radiation) ○ Diseases (such as cancer and immune disorders))

DEFINING CHARACTERISTICS

Subjective: ○ Neurosensory alterations ○ Chilling ○ Itching ○ Insomnia; fatigue; weakness ○ Anorexia

Objective: ○ Deficient immunity ○ Impaired healing ○ Altered clotting ○ Maladaptive stress response ○ Perspiring ○ Dyspnea; cough ○ Restlessness; immobility ○ Disorientation ○ Pressure sores

Note: The purpose of this diagnosis seems to be to provide for the combining of multiple diagnoses under a single heading for ease of planning care when a number of variables may be present, such as:

Extremes of age: Concern may be about Body Temperature, risk for altered/Thermoregulation, or Thought Processes, altered/Sensory-Perceptual alterations; (specify): visual, auditory, kinesthetic, gustatory, tactile, olfactory, as well as Trauma, risk for, Suffocation, risk for, or Poisoning, risk for.

Abnormal blood profile: Suggests possibility of Fluid Volume deficit, Tissue Perfusion, impaired; Gas Exchange, impaired; or Infection, risk for.

Inadequate nutrition: Brings up issues of Nutrition: altered, less than/more than body requirements; Infection, risk for; Thought Processes, altered; or Trauma, risk for.

Alcohol abuse: May be situational or chronic with problems ranging from Breathing Patterns, ineffective; Cardiac Output, decreased; and Fluid Volume deficit to Nutrition: altered, less/more than body requirements; Infection, risk for; Trauma, risk for; or Thought Processes, altered.]

Post-Trauma Syndrome, risk for*

DEFINITION: A risk for sustained maladaptive response to a traumatic, overwhelming event.

RISK FACTORS: ○ Occupation (e.g., police, fire, rescue, corrections, emergency room staff, mental health) ○ Perception of event ○ Exaggerated sense of responsibility ○ Survivor's role in the event ○ Inadequate social support ○ Nonsupportive envi-

---

NOTE: Information appearing in [ ] has been added by the authors to clarify and facilitate the use of nursing diagnoses.

*[Note: A risk diagnosis is not evidenced by signs and symptoms because the problem has not yet occurred, and nursing interventions are directed at prevention. Therefore, risk factors present are noted instead.]

ronment ○ Displacement from home ○ Duration of the event ○ Diminished ego strength

Rape-Trauma Syndrome [specify]

DEFINITION: Sustained maladaptive response to a forced, violent sexual penetration against the victim's will and consent. This syndrome includes the following three subcomponents: Rape trauma (A); Compound reaction (B), and Silent reaction (C). [Note: Although attacks are most often directed toward women, men also may be victims.]

RELATED FACTORS: ○ Rape [actual/attempted forced sexual penetration]

DEFINING CHARACTERISTICS

A: Rape Trauma

Subjective: ○ Shock ○ Fear ○ Anxiety ○ Anger ○ Embarrassment ○ Shame ○ Guilt ○ Humiliation ○ Revenge ○ Self-blame ○ Loss of self-esteem ○ Helplessness ○ Powerlessness ○ Nightmare and sleep disturbances ○ Change in relationships ○ Sexual dysfunction ○ [Changes in lifestyle (change in residence; seeking family support; seeking social network support)]

Objective: ○ Physical trauma (e.g., bruising, tissue irritation) ○ Muscle tension and/or spasms ○ Hyperalertness ○ Confusion ○ Disorganization ○ Inability to make decisions ○ Mood swings ○ Vulnerability ○ Depression ○ Dependence ○ Agitation ○ Aggression ○ Denial ○ Phobias ○ Paranoia ○ Substance abuse ○ Suicide attempts ○ Dissociative disorders

B: Compound Reaction: ○ All defining characteristics listed under rape trauma; in addition:

Acute Phase: ○ Reactivated symptoms of such previous conditions (i.e., physical/psychiatric illness) ○ Reliance on alcohol and/or drugs

C: Silent Reaction: ○ Abrupt changes in relationships with men ○ Increase in nightmares ○ Increasing anxiety during interview, that is, blocking of associations, long periods of silence, minor stuttering, physical distress ○ Pronounced changes in sexual behavior ○ No verbalization of the occurrence of rape ○ Sudden onset of phobic reactions

Relocation Stress Syndrome

DEFINITION: Physiological and/or psychosocial disturbances as a result of transfer from one environment to another.

RELATED FACTORS: ○ Past, concurrent, and recent losses ○ Losses involved with decision to move ○ Feeling of powerlessness ○ Lack of adequate support system ○ Little or no preparation for the move ○ Moderate to high degree of environmental change ○ History and types of previous transfers ○ Impaired psychosocial health status ○ Decreased physical health status

DEFINING CHARACTERISTICS

Subjective: ○ Anxiety ○ Apprehension ○ Depression ○ Loneliness ○ Verbalization of unwillingness to relocate ○ Sleep disturbance ○ Change in eating habits ○ Increased verbalization of needs ○ Gastrointestinal disturbances ○ Insecurity ○ Lack of trust ○ Verbalization of being concerned/upset about transfer ○ Unfavorable comparison of post-/pretransfer staff

Objective: ○ Change in environment/location ○ Increased confusion (elderly population [cognitively impaired]) ○ Dependency ○ Sad affect ○ Vigilance ○ Weight change ○ Withdrawal

Role Performance, altered

DEFINITION: The patterns of behavior and self-expression do not match the environmental context, norms, and expectations.

RELATED FACTORS

Social: ○ Inadequate role socialization (e.g., role model, expectations, responsibilities) ○ Young age, developmental level ○ Lack of resources ○ Low social economic status ○ Poverty ○ Inadequate support system ○ Family conflict ○ Stress and conflict ○ Job schedule demands ○ Lack of rewards ○ Domestic violence ○ Inadequate or inappropriate linkage with the healthcare system

Knowledge: ○ Lack of knowledge about role/role skills ○ Inadequate role preparation (e.g., role transition, skill, rehearsal, validation) ○ Lack of opportunity for role rehearsal ○ Lack of or inadequate role model ○ Education attainment level ○ Role

NOTE: Information appearing in [ ] has been added by the authors to clarify and facilitate the use of nursing diagnoses.

transition ○ Developmental transitions ○ Unrealistic role expectations

Physiological: ○ Health alterations (e.g., physical health, body image, self-esteem, mental health, psychosocial health, cognition, learning style, neurological health) ○ Substance abuse ○ Fatigue ○ Pain ○ Low self-esteem ○ Depression ○ Inadequate/inappropriate linkage with healthcare system

DEFINING CHARACTERISTICS

Subjective: ○ Altered role perceptions ○ Change in self-perception of role/usual patterns of responsibility/capacity to resume role/other's perception of role ○ Role dissatisfaction ○ Role overload ○ Role denial ○ Discrimination [by others] ○ Inadequate opportunities for role enactment

Objective: ○ Inadequate knowledge; role competency and skills; adaptation to change or transition ○ Role conflict; confusion; ambivalence ○ Inadequate confidence; motivation; self-management; coping ○ Inadequate opportunities/external support for role enactment ○ Inappropriate developmental expectations ○ System conflict ○ Uncertainty ○ Role strain ○ Anxiety or depression ○ Pessimistic ○ Powerlessness ○ Domestic violence ○ Harassment

Self-Care deficit (specify): feeding, bathing/hygiene, dressing/grooming, toileting

DEFINITION: Impaired ability to perform or complete feeding, bathing/hygiene, dressing/grooming, or toileting activities for oneself [on a temporary, permanent, or progressing basis.] [**Note:** Self-Care may also be expanded to include the practices used by the patient to promote health, the individual responsibility for self, a way of thinking. Refer to Home Maintenance Management, impaired; Health Maintenance, altered.]

RELATED FACTORS: ○ Weakness or tiredness ○ Decreased or lack of motivation ○ Neuromuscular/musculoskeletal impairment ○ Environmental barriers ○ Severe anxiety ○ Pain ○ Discomfort ○ Perceptual or cognitive impairment ○ Inadequate to perceive body part or spatial relationship (bathing/hygiene) ○ Impaired transfer ability/mobility status (toileting)

DEFINING CHARACTERISTICS

a. Self-Feeding deficit (levels 0–4)†
Inability to: ○ Prepare food for ingestion ○ Open containers ○ Handle utensils ○ Use assistive device ○ Pick up cup or glass ○ Get food onto utensil safely ○ Bring food from a receptacle to the mouth ○ Manipulate food in mouth ○ Chew/swallow food ○ Complete a meal ○ Ingest food in a socially acceptable manner

b. Self-Bathing/Hygiene deficit (levels 0–4)†
Inability to: ○ Get bath supplies ○ Wash body or body parts ○ Obtain or get to water source ○ Regulate temperature or flow of bath water ○ Get in and out of bathroom ○ Dry body

c. Self-Dressing/Grooming deficit (levels 0–4)†
Impaired ability to: ○ Choose clothing ○ Pick up clothing ○ Put on or take off necessary items of clothing (on upper/lower body, socks/shoes) ○ Obtain or replace articles of clothing ○ Fasten clothing/use zippers ○ Use assistive devices ○ Maintain appearance at a satisfactory level

d. Self-toileting deficit (levels 0–4)†
Unable to: ○ Get to toilet or commode ○ Manipulate clothing for toileting ○ Sit on or rise from toilet or commode ○ Carry out proper toilet hygiene ○ Flush toilet or empty commode

Self-Esteem, chronic low

DEFINITION: Long-standing negative self-evaluation/feelings about self or self-capabilities.

RELATED FACTORS: ○ To be developed ○ [Fixation in earlier level of development] ○ [Continual negative evaluation of self/capabilities during childhood] ○ [Personal vulnerability] ○ [Life choices perpetuating failure] ○ [Feelings of abandonment by SO]

DEFINING CHARACTERISTICS

Subjective: ○ Long-standing or chronic ○ Self-negating verbalization ○ Expressions of shame/guilt ○ Evaluates self as unable to deal with events ○ Rationalizes away/rejects positive feedback and exaggerates negative feedback about self

NOTE: Information appearing in [ ] has been added by the authors to clarify and facilitate the use of nursing diagnoses.
†Refer to ND: Mobility, impaired physical, for suggested functional level classification.

Objective: ○ Long-standing or chronic hesitancy to try new things/situations ○ Frequent lack of success in work or other life events ○ Overly conforming, dependent on others' opinions ○ Excessively seeks reassurance ○ Lack of eye contact ○ Nonassertive/passive; indecisive

Self-Esteem disturbance

DEFINITION: Negative self-evaluation/feelings about self or self-capabilities, which may be directly or indirectly expressed. [This is a human need for survival.]

RELATED FACTORS: ○ To be developed ○ [Unsatisfactory parent-child relationship] ○ [Unrealistic expectations (on the part of self and others)] ○ [Unmet dependency needs] ○ [Absent, erratic, or inconsistent parental discipline] ○ [Dysfunctional family system] ○ [Child/sexual abuse or neglect] ○ [Underdeveloped ego and punitive superego, retarded ego development] ○ [Negative role models] ○ [Disorganized or chaotic environments] ○ [Extreme poverty] ○ [Lack of positive feedback, repeated negative feedback resulting in diminished self-worth] ○ [Perceived/numerous failures (learned helplessness); "Failure" at life events, e.g., loss of job, divorce] ○ [Impaired cognition fostering negative view of self] ○ [Aging]

DEFINING CHARACTERISTICS

Subjective: ○ Self-negating verbalization ○ Evaluates self as unable to deal with events ○ Expressions of shame/guilt ○ Rationalizes away/rejects positive feedback and exaggerates negative feedback about self ○ [Inability to accept positive reinforcement]

Objective: ○ Hesitant to try new things/situations ○ Hypersensitive to slight or criticism ○ Grandiosity ○ Denial of problems obvious to others ○ Projection of blame/responsibility for problems ○ Rationalizing personal failures ○ [Not taking responsibility for self-care (self-neglect)] ○ [Lack of follow-through] ○ [Nonparticipation in therapy] ○ [Self-destructive behavior] ○ [Lack of eye contact]

Self-Esteem, situational low

DEFINITION: Negative self-evaluation/feelings about self that develop in response to a loss or change in an individual who previously had a positive self-evaluation.

RELATED FACTORS: ○ To be developed ○ ["Failure" at life events, (e.g., loss of job, relationship problems, divorce)] ○ [Feelings of abandonment by SO] ○ [Maturational transitions, adolescence, aging] ○ [Perceived loss of control in some aspect of life] ○ [Loss of independent functioning] ○ [Loss of capacity for remembering] ○ [Loss of capability for effective verbal communication]

DEFINING CHARACTERISTICS

Subjective: ○ Episodic occurrence of negative self-appraisal in response to life events in a person with a previous positive self-evaluation ○ Verbalization of negative feelings about the self (helplessness, uselessness) ○ Self-negating verbalizations; expressions of shame/guilt ○ Evaluates self as unable to handle situations/events

Objective: ○ Difficulty making decisions

Self-Mutilation, risk for*

DEFINITION: A state in which an individual is at risk to perform an act upon the self to injure, not kill, which produces tissue damage and tension relief.

RISK FACTORS: ○ Groups at risk: Clients with borderline personality disorder, especially females 16 to 25 years of age; clients in psychotic state—frequently males in young adulthood; emotionally disturbed and/or battered children; mentally retarded and autistic children; clients with a history of self-injury, physical, emotional or sexual abuse ○ Inability to cope with increased psychological/physiological tension in a healthy manner ○ Feelings of depression, rejection, self-hatred, separation anxiety, guilt, and depersonalization ○ Fluctuating emotions ○ Command hallucinations ○ Need for sensory stimuli ○ Parental emotional deprivation ○ Dysfunctional family

NOTE: Information appearing in [ ] has been added by the authors to clarify and facilitate the use of nursing diagnoses.

*[**Note:** A risk diagnosis is not evidenced by signs and symptoms because the problem has not yet occurred, and nursing interventions are directed at prevention. Therefore, risk factors present are noted instead.]

Sensory-Perceptual alterations (specify): visual, auditory, kinesthetic, gustatory, tactile, olfactory

DEFINITION: A state in which an individual experiences a change in the amount or patterning of incoming stimuli accompanied by a diminished, exaggerated, distorted, or impaired response to such stimuli.

RELATED FACTORS: ○ Excessive/insufficient environmental stimuli [e.g., therapeutically restricted environments, e.g., isolation, intensive care, bed rest, traction, confining illnesses, incubators; socially restricted environment, e.g., institutionalization, homebound, aging, chronic illness/dying, infant deprivation; stigmatized, e.g., mentally ill/retarded/handicapped; bereaved; excessive noise level, e.g., work environment, patient's immediate environment (intensive care unit with support machinery)] ○ Altered sensory perception, reception, transmission, and/or integration, e.g., neurological disease, trauma, or deficit; altered status of sense organs; inability to communicate, understand, speak, or respond; sleep deprivation; pain, (phantom limb)] ○ Biochemical imbalance ○ Electrolyte imbalance [elevated BUN, elevated ammonia, hypoxia] ○ Biochemical imbalances for sensory distortion (e.g., illusions, hallucinations) [e.g., central nervous system stimulants or depressants, mind-altering drugs] ○ Psychological stress [narrowed perceptual fields caused by anxiety]

DEFINING CHARACTERISTICS

Subjective: ○ Reported change in sensory acuity [e.g., photosensitivity, hypo/hyperesthesias, diminished/altered sense of taste, inability to tell position of body parts (proprioception)] ○ [Pain]

Objective: ○ Measured change in sensory acuity ○ Change in problem-solving abilities, [lack of/poor concentration] ○ Poor concentration ○ Disoriented in time, in place, or with people ○ Altered communication patterns ○ Change in usual response to stimuli, [rapid mood swings, exaggerated emotional responses] ○ Changes in behavior pattern ○ Restlessness ○ Irritability ○ Auditory/visual distortions ○ Hallucinations ○ [Bizarre thinking]

○ [Motor incoordination; altered sense of balance/falls, e.g., Meniere's syndrome]

Sexual dysfunction

DEFINITION: The state in which an individual experiences a change in sexual function that is viewed as unsatisfying, unrewarding, or inadequate.

RELATED FACTORS: ○ Biopsychosocial alteration of sexuality: ○ Ineffectual or absent role models ○ Vulnerability ○ Misinformation or lack of knowledge ○ Physical abuse ○ Values conflict ○ Lack of privacy ○ Altered body structure or function [pregnancy, recent childbirth, drugs, surgery, anomalies, disease process, trauma, radiation, [loss of sexual desire, disruption of sexual response pattern such as premature ejaculation, dyspareunia]) ○ Psychosocial abuse, e.g., harmful relationships ○ Lack of significant other

DEFINING CHARACTERISTICS

Subjective: ○ Verbalization of problem ○ Actual or perceived limitation imposed by disease and/or therapy ○ Inability to achieve desired satisfaction ○ Alterations in achieving perceived sex role ○ Conflicts involving values ○ Alterations in achieving sexual satisfaction ○ Seeking of confirmation of desirability

Objective: ○ Alteration in relationship with significant other ○ Change of interest in self and others

Sexuality Patterns, altered

DEFINITION: The state in which an individual expresses concern regarding his/her sexuality.

RELATED FACTORS: ○ Knowledge/skill deficit about alternative responses to health-related transitions, altered body function or structure, illness or medical treatment ○ Lack of privacy ○ Lack of significant other ○ Ineffective or absent role models ○ Conflicts with sexual orientation or variant preferences ○ Fear of pregnancy or of acquiring a sexually transmitted disease ○ Impaired relationship with a significant other

---

NOTE: Information appearing in [ ] has been added by the authors to clarify and facilitate the use of nursing diagnoses.

DEFINING CHARACTERISTICS

Subjective: ○ Reported difficulties, limitations, or changes in sexual behaviors or activities

Skin Integrity, impaired

DEFINITION: A state in which the individual has altered epidermis and/or dermis. [An interruption in the integumentary system, the largest, multifunctional organ of the body.]

RELATED FACTORS

External: ○ Hyperthermia or hypothermia ○ Chemical substance ○ Radiation ○ Physical immobilization ○ Humidity ○ Moisture ○ Altered fluid status ○ Mechanical factors (e.g., shearing forces, pressure, restraint), [trauma: injury/surgery] ○ Extremes in age ○ Medications

Internal: ○ Altered nutritional state (obesity, emaciation)/metabolic state; circulation; sensation; pigmentation ○ Skeletal   prominence ○ Developmental factors ○ Alterations in turgor (change in elasticity) ○ Immunological deficit ○ [Excretions/ secretions] ○ [Psychogenic] ○ [Presence of edema]

DEFINING CHARACTERISTICS

Subjective: ○ [Reports of itching, pain, numbness of affected/surrounding area]

Objective: ○ Disruption of skin (epidermis) ○ Destruction of skin layers (dermis) ○ Invasion of body structures

Skin Integrity, risk for impaired*

DEFINITION: A state in which the individual's skin is at risk of being adversely altered.

RISK FACTORS

External: ○ Chemical substance ○ Hypothermia or hyperthermia ○ Radiation ○ Physical immobilization ○ Excretions and/or secretions ○ Moisture ○ Humidity ○ Mechanical factors (e.g., shearing forces, pressure, restraint) ○ Extremes of age

Internal: ○ Medication ○ Altered nutritional state (e.g., obesity, emaciation)/metabolic state; cir-

culation; sensation; pigmentation ○ Skeletal prominence ○ Developmental factors ○ Alterations in skin turgor (change in elasticity) ○ Psychogenetic ○ Immunologic ○ [Presence of edema]

Sleep Deprivation

DEFINITION: Prolonged periods of time without sustained natural, periodic suspension of relative unconsciousness [sic].

RELATED FACTORS: ○ Prolonged physical/psychological discomfort ○ Sustained unfamiliar or uncomfortable sleep environment ○ Sleep-related painful reactions ○ Periodic limb movement (e.g., restless leg syndrome, nocturnal myoclonus) ○ Inadequate daytime activities ○ Sustained environmental stimulation ○ Prolonged use of pharmacological or dietary antisoporifics ○ Sustained inadequate sleep hygiene ○ Aging-related sleep stage shifts ○ Non–sleep-inducing parenting practices ○ Sustained circadian synchrony ○ Sundowner's syndrome ○ Dementia ○ Nightmares ○ Sleep walking ○ Sleep terrors ○ Sleep-related enuresis ○ Sleep apnea ○ Idiopathic central nervous system hypersomnolence ○ Narcolepsy ○ Familial sleep paralysis

DEFINING CHARACTERISTICS

Subjective: ○ Daytime drowsiness ○ Tiredness ○ Malaise ○ Decreased ability to function

Objective: ○ Listlessness ○ Lethargy ○ Apathy ○ Slowed reaction ○ Inability to concentrate ○ Irritability ○ Restlessness ○ Hand tremors ○ Mild, fleeting nystagmus ○ Heightened sensitivity to pain ○ Perceptual disorders (e.g., disturbed body sensation, delusions, feeling afloat) ○ Anxious ○ Hallucinations ○ Transient paranoia ○ Acute confusion ○ Agitated or combative

Sleep Pattern disturbance

DEFINITION: Time limited disruption of sleep (natural, periodic suspension of consciousness) amount and quality.

NOTE: Information appearing in [ ] has been added by the authors to clarify and facilitate the use of nursing diagnoses.

*[**Note:** A risk diagnosis is not evidenced by signs and symptoms because the problem has not yet occurred, and nursing interventions are directed at prevention. Therefore, risk factors present are noted instead.]

RELATED FACTORS

Psychological: ○ Daytime activity pattern ○ Social schedule inconsistent with chronotype ○ Daylight/darkness exposure ○ Frequently changing sleep-wake schedule ○ Shift work ○ Aging-related sleep shifts ○ Frequent travel across time zones ○ Thinking about home ○ Circadian asynchrony ○ Fatigue ○ Inadequate sleep hygiene ○ Ruminative presleep thoughts ○ Anticipation ○ Preoccupation with trying to sleep ○ Fear of insomnia ○ Maladaptive conditioned wakefulness ○ Delayed or advanced sleep phase syndrome ○ Dietary ○ Medications ○ Sustained use of antisleep agents ○ Biochemical agents ○ Periodic gender-related hormonal shifts ○ Body temperature ○ Temperament ○ Loneliness ○ Grief ○ Anxiety ○ Fear ○ Boredom ○ Depression ○ Separation from significant others ○ Loss of sleep partner, life change ○ Childhood onset

Environmental: ○ Noise ○ Ambient temperature, humidity ○ Lighting ○ Unfamiliar sleep furnishings ○ Noxious odors ○ Excessive stimulation ○ Privacy control ○ Sleep partner ○ Other-generated awakening ○ Physical restraint ○ Nurse for therapeutics, monitoring, laboratory tests ○ Lack of sleep

Parental: ○ Mother's sleep-wake pattern/emotional support ○ Parent-infant interaction

Physiological: ○ Urinary urgency ○ Gastroesophageal reflux ○ Position ○ Shortness of breath ○ Stasis of secretions ○ Wet ○ Fever ○ Nausea

DEFINING CHARACTERISTICS

Subjective: ○ Verbal reports of: Difficulty falling asleep, not feeling well-rested ○ Dissatisfaction with sleep ○ Sleep onset greater than 30 minutes ○ Awakening earlier or later than desired ○ Three or more nighttime awakenings ○ Prolonged awakenings ○ Early morning insomnia ○ Decreased ability to function ○ [Falls asleep during activities]

Objective: ○ Sleep maintenance insomnia ○ Self-induced impairment of normal pattern ○ Less than age-normed total sleep time ○ Increased proportion of Stage 1 sleep ○ Decreased proportion of Stages 3 and 4 sleep (e.g., hyporesponsiveness, excess sleepiness, decreased motivation) ○ Decreased proportion of REM sleep (e.g., REM rebound, hyperactivity, emotional lability, agitation and impulsivity, atypical polysomnographic features)

Social Interaction, impaired

DEFINITION: The state in which an individual participates in an insufficient or excessive quantity or ineffective quality of social exchange.

RELATED FACTORS: ○ Knowledge/skill deficit about ways to enhance mutuality ○ Communication barriers [including head injury, stroke, other neurological conditions affecting ability to communicate] ○ Self-concept disturbance ○ Absence of available significant other(s) or peers ○ Limited physical mobility [e.g., neuromuscular disease] ○ Therapeutic isolation ○ Sociocultural dissonance ○ Environmental barriers ○ Altered thought processes

DEFINING CHARACTERISTICS

Subjective: ○ Verbalized discomfort in special situations ○ Verbalized inability to receive or communicate a satisfying sense of belonging, caring, interest, or shared history ○ Family report of change of style or pattern of interaction

Objective: ○ Observed discomfort in social situations ○ Observed inability to receive or communicate a satisfying sense of belonging, caring, interest, or shared history ○ Observed use of unsuccessful social interaction behaviors ○ Dysfunctional interaction with peers, family, and/or others

Social Isolation

DEFINITION: Aloneness experienced by the individual and perceived as imposed by others and as a negative or threatened state.

RISK FACTORS: Factors contributing to the absence of satisfying personal relationships, such as: ○ Delay in accomplishing developmental tasks ○ Immature interests ○ Alterations in mental status ○ Altered state of wellness ○ Alterations in physical appearance ○ Unaccepted social behavior/values ○ Inadequate personal resources ○ Inability to en-

NOTE: Information appearing in [ ] has been added by the authors to clarify and facilitate the use of nursing diagnoses.

gage in satisfying personal relationships ○ [Traumatic incidents or events]

DEFINING CHARACTERISTICS

Subjective: Expresses: ○ Feeling of aloneness imposed by others ○ Feelings of rejection ○ Values acceptable to subculture but unacceptable to the dominant cultural group ○ Inability to meet expectations of others ○ Experiencing feelings of difference from others ○ Inadequacy in or absence of significant purpose in life ○ Interests inappropriate to developmental age/stage ○ Insecurity in public

Objective: ○ Absence of supportive significant other(s)—family, friends, group ○ Sad, dull affect ○ Inappropriate or immature interests/activities for developmental age/stage ○ Projects hostility in voice, behavior ○ Evidence of physical/mental handicap or altered state of wellness ○ Uncommunicative, withdrawn, no eye contact ○ Preoccupation with own thoughts, repetitive, meaningless actions ○ Seeks to be alone, or exists in subculture ○ Shows behavior unaccepted by dominant cultural group

Sorrow, chronic

DEFINITION: A cyclical, recurring and potentially progressive pattern of pervasive sadness that is experienced by a client (parent or caregiver, or individual with chronic illness or disability) in response to continual loss, throughout the trajectory of an illness or disability.

RELATED FACTORS: ○ Death of a loved one ○ Person experiences chronic physical or mental illness or disability such as: mental retardation, multiple sclerosis, prematurity, spina bifida or other birth defects, chronic mental illness, infertility, cancer, Parkinson's disease ○ Person experiences one or more trigger events (e.g., crises in management of the illness, crises related to developmental stages and missed opportunities or milestones that bring comparisons with developmental, social, or personal norms) ○ Unending caregiving as a constant reminder of loss

DEFINING CHARACTERISTICS

Subjective: ○ Expresses one or more of the following feelings: anger, being misunderstood, confusion, depression, disappointment, emptiness, fear, frustration, guilt/self-blame, helplessness, hopelessness, loneliness, low self-esteem, recurring loss, overwhelmed

Objective: ○ Client expresses periodic, recurrent feelings of sadness ○ Feelings that vary in intensity, are periodic, may progress and intensify over time, and may interfere with the client's ability to reach his/her highest level of personal and social well-being

Spiritual Distress (distress of the human spirit)

DEFINITION: Disruption in the life principle that pervades a person's entire being and that integrates and transcends one's biologic and psychosocial nature.

RELATED FACTORS: ○ Separation from religious and cultural ties ○ Challenged belief and value system (e.g., due to moral/ethical implications of therapy, due to intense suffering)

DEFINING CHARACTERISTICS

Subjective: ○ Expresses concern with meaning of life/death and/or belief systems ○ Verbalizes inner conflict about beliefs; concern about relationship with deity; does not experience that God is forgiving ○ Questions moral/ethical implications of therapeutic regimen ○ Description of nightmares/sleep disturbances ○ Anger toward God [as defined by the person]; displacement of anger toward religious representatives ○ Questions meaning of suffering ○ Questions meaning of own existence ○ Seeks spiritual assistance ○ Unable to choose [or chooses not to] participate in usual religious practices ○ [Regards illness as punishment] ○ [Unable to accept self; engages in self-blame] ○ [Description of somatic complaints]

Objective: ○ Alteration in behavior or mood evidenced by anger, crying, withdrawal, preoccupation, anxiety, hostility, apathy, and so on ○ Gallows humor

Spiritual Distress, risk for

DEFINITION: At risk for an altered sense of harmonious connectedness with all of life and the uni-

NOTE: Information appearing in [ ] has been added by the authors to clarify and facilitate the use of nursing diagnoses.

verse in which dimensions that transcend and empower the self may be disrupted.

RISK FACTORS: ○ Energy-consuming anxiety ○ Physical or psychological stress ○ Situation/maturational ○ Loss of loved one ○ Natural disasters ○ Physical/mental illness ○ Low self-esteem ○ Blocks to self-love ○ Poor relationships ○ Substance abuse ○ Inability to forgive

Spiritual Well-Being, potential for enhanced

DEFINITION: Spiritual well-being is the process of an individual's developing/unfolding of mystery through harmonious interconnectedness that springs from inner strengths.

RELATED FACTORS: [None listed]

DEFINING CHARACTERISTICS

Subjective: ○ Inner strengths: A sense of awareness, self-consciousness, sacred source, unifying force, inner core, and transcendence ○ Unfolding mystery: one's experience about life's purpose and meaning, mystery, uncertainty, and struggles ○ Harmonious interconnectedness: relatedness, connectedness, harmony with self, others, higher power/God, and the environment

Spontaneous Ventilation, inability to sustain

DEFINITION: A state in which the response pattern of decreased energy reserves results in an individual's inability to maintain breathing adequate to support life.

RELATED FACTORS: ○ Metabolic factors ○ Respiratory muscle fatigue

DEFINING CHARACTERISTICS

Subjective: ○ Dyspnea ○ Apprehensive

Objective: ○ Increased metabolic rate ○ Increased restlessness ○ Increased use of accessory muscles ○ Decreased tidal volume ○ Increased heart rate ○ Decreased Po_2 ○ Decreased Pco_2 ○ Decreased cooperation ○ Decreased Sao_2

Suffocation, risk for*

DEFINITION: Accentuated risk of accidental suffocation (inadequate air available for inhalation).

RISK FACTORS

Internal (Individual): ○ Reduced olfactory sensation ○ Reduced motor abilities ○ Lack of safety education; precautions ○ Cognitive or emotional difficulties [e.g., altered consciousness] ○ Disease or injury process

External (Environmental): ○ Pillow/propped bottle placed in an infant's crib ○ Pacifier hung around infant's head ○ Children playing with plastic bags or inserting small objects into their mouths or noses ○ Children left unattended in bathtubs or pools ○ Discarded or unused refrigerators or freezers without removed doors ○ Vehicle warming in closed garage ○ Household gas leaks ○ Smoking in bed ○ Use of fuel-burning heaters not vented to outside ○ Low-strung clothesline ○ Eating of large mouthfuls [or pieces] of food

Surgical Recovery, delayed

DEFINITION: An extension of the number of postoperative days required for individuals to initiate and perform on their own behalf activities that maintain life, health, and well-being.

RELATED FACTORS: To be developed

DEFINING CHARACTERISTICS

Subjective: ○ Perception more time needed to recover ○ Postpones resumption of work/employment activities ○ Report of pain/discomfort ○ Loss of appetite with or without nausea ○ Fatigue

Objective: ○ Evidence of interrupted healing of surgical area (e.g., red, indurated, draining, immobile) ○ Difficulty in moving about ○ Requires help to complete self-care

Swallowing, impaired

DEFINITION: Abnormal functioning for the swallowing mechanism associated with deficits in oral, pharyngeal, or esophageal structure or function.

NOTE: Information appearing in [ ] has been added by the authors to clarify and facilitate the use of nursing diagnoses.
*[Note: A risk diagnosis is not evidenced by signs and symptoms because the problem has not yet occurred, and nursing interventions are directed at prevention. Therefore, risk factors present are noted instead.]

RELATED FACTORS

Congenital Deficits: ○ Upper airway anomalies ○ Conditions with significant hypotonia ○ Neuromuscular impairment (e.g., decreased or absent gag reflex, decreased strength or excursion of muscles involved in mastication, perceptual impairment, facial paralysis) ○ Cranial nerve involvement ○ Mechanical obstruction (e.g., edema, tracheostomy tube, tumor) ○ History of tube feeding ○ Respiratory disorders ○ Congenital heart disease ○ Behavioral feeding problems ○ Self-injurious behavior ○ Failure to thrive or protein energy malnutrition

Neurological Problems: ○ Acquired anatomic defects ○ External/internal traumas ○ Oral cavity or oropharynx abnormalities ○ Nasal or nasopharyngeal cavity defects ○ Upper airway/laryngeal anomalies ○ Tracheal, laryngeal, esophageal defects ○ Achalasia ○ Gastroesophageal reflux disease ○ Cerebral palsy ○ Premature infants ○ Traumatic head injury ○ Developmental delay

DEFINING CHARACTERISTICS

Subjective: Esophageal Phase Impairment: ○ Food refusal or volume limiting ○ Complaints of "something stuck" ○ Heartburn or epigastric pain ○ Nighttime coughing or awakening

Objective: Oral Phase Impairment: ○ Weak suck resulting in inefficient nippling ○ Lack of tongue action to form bolus ○ Premature entry of bolus ○ Slow bolus formation ○ Incomplete lip closure ○ Food pushed out of/falls from mouth ○ Lack of chewing ○ Coughing, choking, gagging before a swallow ○ Piecemeal deglutition ○ Inability to clear oral cavity ○ Pooling in lateral sulci ○ Nasal reflux ○ Sialorrhea or drooling ○ Long meals with little consumption ○ Abnormality in oral phase of swallow study

Pharyngeal Phase Impairment: ○ Food refusal ○ Altered head positions ○ Delayed/multiple swallows ○ Choking, coughing, or gagging ○ Nasal reflux ○ Gurgly voice quality ○ Inadequate laryngeal elevation ○ Unexplained fevers ○ Recurrent pulmonary infections ○ Abnormality in pharyngeal phase by swallow study

Esophageal Phase Impairment: ○ Observed evidence of difficulty in swallowing (e.g., stasis of food in oral cavity, coughing/choking) ○ Hyperextension of head, arching during or after meals ○ Repetitive swallowing or ruminating ○ Bruxism ○ Unexplained irritability surrounding mealtime ○ Odynophagia ○ Acidic smelling breath ○ Regurgitation of gastric contents or wet burps ○ Vomitus on pillow ○ Vomiting ○ Hematemesis ○ Abnormality in esophageal phase by swallow study

Therapeutic Regimen: Community, ineffective management

DEFINITION: A pattern of regulating and integrating into community processes programs for treatment of illness and the sequelae of illness that are unsatisfactory for meeting health-related goals.

RELATED FACTORS: [None listed]

DEFINING CHARACTERISTICS

Objective: ○ Deficits in persons and programs to be accountable for illness care of aggregates ○ Deficits in advocates for aggregates ○ Deficits in community activities for secondary and tertiary prevention ○ Illness symptoms above the norm expected for the number and type of population ○ Number of healthcare resources are insufficient for the incidence or prevalence of illness(es) ○ Unavailable healthcare resources for illness care ○ Unexpected acceleration of illness(es)

Therapeutic Regimen: Families, ineffective management

DEFINITION: A pattern of regulating and integrating into family processes a program for treatment of illness and the sequelae of illness that is unsatisfactory for meeting specific goals.

RELATED FACTORS: ○ Complexity of healthcare system ○ Complexity of therapeutic regimen ○ Decisional conflicts ○ Economic difficulties ○ Excessive demands made on individual or family ○ Family conflicts

DEFINING CHARACTERISTICS

Subjective: ○ Verbalized desire to manage the treatment of illness and prevention of the sequelae ○ Verbalized difficulty with regulation/integration of one or more effects or prevention of compli-

NOTE: Information appearing in [ ] has been added by the authors to clarify and facilitate the use of nursing diagnoses.

cation ○ Verbalizes that family did not take action to reduce risk factors for progression of illness and sequelae

Objective: ○ Inappropriate family activities for meeting the goals of a treatment or prevention program ○ Acceleration (expected or unexpected) of illness symptoms of a family member ○ Lack of attention to illness and its sequelae

Therapeutic Regimen: Individuals, effective management

DEFINITION: A pattern of regulating and integrating into daily living a program for treatment of illness and its sequelae that is satisfactory for meeting specific health goals.

RELATED FACTORS: [None listed]

DEFINING CHARACTERISTICS

Subjective: ○ Verbalized desire to manage the treatment of illness and prevention of sequelae ○ Verbalized intent to reduce risk factors for progression of illness and sequelae

Objective: Appropriate choices of daily activities for meeting the goals of a treatment or prevention program ○ Illness symptoms are within a normal range of expectation

Therapeutic Regimen: Individuals, ineffective management

DEFINITION: A pattern of regulating and integrating into daily living a program for treatment of illness and the sequelae of illness that is unsatisfactory for meeting specific health goals.

RELATED FACTORS: ○ Complexity of healthcare system; therapeutic regimen ○ Decisional conflicts ○ Economic difficulties ○ Excessive demands made on individual or family ○ Family conflict ○ Family patterns of healthcare ○ Inadequate number and types of cues to action ○ Knowledge deficits ○ Mistrust of regimen and/or healthcare personnel ○ Perceived seriousness; susceptibility; barriers; benefits ○ Powerlessness ○ Social support deficits

DEFINING CHARACTERISTICS

Subjective: Verbalized: ○ Desire to manage the treatment of illness and prevention of sequelae ○ Difficulty with regulation/integration of one or more prescribed regimens for treatment of illness and its effects on prevention of complications ○ Did not take action to include treatment regimens in daily routines/reduce risk factors for progression of illness and sequelae

Objective: ○ Choice of daily living ineffective for meeting the goals of a treatment or prevention program ○ Acceleration (expected or unexpected) of illness symptoms

Thermoregulation, ineffective

DEFINITION: The state in which the individual's temperature fluctuates between hypothermia and hyperthermia.

RELATED FACTORS: ○ Trauma or illness [e.g., cerebral edema, cerebral vascular accident, intracranial surgery, or head injury] ○ Immaturity, aging [e.g., loss/absence of brown adipose tissue] ○ Fluctuating environmental temperature ○ [Changes in hypothalamic tissue causing alterations in emission of thermosensitive cells and regulation of heat loss/production] ○ [Changes in level/action of thyroxone, and catecholamines] ○ [Changes in metabolic rate/activity] ○ [Chemical reactions in contracting muscles]

DEFINING CHARACTERISTICS

Objective: ○ Fluctuations in body temperature above or below the normal range (see also major and minor characteristics present in hypothermia and hyperthermia)

Thought Processes, altered

DEFINITION: A state in which an individual experiences a disruption in cognitive operations and activities.

RELATED FACTORS: To be developed by NANDA ○ [Physiological changes, aging, hypoxia, head injury, malnutrition, infections] ○ [Sleep deprivation] ○ [Psychological conflicts, emotional changes, men-

NOTE: Information appearing in [ ] has been added by the authors to clarify and facilitate the use of nursing diagnoses.

tal disorders] ○ [Biochemical changes, medications, substance abuse]

DEFINING CHARACTERISTICS

Subjective: ○ [Ideas of reference, hallucinations, delusions]

Objective: ○ Inaccurate interpretation of environment ○ Memory deficit/problems, [disorientation to time, place, person, circumstances and events, loss of short-term/remote memory] ○ Hyper/hypovigilance ○ Cognitive dissonance, [decreased ability to grasp ideas, make decisions, problem-solve, reason, abstract or conceptualize, calculate] ○ Distractibility, [altered attention span] ○ Egocentricity ○ Inappropriate/nonreality-based thinking ○ [Confabulation] ○ [Inappropriate social behavior]

Tissue Integrity, impaired

DEFINITION: A state in which an individual experiences damage to mucous membrane, corneal, integumentary, or subcutaneous tissue. It is a state in which an individual has altered body tissue.

RELATED FACTORS: ○ Altered circulation ○ Nutritional deficit/excess [metabolic, endocrine dysfunction] ○ Fluid deficit/excess ○ Knowledge deficit ○ Impaired physical mobility ○ Irritants, chemical (including body excretions; secretions, medications), [infections] ○ Thermal (temperature extremes) ○ Mechanical (e.g., pressure, shear, friction) ○ Radiation (including therapeutic radiation), [surgery]

DEFINING CHARACTERISTICS

Objective: ○ Damaged or destroyed tissue (e.g., cornea, mucous membrane, integumentary, or subcutaneous)

Tissue Perfusion, altered, (specify): cerebral, cardiopulmonary, renal, gastrointestinal, peripheral

DEFINITION: A decrease in oxygen resulting in the failure to nourish the tissues at the capillary level. [Tissue perfusion problems can exist without de-

creased cardiac output; however, there may be a relationship between cardiac output and tissue perfusion.]

RELATED FACTORS: ○ Interruption/mechanical reduction of flow—arterial, venous ○ Exchange problems ○ Hypervolemia ○ Hypovolemia ○ Decreased hemoglobin concentration in blood ○ Altered affinity of hemoglobin for oxygen ○ Impaired transport of the oxygen across alveolar and/or capillary membrane ○ Mismatch of ventilation with blood flow ○ Hypoventilation ○ Enzyme poisoning

DEFINING CHARACTERISTICS

Subjective: Cardiopulmonary: ○ Chest pain ○ [Palpitations] ○ Dyspnea ○ Feelings of impending doom

Renal: ○ Claudication

Objective: Cardiopulmonary: ○ Arrhythmias ○ Capillary refill greater than 3 seconds ○ Altered respiratory rate outside of acceptable parameters ○ Nasal flaring ○ Use of accessory muscles ○ Chest retraction ○ Bronchospasms ○ Abnormal arterial blood gases

Cerebral: ○ Altered mental status ○ Behavioral changes ○ Changes in motor response ○ Extremity weakness or paralysis ○ Speech abnormalities ○ Difficulty in swallowing ○ Changes in pupillary reactions

Renal: ○ Altered blood pressure outside of acceptable parameters ○ Hematuria ○ Oliguria or anuria ○ Elevation in BUN/creatinine ratio ○ Blood pressure changes in extremities ○ Arterial pulsations ○ Bruits ○ Skin color diminished ○ Skin color pale on elevation, color does not return on lowering of leg ○ Slow healing of lesions

Gastrointestinal: ○ Hypoactive or absent bowel sounds ○ Nausea/[vomiting] ○ Abdominal distention/pain or tenderness

Peripheral: ○ Altered skin characteristics (hair, nails, moisture) ○ Skin temperature changes ○ Skin discolorations ○ Weak or absent pulses ○ Altered sensations ○ Edema ○ Positive Homan's sign

NOTE: Information appearing in [ ] has been added by the authors to clarify and facilitate the use of nursing diagnoses.

Transfer Ability, impaired

DEFINITION: Limitation of independent movement between two nearby surfaces.

RELATED FACTORS: To be developed

DEFINING CHARACTERISTICS: ○ Impaired ability to transfer from bed to chair and chair to bed, from chair to car or car to chair, from chair to floor or floor to chair, from standing to floor or floor to standing, on or off a toilet or commode, in and out of tub or shower, between uneven levels

Trauma, risk for*

DEFINITION: Accentuated risk of accidental tissue injury (e.g., wound, burn, fracture).

RISK FACTORS [include but are not limited to]

Internal (Individual): ○ Weakness ○ Poor vision ○ Balancing difficulties ○ Reduced temperature and/or tactile sensation ○ Reduced large, or small, muscle coordination/hand/eye coordination ○ Lack of safety education/precautions ○ Insufficient finances to purchase safety equipment or effect repairs ○ Cognitive or emotional difficulties ○ History of previous trauma

External (Environmental): ○ Slippery floors (e.g., wet or highly waxed) ○ Snow or ice collected on stairs, walkways ○ Unanchored rugs ○ Bathtub without hand grip or antislip equipment ○ Use of unsteady ladder or chairs ○ Entering unlighted rooms ○ Unsturdy or absent stair rails ○ Unanchored electric wires ○ Litter or liquid spills on floors or stairways ○ High beds ○ Children playing without gates at top of stairs ○ Obstructed passageways ○ Unsafe window protection in homes with young children ○ Inappropriate call-for-aid mechanisms for bed-resting client ○ Pot handles facing toward front of stove ○ Bathing in very hot water (unsupervised bathing of young children) ○ Potential igniting gas leaks ○ Delayed lighting of gas burner or oven ○ Experimenting with chemical or gasoline ○ Unscreened fires or heaters ○ Wearing plastic apron or flowing clothing around open flame ○ Children playing with matches, candles, ciga-

rettes ○ Inadequately stored combustibles or corrosives (e.g., matches, oily rags, lye) ○ Highly flammable children's toys or clothing ○ Overloaded fuse boxes ○ Contact with rapidly moving machinery, industrial belts, or pulleys ○ Sliding on coarse bed linen or struggling within bed restraints ○ Faulty electric plugs, frayed wires, or defective appliances ○ Contact with acids or alkalis ○ Playing with fireworks or gunpowder ○ Contact with intense cold ○ Overexposure to sun, sun lamps, radiotherapy ○ Use of cracked dishware or glasses ○ Knives stored uncovered ○ Guns or ammunition stored unlocked ○ Large icicles hanging from roof ○ Exposure to dangerous machinery ○ Children playing with sharp-edged toys ○ High-crime neighborhood and vulnerable clients ○ Driving a mechanically unsafe vehicle ○ Driving after partaking of alcoholic beverages or drugs ○ Driving at excessive speeds ○ Driving without necessary visual aids ○ Children riding in the front seat of car ○ Smoking in bed or near oxygen ○ Overloaded electric outlets ○ Grease waste collected on stoves ○ Use of thin or worn pot holders [or mitts] ○ Nonuse or misuse of necessary headgear for motorized cyclists [bicyclists/rollerbladers]/or young children carried on adult bicycles ○ Unsafe road or road-crossing conditions ○ Play or work near vehicle pathways (e.g., driveways, lanes, railroad tracks) ○ Nonuse or misuse of seat restraints/[unrestrained or improperly restrained children riding in car]

Unilateral Neglect

DEFINITION: A state in which an individual is perceptually unaware of and inattentive to one side of the body [and the immediate unilateral territory/space].

RELATED FACTORS: ○ Effects of disturbed perceptual abilities (e.g., [homonymous] hemianopsia, [or visual inattention]) ○ One-sided blindness; neurological illness or trauma ○ [Impaired cerebral blood flow]

DEFINING CHARACTERISTICS

Subjective: ○ [Reports of feeling that part does not belong to own self]

NOTE: Information appearing in [ ] has been added by the authors to clarify and facilitate the use of nursing diagnoses.
*[Note: A risk diagnosis is not evidenced by signs and symptoms because the problem has not yet occurred, and nursing interventions are directed at prevention. Therefore, risk factors present are noted instead.]

Objective: ○ Consistent inattention to stimuli on an affected side ○ Inadequate self-care [inability to satisfactorily perform activities of daily living] ○ [Lack of] Positioning and/or safety precautions in regard to the affected side ○ Does not look toward affected side ○ Leaves food on plate on the affected side ○ [Does not touch affected side] ○ [Failure to use the affected side of the body without being reminded to do so]

Urinary Elimination, altered

DEFINITION: The state in which an individual experiences a disturbance in urine elimination.

RELATED FACTORS: Multiple causality, including: ○ Sensory motor impairment ○ Anatomical obstruction ○ Urinary tract infection ○ Mechanical trauma ○ [Fluid/volume states] ○ [Psychogenic factors] ○ [Surgical diversion]

DEFINING CHARACTERISTICS

Subjective: ○ Frequency ○ Hesitancy ○ Dysuria

Objective: ○ Nocturia, [Enuresis] ○ Urgency ○ Incontinence ○ Retention

Urinary Incontinence, functional

DEFINITION: Inability of usually continent person to reach toilet in time to avoid unintentional loss of urine.

RELATED FACTORS: ○ Altered environmental factors [e.g., poor lighting or inability to locate bathroom] ○ Impaired cognition [e.g., inattentiveness to urge to void, use of sedation] neuromuscular limitations [including difficulty in removing clothes] ○ Impaired vision ○ Weakened supporting pelvic structures ○ Psychological factors

DEFINING CHARACTERISTICS

Subjective: ○ Senses need to void

Objective: ○ May only be incontinent in early morning ○ Loss of urine before reaching toilet ○ Amount of time required to reach toilet exceeds length of time between sensing urge and uncontrolled voiding ○ Able to completely empty bladder

Urinary Incontinence, reflex

DEFINITION: An involuntary loss of urine at somewhat predictable intervals when a specific bladder volume is reached.

RELATED FACTORS: ○ Neurological impairment above level of sacral micturition center or pontine micturition center ○ Tissue damage from radiation cystitis, inflammatory bladder conditions, or radical pelvic surgery

DEFINING CHARACTERISTICS

Subjective: ○ No sensation of bladder fullness/urge to void/voiding ○ Sensation to urge without voluntary inhibition of bladder contraction

Objective: ○ Predictable pattern of voiding ○ Unable to cognitively inhibit or initiate voiding ○ Complete emptying with lesion above pontine micturition center ○ Incomplete emptying with lesion above sacral micturition center ○ Sensations associated with full bladder such as sweating, restlessness, and abdominal discomfort

[Urinary] Incontinence, stress

DEFINITION: The state in which an individual experiences a loss of urine of less than 50 ml occurring with increased abdominal pressure.

RELATED FACTORS: ○ Degenerative changes in pelvic muscles and structural supports associated with increased age ○ High intra-abdominal pressure (e.g., obesity, gravid uterus) ○ Incompetent bladder outlet ○ Overdistention between voidings ○ Weak pelvic muscles and structural supports

DEFINING CHARACTERISTICS

Subjective: ○ Reported dribbling with increased abdominal pressure [e.g., coughing, sneezing, lifting, impact aerobics, changing position] ○ Urinary urgency/frequency (more often than every 2 hours)

Objective: ○ Observed dribbling with increased abdominal pressure

[Urinary] Incontinence, total

DEFINITION: The state in which an individual experiences a continuous and unpredictable loss of urine.

NOTE: Information appearing in [ ] has been added by the authors to clarify and facilitate the use of nursing diagnoses.

RELATED FACTORS: ○ Neuropathy preventing transmission of reflex [signals to the reflex arc] indicating bladder fullness ○ Neurological dysfunction causing triggering of micturition at unpredictable times [cerebral lesions] ○ Independent contraction of detrusor reflex due to surgery ○ Trauma or disease affecting spinal cord nerves [destruction of sensory or motor neurons below the injury level] ○ Anatomic (fistula)

DEFINING CHARACTERISTICS

Subjective: ○ Constant flow of urine occurs at unpredictable times without distention or uninhibited bladder contractions/spasm ○ Nocturia ○ Lack of perineal or bladder filling awareness ○ Unawareness of incontinence

Objective: ○ Unsuccessful incontinence refractory treatments

Urinary Incontinence, risk for urge

DEFINITION: Risk for involuntary loss of urine associated with a sudden, strong, sensation or urinary urgency.

RELATED FACTORS: ○ Effects of medications; caffeine; alcohol ○ Detrusor hyperreflexia from cystitis, urethritis, tumors, renal calculi ○ Central nervous system disorders above pontine micturition center; detrusor muscle instability with impaired contractility; involuntary sphincter relaxation ○ Ineffective toileting habits ○ Small bladder capacity

[Urinary] Incontinence, urge

DEFINITION: The state in which an individual experiences involuntary passage of urine occurring soon after a strong sense of urgency to void.

RELATED FACTORS: ○ Decreased bladder capacity (e.g., history of pelvic inflammatory disease [PID], abdominal surgeries, indwelling urinary catheter) ○ Irritation of bladder stretch receptors causing spasm (e.g., bladder infection); alcohol; caffeine; increased fluids; increased urine concentration; overdistention of bladder

DEFINING CHARACTERISTICS

Subjective: ○ Urinary urgency ○ Frequency (voiding more often than every 2 hours) ○ Bladder contracture/ spasm ○ Nocturia (more than two times per night)

Objective: ○ Inability to reach toilet in time ○ Voiding in small amounts (less than 100 ml) or in large amounts (more than 550 ml)

Urinary Retention [acute/chronic]

DEFINITION: The state in which the individual experiences incomplete emptying of the bladder. [High urethral pressure inhibits voiding until increased abdominal pressure causes urine to be involuntarily lost, or high urethral pressure inhibits timely/complete emptying of bladder.]

RELATED FACTORS: ○ High urethral pressure caused by weak detrusor [absent detrusor] ○ Inhibition of reflex arc ○ Strong sphincter; blockage [e.g., benign prostatic hypertrophy, perineal swelling] ○ [Habituation of reflex arc] ○ [Infections] ○ [Neurological diseases/trauma] ○ [Use of medications with side effects of retention, e.g., atropine, belladonna, psychotropics, antihistamines, opiates]

DEFINING CHARACTERISTICS

Subjective: ○ Sensation of bladder fullness ○ Dribbling ○ Dysuria

Objective: ○ Bladder distention ○ Small, frequent voiding or absence of urine output ○ Residual urine [150 ml or more] ○ Overflow incontinence ○ [Reduced stream]

Ventilatory Weaning Response, dysfunctional (DVWR)

DEFINITION: A state in which a patient cannot adjust to lowered levels of mechanical ventilator support, which interrupts and prolongs the weaning process.

RELATED FACTORS:

Physical: ○ Ineffective airway clearance ○ Sleep pattern disturbance ○ Inadequate nutrition ○ Uncontrolled pain or discomfort ○ [Immobility] ○ [Muscle weakness/fatigue, inability to control respiratory muscles]

NOTE: Information appearing in [ ] has been added by the authors to clarify and facilitate the use of nursing diagnoses.

Psychological: ○ Knowledge deficit of the weaning process, patient role ○ Patient perceived inefficacy about the ability to wean ○ Decreased motivation ○ Decreased self-esteem ○ Anxiety: moderate, severe ○ Fear ○ Hopelessness ○ Powerlessness ○ Insufficient trust in the nurse

Situational: ○ Uncontrolled episodic energy demands or problems ○ Inappropriate pacing of diminished ventilator support ○ Inadequate social support ○ Adverse environment (noisy, active environment, negative events in the room, low nurse-patient ratio, extended nurse absence from bedside, unfamiliar nursing staff) ○ History of ventilator dependence for more than 1 week ○ History of multiple unsuccessful weaning attempts

DEFINING CHARACTERISTICS:
Responds to lowered levels of mechanical ventilator support with:

Mild DVWR

Subjective: ○ Expressed feelings of increased need for oxygen/breathing ○ Queries about possible machine malfunction

Objective: ○ Restlessness ○ Slight increased respiratory rate from baseline ○ Increased concentration on breathing

Moderate DVWR

Subjective: ○ Apprehension

Objective: ○ Slight increase from baseline BP (less than 20 mm Hg) ○ Slight increase from baseline heart rate (less than 20 bpm) ○ Baseline increase in respiratory rate (less than 5 breaths/min) ○ Hypervigilance to activities ○ Inability to respond to coaching ○ Inability to cooperate ○ Diaphoresis ○ Eye widening "wide-eyed look" ○ Decreased air entry on auscultation ○ Color changes; pale, slight cyanosis ○ Slight respiratory accessory muscle use

Severe DVWR

Objective: ○ Agitation ○ Deterioration in ABGs from current baseline ○ Increase from baseline BP (greater than 20 mm Hg) ○ Increase from baseline heart rate (greater than 20 bpm) ○ Respiratory rate increase significantly from baseline ○ Profuse diaphoresis ○ Full respiratory accessory muscle use ○ Shallow, gasping breaths ○ Paradoxical abdominal breathing ○ Discoordinated breathing with the ventilator ○ Decreased level of consciousness ○ Adventitious breath sounds, audible airway secretions ○ Cyanosis

Violence, [actual]/risk for directed at others*

DEFINITION: Behaviors in which an individual demonstrates that he/she can be physically, emotionally, and/or sexually harmful to others.

[RELATED OR] RISK FACTORS: ○ Antisocial character ○ Catatonic/manic excitement ○ Panic states; rage reactions ○ Suicidal behavior ○ Toxic reactions to medication [including illicit drug/alcohol] ○ Battered women[/spouse abuse]; child abuse ○ Organic brain syndrome; temporal lobe epilepsy ○ [Negative role modeling] ○ [Developmental crisis] ○ [Hormonal imbalance, e.g., PMS, postpartal depression/psychosis]

DEFINING CHARACTERISTICS [OR INDICATORS]†:
○ History of violence: Against others (hitting, kicking, scratching, biting or spitting, or throwing objects at someone; attempted rape, rape, sexual molestation; urinating/defecating on a person ○ Threats (verbal threats against property/person, social threats, cursing, threatening notes/letters or gestures, sexual threats) ○ Antisocial behavior (stealing, insistent borrowing, insistent demands for privileges, insistent interruption of meetings; refusal to eat or to take medication, ignoring instructions) ○ Indirect (tearing off clothes, urinating/defecating on floor, stamping feet, temper tantrum; running in corridors, yelling, writing on walls, ripping objects off walls, throwing objects, breaking a window, slamming doors; sexual advances) ○ Other factors: Neurological impairment (positive EEG, CAT, or MRI; head trauma; positive neurological findings; seizure disorders ○ Cognitive impairment (learning disabilities, attention deficit disorder, decreased intellectual functioning) ○ History of childhood abuse/witnessing family violence; cruelty to animals; firesetting ○ Prenatal and perinatal

---

NOTE: Information appearing in [ ] has been added by the authors to clarify and facilitate the use of nursing diagnoses.

†Although a risk diagnosis does not have defining characteristics (signs and symptoms), the ones identified here can be used to denote an actual diagnosis or as indicators of risk for/escalation of violence.

complications/abnormalities ○ History of drug/alcohol abuse; pathological intoxication ○ Psychotic symptomatology (auditory, visual, command hallucinations; paranoid delusions; loose, rambling, or illogical thought processes) ○ Motor vehicle offenses (frequent traffic violations, use of motor vehicle to release anger) ○ Suicidal behavior; impulsivity; availability and/or possession of weapon(s) ○ Body language: rigid posture, clenching of fists and jaw, hyperactivity, pacing, breathlessness, and threatening stances ○ [Almost continuous thoughts of violence] ○ [Expressed intent/desire to harm others directly or indirectly]

Violence, [actual]/risk for self-directed*

DEFINITION: Behaviors in which an individual demonstrates that he/she can be physically, emotionally, and/or sexually harmful to self.

[RELATED OR] RISK FACTORS: ○ Antisocial character ○ Catatonic/manic excitement ○ Panic states; rage reactions ○ Suicidal behavior ○ Toxic reactions to medication [including illicit drug/alcohol] ○ Battered women[/spouse abuse]; child abuse ○ Organic brain syndrome; temporal lobe epilepsy ○ [Negative role modeling] ○ [Developmental crisis] ○ [Hormonal imbalance, e.g., PMS, postpartal depression/psychosis]

DEFINING CHARACTERISTICS [OR INDICATORS]†: ○ Suicidal ideation: frequent, intense prolonged; plan: clear and specific; lethality: method and availability of destructive means ○ Age 15–19; over age 45 ○ Marital status; single, widowed, divorced ○ Employment: unemployed, recent job loss/failure; occupation: executive, administrator/owner of business, professional, semiskilled worker ○ Interpersonal relationships: conflictual ○ Family background: chaotic or conflictual, history of suicide ○ Sexual orientation: bisexual (active), homosexual (inactive) ○ Physical health: hypochondriac, chronic or terminal illness ○ Mental health: severe depression, psychosis, severe personality disorder, alcoholism, or drug abuse ○ Emotional status: hopelessness, [lifting of depressed mood], despair, increased anxiety, panic, anger, hostility; history of multiple attempts ○ Personal resources: poor achievement, poor insight, affect unavailable and poorly controlled ○ Social resources: poor rapport, socially isolated, unresponsive family ○ Verbal clues: talking about death, "better off without me," asking questions about lethal dosages of drugs ○ Behavioral clues: writing forlorn love notes, directing angry messages at a significant other who has rejected the person, giving away personal items, taking out a large life insurance policy; engaging in autoerotic sexual acts [e.g., asphyxiation]

Walking, impaired

DEFINITION: Limitation of independent movement within the environment on foot.

RELATED FACTORS: To be developed

DEFINING CHARACTERISTICS

Subjective: ○ Impaired ability to walk required distances, walk on an incline/decline, or on uneven surfaces, to navigate curbs, climb stairs

---

NOTE: Information appearing in [ ] has been added by the authors to clarify and facilitate the use of nursing diagnoses.

*[Note: A risk diagnosis is not evidenced by signs and symptoms because the problem has not yet occurred, and nursing interventions are directed at prevention. Therefore, risk factors present are noted instead.]

†Although a risk diagnosis does not have defining characteristics (signs and symptoms), the ones identified here can be used to denote an actual diagnosis or as indicators of risk for/escalation of violence.

Assessment Tools

The following are suggested guides/tools for development by an individual/institution to create databases reflecting Diagnostic Divisions of Nursing Diagnoses in any care setting. Although the divisions are alphabetized for ease of presentation, they can be prioritized or rearranged to meet individual needs.

Adult Medical/Surgical Assessment Tool

GENERAL INFORMATION

Name: _____ Age: _____ DOB: _____ Gender: _____ Race: _____
Admission Date: _____ Time: _____ From: _____
Source of Information: _____ Reliability (1–4 with 4 = very reliable): _____

Activity/Rest

Subjective (Reports)

Occupation: _____ Usual activities/hobbies: _____
  Leisure time activities: _____
Feelings of boredom/dissatisfaction: _____
Limitations imposed by condition: _____
Sleep: Hours: _____ Naps: _____
  Aids: _____ Insomnia: _____
  Related to: _____
  Rested on awakening: _____
  Excessive grogginess: _____

Objective (Exhibits)

Observed response to activity:
  Cardiovascular: _____
  Respiratory: _____
Mental status (i.e., withdrawn/lethargic): _____
Neuro/muscular assessment:
  Muscle mass/tone: _____ Posture: _____
  Tremors: _____ ROM: _____ Strength: _____
  Deformity: _____

Circulation

Subjective (Reports)

History of: Hypertension: _____
  Heart trouble: _____ Rheumatic fever: _____
  Ankle/leg edema: _____ Phlebitis: _____
  Slow healing: _____ Claudication: _____
  Dysreflexia: _____

Objective (Exhibits)

BP: R and L: Lying: _____ Sit: _____ Stand: _____
  Pulse pressure: _____
  Auscultatory gap: _____
Pulse (palpation): Carotid: _____ Temporal: _____
  Jugular: _____ Radial: _____ Femoral: _____

Bleeding tendencies/episodes: _____
Palpitations: _____ Syncope: _____
Extremities: Numbness: _____ Tingling: _____
Cough/hemoptysis: _____
Change in frequency/amount of urine: _____
Other: _____

Popliteal: _____ Post-tibial: _____
Dorsalis pedis: _____
Cardiac (palpation): Thrill: _____ Heaves: _____
Heart sounds: Rate: _____ Rhythm: _____
Quality: _____ Friction rub: _____
Murmur: _____
Breath sounds: _____
Vascular bruit: _____ Jugular vein distention: _____
Extremities: Temperature: _____ Color: _____
Capillary refill: _____ Homan's sign: _____
Varicosities: _____ Nail abnormalities: _____
Edema: _____ Distribution/quality of hair: _____
Trophic skin changes: _____
Color: General: _____ Mucous membranes: _____
Lips: _____ Nailbeds: _____ Conjunctiva: _____
Sclera: _____
Diaphoresis: _____

Ego Integrity

Subjective (Reports)

Stress factors: _____
Ways of handling stress: _____
Financial concerns: _____
Relationship status: _____
Cultural factors/ethnic ties: _____
Religion: _____
Practicing: _____
Lifestyle: _____ Recent
changes: _____
Sense of connectedness/harmony with
self: _____
Feelings of: Helplessness _____
Hopelessness: _____
Powerlessness: _____

Objective (Exhibits)

Emotional status (check those that apply):
Calm: _____ Anxious: _____
Angry: _____ Withdrawn: _____
Fearful: _____ Irritable: _____
Restive: _____ Euphoric: _____
Observed physiological response(s):
_____
Changes in energy field:
Temperature: _____ Color: _____
Distribution: _____ Movement: _____
Sounds: _____

Elimination

Subjective (Reports)

Usual bowel pattern: _____
Laxative use: _____
Character of stool: _____ Last BM: _____
History of bleeding: _____ Hemorrhoids: _____
Constipation: _____ Diarrhea: _____
Usual voiding pattern: _____
Incontinence/when: _____ Urgency: _____
Frequency: _____ Retention: _____
Character of urine: _____
Pain/burning/difficulty voiding: _____
History of kidney/bladder disease: _____
Diuretic use: _____

Objective (Exhibits)

Abdomen: Tender: _____
Soft/firm: _____ Palpable mass: _____
Size/girth: _____
Bowel sounds: Location/type: _____
Hemorrhoids: _____
Bladder palpable: _____ Overflow voiding: _____
CVA tendencies: _____
Stool guaiac: _____

Food/Fluid

Subjective (Reports)

Usual diet (type): _____
Carbohydrate/protein/fat intake: _____
Vitamin/food supplement use: _____
Food preferences: _____ Prohibitions: _____
No. of meals daily: _____
Dietary pattern/content: B: _____
 L: _____ D: _____
Last meal/intake: _____
Loss of appetite: _____
Nausea/vomiting: _____
Heartburn/indigestion: _____
 Related to: _____
 Relieved by: _____
Allergy/food intolerance: _____
Mastication/swallowing problems: _____
 Dentures: _____
Usual weight: _____ Changes in weight: _____
Diuretic use: _____

Objective (Exhibits)

Current weight: _____ Height: _____
 Body build: _____
Skin turgor: _____ Mucous membranes
 moist/dry: _____
Edema: General: _____ Dependent: _____
 Periorbital: _____ Ascites: _____
Jugular vein distention: _____
Breath sounds: _____ Crackles: _____
 Wheezes: _____
Thyroid enlarged: _____
Halitosis: _____ Condition of teeth/gums: _____
 Appearance of tongue: _____
 Mucous membranes: _____
Bowel sounds: _____ Hernia/masses: _____
Urine S/A or Chemstix: _____
Serum glucose (Glucometer): _____

Hygiene

Subjective (Reports)

Activities of daily living:
 Independent/dependent (level):
 Mobility: _____ Feeding: _____ Hygiene: _____
 Dressing: _____ Toileting: _____
Preferred time of personal care/bath: _____
Equipment/prosthetic devices required: _____
Assistance provided by: _____

Objective (Exhibits)

General appearance: _____
Manner of dress:_____ Personal habits: _____
 Body odor: _____ Condition of scalp: _____
 Presence of vermin: _____

Neurosensory

Subjective (Reports)

Fainting spells/dizziness: _____
Headaches: Location: _____ Frequency: _____
Tingling/numbness/weakness (location): _____
Stroke/brain injury (residual effects): _____
Seizures: _____ Type: _____ Aura: _____
 Frequency: _____ Postictal state: _____
 How controlled: _____
Eyes: Vision loss: _____ Last exam: _____
 Glaucoma: _____ Cataract: _____
Ears: Hearing loss: _____ Last exam: _____
Epistaxis: _____ Sense of smell: _____
Other: _____

Objective (Exhibits)

Mental status: (note duration of change)
 Oriented/disoriented: Time: _____ Place: _____
 Person: _____ Situation: _____
 Alert: _____ Drowsy: _____ Lethargic: _____
 Stuporous: _____ Comatose: _____
 Cooperative: _____ Combative: _____
 Delusions: _____ Hallucinations: _____
 Affect (describe): _____
 Memory: Recent: _____ Remote: _____
Glasses: _____ Contacts: _____ Hearing aids: _____
Pupil shape: _____ Size/reaction: R/L: _____
Facial droop: _____ Swallowing: _____
Handgrasp/release, R/L: _____
Posturing: _____
Deep tendon reflexes: _____ Paralysis: _____

Pain/Discomfort

Subjective (Reports)

Primary focus: _____
  Location: (Intensity (0–10 with 10 most
  severe): _____ Frequency: _____
  Quality: _____ Duration: _____ Radiation: _____
  Precipitating factors: _____ How relieved: _____
  Associated symptoms: _____
  Effect on activities: _____ Relationships: _____
Additional focus: _____

Objective (Exhibits)

Facial grimacing: _____
Guarding affected area: _____
Emotional response: _____
Narrowed focus: _____
Change in BP: _____ Pulse: _____

Respiration

Subjective (Reports)

Dyspnea/related to: _____
Cough/sputum: _____
History of bronchitis: _____ Asthma: _____
  Tuberculosis: _____ Emphysema: _____
  Recurrent pneumonia: _____ Exposure to noxious
  fumes: _____
Smoker, packs/day: _____ No. of pack years: _____
Use of respiratory aids: _____ Oxygen: _____

Objective (Exhibits)

Respiratory: Rate: _____ Depth: _____
  Symmetry: _____
Use of accessory muscles: _____ Nasal flaring: _____
Fremitus: _____
Breath sounds: _____ Egophony: _____
Cyanosis: _____ Clubbing of fingers: _____
Sputum characteristics: _____
Mentation/restlessness: _____

Safety

Subjective (Reports)

Allergies/sensitivity: _____ Reaction: _____
Exposure to infectious diseases: _____
Previous alteration of immune system: _____
  Cause: _____
History of sexually transmitted disease
  (date/type): _____
  Testing: _____
High risk behaviors: _____
Blood transfusion/number: _____ When: _____
  Reaction: _____ Describe: _____
Geographic areas lived in/visited: _____
Seat belt/helmet use: _____
History of accidental injuries: _____
  Fractures/dislocations: _____
Arthritis/unstable joints: _____
  Back problems: _____
Changes in moles: _____
  Enlarged nodes: _____
Delayed healing: _____
Cognitive limitations: Impaired vision/
  hearing: _____
Prosthesis: _____
Ambulatory devices: _____

Objective (Exhibits)

Temperature: _____ Diaphoresis: _____
Skin integrity: _____ Scars: _____ Rashes: _____
  Lacerations: _____ Ulcerations: _____
  Ecchymosis: _____ Blisters: _____
  Burns: (degree/percent): _____ Drainage: _____
Mark location of above on diagram:

General strength: _____ Muscle tone: _____
  Gait: _____ ROM: _____
  Paresthesia/paralysis: _____
Results of cultures: _____ Immune system
  testing: _____
Tuberculosis testing: _____

Sexuality [Component of Social Interaction]

Subjective (Reports)

Sexually active: _____
Use of condoms: _____
Birth control method: _____
Sexual concerns/difficulties: _____
Recent change in frequency/interest: _____

Female

Age at menarche: _____ Length of cycle: _____
   Duration: _____ Number of pads used/day: _____
   Last menstrual period: _____
   Pregnant now: _____
Bleeding between periods: _____
Menopause: _____ Vaginal lubrication: _____
Vaginal discharge: _____
Surgeries: _____
Hormonal therapy/calcium use: _____
Practices breast self-exam: _____
Mammogram: _____ Last PAP smear: _____

Male

Penile discharge: _____
Prostate disorder: _____
Circumcised: _____ Vasectomy: _____
Practice self-exam: Breast: _____
   Testicles: _____
Last proctoscopic/prostate exam: _____

Objective (Exhibits)

Comfort level with subject matter:
_____

Breast exam: _____
Genital warts/lesions: _____
Discharge: _____

Breast: _____
Penis: _____
Testicles: _____
Genital warts/lesions: _____
Discharge: _____

Social Interactions

Subjective (Reports)

Marital status: _____ Years in relationship: _____
   Perception of relationship: _____
   Living with: _____
   Concerns/stresses: _____
Extended family: _____ Other support
   person(s): _____
Role within family structure: _____
Perception of relationship with family
   members: _____
Ethnic affiliation: _____
Strength of ethnic identity: _____
Lives in ethnic community (Y/N): _____
Feelings of: Mistrust: _____ Rejection:_____
   Unhappiness: _____ Loneliness/isolation: _____
Problems related to illness/condition: _____
Problems with communication: _____
   Use of communication aids: _____
Genogram: _____

Objective (Exhibits)

Speech: Clear: _____ Slurred: _____
   Unintelligible: _____ Aphasic: _____
   Unusual speech pattern/impairment: _____
   Use of speech/communication aids: _____
   Laryngectomy present: _____
Verbal/nonverbal communication with
   family/SO(s): _____
Family interaction (behavioral)
   pattern: _____

Teaching/Learning

Subjective (Reports)

Dominant language (specify): _____
  Second language: _____ Literate: _____
  Education level: _____ Learning disabilities
  (specify): _____
  Cognitive limitations: _____
Where born: _____ If immigrant, how long in this
  country: _____
Health and illness beliefs/practices/customs:

_____

Special healthcare concerns (e.g., impact of reli-
  gious/cultural practices): _____
  Health Goals: _____
Familial risk factors (indicate relationship):
  Diabetes: _____ Thyroid (specify): _____
  Tuberculosis: _____ Heart disease: _____
  Strokes: _____ High BP: _____ Epilepsy: _____
  Kidney disease: _____ Cancer: _____
  Mental illness: _____ Other: _____
Prescribed medications:
  Drug: _____ Dose: _____
  Times (*circle* last dose): _____
  Take regularly: _____ Purpose: _____
  Side effects/problems: _____
Nonprescription drugs:
  OTC drugs: _____
  Street drugs: _____ Tobacco: _____
  Smokeless tobacco: _____
  Alcohol (amount/frequency): _____
Admitting diagnosis per provider: _____
Reason for hospitalization per
  patient: _____
History of current complaint: _____
Patient expectations of this
  hospitalization: _____
Previous illnesses and/or hospitalizations/surgeries:

_____

Evidence of failure to improve: _____
Last complete physical exam: _____

Discharge Plan Considerations

DRG projected mean length of stay: _____
Date information obtained: _____
Anticipated date of discharge: _____
Resources available: Persons: _____
  Financial: _____ Community supports: _____
  Groups: _____
  Socialization: _____
Areas that may require alteration/assistance: Food
  preparation: _____ Shopping: _____
  Transportation: _____ Ambulation: _____
  Medication/IV therapy: _____ Treatments: _____
  Wound care: _____ Supplies: _____
  Self-care (specify): _____ Homemaker/
  maintenance (specify): _____
Physical layout of home (specify): _____
Anticipated changes in living situation after dis-
  charge: _____
Living facility other than home
  (specify): _____
Referrals (date, source, services):
  Social services: _____
  Rehab services: _____
  Dietary: _____
  Home care: _____
  Resp/O_2: _____
  Equipment: _____
  Supplies: _____
  Other: _____

Excerpt from Psychiatric Nursing Assessment Tool

Ego Integrity

Subjective (Reports)

What kind of person are you (positive/negative,
  etc.)? _____
What do you think of your body?

_____

Objective (Exhibits)

Emotional status (check those that apply):
  Calm: _____ Friendly: _____ Cooperative: _____
  Evasive: _____ Fearful: _____ Anxious: _____
  Irritable: _____ Withdrawn: _____

How would you rate your self-esteem (1–10; with 10 the highest): _____

What are your moods:

Depressed: _____ Guilty: _____ Unreal: _____

Ups/downs: _____ Apathetic: _____

Separated from the world: _____ Detached: _____

Are you a nervous person? _____

Are your feelings easily hurt? _____

Report of stress factors: _____

Previous patterns of handling stress: _____

Financial concerns: _____

Relationship status: _____

Work history/Military service: _____

Cultural factors: _____

Religion: _____ Practicing: _____

Lifestyle: _____ Recent changes: _____

Significant losses/changes (date): _____

Stages of grief/manifestations of loss: _____

Feelings of: Helplessness: _____ Hopelessness: _____

Powerlessness: _____

Restive: _____ Passive: _____

Dependent: _____ Euphoric: _____

Angry/hostile: _____ Other (specify) _____

Defense mechanisms: Projection: _____

Denial: _____ Undoing: _____

Rationalization: _____ Passive/aggressive: _____

Repression: _____ Intellectualization: _____

Somatization: _____ Regression: _____

Identification: _____ Introjection: _____

Reaction formation: _____ Isolation: _____

Displacement: _____ Substitution: _____

Sublimation: _____

Consistency of behavior: Verbal: _____

Nonverbal: _____

Characteristics of speech: _____

Motor behaviors: _____

Posturing: _____

Under/overactive: _____

Stereotypic: _____

Observed physiological response(s): _____

Neurosensory

Subjective (Reports)

Dreamlike states: _____ Walking in sleep: _____

Automatic writing: _____

Believe/feel you are another person: _____

Perception different than others: _____

Ability to follow directions: _____

Perform calculations: _____

Accomplish ADL: _____

Objective (Exhibits)

Mental Status: (note duration of change)

Oriented/disoriented: Time: _____

Place: _____ Person: _____

Check all that apply:

Alert: _____ Drowsy: _____ Lethargic: _____

Stuporous: _____ Comatose: _____

Cooperative: _____ Combative: _____

Delusions: _____ Hallucinations: _____ Affect (describe): _____ Memory: Immediate: _____

Recent: _____ Remote: _____

Comprehension: _____

Thought processes (assessed through speech): Patterns of speech (spontaneous/sudden silences): _____ Content: _____ Change in topic: _____ Delusions: _____

Hallucinations: _____ Illusions: _____

Rate or flow: _____ Clear, logical progression: _____ Expression: _____

Mood: _____ Affect: _____

Appropriateness: _____

Intensity: _____

Range: _____

Insight: _____

Misperceptions: _____

Attention/calculation skills: _____
Judgment: _____
Ability to follow directions: _____
Problem solving: _____

Excerpt from Prenatal Assessment Tool

Safety

Subjective

Allergies/Sensitivity: _____
  Reaction: _____
Previous alteration of immune system: _____
  Cause: _____
History of sexually transmitted diseases/gynecologic
  infections (date/type): _____
  High-risk behaviors: _____
  Testing: _____
Blood transfusion/number: _____
  When: _____ Reaction: _____
  Describe: _____
Childhood diseases: _____
  Immunization history: _____
Recent exposure to german measles: _____ Other
  viral infections: _____ X-ray/radiation: _____
  House pets: _____
Previous obstetric problems: PIH: _____
  Kidney: _____ Hemorrhage: _____ Cardiac: _____
  Diabetes: _____ Infection/UTI: _____
  ABO/Rh sensitivity: _____ Uterine surgery: _____
  Anemia: _____
Length of time since last pregnancy: _____ Type of
  previous delivery: _____
History of accidental injuries:
  Fractures/dislocations: _____
  Physical abuse: _____ Arthritis/unstable
  joints: _____ Back problems: _____
Changes in moles: _____ Enlarged nodes: _____
Impaired vision: _____ Hearing: _____
Prosthesis: _____
  Ambulatory devices: _____

Objective

Temperature: _____ Diaphoresis: _____
  Skin integrity: _____ Scars: _____ Rashes: _____
  Ecchymosis: _____ Vaginal warts/lesions: _____
General strength: _____ Muscle tone: _____
  Gait: _____ ROM: _____
  Paresthesia/paralysis: _____
Fetal: Heart rate: _____ Location: _____
  Method of auscultation: _____
  Fundal height: _____ Estimated gestation: _____
  Movement: _____ Ballottement: _____
Results of fetal testing: _____ AFT: _____
Results of cultures, cervical/rectal: _____
  Immune system testing: _____
Blood type: Maternal: _____ Paternal: _____
Screenings, i.e., Serology: _____ Syphilis: _____
  Sickle cell: _____ Rubella: _____
  Hepatitis: _____ HIV: _____

Sexuality (Component of Social Interactions)

Subjective

Sexual concerns: _____ Menarche: _____ Length of
  cycle: _____ Duration: _____ First day of last menstrual period: _____ Amount: _____
Bleeding/cramping since LMP: _____ Vaginal discharge: _____

Objective

Pelvic: Vulva: _____ Perineum: _____ Vagina: _____
  Cervix: _____ Uterus: _____ Adnexal: _____
  Diagonal conjugate: _____ Transverse
  diameter: _____ Outlet (cm): _____
  Shape of sacrum: _____ Arch: _____

Client's belief of when conception occurred: _____
Estimated date of delivery: _____
Practices breast self-exam (Y/N): _____
    Last PAP smear: _____
Recent contraceptive method: _____
Ob history: GPTPAL: Gravida: _____ Para: _____
    Term: _____ Preterm: _____ Abortions: _____
    Living: _____ Multiple births: _____
Delivery History: Year: _____
    Place of delivery: _____
    Length of gestation: _____ Length of labor: _____
    Type of delivery: _____ Born (alive or dead): _____
    Weight: _____ Apgar scores: _____
Complications (maternal/fetal): _____

Coccyx: _____ SS Notch: _____ Ischial spines: _____
    Adequacy of inlet: _____ Mid: _____ Outlet: _____
Prognosis for delivery: _____
Breast exam: _____ Nipples: _____
Pregnancy test: _____ Serology test (date): _____
PAP smear results: _____

Excerpt from Intrapartal Assessment Tool

Pain/Discomfort

Subjective

Uterine contractions began: _____ Became regular:
    _____ Character: _____ Frequency: _____
    Duration: _____
Location of contractile pain: Front: _____
    Sacral area: _____
Degree of discomfort: Mild: _____ Moderate: _____
    Severe: _____ How relieved:
    Breathing/relaxation techniques: _____
    Positioning: _____ Sacral rubs: _____
    Effleurage: _____ Other: _____

Objective

Facial expression: _____ Narrowed focus: _____
    Body movement: _____
Change in BP: _____ Pulse: _____

Safety

Subjective

Allergies/Sensitivity: _____
    Reaction (specify): _____
    History of STD (date/type): _____
Health status of living children: _____
Month of first prenatal visit: _____
Previous/current obstetric problems/treatment:
    PIH: _____ Kidney: _____ Hemorrhage: _____
    Cardiac: _____ Diabetes: _____
    Infection/UTI: _____ ABO/Rh sensitivity: _____
    Uterine surgery: _____ Anemia: _____
Length of time since last pregnancy: _____
Type of previous delivery: _____
Blood transfusion: _____ When: _____
    Reaction (describe): _____
Maternal stature/build: _____
Fractures/dislocations: _____

Objective

Temperature: _____
Skin integrity: _____ Rashes: _____ Sores: _____
    Bruises: _____ Scars: _____
Paresthesia/paralysis: _____
Fetal status: Heart rate: _____ Location: _____
    Method of auscultation: _____
    Fundal height: _____ Estimated gestation: _____
    Activity/movement: _____ Fetal assessment testing (Y/N): _____ Date: _____ Test: _____
    Results: _____
Labor status: Cervical dilation: _____
    Effacement: _____ Fetal descent: _____
    Engagement: _____ Presentation: _____
    Lie: _____ Position: _____
Membranes: Intact: _____ Ruptured/time: _____
    Nitrazine test: _____ Amount of drainage: _____

Pelvis: _____

Arthritis/Unstable joints: _____

Spinal problems/deformity:

    Kyphosis: _____   Scoliosis: _____   Trauma: _____

    Surgery: _____

    Prosthesis: _____   Ambulatory devices: _____

Character: _____

Blood Type/Rh: Maternal: _____ Paternal: _____

Screens: Sickle cell: _____ Rubella: _____

    Hepatitis: _____ HIV: _____

Serology: Syphilis: Pos _____ Neg _____

Cervical/Rectal culture: Pos _____ Neg _____

Vaginal warts/lesions: _____

Perineal varicosities: _____

North American Nursing Diagnosis Association (NANDA) Nursing Diagnoses Organized According to Maslow's Hierarchy of Needs and Nursing Framework: A Health Outcome Classification for Nursing Diagnosis

Self-Actualization

Community Coping, potential for enhanced
Development, risk for altered
Family Coping: potential for growth
Growth and Development, altered
Growth, risk for altered
Health-Seeking Behaviors [specify]
Spiritual Distress (distress of the human spirit)
Spiritual Distress, risk for

Spiritual Well-Being, potential for enhanced
Therapeutic Regimen: Individual, effective management

Self-Esteem

Adjustment, impaired
Body Image disturbance
Coping, defensive
Coping, Individual, ineffective

Decisional conflict (specify)
Denial, ineffective
Diversional Activity deficit
Hopelessness
Noncompliance [Compliance, altered] (specify)
Nutrition: altered, more than body requirements
Nutrition: altered, risk for more than body requirements
Personal Identity disturbance
Post-Trauma Syndrome
Post-Trauma Syndrome, risk for
Powerlessness
Rape-Trauma Syndrome
Self-Esteem, chronic low
Self-Esteem, disturbance
Self-Esteem, situational low
Self-Mutilation, risk for
Violence, risk for directed at others
Violence, risk for self-directed

Love and Belonging

Family Coping, ineffective: compromised
Family Coping, ineffective: disabling
Family Processes, altered
Family Processes, altered: alcoholism
Loneliness, risk for
Parent/Infant/Child attachment, risk for altered
Parental Role conflict
Parenting, altered
Role Performance, altered
Social Interaction, impaired
Social Isolation

Safety and Security

[Autonomic] Dysreflexia
Autonomic Dysreflexia, risk for
Anxiety [mild, moderate, severe, panic]
Anxiety, death
Caregiver Role Strain
Caregiver Role Strain, risk for
Communication, impaired verbal
Community Coping, ineffective
Confusion, acute
Confusion, chronic
Disuse Syndrome, risk for
Environmental Interpretation Syndrome, impaired
Fear

Grieving, anticipatory
Grieving, dysfunctional
Health Maintenance, altered
Home Maintenance Management, impaired
Infant Behavior, organized, potential for enhanced
Infection, risk for
Injury, risk for
Knowledge deficit [Learning Need] (specify)
Latex Allergy
Latex Allergy, risk for
Memory, impaired
Mobility, impaired bed
Mobility, impaired wheelchair
Perioperative Positioning, risk for injury
Protection, altered
Sorrow, chronic
Therapeutic Regimen: Community, ineffective management
Therapeutic Regimen: Families, ineffective management
Therapeutic Regimen: Individual, ineffective management
Transfer Ability, impaired
Trauma, risk for
Unilateral Neglect
Walking, impaired

Physiological Needs

Activity intolerance [specify level]
Adaptive Capacity: Intracranial, decreased
Airway Clearance, ineffective
Aspiration, risk for
Body Temperature, risk for altered
Bowel Incontinence
Breastfeeding, effective
Breastfeeding, interrupted
Breathing Pattern, ineffective
Cardiac Output, decreased
Constipation
Constipation, perceived
Constipation, risk for
Dentition, altered
Diarrhea
Energy Field disturbance
Failure to Thrive, adult
Fatigue
Fluid Volume deficit

Fluid Volume, excess
Fluid Volume, risk for deficit
Fluid Volume, risk for imbalance
Gas Exchange, impaired
Hyperthermia
Hypothermia
Infant Behavior, disorganized
Infant Behavior, risk for disorganized
Infant Feeding Pattern, ineffective
Mobility, impaired physical [specify level]
Nausea
Nutrition, altered, less than body requirements
Oral Mucous Membrane, altered
Pain [acute]
Pain, chronic
Protection, altered
Self-Care deficit (specify): feeding, bathing/hygiene, dressing/grooming, toileting
Sensory-Perceptual alterations (specify): visual, auditory, kinesthetic, gustatory, tactile, olfactory
Sexual dysfunction
Sexuality Patterns, altered
Skin Integrity, impaired
Sleep Deprivation
Sleep Pattern disturbance
Spontaneous Ventilation, inability to sustain
Suffocation, risk for
Surgical Recovery, delayed
Swallowing, impaired
Thermoregulation, ineffective
Thought Processes, altered
Tissue Integrity, impaired
Tissue Perfusion, altered (specify): cerebral, cardiopulmonary, renal, gastrointestinal, peripheral
Urinary Elimination, altered
Urinary Incontinence, functional
Urinary Incontinence reflex
Urinary Incontinence, risk for urge
[Urinary] Incontinence stress
[Urinary] Incontinence, total
[Urinary] Incontinence, urge
Urinary Retention [acute/chronic]
Ventilatory Weaning Response, dysfunctional (DVWR)

Nursing Framework: A Health Outcome Classification for Nursing Diagnoses*

SELF-CARE TAXONOMY OF NURSING DIAGNOSES

I. Physiological Homeostasis

1.1.0. Alterations in oxygenation
  1.1.1. Impaired gas exchange
  1.1.2. Ineffective airway clearance
    1.1.2.1. Risk for aspiration
    1.1.2.2. Risk for suffocation
  1.1.3. Ineffective breathing pattern
    1.1.3.1. Inability to sustain spontaneous ventilation
    1.1.3.2. Dysfunctional ventilatory weaning response
1.2.0. Alterations in circulation
  1.2.1. Altered tissue perfusion
  1.2.2. Altered fluid volume
    1.2.2.1. Deficit
    1.2.2.2. Excess
  1.2.3. Decreased cardiac output
1.3.0. Alterations in protective mechanisms
  1.3.1. Risk for infection
  1.3.2. [Bleeding tendency]
  1.3.3. Risk for peripheral neurovascular dysfunction
  1.3.4. Dysreflexia
1.4.0. Ineffective thermoregulation
  1.4.1. Risk for altered body temperature
    1.4.1.1. Hypothermia
    1.4.1.2. Hyperthermia
1.5.0. Sensory-perceptual alterations
  1.5.1. Specific sensory deficit
    1.5.1.1. Impaired vision
    1.5.1.2. Impaired hearing [auditory]
    1.5.1.3. Impaired touch [tactile]
    1.5.1.4. Impaired taste [gustatory]
    1.5.1.5. Impaired smell [olfactory]
    1.5.1.6. Impaired sense of movement [kinesthetic]
    1.5.1.7. [Altered proprioception]
  1.5.2. [Altered consciousness]
  1.5.3. Discomfort/pain

---

*Modified from Jenny, J: Classification of Nursing Diagnoses: NANDA Proceedings from the 8th Conference. JB Lippincott, Philadelphia, 1989; and Jenny, J: Classifying Nursing Diagnoses: A self-care approach. Nursing and Health Care 10(2): 1983–1988.

1.5.3.1. Chronic pain

II. Bodily Comfort

2.1.0. Alterations in nutrition
  2.1.1. More than body requirements
  2.1.2. Less than body requirements
  2.1.3. Effective breastfeeding
  2.1.4. Feeding difficulties
    2.1.4.1. Impaired swallowing
    2.1.4.2. Ineffective infant feeding pattern
      2.1.4.2.1. Ineffective breastfeeding
      2.1.4.2.2. Interrupted breastfeeding
  2.1.5. Delayed growth
2.2.0. Alterations in elimination
  2.2.1. Bowel
    2.2.1.1. Constipation
      2.2.1.1.1. Colonic
      2.2.1.1.2. Perceived
    2.2.1.2. Diarrhea
    2.2.1.3. Incontinence
  2.2.2. Bladder
    2.2.2.1. Incontinence
      2.2.2.1.1. Functional
      2.2.2.1.2. Reflex
      2.2.2.1.3. Stress
      2.2.2.1.4. Total
      2.2.2.1.5. Urge
    2.2.2.2. Retention
    2.2.2.3. Altered urination pattern
  2.2.3. [Skin]
  2.2.4. Toileting difficulties
2.3.0. Impaired tissue integrity
  2.3.1. Impaired skin integrity
  2.3.2. Impaired oral mucous membrane
2.4.0. Alterations in activity
  2.4.1. Impaired physical mobility
    2.4.1.1. [Hyperactivity]
    2.4.1.2. Activity intolerance
    2.4.1.3. Risk for disuse syndrome
  2.4.2. Sleep pattern disturbance
  2.4.3. Fatigue
  2.4.4. Diversional activity/recreation deficit
2.5.0. Altered grooming pattern
  2.5.1. Specific grooming difficulties
    2.5.1.1. Bathing/perineal care
    2.5.1.2. [Mouth care]
    2.5.1.3. Dressing
  2.5.2. [Self-neglect]
    2.5.2.1. Neglect, unilateral

III. Ego Integrity

3.1.0. Altered self-concept
  3.1.1. Disturbance in body image
  3.1.2. Disturbance in self-esteem
    3.1.2.1. Chronic low
    3.1.2.2. Situational low
  3.1.3. Disturbance in personal identity
3.2.0. Altered thought processes
  3.2.1. [Impaired information processing]
  3.2.2. [Memory loss]
  3.2.3. [Confusion]
  3.2.4. [Impaired learning]
  3.2.5. [Impaired self-orientation]
3.3.0. [Diminished feelings of personal control]
  3.3.1. Anxiety
  3.3.2. Fear
  3.3.3. Grieving
    3.3.3.1. Anticipatory
    3.3.3.2. Dysfunctional
  3.3.4. Risk for violence
    3.3.4.1. Risk for self-mutilation
  3.3.5. Post-trauma response
    3.3.5.1. Rape-trauma syndrome
      3.3.5.1.1. Compound reaction
      3.3.5.1.2. Silent reaction
  3.3.6. Powerlessness
  3.3.7. Hopelessness
3.4.0. Spiritual distress

IV. Social Interaction

4.1.0. [Alterations in communication]
  4.1.1. Verbal, impaired
  4.1.2. [Nonverbal, impaired]
4.2.0. [Alterations in relationships]
  4.2.1. Social isolation
  4.2.2. [Social withdrawal]
  4.2.3. Altered sexuality pattern
    4.2.3.1. Sexual dysfunction
4.3.0. Alterations in role
  4.3.1. Impaired parenting
    4.3.1.1. Parental role conflict
  4.3.2. [Impaired work functioning]
    4.3.2.1. Caregiver role strain
4.4.0. Alterations in family process
  4.4.1. Family coping, potential for growth
  4.4.2. Ineffective family coping
    4.4.2.1. Compromised
    4.4.2.2. Disabling

4.4.3. [Risk for abuse]
4.5.0. Developmental delay

V. Health Protection

5.1.0. Health-seeking behaviors
5.2.0. Altered health maintenance
    5.2.1. [Inadequate self-monitoring]
    5.2.2. [Inadequate self-protection]
    5.2.3. [Reduced use of health services]
5.3.0. [Ineffective stress management]
    5.3.1. Ineffective individual coping
        5.3.1.1. Decisional conflict
        5.3.1.2. Ineffective denial
        5.3.1.3. Coping defensive
5.4.0. Risk for injury
    5.4.1. Risk for trauma
    5.4.2. [Risk for abuse]

VI. Health Restoration

6.1.0. Ineffective management of therapeutic regimen
    6.1.1. Noncompliance [specify]
    6.1.2. Impaired adjustment
    6.1.3. [Risk for transmitting infection]

VII. Environmental Management

7.1.0. Impaired home maintenance management
    7.1.1. [Coping with dysfunctional facilities]
    7.1.2. [Inability to perform household tasks]
7.2.0. [Exposure to hazards]
7.3.0. [Separation from community services/ resources]
7.4.0. Relocation stress syndrome

Code for Nurses

1. The nurse provides services with respect for human dignity and the uniqueness of the client, unrestricted by considerations of social or economic status, personal attributes, or the nature of health problems.
2. The nurse safeguards the client's right to privacy by judiciously protecting information of a confidential nature.
3. The nurse acts to safeguard the client and the public when healthcare and safety are affected by the incompetent, unethical, or illegal practice of any person.
4. The nurse assumes responsibility and accountability for individual nursing judgments and actions.
5. The nurse maintains competence in nursing.
6. The nurse exercises informed judgment and uses individual competence and qualifications as criteria in seeking consultation, accepting responsibilities, and delegating nursing activities to others.

7. The nurse participates in activities that contribute to the ongoing development of the profession's body of knowledge.
8. The nurse participates in the profession's efforts to implement and improve standards of nursing.
9. The nurse participates in the profession's efforts to establish and maintain conditions of employment conducive to high quality nursing care.
10. The nurse participates in the profession's effort to protect the public from misinformation and misrepresentation and to maintain the integrity of nursing.
11. The nurse collaborates with members of the health professions and other citizens in promoting community and national efforts to meet the health needs of the public.

Reprinted with permission from Code for Nurses with Interpretive Statements, 1985, American Nurses Association, Washington, DC.

Lunney's Ordinal Scale for Degrees of Accuracy of a Nursing Diagnosis

VALUE	CRITERIA
+5	Diagnosis is consistent with all of the cues, supported by highly relevant cues, and precise.
+4	Diagnosis is consistent with most or all of the cues and supported by relevant cues but fails to reflect one or a few highly relevant cues.
+3	Diagnosis is consistent with many of the cues but fails to reflect the specificity of available cues.
+2	Diagnosis is indicated by some of the cues but there are insufficient cues relevant to the diagnosis and/or the diagnosis is lower priority than other diagnoses.
+1	Diagnosis is only suggested by one or a few cues.
0	Diagnosis is not indicated by any of the cues. No diagnosis is stated when there are sufficient cues to state a diagnosis.
	The diagnosis can not be rated.
−1	Diagnosis is indicated by more than one cue but should be rejected based on the presence of at least two disconfirming cues.

Reprinted with permission from Lunney, M. (1990). Accuracy of Nursing Diagnosis: Concepts and Developments. Nursing Diagnosis 1:12–17.

Self-Monitoring of Accuracy Using the Integrated Model: A Guide

1. Pre-encounter data
   a. What data did I collect before seeing the patient? Did I collect enough (or too much) data at this point?
   b. How did I interpret the data before seeing the patient (e.g., relevance of data, priority of data, nursing responsibilities related to data, health status of patient)? What were my biases?
   c. Did I cluster two or more cues, before contact with the patient, as having specific meaning when occurring together?
   d. Was I naming hypotheses before I saw the patient? Should I have connected the data with hypotheses?
2. Entering the data search field and shaping the direction of data gathering
   a. In what ways did seeing the patient affect my initial assessment?
   b. How did I interpret the data that I initially collected in relation to other data, previous expectations, priorities, my responsibilities, or specific hypotheses? How did the patient interpret my behavior?
   c. Did I rearrange any clusters that existed (in my mind) before seeing the patient?
   d. For which hypotheses was I collecting data? Did I consider hypotheses related to the individuality of the patient? Did the patient express diagnostic hypotheses? Were the diagnoses the same as those that were generated by pre-encounter data, or did seeing the patient revise the names that I was considering?
3. Coalescing the cues into clusters or chunks
   a. To what extent did the clustering of cues make me aware of the need for further data collection?
   b. Did I assign validity and reliability estimates to the data while coalescing them into clusters or chunks?
   c. Did the clusters or chunks of data have meanings that can be validated through the literature?

d. To what extent would other nurses agree with the names that I was considering for the clusters or chunks?

4. Activating possible diagnostic explanations
   a. What data did I collect to support hypotheses? If the answer is none, did I close data collection prematurely? Did limitations in my knowledge prevent me from collecting data for certain diagnoses?
   b. How did I judge the relevance of the data that activated diagnostic hypotheses, for example, were they relevant enough to validate the diagnosis or just predictive? Was my judgment consistent with the judgment of the patient?
   c. Considering the literature on diagnostic concepts, how well did the clusters support the activation of diagnostic hypotheses? Did I consider the unique aspects of this patient when clustering the data for hypotheses?
   d. Did I consider the names of the important hypotheses?

5. Hypothesis- and data-directed searching of the data field
   a. Was my data collection efficient enough to produce high relevant data for high priority diagnoses as well as to rule out competitive diagnoses? Was I able to obtain the greatest amount of relevant data with the least amount of cost to the patient and myself (cost equals time spent, time lost, and effort expended)?
   b. Was I able to interpret the data in relation to many conflicting hypotheses? Was my interpretation specific enough to direct me to precise diagnoses? Was I able to identify the need for further data?
   c. Were previous clusters used, or were they rearranged to produce new clusters?
   d. What diagnostic concepts were considered relevant and valid for testing the goodness of fit after a search of the data field? Were there concepts that I considered briefly during the previous steps but did not pursue?

6. Testing diagnostic hypotheses for goodness of fit
   a. What cues were used to test the goodness of fit?
   b. Were my interpretations of these cues derived from legitimate sources of information: theory, research, norms, and the unique patterns of the patient?
   c. Were the clusters of cues sufficiently well developed for testing the goodness of fit?
   d. Did the diagnostic label fulfill the criteria for goodness of fit?

Clinical (Critical) Pathways: A Sample

Clinical pathways may be used as a standardized plan of care or as a guideline for developing an individualized plan for a specific patient. Pathways are best used for acute problems for which there are predictable outcomes that must be achieved within a specific time frame. For example, Donald may be admitted initially to a medical, or step-down unit, during the acute phase of alcohol withdrawal. Following is a sample clinical pathway for his 7-day length of stay. After completing this phase, he would be transferred to the Behavioral Unit for the rehabilitation program, and a new clinical pathway would be implemented.

CLINICAL PATHWAY: ALCOHOL WITHDRAWAL—LOS: 7 DAYS

Nursing Diagnoses and Categories of Care	Time Dimension	Goals and/or Actions	Time Dimension	Goals and/or Actions	Time Dimension	Discharge Outcome
Risk for injury related to central nervous system agitation					Day 7	Patient shows no evidence of injury incurred during ETOH withdrawal
Referrals	Day 1	Psychiatrist Assess need for: Neurologist, Cardiologist, Internist			Day 7	Discharge with follow-up appointments as required
Diagnostic studies	Day 1	Blood alcohol level Drug screen SMAC 27 Urinalysis Chest x-ray ECG	Day 4	Repeat selected diagnostic studies as necessary		
Additional assessments	Day 1 Day 1–5 ongoing ongoing	VS q4h I&O Restraints PRN Assess withdrawal symptoms: tremors, nausea/vomiting, tachycardia, sweating, high blood pressure, seizures, insomnia, hallucinations	Day 2–3 Day 4–7 Day 6 Day 4 (G)	VS q8h if stable DC I&O Marked decrease in objective symptoms	Day 7	VS bid; remain stable Discharge: absence of objective withdrawal symptoms

Category	Day(s)		Day(s)		Day	Outcome
Medications	Day 1	Librium 200 mg	Day 3	Librium 120 mg		
	Day 2	Librium 160 mg	Day 4	Librium 80 mg		
	Day 1–6	Librium prn	Day 5	Librium 40 mg		
	Day 1–7	Maalox ac and hs	Day 6	DC Librium		
Patient education			Day 5	Discuss goals of Alcoholics Anonymous (AA) and need for ongoing therapy	Day 7	Discharge with information regarding AA attendance or outpatient treatment or transfer to Behavioral Unit
Altered nutrition: Less than body requirements						
Referrals	Day 1	Consult Dietitian	Day 1–7 (G)	Fulfill nutritional needs	Day 7	Nutritional condition has stabilized
Diet	Day 1	Bland as tolerated; fluids as tolerated	Day 2–3	Frequent, small meals; easily digested foods; advanced as tolerated		
Additional assessments	Day 1–7	Weight, I&O, Skin turgor, Color of mucous membrane	Day 4–7	High-protein, high-carbohydrate diet		
Medications	Day 1–4	Thiamine 100 mg injections	Day 2–7	Multiple vitamin tablet		
Patient education			Day 5	Principles of nutrition; foods for maintenance of wellness		
			Day 6–7 (G)	Demonstrates ability to select appropriate foods for healthy diet		

255

Common Medical Abbreviations

Abbreviations are used as a time and space saver when writing notes. In order to assure that everyone in the hospital/agency can understand what has been written by others, most facilities have a list of abbreviations approved by the medical record department for use in that particular facility. Therefore, the list of acceptable abbreviations varies from one facility to the next. The following is a representation of common abbreviations used by nurses. **Note:** The context of use determines the appropriate choice when more than one definition is provided.

A	assessment	ASAP	as soon as possible
ABD	abdomen	ASHD	arteriosclerotic heart disease
ac	before meals	assist.	assistance
ACTH	adrenocorticotrophic hormone	as tol	as tolerated
ad lib	at discretion	AV	atrioventricular; arteriovenous
ADL	activities of daily living		
adm	admission	bid	twice a day
AFO	ankle-foot orthosis	bilat.	bilateral
AK	above knee	BK	below knee
AM	morning	BM	bowel movement
AMA	against medical advice	BP	blood pressure
Amb	ambulate, ambulatory	bpm	beats per minute
AP	anterioposterior	BR	bedrest
AROM	active range of motion	BRP	bathroom privileges
ASA	aspirin	BS	blood sugar

B/S	bedside		HHA	home health agency
BUN	blood urea nitrogen (blood test)		HNP	herniated nucleus pulposus
			HOB	head of bed
C	Centigrade		HR	heart rate
C & S	culture and sensitivity		hr	hour
CA	carcinoma, cancer; cardiac arrest		hs	at bedtime
CABG	coronary artery bypass graft		ht	height
CAD	coronary artery disease		Ht	hematocrit
cal	calories		Htn	hypertension
CBC	complete blood count		Hx, hx	history
CBS	chronic brain syndrome			
CC, C/C	chief complaint		I&O	intake and output
cc	cubic centimeter		ICU	intensive care unit
CCU	coronary care unit		IDDM	insulin-dependent diabetes mellitus
CHF	congestive heart failure		IM	intramuscular
cm	centimeter		imp.	impression
CNS	central nervous system		in	inches
c/o	complains of		IPPB	intermittent positive-pressure
CO_2	carbon dioxide			breathing
COLD	chronic obstructive lung disease		IV	intravenous
cont.	continue			
COPD	chronic obstructive pulmonary disease		JVP	jugular venous pressure
CP	cerebral palsy		kcal	kilocalories
CSF	cerebrospinal fluid		kg	kilogram
CVA	cerebrovascular accident; costovertebral angle		KUB	kidney, ureter, bladder
CVP	central venous pressure		L, l	liter
			lb	pound
DAR	data, action, response (charting)		LBP	low back pain
D & C	dilation & curettage		LE	lower extremity
DOB	date of birth		LOC	loss of consciousness; locus of control
Dx	diagnosis		LP	lumbar puncture
			L & W	living & well
ECG	electrocardiogram			
EDD	expected date of delivery		m	meter
EEG	electroencephalogram		MD	medical doctor; doctor of medicine
ER/D	emergency room/department		Meds	medications
			mEq	millequivalent
FBS	fasting blood sugar		mg	milligram
FHT	fetal heart tones		MI	myocardial infarction
Fx	fracture		mL	milliliter
			mm	millimeter
GU	genitourinary		Mn	midnight
			MRI	magnetic resonance imaging
HA, H/A	headache		MSW	medical social worker
Hb, Hgb	hemoglobin			
HCVD	hypertensive cardiovascular disease		NA	nurse's aide
HEENT	head, ear, eyes, nose, throat		neg	negative

NG	nasogastric		sig	directions for use, give as follows, let it be labeled
NIDDM	non–insulin-dependent diabetes mellitus		SLE	systemic lupus erythematosus
			SLR	straight leg raise
O_2	oxygen		SNF	skilled nursing facility
OOB	out of bed		SO(s)	significant other(s)
OR	operating room		SOAP	subjective, objective, assessment, plan (charting)
OTC	over-the-counter		S/P	status post
PEEP	positive end-expiratory pressure		spec	specimen
PERRLA	pupils equal, round, and reactive to light and accommodation		STD	sexually transmitted disease
			stat	immediately, at once
PO	per os (by mouth)		Sx	symptoms
POMR	problem-oriented medical record			
pos	positive		T	temperature
poss	possible		T & A	tonsillectomy and adenoidectomy
post op	after surgery (operation)		tab	tablet
pre op	before surgery (operation)		TB	tuberculosis
PROM	passive range of motion; premature rupture of membranes		tbsp	tablespoon
			TENS, TNS	transcutaneous electrical nerve stimulator
prn	whenever necessary		THR	total hip replacement
PT	physical therapy, physical therapist		TIA	transient ischemic attack
Pt., pt.	patient		tid	three times daily
PVD	peripheral vascular disease		TKR	total knee replacement
PWB	partial weight bearing		TMJ	temporomandibular joint
			t.o.	telephone order
q	every		TPR	temperature, pulse, and respiration
qd	every day		tsp	teaspoon
qh	every hour		TUR	transurethral resection
qid	four times a day			
qn	every night		UA	urine analysis
qod	every other day		UE	upper extremity
qs	sufficient quantity		UMN	upper motor neuron
qt	quart		URI	upper respiratory infection
			US	ultrasound
RA	rheumatoid arthritis		UTI	urinary tract infection
RBC	red blood cell count		UV	ultraviolet
RD	registered dietician			
re:	regarding		VD	venereal disease
resp	respiratory, respiration		vo	verbal orders
RN	registered nurse		vol	volume
R/O	rule out		vs	vital signs
ROM	range of motion			
ROS	review of systems		WBC	white blood cell count
RT	respiratory therapist		w/c	wheelchair
Rx	treatment, prescription, therapy		WIC	women, infants and children (program)
sec	seconds		wk	week
sc	subcutaneous			

WNL	within normal limits	y/o	years old
wt	weight	yd	yard
		yr	year
X	number of times performed (X2 = twice)		

Glossary

Analysis: The process of examining and categorizing information to reach a conclusion about a patient's needs.

Assessment: The first step of the nursing process, during which data are collected.

Baseline Assessment: Initial data collection done at the time of admission/beginning of shift, and so on, with which future assessments are compared.

Charting: The written record of relevant details of the care given to a patient and the patient's response, including observations and changes in the patient's condition.

Collaborative Problem: A need identified by another discipline that will contain a nursing component requiring nursing intervention and/or monitoring.

Cue(s): A signal that indicates a possible need/direction for care.

DAR: Format for charting—data, actions, response (called Focus Charting™).

Defining Characteristics: Clinical criteria that represent the presence of a diagnostic category; cluster of signs and symptoms indicating a specific nursing diagnosis.

Diagnosis: Identification of a disease/condition or human response by a scientific evaluation of signs/symptoms, history, and diagnostic studies.

Diagnostic Error: A mistaken assumption leading to a wrong conclusion.

Diagnostic Reasoning: Process of problem identification used during the second step of the nursing process: problem-sensing, rule-out process, synthesizing the data, evaluation or confirming the hypothesis, listing patient problems/needs.

Etiology: Identified causes and/or contributing factors responsible for the presence of a specific patient problem/need.

Evaluation: The fifth step of the nursing process during which the patient's movement toward specified outcomes is determined and the plan of care is modified or care is terminated depending on the findings.

Focus Assessment: Gathering of data narrowed to a specific area/topic.

Goal: Broad guidelines indicating the overall direction for movement as a result of the interventions of the healthcare team; divided into long-term and short-term goals.

Implement/Implementation: The fourth step of the nursing process in which the plan of care is put into action; performing identified interventions/activities.

Inference: To conclude/deduce from evidence presented.

Intuition: A sense of something that is not clearly evidenced by known facts.

JCAHO (Joint Commission on Accreditation of Healthcare Organizations): Surveying body that certifies clinical and organization performance of an institution following established guidelines.

Long-Term Goals: May not be achieved before discharge from care.

Measureable Verb: An action/behavior that can be quantified by specific amounts of time and can be seen or heard.

Medical Diagnosis: Illness/condition for which treatment is directed by a licensed physician; medical diagnosis focuses on correction/prevention of pathology of specific organs/body systems.

NANDA (North American Nursing Diagnosis Association): International group responsible for the development of nursing diagnoses.

Nurse-Patient Relationship: A therapeutic relationship built on a series of interactions, developing over time, and meeting the needs of the patient.

Nursing Audit: Procedure to evaluate the quality of nursing care provided, using established criteria/standards. Concurrent audit is done while nursing care is being performed. Retrospective audit is done after the patient is discharged from care.

Nursing Diagnosis: *Noun:* a label approved by NANDA identifying specific patient/problems/needs. The means of describing health problems amenable to treatment by nurses; may be physical, sociologic, or psychological. *Verb:* process of identifying specific patient problems/needs, used by some as the title of the second step of the nursing process.

Nursing Interventions: Prescriptions for specific behaviors expected for the patient, and/or actions to be carried out by nurses to promote, maintain, or restore health.

Nursing Process: An orderly, logical five-step problem-solving approach for administering nursing care. Composed of assessment, problem identification, planning, implementation, and evaluation.

Nursing Standard: Identified criterion against which nursing care is compared and evaluated; generally reflects the minimum level for nursing care.

Objective Data: What can be observed, for example: vital signs, behaviors, diagnostic studies.

Outcome: The result of actions undertaken to achieve a broader goal; measurable steps to achieve the goals of treatment and to meet discharge criteria.

Patient Database: The compilation of data collected about a patient; it consists of the nursing history, physical examination, and results of the diagnostic studies.

Patient Diagnostic Statement: The outcome of the diagnostic reasoning process; a three-part statement identifying the patient's problem/need, etiology of the problem/need, and the associated signs/symptoms.

PES: Format for combining a patient problem label, etiology, and signs/symptoms to create an individualized diagnostic statement.

Planning: The third step of the nursing process during which goals/outcomes are determined and interventions chosen.

Plan of Care: Written evidence of the second and third steps of the nursing process that identifies the patient's problems/needs, goals/outcomes of care, and interventions to treat the problems/needs.

POMR or PORS (Problem-Oriented Medical Record): A method of recording data about the health status of the patient relative to specific problems.

Problem Identification: The second step of the nursing process in which the data collected are analyzed and, through the process of diagnostic reasoning, specific patient diagnostic statements are created.

Protocol: Written guidelines of steps to be taken for providing patient care in a particular situation/condition.

Related Factor: The conditions/circumstances that contribute to the development/maintenance of a nursing diagnosis; forms the *related to* component of the patient diagnostic statement.

Risk Factor: The environmental factors and physiological, psychological, genetic, or chemical elements that increase the vulnerability of an individual, family, or community to an unhealthful event.

Risk Nursing Diagnosis: A problem that may occur/recur, particularly if intervention is not undertaken. Because it has not yet occurred, there are no signs/symptoms when writing the patient diagnostic statement; instead, risk factors are identified.

Short-Term Goals: Those goals that usually must be met before discharge or movement to a less acute level of care.

SOAP: Format for documentation—subjective, objective, analysis, plan.

SOAPIER: Format for documentation—subjective, objective, analysis, plan, implementation, evaluation, revision.

Sign: Objective or observable evidence or manifestation of a health problem.

Subjective Data: What the patient reports, believes, or feels.

Symptom: Subjectively perceptible change in the body or its functions that indicates disease or the kind or phases of disease.

Synthesize: Viewing all data as a whole to provide a comprehensive picture of the patient.

Validating: The process of assuring that data is factual.

Wellness: A state of optimal health, physical and psychosocial.

Nursing Outcomes Classification

The Nursing Outcomes Classification (NOC) uses the following 16 different Likert scales to measure variability in the patient state, behavior, or perception depicted in the outcome:

Scale No. 1: 1—Extremely compromised; 2—Substantially compromised; 3—Moderately compromised; 4—Mildly compromised; 5—Not compromised—used to measure outcomes such as Bowel Elimination, Cognitive Ability, Well Being

Scale No. 2: 1—Extreme deviation from expected range to 5—No deviation from expected range, to measure Growth, Physical Aging Status, or Vital Signs Status

Scale No. 3: 1—Dependent, does not participate to 5—Completely independent, for outcomes such as Balance, Self-Care, and Transfer Performance

Scale No. 4: 1—No motion to 5—Full motion for Joint Movement outcomes

Scale No. 5: 1—Not at all to 5—To a very great extent, for outcomes such as Dignified Dying, Energy Conservation, Immune Hypersensitivity Control

Scale No. 6: 1—Not adequate to 5—Totally adequate, measuring Abuse Protection, Breastfeeding, Role Performance

Scale No. 7: 1—Over 9 to 5—None, for Safety Status: Falls Occurrence

Scale No. 8: 1—Extensive to 5—None, for Caregiver Stressors and Loneliness

Scale No. 9: 1—None to 5—Extensive, for outcomes such as Abuse Recovery, Knowledge, and Social Support

Scale No. 10: 1—None to 5—Complete, for Bone Healing and Wound Healing

Scale No. 11: 1—Never positive to 5—Consistently positive, measuring Body Image and Self-Esteem

Scale No. 12: 1—Very weak to 5—Very strong, for Health Beliefs and Health Orientation

Scale No. 13: 1—Never demonstrated to 5—Consistently demonstrated, for outcomes such as Aggression Control, Memory, Suicide Self-Restraint

Scale No. 14: 1—Severe to 5—None, to measure Infection Status, Pain Level, Substance Addiction Consequences

Scale No. 15: 1—No evidence to 5—Extensive evidence, for Abuse Cessation and Neglect Cessation

Scale No. 16: 1—Extreme delay from expected range to 5—No delay from expected range, to measure Child Development outcomes

Sample of NOC Outcome Measurement:

PAIN CONTROL BEHAVIOR

	Never 1	Rarely 2	Sometimes 3	Often 4	Consistently Demonstrated 5
Indicators:					
Reports symptoms to healthcare professional				✓	
Uses preventive measures			✓		
Uses non-analgesic relief measures				✓	
Reports pain controlled					✓

Keys to Practice Activities

Key for Practice Activity 2–1: Determining Types of Data

1. Identify subjective (S) versus objective (O) data:

   <u>O</u>   Skin cool/damp

<u>S or O</u> Sputum pale yellow

   <u>S</u>   Allergic to eggs and sulfa

   <u>O</u>   Pitting edema of feet and ankles

   <u>S</u>   Usually voids three times per day

   <u>S</u>   Chest pain lasting 15 minutes

2. Match the technique in column A to the statements in column B:

Column A	**Column B**	
a. Open-ended question	<u>B</u>	The next time this comes up, what would you do to handle it?
b. Hypothetical question		
c. Reflection	<u>C</u>	That feeling in your chest, can you describe it more fully?
d. Closed-ended question		
e. Leading question	<u>D</u>	Do you use alcohol regularly?
	<u>A</u>	What would you like to talk about?
	<u>E</u>	You're feeling better today, aren't you?

3. Rewrite the following using effective data collection techniques (see Box 2–3):

   a. You felt like crying, didn't you? *You're sad about what happened and are concerned about what you can do.*

   b. You're in pain again? *I notice you seem to be in pain, tell me about it.*

   c. Do you want to change occupations? *I'd like to hear more about your interests, what you would enjoy doing.*

   d. Since your doctor has talked with you, you don't have any questions, do you? *What is your understanding of what the doctor told you?*

   e. Did you eat lunch? *Tell me what you ate for lunch.*

Key to Practice Activity 2–2: Organizing Data: Diagnostic Divisions and Functional Health Patterns

Donald has been admitted to the psychiatric hospital inpatient substance abuse unit for treatment of depression and withdrawal from alcohol.

Organize the data below according to diagnostic divisions and functional health patterns. Place the number of the listed data next to the category where you believe it fits (see Table 2–1).

1. 46-year-old male

2. Divorced, not currently involved in a relationship

3. Loan banker, laid off 7 months ago

4. Unsteady gait

5. Clothes rumpled, has not shaved for 2 days, dry skin

6. Eats one or two meals a day—donuts, sandwiches, meat and potatoes, no vegetables or fruits; coffee 4 + cups/day

7. Stools have been loose, 3–4/day

8. BP 136/82, right arm/sitting; radial pulse 92

9. Alert and oriented

10. Catholic, not practicing

11. Sleeps usually 3–4 hours a night, awakens around 5:00 AM

12. "I've been drinking a lot lately." Bourbon one fifth/day

13. Worries about financial situation, unable to make child support payments

14. Congested nonproductive cough

15. Reports constant throbbing pain, left knee—old sports injury

16. Genogram:

Diagnostic Divisions

Activity/Rest: _3, 11_
Circulation: _8_
Ego Integrity: _2, 10, 13_
Elimination: _7_
Food/Fluid: _6_
Hygiene: _5_
Neurosensory: _9_
Pain/Discomfort: _15_
Respiration: _14_
Safety: _4, 15_
Sexuality: _1, 2_
Social Interaction: _2, 16_
Teaching/Learning: _12_

Functional Health Patterns

Health Perception/Health
  Management: _4,_
  _12, 15_
Nutritional/Metabolic: _6, 8, 14_
Elimination: _7_
Activity/Exercise: _4, 5_
Cognitive/Perceptual: _9_
Sleep/Rest: _11_
Self-Perception/Self-Concept: _13_
Role/Relationship: _1, 2, 3, 16_
Sexuality/Reproductive: _2_
Coping/Stress Tolerance: _12, 13_
Value/Belief: _10_

GENOGRAM: graphic representation of a family (may include several generations) reflecting medical data and relationships/roles.

Key to Practice Activity 3–1: Activity Intolerance (Level II)

Patient's medical diagnosis: *Pneumonia, recurrent*
Assessment
Subjective data entry:
Reports being weak most of the time. Stays at home; activity limited to short walks and watching baseball on TV. Shortness of breath has contributed to activity limitations. History of smoking 49 pack years. Dyspnea when walking too long and in closed places.
Objective data entry:
BP 178/102, P 100 after short walk on unit. Leans forward to help him breathe while in a sitting position. Respirations at rest are 28 and shallow. AP chest diameter is increased.

Key to Practice Activity 3–2: Identifying the PES Components of the Patient Diagnostic Statement

Instructions (questions 1 through 5): Identify the "PES" components of each of these diagnostic statements:

1. Anxiety, severe, related to changes in health status of fetus/self and threat of death as evidenced by restlessness, tremors, focus on self/fetus.
   P = *Anxiety, severe*
   E = *Changes in health status of fetus/self and threat of death*
   S = *Restlessness, tremors, focus on self/fetus*

2. Thought Processes, altered, related to pharmacological stimulation of the nervous system as evidenced by altered attention span, disorientation, and hallucinations.
   P = *Thought processes, altered*
   E = *Pharmacological stimulation of the nervous system*
   S = *Altered attention span, disorientation, and hallucinations*

3. Coping, Individual, ineffective, related to maturational crisis as evidenced by inability to meet role expectations and alcohol abuse.
   P = *Coping, Individual, ineffective*
   E = *Maturational crisis*
   S = *Inability to meet role expectations and alcohol abuse*

4. Hyperthermia related to increased metabolic rate and dehydration as evidenced by elevated temperature, flushed skin, tachycardia, and tachypnea.
   P = *Hyperthermia*
   E = *Increased metabolic rate and dehydration*
   S = *Elevated temperature, flushed skin, tachycardia, and tachypnea*

5. Pain [acute] related to tissue distention and edema as evidenced by verbal reports, guarding behavior, and changes in vital signs.
   P = *Pain [acute]*
   E = *Tissue distention and edema*
   S = *Verbal reports, guarding behavior, and changes in vital signs*

6. Explain the difference between actual and risk diagnoses: *An actual diagnosis is one that is currently present and manifested by signs and symptoms. In recording the problem/need, you would use a three-part problem statement. A risk diagnosis is one that you believe could develop, but because it has not occurred yet, there are no signs or symptoms, only "risk factors." Therefore the problem would be written as a two-part problem statement.*

7. Give an example of an actual and a risk problem for a patient with second-degree burns of the hand.
   Actual: Skin Integrity, impaired; Pain [acute]; Self-Care deficit; Knowledge deficit: treatment needs
   Risk: Infection, risk for; Adjustment, risk for impaired; Body Image risk for disturbance

Practice Activity 3–3: Identifying Correct and Incorrect Patient Diagnostic Statements

Label each patient diagnostic statement as correct or incorrect. Identify why a statement is incorrect:

____correct____ 1. Airway Clearance, ineffective, related to increased pulmonary secretions and bronchospasm as evidenced by wheezing, tachypnea, and ineffective cough.

____correct____ 2. Thought Processes, altered, related to delusional thinking or reality base as evidenced by persecutory thoughts of "I am victim," and interference with ability to think clearly and logically.

____incorrect____ 3. Gas Exchange, impaired, related to bronchitis as evidenced by rhonchi, dyspnea, and cyanosis. *Related to medical diagnosis. In considering the pathophysiology of bronchitis, the underlying problem may actually be Airway Clearance, ineffective, related to excessive, thickened mucous secretions as evidenced by rhonchi, dyspnea, and cyanosis.*

____incorrect____ 4. Knowledge deficit, diabetic care, related to inaccurate follow-through of instructions as evidenced by information misinterpretation and lack of recall. *"Related to" and "evidenced by" statements are reversed.*

_____correct_____   **5.** Pain, related to tissue distention and edema as evidenced by reports of severe colicky pain in right flank, elevated pulse and respirations, and restlessness.

Key to Practice Activity 4–1: Prioritizing Nursing Diagnoses

Instructions: Prioritize the nursing diagnoses listed in each separate set by using the Maslow and Kalish models. Rank the four diagnoses by using 1 to designate the most basic or more immediate patient need and continuing to 4, which designates the highest-level need (but least in priority). Review Appendix A as needed to compare definitions of these nursing diagnoses.

a. __2__ Incontinence, stress
   __4__ Sexuality Patterns, altered
   __1__ Airway Clearance, ineffective
   __3__ Skin Integrity, risk for impaired
b. __1__ Gas Exchange, impaired
   __4__ Knowledge deficit
   __2__ Hypothermia
   __3__ Infection, risk for
c. __1__ Pain [acute]
   __4__ Self-Esteem, chronic low
   __2__ Physical Mobility, impaired
   __3__ Social Isolation

Practice Activity 4–2: Identifying Correctly Stated Outcomes

Instructions: Identify which of the following outcome statements are written correctly, or state why it is not correct. Modify those statements that are not correct.

1. Patient will: List individual risk factors and appropriate interventions. _Incorrect—RATIONALE: There is no time frame indicated. Corrected example: Patient will: List individual risk factors and appropriate interventions within 72 hours._

2. Patient will: Identify four adaptive/protective measures for individual situation by discharge. _Correct—RATIONALE: All elements of a measurable outcome are present._

3. Patient will: Understand behaviors, lifestyle changes necessary to promote physical safety within 72 hours. _Incorrect—RATIONALE: "Understands" is not a measurable verb. Corrected example: Patient will: Verbalize understanding of behaviors, lifestyle changes necessary to promote physical safety within 72 hours._

4. Airway patent, aspiration prevented, ongoing. _Incorrect—RATIONALE: There is no active verb, no subject, and this may represent two separate outcomes. Corrected example: Patient will: maintain patent airway, ongoing. OR Patient will: demonstrate techniques to prevent aspiration, within 24 hours._

5. Patient will: Assume responsibility for own learning by participating in group discussions twice a day no later than 10/29/99. _Correct—RATIONALE: All elements of a measurable outcome are present._

Practice Activity 4–3: Identifying Correctly Stated Interventions

Instructions: Identify which of the following interventions are correctly stated, and rewrite those that are not.

1. Walk length of hall 2 ×/day with assistance from two staff members. *Correct.*

2. Force fluids. *Incorrect—RATIONALE: The quantity of fluid is not indicated. Corrected example: Force fluid to a minimum of 2000 ml/day.*

3. Pericare after each BM. *Incorrect—RATIONALE: No verb and no indication of who is responsible for the activity. Corrected example: Provide [nurse], OR Assist with [nurse and patient] OR Encourage [patient] pericare after each BM.*

4. Encourage deep-breathing exercises and cough q2h. *Correct.*

5. Reduce environmental stimuli. *Incorrect—RATIONALE: How/what? Corrected example: Maintain low lighting in room, OR Keep hallway door closed.*

6. Provide written handout for side effects of medications before discharge. *Correct.*

Practice Activity 4–4

Does not require a key because student is simply copying information from Box 4–3 into a 5-column form.

Practice Activity 4–5

Desired Outcome and Patient Criteria:	**The Patient will:** *Report measurable increase in activity level.* *Demonstrate a decrease in physiological signs of intolerance.*
TIME OUT!	The desired outcome must meet criteria to be accurate. The outcome must be specific, realistic, measurable, and include a time frame for completion. Does the action verb describe the patient's behavior to be evaluated? Can the outcome be used in the evaluation step of the nursing process to measure the patient's response to the nursing interventions listed below?

Interventions	Rationale for Selected Intervention and References
Measure vital signs before/during/after activity.	*Determines pt's response to physical activity & appropriateness of activity.*
Adjust activities to pt. tolerance.	*Prevents overexertion.*
Teach energy-conserving methods.	*May enhance pt's ability to perform ADLs.*
Plan care with rest periods between activities.	*Reduces fatigue, enhances sense of well-being.*
Encourage participation in social activities.	*Provides stimulation, opportunities to form new relationships, and maximizes cognitive function.*

TIME OUT! Do your interventions assist in achieving the desired outcome? Do your interventions address further monitoring of the patient's response to your interventions and to the achievement of the desired outcome? Are qualifiers: **when, how, amount, time,** and **frequency** used? Is the focus of the action's verb on the nurse's actions and not on the patient? Do your rationales provide sufficient reason and directions?

What was your patient's response to the interventions?

Was the desired outcome achieved?
☐ Yes ☐ No

... revisions to either the desired outcome or interventic... you make?

Documentation Focus: Now tha... low to enter your progress n...

...valuation, the next step is to docume...

...assessment Data:

P L A N N I N G

E V A L U A T I O N

Key to Practice Activity 5–1: Setting Your Work Schedule for Implementing the Plan of Care

Vignette: Michelle incurred compound fractures of the right lower leg 3 days ago. In reviewing the plan of care, you note the following:

○ Assist with bed bath ○ Calculate I&O every 8 hours (2 PM) ○ Change dressing twice a day and prn (9 AM) ○ Assess vital signs every 4 hours (8 AM, 12 noon) ○ Monitor circulation/nerve function R lower leg every hour × 24 hr, then every 4 hr and prn ○ IV medications (8 AM, 2 PM) ○ Up in chair with meals (7:30 AM, 12 noon) ○ Walk in halls 3 times a day after instructed in crutch walking.

1. Organize the above interventions and activities on the following worksheet:

Worksheet

Pt.	7	8	9	10	11	12	1	2	3	Comments
Michelle	Chair	VS Circ ✓ Med	Bath Dress	Walk	VS Circ ✓ Chair			I&O Med Walk		

2. During nursing rounds, just after the change-of-shift report on 6/13, you find Michelle is crying and she reports sudden throbbing pain in her R lower leg. How will this affect your work plan?

The plan needs to be reordered because after you assess Michelle's pain and administer medication, she requires time to relax and for the medication to take effect. For example: You may choose to leave Michelle in bed for her breakfast and have her up in the chair after her bath or following her walk.

Key to Practice Activity 5–2: Legal and Ethical Concerns of Care

As noted, Robert had completed a form directing healthcare providers to withhold advanced life support measures including the use of a mechanical ventilator.

1. Have you and your family members completed advance directives stating specific healthcare desires? Self-answer _____

If not, why: Self-answer _____

2. As a nurse, how do you feel about adhering to advance directives as stipulated by an elderly patient? Self-answer _____

for a premature infant as stipulated by the parents? Self-answer _____

3. Review the Code for Nurses (see Appendix D) and choose two principles you believe may address your responsibility to patients/guardians in regard to their decisions to limit care.

a. *No. 1—A patient has the moral right to determine their own care by accepting, rejecting, or terminating treatment based on their own value system and lifestyle. Nurses have an obligation to be knowledgeable about the moral and legal rights of the patient and to protect and support those rights.*

b. *No. 3—Denying or negating the patient's rights (moral and/or legal) results in unethical or illegal practice. The nurse has a duty to be knowledgeable regarding agency policies and procedures, nursing standards of practice, the Code for Nurses, and laws governing nursing and healthcare practices to protect and advocate for the patient.*

c. *No. 4—The professional nurse bears the primary responsibility for nursing care provided (or not provided) and neither physicians' orders nor agency policies relieve the nurse of accountability for actions taken and judgments made.*

Key to Practice Activity 5–3: Communicating Nursing Information to Other Caregivers

Work through the questions below.

1. Two methods of communicating your observations about patient care and activities to other nurses are by:

   a. *Written record*   b. *Verbal report*

2. Discuss the benefits of nursing rounds: *Aids in verifying the status of invasive treatments, appearance of wounds/dressings, and the current condition of the patient.*

3. Underline the information listed below that you would include in your change-of-shift report:
   Sally   Ate well   *Age 30*   *Dr. Jefferson*
   Weak and unsteady while up in hall
   Episiotomy reddened, slight edema, no drainage second day postpartum
   Scheduled for discharge tomorrow
   Received oral pain medication at 11 AM with reported relief
   Does not want to go home
   Sister in to visit at lunchtime
   Coordination for home care services in progress with the discharge planner
   Spent afternoon talking on phone
   Has not named Baby B and at times has ignored infant cues

4. The wife of a prominent local politician is admitted for treatment of alcoholism. You could discuss her admission and course of therapy with which of the following people? (check any answers that seem appropriate)
   __x__ attending/primary physician
   __x__ nursing supervisor
   _____ pediatric nurse (her best friend)
   _____ your husband
   _____ patient's son
   _____ interested newspaper reporter
   __x__ other nurses on your unit

   Note: Patient permission is required for release of information even to family members.

Key to Practice Activity 6–1: Evaluating Patient Outcomes

Read over the case study information below. It has been used to develop a plan of care for Michelle.

When Michelle was admitted to the hospital the evening of 6/11, a physiological (Maslow's) or survival (Kalish's) need of pain avoidance was identified (i.e., Pain [acute]). A higher-level problem of safety or stimulation was noted (i.e., Impaired Physical Mobility) as was a safety need of protection (i.e., Risk For Infection).

The following morning (6/12) during the 8 AM assessment, Michelle indicates she was successful in obtaining relief of pain following periodic injection of analgesics. Michelle also found that deep-breathing exercises and focusing her attention on the scenic picture at the foot of her bed helped to minimize the severity of recurrent muscle spasms in her right leg. In addition, frequent weight shifts using the overhead trapeze and range-of-motion exercises reduced general aches and joint stiffness and meditation enhanced general relaxation.

The nurse noticed that most of Michelle's breakfast tray was untouched. Michelle reported she was not very hungry but did want fruit juice and other fluids. Following the morning bed bath, the dressings were changed and the right leg wound was evaluated. Skin edges were pink and serous drainage was odorless. Pin sites were also cleaned and no signs of inflammation noted. At lunch, Michelle's intake was poor. She indicated she was having difficulty opening her mouth and chewing and had an aching sensation located in the right temple and ear.

During the afternoon assessment at 4:30 PM, Michelle's nurse verified that Michelle understood and was using infection control techniques of proper handwashing and avoidance of contact with wound and pin sites.

When Michelle was set up on the side of the bed before her dinner, she reported dizziness and sharp pain in her right leg, and she became pale and diaphoretic. She was returned to the supine position and a focused assessment was performed, revealing a BP of 92/60. Within 20 minutes, Michelle's color had improved, the dizziness was gone, and the pain was relieved with medication.

In reviewing the excerpts from Michelle's plan of care, complete the status column denoting whether the outcomes have been met (m), partially met (pm), or not met (nm) appropriately for the timeframes indicated.

Practice Activity 6–1 Plan of Care: Michelle

Patient: Michelle Age: 14—03/2/85 Sex: F Admitted: 6/11/99 5:30 PM Dx: Compound Fx R Tibia/Fibula, closed head injury/mild concussion

Date	Patient Diagnostic Statement	Goal	Interventions	Outcomes	Status
6/11/99	Pain [acute], related to movement of bone fragments, soft tissue injury/edema evidenced by verbal reports, guarding, muscle tension, narrowed focus, and tachycardia.	Pain-free or controlled by discharge.	1. Maintain limb rest R leg × 24 hr to 5 PM 6/12. 2. Elevate lower leg with folded blanket. 3. Apply ice to area as tolerated × 48 hr to 5 PM 6/13. 4. Place cradle over foot of bed. 5. Document reports and characteristics of pain. 6. Medicate with Demerol 75 mg and Phenergan 25 mg IM q4h prn or Vicodin 5 mg PO q4h prn. 7. Demonstrate/encourage use of progressive relaxation techniques, deep-breathing exercises, visualization. 8. Provide alternate comfort measures, position change, backrub. 9. Encourage use of diversional activities.	Verbalizes relief of pain within 30–60 minutes of administration of medication. Identifies methods that provide relief by 9 AM 6/12. Uses relaxation skills to reduce level of pain by 9 AM 6/12.	*M 6/12* *M 6/12*

Continued

Date	Nursing Diagnosis	Desired Outcome	Nursing Interventions	Evaluation	
6/11/99	Risk for Infection: risk factors of broken skin, traumatized tissues, decreased hemoglobin, invasive procedures, environmental exposure.	Free of infection.	1. Monitor temp, VS, q4h. 2. Aseptic dressing change bid 9 AM, 9 PM, and prn. 3. Pin care per protocol bid 9 AM, 9 PM. 4. Routine IV site care daily. 5. Document condition of wound, IV, and pin sites q4h. 6. Review ways patient can reduce risk of infection. 7. Cefoxitin 2 g IV piggyback q8h (8 AM, 4 PM, 12 AM).	Identifies and practices interventions to reduce risk of infection by 5 PM 6/12. Identifies signs/symptoms requiring medical evaluation by 9 AM 6/13. Displays initial wound healing free of purulent drainage/signs of infection by discharge.	M 6/12
6/11/99	Impaired Physical Mobility: related to musculoskeletal impairment and pain, evidenced by reluctance to attempt movement and imposed restrictions.	Ambulates safely with assistive device.	1. Monitor circulation/nerve function R leg q1h × 24 hr, then q4h prn. 2. Support R leg fixator during movement. 3. Support feet with footboard. 4. Encourage use of side rails/overhead trapeze for position change. 5. Demonstrate/assist with ROM exercises to unaffected limbs q2h. 6. Assist out of bed, non–weight-bearing 6 PM 6/12. 7. Instruct in/monitor use of crutches 6/13.	Participates in activities to maintain muscle strength by 9 AM 6/12. Increases level of activity beginning 6 PM 6/12 and ongoing. Demonstrates techniques/behaviors that enable resumption of activities by 6 PM 6/13. Maintains position of function R leg, free of foot drop—ongoing.	M 6/12

Pain [acute]

Although Michelle is reporting relief of pain following administration of medication, this is an ongoing outcome and will remain active. Michelle has identified methods that enhance pain relief and is successfully using relaxation techniques; thus the second and third outcomes have been met.

Infection, risk for

Michelle is able to identify and is practicing interventions to reduce risk of infection, meeting the first outcome.

Physical Mobility, impaired

Michelle is participating in activities to maintain muscle strength meeting the first outcome. However, the initial attempt to get Michelle out of bed was unsuccessful, and the second outcome is not met.

Key to Practice Activity 6–2: Modification of the Plan of Care

Based on your evaluation, how would you alter Michelle's plan of care from Practice Activity 6–1?

Michelle has learned ways to control her pain, and she seeks pharmacological relief appropriately. The problem will remain active for the duration of this admission, although at a lesser level of concern. Intervention 1 can be deleted.

At this time, Michelle's wounds show no signs of infection, and Michelle is aware of ways to help reduce the risk of infection. Components of this problem will remain active for the duration of this hospitalization. Intervention 6 can be deleted.

Michelle is able to reposition herself and participates in activities/behaviors to maintain function. Michelle's initial attempt to be out of bed was not successful. The timeframe will need to be extended while Michelle is evaluated for adequacy of circulation and appropriateness of premedication before activity is initiated again.

A problem of nutrition has also been identified. Assessing the integrity of Michelle's jaws/teeth and TM joint and providing a semisoft diet may help improve her intake. In addition, Michelle's knowledge of her nutritional needs will need to be assessed, because a proper diet can promote healing and reduce risk of infection. Obtain a baseline weight for future comparison.

Key for Practice Activity 7–1: Elements of Progress Notes

Give a brief explanation of how progress notes provide for the following elements of the nurse/patient relationship.

1. Staff communication: *Recorded information can be reviewed by other staff members/healthcare providers at any time.*

2. Evaluation: *Tracks the patient's responses to treatment, progress toward outcomes, and interventions used to obtain these outcomes to determine quality of care provided.*

3. Relationship monitoring: *Documents patient's interactions with others, which may have an impact on well-being, recovery, and independence.*

4. Reimbursement: *Proof of services necessary for payment.*

5. Legal documentation: *Verifies implementation of the plan of treatment, events, activities, and progress toward outcomes.*

6. Accreditation: *Meets standards necessary to gain accreditation.*

7. Training/Supervision: *A model for coworkers; gives an impression of abilities and identifies areas for additional training or supervision.*

Practice Activity 7–2: Writing Nonjudgmental Statements

Circle either the J or O/B for each of the following statements to identify either judgmental (J) or observational/behavioral (O/B) documented statements. If the statement is judgmental, rewrite to reflect observation/behavioral language:

1. Mrs. Jewel has a poor body image since undergoing a mastectomy. ⏌ Example of behavioral language: *Mrs. Jewel says she thinks her husband will not want to look at her body, and she doesn't feel like a woman anymore.*

2. Mr. Dunn needs to be evaluated regarding his competence to manage his household affairs because of his left-sided weakness since his stroke. O/B

3. Miss Janus usually practices breast self-examination. ⏌ Example of behavioral language: *Miss Janus performs her breast examination 10 or more times a year.*

4. Mary Bird does not eat enough for her current level of activity. ⏌ Example of behavioral language: *Mary Bird's caloric intake is 1000 calories, which represents maintenance level and is not sufficient to maintain her weight at her current level of activity.*

5. Mr. Lambert stops taking his medication; then when he has a seizure, he presents at the doctor's office for treatment. O/B

6. It has been a long time since Mr. Babbitt has had his medications evaluated. ⏌ Example of behavioral language: *Mr. Babbitt has not had his medications evaluated since last November.*

Keys to Chapter Work Pages

Key to Work Page: Chapter 1

1. The ANA has defined nursing as:
   The diagnosis and treatment of human responses to actual or potential health problems.
2. My own definition of nursing is: *Self-answer*
3. How has the information in this chapter affected your definition? *Self-answer*
4. The ANA Social Policy Statement defines the phenomena of concern for nurses as: *human responses to health and illness.*
5. The definition of nursing process is: *an orderly, logical five-step problem-solving approach for administering nursing care.*
6. Name and define the five steps of the nursing process and provide an example of each step:

Steps	Definition	Example
a. *Assessment*	*Systematic collection of data.*	*Low BP, thirst, dry mouth, dark urine.*
b. *Problem Identification*	*Analysis of data to identify patient's problems/needs.*	*Fluid volume deficit.*
c. *Planning*	*Setting goals/outcomes and choosing interventions.*	*Increase circulating volume. Encourage oral fluids.*
d. *Implementation*	*Putting the plan into action.*	*Place water and juice of choice at bedside.*
e. *Evaluation*	*Assessing the effectiveness of the plan and changing the plan if indicated.*	*Monitor BP, urine output, and mucous membranes to note improvement.*

7. List the three advantages of using nursing process:
   a. *Provides framework for meeting individual needs of the patient, family, and community.*
   b. *Focuses attention on individual human responses to provide holistic care.*
   c. *Provides an organized, systematic method of problem solving.*
   d. *Promotes active involvement of the patient.*
   e. *Enables the nurse to exert greater control over own practice.*
   f. *Provides a common language for practice.*

g. *Provides a means for assessing nursing's economic contribution to patient care.*

8. List two of the fundamental philosophical beliefs that you believe are basic to decision making within the nursing process:

Patient is a human being who has worth and dignity.

If basic human needs are not met, intervention is required until individual can resume responsibility for self.

Patients have a right to quality health and nursing care with a focus on wellness and prevention.

Therapeutic nurse-patient relationship is important to this process.

9. Identify the steps of the nursing process by placing the appropriate number of the activity in the space following the data presented in the following vignette:

1 = Assessment; 2 = Problem/Need Identification; 3 = Planning; 4 = Implementation; 5 = Evaluation

VIGNETTE:

Robert, a 72-year-old African-American male, is admitted with recurrent bilateral lower lobe pneumonia. __1__

He reports this is his second episode in 6 months. __1__

Temperature is 101°F; skin hot and flushed. __1__

He reports frequent, hacking cough with moderate amount of thick greenish mucus. __1__

Auscultation of the chest reveals scattered rhonchi throughout. __1__

His mucous membranes are pale, and his lips are dry and cracked. __1__

He says when he was sick last month, the doctor prescribed an antibiotic which he discontinued after 6 days because he was feeling better. __1__

You determine Robert has an airway clearance problem, a fluid volume deficit, and is not managing his therapeutic regimen effectively, which will require teaching to promote adequate self-care and to prevent recurrence. __2__

You establish the following outcomes:

Expectorates secretions completely with breath sounds clear and respirations noiseless. __3__

Demonstrates adequate fluid balance with moist mucous membranes and loose respiratory secretions. __3__

Verbalizes understanding of cause of condition and therapeutic regimen. __3__

You decide to set up a regular schedule for respiratory activities and fluid replacement. __3__

In addition, you formulate a teaching plan to cover the identified concerns for self-care and illness prevention. __3__

You provide a tube of petroleum jelly for Robert to use on his lips. __4__

Every 2 hours you visit Robert to encourage him to deep breathe, cough, change his position, and drink a glass of fluid of his choice. __4__

You use this time to discuss avoidance of crowds and individuals with upper respiratory infections and necessity of continuing the treatment plan after discharge. __4__

The following day, Robert's skin is no longer hot and flushed, temperature is 99°F, secretions are loose and readily expectorated, and breath sounds are clearing. __5__

Robert's lips and oral mucous membranes are moist. He is able to explain in his own words how to care for himself and ways to prevent pneumonia. __5__

You decide the current treatment plan is achieving the identified outcomes and to continue the plan as written. __5__

Key to Work Page: Chapter 2

1. Rewrite the following questions so that they are open-ended:
   a. You're feeling better after the respiratory treatment, aren't you? *How are you feeling after your respiratory treatment?*
   b. Have you taken your medicine today? *Tell me about your medication schedule. How is that working for you?*
   c. Do you understand these directions? *Explain your understanding of these directions.*
2. Using the technique of reflection, write a response to clarify these patient statements:
   a. Do you think I should tell my doctor about my concern?
      What do you think you need to do?
   b. What do you want to talk about today?
      I'm interested in what your concerns are.
   c. I don't think I can go on without my husband.
      It seems difficult without him.
   d. Do you think it is important to get married?
      I'd be interested in your thoughts about that.
3. When might a closed-ended question be helpful?
   In an emergency.
4. Describe the three components of the patient database:
   a. *Patient history*
   b. *Physical examination*
   c. *Diagnostic studies*
5. The four activities involved in the physical assessment are:
   a. Inspection
   b. Percussion
   c. Auscultation
   d. Palpation
6. The patient database is important to the provision of patient care because *it provides a profile of the patient's health status on which problem identification is based.*
7. For assessment purposes the difference between subjective data and objective data is: *Subjective data are what the patient/significant other(s) say that reflects their thoughts, feelings, perceptions. Objective data are observable and measurable and include data gathered from other sources.*
8. Underline the subjective data, and circle the objective data in the following vignette:

VIGNETTE:

Sally comes to the obstetric department for evaluation of her stage of labor. Back pains began about 3 hours ago (8 PM) while on her job as a respiratory therapist. Contractions are 5 minutes apart, lasting 30 seconds for the last 45 minutes. BP 146/84, left arm/lying; P 110; respirations 24. Weight 155 pounds (up 4 pounds this week). Cervix dilated 4 cm, membranes intact. Fetal head engaged, heart tones slightly muffled in right lower quadrant, rate 132. Nauseated since a dinner of fried chicken 4 hours ago. Appears anxious and seems irritated that her physician is not here. Voided 1 hour ago, has not had a bowel movement for 2 days. Stopped smoking 8 months ago. Lungs clear. No allergies. Married, husband plans to attend the birth. Two children are in the care of their grandmother tonight. Appearance is well-groomed with a well-fitting maternity uniform and low-heeled shoes. Requests to leave contacts in to observe the birth. Last physical examination 1 week ago. Gestation 37 weeks, with due date 3 weeks off—3/11/99.

9. An important benefit of doing "research" or reviewing available information before an interview is *to gather information and generate questions.*

10. An interview should be "requested" because *it promotes a more positive interaction.*
11. Check those information resources that can be useful in helping the nurse to prepare for the interview:
    - _X_ Family/significant other   _X_ Physician notes
    - _X_ Old medical records   _X_ Textbooks/reference journals
    - _X_ Diagnostic studies   _X_ Other nurse/healthcare providers
12. Sensitivity of the nurse is important during the interview process to *respect the patient's right to privacy and enhance trust.*
13. List three abilities of the nurse that are necessary in order to collect a relevant patient database.
    a. *Knowledge base*
    b. *Choice of questions to be asked*
    c. *Method of asking questions*
    d. *Ability to give meaning to response*
14. In the following vignette, cluster and record the assessed data (following the numbers) into the appropriate diagnostic divisions listed below. Refer to Table 2–1 as needed for the type of data included in the specific divisions to assist you in clustering the data.

VIGNETTE:

Robert, a 72-year-old (1) African-American (2) male admitted to the medical unit at 1 PM for (3) bilateral lower lobe pneumonia. (4) Has had liquids only by mouth for several days. (5) Last BM—2 days ago, brown/formed stool, (6) voided at 1:20 PM—clear, dark amber. He reports (7) "My chest hurts," as he splints chest while coughing. (8) Small amount, thick, yellow sputum expectorated with cough. (9) Appears anxious, fidgeting with sheets, face tense, watching nurse intently. (10) Tympanic temperature (TMT) 101°F, (11) BP 178/102 (left arm/lying), P 100/regular, (12) respirations 28/shallow. (13) Skin warm, moist, color pale. (14) Has difficulty hearing questions, left hearing aid (R ear) at home. (15) Reports "This is the second episode in a month." (16) Doctor did prescribe antibiotic (drug unknown) a month ago, patient did not complete treatment. (17) States he lives alone (widower), and (18) is responsible for meeting own needs. In reviewing diagnostic studies, you note the (19) chest x-ray reveals infiltrates both lower lobes and a (20) Gram stain of the sputum reveals Gram-negative bacteria.

Diagnostic Divisions

Activity/Rest: _none_   Hygiene: _18_   Safety: _10, 14, 20_
Circulation: _8, 11, 13_   Neurosensory: _14_   Sexuality: _2_
Ego Integrity: _9_   Pain/Discomfort: _7_
Social Interaction: _1, 17_   Elimination: _5, 6_
Respiration: _8, 12, 19_   Teaching/Learning: _3, 15, 16_
Food/Fluid: _4_

Key to Work Page: Chapter 3

1. What is the definition of Problem/Need Identification? *The process of data analysis using diagnostic reasoning to determine if nursing intervention is indicated.*
2. What two factors influenced the development and acceptance of nursing diagnosis as the language of nursing? *ANA Social Policy Statement and ANA Standards of Practice.*
3. List three reasons for using nursing diagnosis:
    a. *Provides a common language for improved communication.*
    b. *Promotes identification of appropriate goals and interventions and provides guidance for evaluation.*
    c. *Provides framework for patient classification system for staffing needs and third-party reimbursement.*
    d. *Can be a standard for nursing practice.*
    e. *Provides opportunity for documentation and validation of process.*

4. List the six steps of diagnostic reasoning:
   a. *Problem-sensing*
   b. *Rule-out process*
   c. *Synthesizing data*
   d. *Evaluating/confirming the hypothesis*
   e. *List patient's problems/needs*
   f. *Re-evaluate the problem list*

5. Name the components of the Patient Diagnostic Statement:
   a. *Problem*
   b. *Etiology*
   c. *Signs/Symptoms*

6. If a risk diagnosis is identified, how is the patient diagnostic statement altered? *Etiology and signs/symptoms are replaced by risk factors.*

7. What is the difference between a medical and a nursing diagnosis? *Medical diagnoses are illnesses/conditions while nursing diagnoses are human responses to actual or potential health problems/life processes that are amenable to treatment by nurses.*

8. Which of these patient diagnostic statements are stated correctly? Indicate by placing a C before correct, or an I before incorrect statements. Then, differentiate actual (A) from risk (R) problems by placing an A or R by each statement.
   <u>C/A</u>   a. Knowledge deficit, drug therapy related to misinterpretation and unfamiliarity with resources as evidenced by request for information and statement of misconception.
   <u>C/R</u>   b. Infection, risk, for risk factors of altered lung expansion, decreased ciliary action, decreased hemoglobin, and invasive procedures.
   <u>I/A</u>   c. Urinary Elimination, altered, related to indwelling catheter as evidenced by inability to void.
   <u>C/A</u>   d. Anxiety [moderate] related to change in health status, role functioning, and socioeconomic status as evidenced by apprehension, insomnia, and feelings of inadequacy.

9. Underline the cues in the patient database below that indicate that a problem may exist, and write a patient diagnostic statement based on your findings:

VIGNETTE:

Sally is 2 days postdelivery. She reports her bowels have not moved but says she has been drinking plenty of fluids, including fruit juices, and has been eating a balanced diet.

Elimination (Excerpt from the Patient Database)

Subjective

Usual bowel patterns: Every morning
Laxative use: Rare/MOM PM
Character of stool: Brown, formed   **Last BM:** <u>4 days ago</u>
History of bleeding: No   **Hemorrhoids:** <u>Last 5 weeks</u>
Constipation: <u>Since delivery</u>   **Diarrhea:** No
Usual voiding pattern: 3–4 ×/day   **Incontinence:** No   **Urgency:** No
Character of urine: Yellow   **Pain/burning/difficulty voiding:** No
History of kidney/bladder disease: Several bladder infections, last one 6 years ago
Associated complaints: <u>Pain with stool, nausea, "I just can't go no matter what I do."</u>

Objective

Abdomen tender: Yes   **Soft/firm:** <u>Somewhat firm</u>
Palpable mass: No   **Size/girth:** Enlarged/postpartal

Bowel sounds: Present all four quadrants, <u>hypoactive, every 1 to 2 minutes</u>
Hemorrhoids: Visual examination not done

Now, write the Patient Diagnostic Statement. (Refer to the listing of nursing diagnoses in Appendix A to compare diagnostic labels addressing bowel elimination.) *Constipation related to weak abdominal muscula-ture and pain on defecation evidenced by decreased frequency of stool, abdominal fullness, nausea, and hypoac-tive bowel sounds.*

Key to Work Page: Chapter 4

1. List three reasons why the plan of care is important:
   a. *Provides continuity of care*
   b. *Enhances communication*
   c. *Assists with determining unit priorities*
   d. *Supports documentation of the nursing process*
   e. *Serves as a teaching tool*
2. Briefly explain why setting priorities is necessary:
   Helps ensure that basic needs are met first, then other needs in order of importance.
3. What is the difference between a goal and an outcome?
   A goal is stated broadly, reflecting the general direction in which the patient is expected to progress. An outcome is a specific measurable step taken toward achieving the goal.
4. Identify five important components of patient outcomes:
   a. *Specific*
   b. *Realistic*
   c. *Consider the patient's circumstances and desires*
   d. *Indicate a time frame*
   e. *Provide measurable evaluation criteria*
5. List four types of information that nursing interventions need to contain:
   a. *Date intervention is written*
   b. *Action verb reflecting activity to be performed*
   c. *Qualifiers of how, when, where, time/frequency, and amount*
   d. *Signature and/or initials of the nurse*
6. Explain the difference between a measurable and a nonmeasurable verb and give an example of each:
   Measurable verbs describe an action that can be observed and/or quantified, for example, "verbalizes," "am-bulates"; nonmeasurable verbs cannot be observed, for example, "understands."
7. When does discharge planning begin? *When the patient is admitted.*
8. How is the plan of care documented? *On a single or multipage form that is kept in a Kardex, the patient's chart, or at the bedside.*
9. Identify two additional problems facing Michelle; then set a goal with one outcome and two interven-tions for each problem.

VIGNETTE:

Michelle, the 14-year-old female with a compound fracture of the right lower leg and a mild concussion, has other problems in addition to Pain [acute], previously discussed.

Her wound was contaminated by dirt and she had significant blood loss before paramedics arrived. Al-though the wound was flushed with sterile saline and antibiotic solution before being packed and dressed, a cast was not applied because of tissue swelling and concerns about the wound and bone. Instead, an ex-ternal fixation device (a metal frame with pins extending through the skin and bone) is currently being used for immobilization of the tibia and fibula. The device is heavy and awkward for Michelle to move without causing increased pain, and she is to remain on bedrest for 24 hours. In addition, IV antibiotics are to be administered q4h.

a. Problem: *Infection, risk for, risk factors of broken skin, traumatized tissues, decreased hemoglobin, invasive procedures, increased environmental exposure.*
Goal: *Free of infection.*
Outcome: *Patient will achieve timely wound healing free of purulent drainage and be afebrile by discharge.*

OR

Outcome: *Patient will identify behaviors to reduce risk of infection within 24 hours.*
Interventions:

○ *Monitor temperature/vital signs* ○ *Maintain aseptic technique with dressing change* ○ *Assess/document wound condition and pin sites* ○ *Administer antibiotic—monitor response* ○ *Instruct patient in ways to reduce risk of infection.*

b. Problem/Need: *Mobility, impaired physical related to musculoskeletal/impairment and pain as evidenced by reluctance to attempt movement, imposed restrictions of movement.*
Goal: *Ambulates safely with assistive device.*
Outcome: *Patient will maintain position of function R leg, free of footdrop—ongoing.*

OR

Outcome: *Patient will increase level of activity within 24 hours.*
Interventions:

○ *Monitor circulation/nerve function of R leg* ○ *Support foot in upright position with bed board/blanket roll* ○ *Assist out of bed* ○ *Instruct in/monitor use of crutches.*

c. Problem/Need: *Knowledge deficit, self-care/treatment needs related to lack of exposure to resources evidenced by request for information.*
Goal: *Managing own care effectively.*
Outcome: *Patient will verbalize understanding of condition and treatment needs within 3 days.*

OR

Outcome: *Patient will list signs/symptoms requiring medical evaluation/intervention, within 36 hours.*
Interventions:

○ *Review appropriate pathophysiology of injury in lay terms* ○ *Demonstrate proper wound and pin care* ○ *Identify signs/symptoms suggestive of complications* ○ *Discuss actions, side-effects, and possible adverse reactions of medications.*

Key to Work Page: Chapter 5

1. Identify three activities involved in implementing the plan of care:
   a. *Identifying priorities*
   b. *Providing patient care*
   c. *Ongoing data collection*
   d. *Documentation*
   e. *Communication*
2. Discuss the importance of understanding the expected effect and potential hazards of the interventions you will implement:
   It is important to understand the expected effect and potential hazards of the interventions you will implement to be sure the intervention will be beneficial, that you are achieving the desired effects, or that you have allowed for changes necessary to provide for specific needs/safety.
3. Explain the purpose for ongoing data collection throughout the implementation step of the nursing process:

Provides information that will be used to determine appropriateness of care; need to alter interventions, and/or refer to other resources; necessity of shifting priorities, development of new patient problems/needs.

4. List two reasons why documentation of the care provided is important:
   a. *Legal requirement for all healthcare settings*
   b. *Communication tool*
   c. *Resource to aid in determining effectiveness of care*
   d. *Assisting in setting priorities for ongoing care*

5. Name three activities you might use to carry out interventions for planned patient care:
   a. *"Hands-on" care*
   b. *Assisting the patient with care*
   c. *Instructing*
   d. *Counseling*
   e. *Monitoring*

6. What is the advantage of reporting "by exception"? *Provides for giving important information in a brief, concise manner that saves time.*

7. When and where is patient confidentiality important? *When discussing the patient in any area/situation where the conversation can be overheard by others who are not involved in the patient's care.*

8. Flexibility in providing patient care is important because: *it allows the nurse to respond to changed circumstances, interruptions, and so on, in a timely manner.*

VIGNETTE:

Robert signed advance directives asking that no extraordinary means (e.g., intubation and mechanical ventilation) be used to prolong his life. When his condition changed, his daughter was notified as required. While visiting with her father, she is surprised to learn of his decision. She is very upset and a confrontation develops. Robert tells her "it is none of your business" and refuses to enter into further conversation.

9. What can you do now? *Ask the daughter to step out of the room with you, making sure that the patient is "settled" before leaving the room. Find a quiet, private area, offer something to drink and sit down facing the daughter. Acknowledge her feelings of distress and encourage her to talk about the situation. Answer questions and provide information, as indicated, in verbal and written form regarding advanced directives. Review what will be done for her father under advanced directives. Facilitate a conference between father and daughter if both are agreeable, helping with clarification of terms and promoting understanding. If necessary, refer to a clinical nurse specialist or social worker for additional conflict resolution.*

Key to Work Page: Chapter 6

1. What is the difference between assessment and evaluation? *Assessment identifies the patient's current status, and evaluation determines the patient's movement toward specified outcomes.*

2. What is the primary purpose of the evaluation process? *Determines effectiveness of the plan of care.*

3. The evaluation process provides what three opportunities for the patient and nurse:
   a. *Provides positive feedback to patient and caregivers for efforts to date.*
   b. *Provides encouragement to continue to strive for higher level of functioning.*
   c. *Provides for problem solving.*
   d. *Provides for personal growth.*

4. List the three methods by which patient outcomes may be evaluated, and give an example for each:
   a. *Direct observation.   Ambulated the length of the hall without difficulty.*
   b. *Patient interview.   Reports decreased level of pain.*
   c. *Review of records.   Temperature has remained within normal range.*

5. Because it is advisable to deal with only three to five nursing diagnoses at a time, how are needs prioritized? *According to the hierarchy of needs, meeting basic needs first.*

6. When is consideration of discharge planning begun? *On admission.*

7. VIGNETTE:

Today is Donald's fifth hospital day. At the start of the shift, you have completed a focused assessment to evaluate progress/changes in status of the identified patient problems. Donald's initial nausea has resolved and his intake yesterday was approximately 3000 calories. During rounds you notice he has eaten all of the food on his breakfast tray. He fills out the next day's menu, neglecting to include any vegetables and selecting only one fruit.

Later, during group, Donald talks about his options for employment and says he knows an employment agency and a business where he can check about possible jobs. He also mentions a friend who he believes might be willing to help him. He says he is realizing that he is really OK, even though the loss of his job was a devastating event for him following so soon after his divorce. He acknowledges that his feelings of anxiety led to an increase in his drinking. He further says he still has feelings of sadness and occasionally feels a sense of despair but believes he will feel better as he begins to get his life back together again. He seems tentative in accepting his need to be involved in AA, saying he doesn't know "where they meet, or anyone who attends the meetings."

a. **Evaluation:** Based on the above information, evaluate Donald's progress regarding his problems of Altered Nutrition: less than body requirements, Ineffective Individual Coping, and Altered Role Performance as outlined in the Plan of Care.

Problem 4: Donald's intake is meeting daily caloric requirements, achieving the second outcome. However, his menu choices do not include all appropriate food groups; therefore, the first outcome is only partially met.

Problem 5: Donald recognizes the impact that his loss of employment and recent divorce have had on his current feelings of anxiety and helplessness, meeting the first outcome.

Problem 6: Donald is expressing awareness of feelings related to his situation and has some optimism for the future. This meets the first outcome. In addition, Donald has developed a realistic plan with two job-hunting strategies, meeting the second outcome.

b. **Modification:** How would you change Donald's plan of care? *Investigate Donald's menu choices and how he plans to meet dietary needs without adequate intake of fruits and vegetables.*

c. **Termination:** How might new concerns regarding the patient affect your discharge plans? *Identify a contact person from AA to provide support for Donald to promote continued involvement in the treatment plan.*

Key to Work Page: Chapter 7

1. You are writing a paper regarding documentation. Identify three goals of the documentation process you will include:

a. *Facilitate the quality of patient care.*

b. *Ensure documentation of progress with regards to patient-focused outcomes.*

c. *Facilitate interdisciplinary consistency and communication of treatment goals and progress.*

2. Steps of the Nursing Process are documented on which form:

Steps		Form
_c_	Assessment	a. Plan of care
_a_	Problem identification	b. Progress notes
_a_	Planning	c. Patient database
_b, d_	Implementation	d. Flow sheets
_a, b_	Evaluation	

3. List five functions of progress notes:
   a. *Staff communication*
   b. *Legal documentation*
   c. *Evaluation*
   d. *Accreditation*
   e. *Training and supervision*
   f. *Reimbursement*
   g. *Relationship monitoring*

4. Complete the following statements describing the JCAHO's standards for documentation.
   a. A medical record is *initiated* and *maintained* for every individual assessed or treated. The medical record incorporates information from subsequent contacts between the *patient* and *the organization*.
   b. The medical record contains *sufficient information* to *identify* the patient, support the *diagnosis*, justify the *treatment*, document the course and results accurately, and facilitate *continuity* of care among healthcare providers.

5. When documenting for reimbursement, five factors need to be included: *These are the when, where, how, what, and who of services.*

6. Two ways in which the plan of care can be used for supervision are: *the identification of employees' abilities identifying the need for further supervision, training, or education.*

7. The best way to ensure clarity of the progress notes is: *to use descriptive/observational statements.*

8. Rewrite the following judgmental statements to make them nonjudgmental:
   a. He is uncooperative today.
      Mr. Jones refused his bath and did not want to get out of bed this morning.
   b. He is a manipulative patient.
      Mr. Smith told me I was the only nurse who listened to him and wanted me to let him skip his medication and not tell the doctor.
   c. She had a bad attitude about taking her medication this morning.
      Mrs. Wharton stated she was tired of taking her medicine and threw the cup across the room this morning.
   d. The new patient is really difficult.
      Mr. Bemish did not want to go to bed and cursed when I went in to obtain his admitting information.

9. List three types of judgmental statements:
   a. *Contain undefined periods of time*
   b. *Contain undefined quantities*
   c. *Contain undefined qualities*
   d. *Fail to specify any objective basis for the judgment made*

10. Name three types of data that are important to record in the progress note:
    a. *Unsettled or unclear problems that need to be dealt with*
    b. *Noteworthy incidents or interview*
    c. *Significant phone calls, home visits, and family interactions; additional critical incident data*
    d. *Care or observations not recorded elsewhere*

11. List five additional factors that can enhance accurate communication:
    a. *Correct grammar and spelling*
    b. *Legible writing, use of nonerasable ink*
    c. *Avoidance of repetition of data*
    d. *Avoidance of abbreviations*
    e. *Brevity*

12. What actions can be taken to correct an error in charting? *Draw a line through the error, write "error," and initial.*

13. Name three charting formats:
    a. *Block*

    b. *POMR/SOAP*

    c. *FOCUS™ CHARTING/DAR*

    d. *Narrative—time.*

14. Read the following vignette and record the patient data using the SOAP and DAR formats, and the format used in your facility/agency, if different.

VIGNETTE:

Sally was discharged home with the twins on the evening of her third postpartal day. On the morning of day 5, she is visited by the public health nurse specializing in maternal/newborn care.

Sally is dressed in a robe and slippers, her hair is uncombed, her color is pale, and she has dark circles under her eyes. She is sitting in a recliner, bottle feeding Baby A. The grandmother is sitting on the couch feeding Baby B. Living area is noted to be clean and neat with comfortable ambient temperature. The two older children are reported to be at preschool from 9 AM to 2:30 PM daily.

Postpartal assessment form is completed with physical findings within normal limits. Sally reports her bowels are working "slowly" (small firm BM this AM) with fluid intake approximately 2 L/day and moderate appetite—"just too tired to really eat or do anything else." Sally's mother indicates she is providing household assistance—cooking, cleaning, and child care. Sally and her mother agree fatigue is a major concern for Sally. Both Sally and her mother are up twice during the night to feed the twins. Sally does take short naps during the day. Sally is observed to display usual attachment behaviors toward Baby A (Laura); however, her interaction with Baby B (unnamed) is of short duration, appears to lack warmth, and is restricted to caretaking activities.

You provide Sally with a teaching sheet describing postpartal fatigue and discussing dietary needs/supplements, energy conservation techniques, and the importance of balanced activity/exercise and rest. You suggest Sally's husband might get up for one feeding during the night to allow her a longer period of uninterrupted sleep and to provide him additional opportunity for interaction with his daughters.

Next, you ask Sally how she feels about being the mother of twins. Sally becomes tearful and states "I just don't know what I'm going to do when Mom goes home." You ask if she would like to have a visit from a member of the Mothers of Multiples group. You also suggest having a family meeting to problem-solve her concerns. You then discuss your observation that Sally appears more comfortable with Laura than with her twin, asking Sally to describe her perceptions of and feelings for Baby B. After reflecting on the question, Sally says she has felt so overwhelmed that she has not truly accepted the reality of having twins. She is visibly upset, berating herself for being a "poor mother." You tell her that it is not unusual to be overwhelmed by the reality of a multiple birth, even when planned for in advance of delivery.

You ask Sally to think about what she needs to help her resolve this situation. Sally decides she needs to spend more time getting to know Baby B, allowing other family members to care for and interact with Laura. After a discussion about the individual characteristics of her other children, Sally says Baby B is unique in her level of alertness and "her acceptance" of anyone who cares for her. "She deserves a name reflecting family ties and thanksgiving for the special gift of twins." You encourage Sally to read the literature about twins provided before her discharge and to apply techniques she has found successful in dealing with previous stressful situations. You schedule a follow-up visit for 1 week and leave a contact number if Sally has any questions or needs assistance before your next visit. When you depart, Sally appears focused on ways to improve her current situation, displaying a lighter mood, smiling, and giving a firm handshake.

The SOAP format requires that chart entries be tied to a problem. In reviewing this vignette, you might choose to address the problem of constipation as follows:

SOAP: Problem #4 (Constipation)

    S: Bowels working slowly.

    O: Small firm BM this AM.

A: Constipation beginning to resolve.

P: Continue oral fluid intake of 2 + L/day and monitor diet for adequate bulk and roughage.

I: Verified Sally has reviewed teaching sheet.

E: States she understands interventions.

R: Reassess on next visit. Or you might choose to address the problem of fatigue:

SOAP: Problem #6 (Fatigue)

S: "Too tired to eat or do anything else." Concern expressed about coping once her mother leaves.

O: Tearful. Color pale with dark circles under her eyes.

A: Postpartum fatigue.

P: Provide information, review activity schedule, identify possible role model.

I: Teaching sheet regarding postpartal fatigue provided. Discussed dietary needs/supplements, energy conservation techniques, and activity/rest program. Suggested family meeting to problem-solve concerns and to involve husband more in provision of care for infants. Referral made to Mothers of Multiples group.

E: Sally appears receptive to plan and with mother's assistance will likely follow through. Will reassess at next visit in 1 week.

The DAR format provides for chart entries to be tied to a problem sign/symptom, event, or specific standard of care. Therefore, an initial entry addressing the home visit is acceptable, or you could choose to address the problem of fatigue.

DAR: Home Visit

D: See Postpartal Assessment form attached. Reports constipation slowly resolving. Primary concern is fatigue and whether she will be able to cope once mother leaves. Bonding with Baby B appears weak, interaction is of short duration and restricted to caretaking activities, appears uncomfortable and lacks warmth. Tearful, berated self for being a "poor" mother.

A: Provided teaching sheet re Postpartal Fatigue. Discussed dietary needs/supplements, energy conservation techniques, activity/rest program. Suggested family meeting to problem-solve concerns and to have husband increase infant care activities. Encouraged Sally to identify special/individual characteristics of Baby B and review discharge literature re twins. Noted successful coping skills previously used and referral to Mothers of Multiples group provided. Follow-up visit scheduled for 1 week.

R: Sally has clarified current needs. She is focused on problem-solving activities and has identified actions to improve interactions and relationship with Baby B. Mood lighter, smiling, and handshake firm.

Key to Work Page: Chapter 8: Possible Nursing Diagnoses for Mr. R. Simmons

6/28 PATIENT DIAGNOSTIC STATEMENT (NURSING DIAGNOSIS)

Impaired Skin Integrity related to pressure, altered metabolic state, circulatory impairment, and decreased sensation as evidenced by draining wound L foot.

DESIRED OUTCOMES: PATIENT WILL:

Demonstrate correction of metabolic state as evidenced by blood glucose within normal limits within (time frame).

Be free of purulent drainage within (time frame).

Display signs of healing with wound edges clean/pink by (time frame).

INTERVENTIONS

Obtain culture of wound drainage on admission.
Administer dicloxacillin 500 mg PO starting 10 PM.
Observe for signs of hypersensitivity (i.e., pruritus, urticaria, rash).
Irrigate foot wound with room temperature sterile NS tid.
Dress wound with wet-to-dry sterile dressing; use paper tape.
Administer 10 U NPH insulin sc q AM after daily FBS drawn and q hs.
Administer Dicloxacillin 500 mg PO q6h—begin 12 AM.

6/28 PATIENT DIAGNOSTIC STATEMENT (NURSING DIAGNOSIS)

Pain related to physical agent (wound L foot) as evidenced by verbal report of discomfort and guarding behavior.

DESIRED OUTCOMES: PATIENT WILL:

Report pain is minimized/relieved within 1 hour of analgesic administration (time frame).
Ambulate normally, full weight bearing by (time frame).

INTERVENTIONS

Determine pain characteristics through patient's description.
Place foot cradle on bed/encourage use of loose-fitting slipper, when up.
Administer Darvocet-N 100 mg PO q4h as needed. Document effectiveness.

6/28 PATIENT DIAGNOSTIC STATEMENT (NURSING DIAGNOSIS)

Altered peripheral tissue perfusion related to decreased arterial flow as evidenced by decreased pulses, pale/cool feet, thick brittle nails, numbness/tingling of feet "when walks 1/4 mile."

DESIRED OUTCOMES: PATIENT WILL:

Verbalize understanding of relationship between chronic disease (diabetes mellitus) and circulatory changes by (time frame).
Demonstrate awareness of safety factors/proper foot care within (time frame).

INTERVENTIONS

Elevate feet when up in chair.
Avoid long periods with feet dependent.
Assess for signs of dehydration.
Monitor I&O. Encourage oral fluids.
Instruct patient to avoid constricting clothing/socks and ill-fitting shoes.
Reinforce safety precautions regarding use of heating pads, hot water bottles/soaks.
Discuss complications of disease that results in vascular changes (e.g., ulceration, gangrene, muscle or bony structure changes).
Review proper foot care as outlined in teaching plan.

6/28 PATIENT DIAGNOSTIC STATEMENT (NURSING DIAGNOSIS)

Knowledge deficit regarding diabetic condition related to misinterpretation of information and/or lack of recall evidenced by inaccurate follow-through of instructions regarding home glucose monitoring and foot care, and failure to recognize signs/symptoms of hyperglycemia.

DESIRED OUTCOME: PATIENT WILL:

Verbalize basic understanding of disease process and treatment within (time frame).
Perform procedure of home glucose monitoring and insulin administration correctly (time frame).

INTERVENTIONS

Determine patient's level of knowledge, priorities of learning needs, and desire/need for including wife in instruction.
Review factors related to/altering diabetes control (e.g., stress, illness, exercise).
Review signs/symptoms of hyperglycemia, discuss prevention and evaluation of situation and when to seek medical care.
Review and provide information about routine examination of feet.
Instruct regarding prescribed insulin therapy.
Demonstrate, then observe patient in: drawing insulin into syringe, reading syringe markings, and administering dose. Assess for accuracy.
Instruct in signs/symptoms of insulin reaction/hypoglycemia.
Review "Sick Day Rules."
Recommend R.S. maintain record of fingerstick testing, insulin dosage/site, unusual physiological response, dietary intake.
Refer to dietician for revision of diet.

Index

Numbers followed by an "f" indicate figures; numbers followed by a "t" indicate tabular material.

A

Abbreviations, common medical, 257–260
Accreditation
    Joint Commission on, of Healthcare Organizations, 89, 131, 133, 134, 164, 261
    progress notes and, 134
Accuracy
    Lunney's Ordinal Scale for Degrees of, of a Nursing Diagnosis, 249
    self-monitoring of, using integrated model, 251–252
Acquired immunodeficiency syndrome (AIDS), 57
Action verbs useful in writing measurable outcomes, 80
Active-listening
    definition of, 22
    nursing interview and, 22
Activity intolerance, 83, 87, 88, 183–184, 269
    definition of, 82
    risk for, 184
Activity/rest, 43, 48, 158t, 167, 231
Actual diagnosis, 54
Acuity information, nursing diagnosis and, 41–42
Adaptive capacity, intracranial, decreased, 184
Adjustment, impaired, 184
Admitting physician's orders, 167
Agency-based nursing audit committees, 125
Agreeing, interview and, 20
AIDS. *See* Acquired immunodeficiency syndrome
Airway clearance, ineffective, 184–185
Alcohol withdrawal, clinical pathway for, 254–255
American Nurses Association (ANA)
    Code for Nurses, 5, 247
    Nursing's Social Policy Statement, 1–2
    Social Policy Statement, 38
    Standard I, Assessment, 32
    Standard II, Measurement, 66
    Standard III, Outcome identification, 95
    Standard IV, Planning, 95
    Standard V, Implementation, 111
    Standard VI, Evaluation, 126
    Standards of Clinical Nursing Practice, 5–6, 6t, 95
ANA. *See* American Nurses Association
Analysis, 37–73, 261. *See also* Patient database; Problem/need identification step, nursing process
    definition of, 37

Antidysrhythmic medication, discharge education for, 125
Anxiety, 58, 61f, 121
    death, 185–186
    mild, 185
    moderate, 185
    severe, 185
Aspiration, risk for, 186
Assessment, 3, 131–132, 261
    abnormalities/changes in, 109
    baseline, 261
    definition of, 13
    focus, 261
    nursing framework and, 30–31
    physical examination and, 24
    trifocal model for, 61f
Assessment step, nursing process, 13–36. *See also* Interview; Assessment tools
    laboratory tests and diagnostic procedures in, 25–26
    nursing interview in, 19–23
    organizing information elements in, 26–29, 30–31, 32
    patient database in, 13–19, 20, 21
    physical examination in, 23–25
Assessment tools, 231–240
    adult medical/surgical, 231–236
    intrapartal, 239–240
    prenatal, 238–239
    psychiatric, 236–238
Assumptions, patient diagnostic statement errors and, 63
Audit, nursing, 262
Audit committees, nursing, 125
Auditory sensory-perceptual alterations, 218
Auscultation, assessment and, 24
Autonomic dysreflexia, 186
    risk for, 186

B

Baseline assessment, 261
Bathing self-care deficit, 216
Bedpans, 105–106
Behavior
    infant. *See* Infant behavior
    Omaha System Problem Rating Scale for Outcomes and, 119, 120